RUSSIAN ENERGY CHAINS

WOODROW WILSON CENTER SERIES

Wilson Center

WOODROW WILSON CENTER SERIES

The Woodrow Wilson International Center for Scholars was chartered by the U.S. Congress in 1968 as the living memorial to the nation's twenty-eighth president. It serves as the country's key nonpartisan policy forum, tackling global challenges through independent research and open dialogue. Bridging the worlds of academia and public policy, the Center's diverse programmatic activity informs actionable ideas for Congress, the administration, and the broader policy community.

The Woodrow Wilson Center Series shares in the Center's mission by publishing outstanding scholarly and public policy-related books for a global readership. Written by the Center's expert staff and international network of scholars, our books shed light on a wide range of topics, including U.S. foreign and domestic policy, security, the environment, energy, and area studies. Conclusions or opinions expressed in Center publications and programs are those of the authors and speakers and do not necessarily reflect the views of the Center staff, fellows, trustees, advisory groups, or any individuals or organizations that provide financial support for the Center.

Please visit us online at www.wilsoncenter.org.

William H. Hill, *No Place for Russia: European Security Institutions Since 1989*
Donald R. Wolfensberger, *Changing Cultures in Congress: From Fair Play to Power Plays*
Samuel F. Wells Jr., *Fearing the Worst: How Korea Transformed the Cold War*
Abraham M. Denmark, *U.S. Strategy in the Asian Century: Empowering Allies and Partners*

RUSSIAN
ENERGY CHAINS

*The Remaking of Technopolitics from
Siberia to Ukraine to the European Union*

Margarita M. Balmaceda

Columbia University Press
New York

Columbia University Press
Publishers Since 1893
New York   Chichester, West Sussex
cup.columbia.edu
Copyright © 2021 Columbia University Press
All rights reserved

Library of Congress Cataloging-in-Publication Data

Names: Balmaceda, Margarita Mercedes, 1965- author.
Title: Russian energy chains : the remaking of technopolitics from Siberia
to Ukraine to the European Union / Margarita M. Balmaceda.
Description: New York : Columbia University Press, [2021] |
Series: Woodrow Wilson center series | Includes bibliographical
references and index.
Identifiers: LCCN 2020042517 (print) | LCCN 2020042518 (ebook) |
ISBN 9780231197489 (hardback) | ISBN 9780231197496 (trade paperback) |
ISBN 9780231552196 (ebook)
Subjects: LCSH: Energy policy—Russia (Federation) | Energy development—
Russia (Federation) | Energy industries—Russia (Federation)
Classification: LCC HD9502.R82 B368 2021 (print) |
LCC HD9502.R82 (ebook) | DDC 333.790947—dc23
LC record available at https://lccn.loc.gov/2020042517
LC ebook record available at https://lccn.loc.gov/2020042518

Cover design: Milenda Nan Ok Lee
Cover photo: Christian Lagerek © Shutterstock

To Marianne Sághy

Contents

Acknowledgments

IF THE CHAINS covered by this book are long, even longer are the chains of gratitude that tie me to all those without whose help this book would not have been possible. These chains extend across several continents and many countries, from the dark night in Oslo in late 2013 when the idea for the book first appeared to me, to this day. This book started with a very strong hunch, a very pressing question, but no idea of how I would get there. If it had not been for the many talented and generous people who helped me along this journey, I might never have gotten there.

In 2013, during a presentation I did at the Stiftung Wissenschaft und Politik (SWP) in Berlin, Susan Stewart—today head of the SWP's Eastern Europe and Eurasia Division—asked a question that set the ball rolling in the back of my mind, to become an actual question during a long sleepless night in Oslo a few months later. I am forever thankful for that question and for the warm welcome of my colleagues at the division during my research visit in 2013, and especially to Sabine Fischer, then head of the division, for cultivating this unique discussion space.

The prehistory of this book is connected to two long research stays at the Aleksanteri Institute in Helsinki, where I finished two previous books and unconsciously prepared myself for this new challenge. I am deeply indebted to Anna Korhonen, Aleksanteri's head of international affairs, for her inspiration and encouragement over many years, and for working with me through a major grant application related to an earlier version of this project. Although it was not funded, work on this application gave me the impetus, energy, and think-big ambition that nevertheless helped propel the project forward. Also at Aleksanteri, I am indebted to the Finnish Centre of Excellence on Choices of Russian Modernization—and, personally, to Pami Aalto, Markku Kivinen, and Sari Autio-Sarasmo—who welcomed me as a member and cofinanced workshops in Moscow, Oslo, Cambridge (Massachusetts), and Delmenhorst—where many of the ideas for this book were developed.

Two year-long fellowships allowing for dedicated, intensive work on the project gave it a strong start: a Woodrow Wilson Fellowship at the Woodrow Wilson International Center for Scholars in Washington and an EURIAS Senior Fellowship at the Hanse Wissenschaftskolleg (HWK) in Delmenhorst, Germany. At the Wilson Center, I am especially indebted to Arlyn Charles, Lindsay Collins, Kimberly Conner, Robert Litwak, and Janet Spikes, and to the 2015–16 Class of Woodrow Wilson Fellows, who inspired me with their strong work ethic, intellectual curiosity, and commitment to finding actionable answers to contemporary policy challenges. A series on writing and its challenges co-organized with then–executive vice president Andrew Seele kept me motivated for the huge task ahead. At the Kennan Institute, I am indebted to director Matthew Rojansky and deputy director William Pomeranz for their ongoing support and their contribution to keeping work on the former Soviet Union vibrant and relevant despite changing political conditions.

At the HWK—one of only two institutes of advanced studies worldwide with a dedicated energy program—I had the opportunity to learn firsthand from natural scientists, physicists, and visual artists looking at energy, broadly understood, from a wide diversity of perspectives. I am indebted to Wolfgang Stenzel, head of the HWK's Energy Program, for shaping this agenda and bringing it into dialogue with the social sciences, and for helping me develop new and exciting partnerships. That I always looked—and continue to look— forward with excited anticipation to return to the HWK's "mother ship" has much to do with Dorothe Peggel's personal and intellectual support, and with Christine Gehrking, Kerstin Labusch, and Christina Thiel's always warm welcome and efficient organization. Located in Niedersachsen, already for centuries one of Germany's top regions for wind energy, my stay at the HWK did much to challenge my fossil-fuel centered view of energy shaped by the predominance of these resources in the Soviet context.

I am enormously indebted to the HWK for making possible a dedicated workshop in June 2017, where I had the opportunity to discuss in depth a full first draft of the book with a dream team of experts on Soviet and post-Soviet energy politics: Simon Blakey, Per Högselius, Heiko Pleines, Andrian Prokyp, Doug Rogers, Peter Rutland, and Thane Gustafson. In particular, I am indebted to Doug Rogers and Thane Gustafson for helping me get through what seemed insurmountable methodological hurdles through their refreshing suggestions on how to conceptualize exemplary value chains and nonphysical nodes.

I was fortunate to receive support from the HWK to lead a study group on "Energy Materiality: Infrastructure, Spatiality, and Power" that brings together, in twice-yearly meetings, six scholars from around the world and across the social sciences (one anthropologist, one geographer, one specialist in environmental studies, one historian of technology, and two political scientists) to rethink the meaning of materiality in a world that must decarbonize its energy system in order to survive. I thank my study group members—Corey Johnson, Per Högselius, Heiko Pleines, Doug Rogers, and Veli-Pekka Tynkkynen—for ongoing inspiration and constructive criticism.

I am indebted to the Research Centre for East European Studies (Forschungsstelle Osteuropa) in Bremen, with which I was affiliated during my stay at the HWK. Its director, Susanne Schattenberg, deputy director, Heiko Pleines, science manager, Anastasia Stoll, and all members of the community made me truly feel like a member of the family on each of my visits there. And it was at the institute's Research Colloquium—where I had the opportunity to present research related to this book on several occasions—where I received some of the most relentless and academically rigorous criticism. Karen Smith Stegan of Jacobs University in Bremen provided additional inspiration.

A Renewed Research Stay Fellowship from the Alexander von Humboldt Foundation (AvH), tenable at the Alfried Krupp Institute for Advanced Studies in Greifswald, Germany—20 kilometers away from the end point of the Nord Stream pipeline—in the summer of 2018 made it possible to get back to writing after two years of full-time teaching, a task that was made much sweeter by the warm welcome of academic coordinator Christian Suhm and scientific director Bärbel Friedrich. I am especially indebted to Steffen Mehlich, head of networking and support at the AvH, for his continued assistance since 2004, and for keeping the Humboldt family always relevant and always

welcoming. The unique atmosphere of the Center for Eastern European and International Studies (ZOiS) in Berlin opened new horizons
in my research, which I experienced through an eight-week research
visit in the summer of 2019. At ZOiS, I am especially indebted to
director Gwendolyn Sasse and managing director Christian Schaich
for their warm welcome, and to Tsypylma Darieva, Nadja Douglas,
and Sabine von Lewis for inspiring research insights.

Research in Russia was made possible by the kind invitation of
the Institute of Comparative Studies of International Development
at the Higher School of Economics and its director, Andrei Yakov-
lev. Research in Ukraine was made possible by a visiting affiliation at
the National Academy of Public Administration under the President
of Ukraine, Kyiv, and the warm welcome of Professor Lilia Gonyu-
kova and Vice-President Maryna Bilynska. I am also thankful to Olena
Viter, the Dixi Group led by her, and Andrian Prokip for their keen
insights and intellectual generosity over the years. I had the privilege of
studying the Ukrainian language for coal mining and metallurgy with
the gifted teacher Valentyna Nevoit, whom I first met while studying
Ukrainian for energy issues more than a decade ago.

My home institution, the School of Diplomacy and International
Relations at Seton Hall University, has long provided the strong basis
and continued assistance without which none of my research projects
would have been able to take off. At the school, I have been fortunate
to count on the unqualified support and encouragement of a won-
derful set of colleagues, including deans Andrea Bartoli and Court-
ney Smith, chairs Benjamin Goldfrank and Martin Edwards, school
secretary Susan Malcolm, and director of marketing and communica-
tions Gwen DiBenedetto. Elsewhere at Seton Hall, I am indebted to
Nathaniel Knight and Olessia Vovina for stoking the fires of my love
of learning through unforgettable—albeit far too rare—evenings filled
with history, anthropology, and music.

At Harvard University, I am indebted to the Davis Center for Russian and Eurasian Studies for making me part of a vibrant community
of scholars studying all aspects of Soviet and post-Soviet life, and in
particular to director Rawi Abdelal and executive director Alexandra
Vacroux. The Workshop on Post-Communist Politics and Economics
(aka PostComm) at Davis and its longtime chairs, Dimitry Gorenburg
and Oxana Shevel, as well as long-term participants Linda Cook and
Mark Kramer, has been my core peer review community for many

years and has provided valuable feedback on numerous papers related to all stages of this project. Bringing together a critical mass of ambitious scholars at all stages of their academic careers for rigorous and constructive peer-review of ongoing work, PostComm is a gold nugget and secret tip.

The Harvard Ukrainian Research Institute has made me a part of their family for over twenty years and has provided a home to my Ukrainian studies self. For this and much more, thanks to the director, Serhii Plokhii, the managing director, Timysh Holowinsky, and the director of the Temerty Contemporary Ukraine Program, Emily Channell-Justice. My special thanks go to Halyna Hryn, editor of *Harvard Ukrainian Studies*, for help in crises small and big, and to Lubomyr Hajda, the institute's long-term associate director and the first person to welcome me to Harvard, for his wisdom and support over more than two decades. Perched in Cambridge between Harvard and the Massachusetts Institute of Technology, the 1369 Coffee House in Inman Square gave me a good reason to get up early every working day and stick to my writing schedule.

Portions of chapter 3 first appeared as "Differentiation, Materiality, and Power: Towards a Political Economy of Fossil Fuels," *Energy Research and Social Sciences* 39 (2018): 130–40, and are reprinted with permission.

I am indebted to Stacy Closson and Peter Rutland for their detailed comments on a second, full draft of the book. Kathleen Hancock from the Colorado School of Mines was the catalyst who—through her insightful comments and three highly useful workshops in Berlin, Hamburg, and Baltimore—marked my incorporation into the community of energy studies scholars working on energy issues above and beyond the regional context.

Special thanks to research assistants Marc Weilenmann at the Woodrow Wilson Center, Mikola Yakovenko in Kyiv, and James Janos and Emanuel Hernández at Seton Hall for their high level of professionalism and efficiency and help with myriad tasks related to this book. Each of them is now firmly on their way to a rewarding professional career, and I am fortunate to have worked with them on this project.

Keeping my sanity during the last stretch of work on this book was made possible by the very efficient work and support of Alfred Imhoff, seasoned consulting managing editor for the Woodrow Wilson Center's book series, who was always positive and forward-looking and always had creative solutions to what at first seemed like daunting crises. At Columbia University Press, it was a pleasure working with my editor, Stephen Wesley, and associate editor, Christian Winting. I am also very indebted to Matthias Newman for work on innumerable versions of the maps and figures in this book.

Finishing this book would not have been possible without a strong personal front. My extended family, including my parents, Margarita Sastre de Balmaceda and Eudoro Balmaceda, siblings Eddie and Casilda Balmaceda, Casilda's partner Gabriel Faingolz, and friends Luis Girón and Srinivas Ghandi, kept me grounded and motivated. Maren Jochimsen was with me at every step of the way—with cheerful comments but also serious reality checks—as she has been for each of my previous books and for each life and professional challenge, since 1997. Thank you!

I dedicate this book to Marianne Sághy—talented medievalist, superlative university teacher, and big love of my youth—who, in 2018, cancer took away from the prime of life and the dream of an old age together hiking the Budapest Hills, but who in the previous six years—after her victory over breast cancer in 2012—had taught me everything about enjoying life to the fullest. The gift of an unexpected reconnection with her former PhD student, the renaissance woman Andra Juganaro, did much to bring me back to life, and convinces me that Marianne's work goes on through a new generation touched and inspired by her.

This list of necessity is incomplete. To all who supported this project, thank you!

A Note on How to Read This Book

THIS BOOK has many levels, and it can be read in many different ways. I strongly recommend that you read it from beginning to end, so you can see the whole picture of fossil fuels, politics, and technology from Siberia to the European Union. But if you are short of time and are reading the book with a specific goal in mind, one of the following strategies may be the right one. If you are a student or scholar of political science, international relations, or a related field, read the theoretical chapters, 1 through 3, and then turn to the empirical case study chapters, 4 through 6, as examples of the issues discussed in the theoretical chapters. If you are using the book as part of an undergraduate course, I recommend that you assign all its chapters and encourage your students—as they work through the empirical chapters—to actively make use of appendices A (key technical terms), B (key actors), and C (chronology), and also to pay close attention to the explanatory notes. In particular, if you are using the book as part of an undergraduate course on energy politics, I encourage you to use appendix A as the basis for assignments on the impact of the use of different energy technologies. If you are reading the book for pleasure and out of a general interest in the region, I recommend that you read chapter 1 and then move directly to the empirical case study chapters, letting your imagination roam the road between Siberia and Germany, and returning to chapters 2 and 3 once that road trip has left you craving more theoretical explanations.

A Note on Transliteration and Measurement Units

PERSONAL NAMES in the main text are rendered per common usage in English-language publications (e.g., Boris Yeltsin, not Boris El'cin, as the transliteration from Russian would render it); names of companies are rendered per their names on their official websites. (Thus, it is possible that a person's name may be spelled differently in the text and the bibliographic reference.) Bibliographic sources in Russian and Ukrainian were transliterated from the Cyrillic script using the online tools for transliteration (e.g., https://www.translitteration.com/transliteration/en/ukrainian/iso-9/ and https://www.translitteration.com/transliteration/en/russian/iso-9/), which make it possible for the reader desiring to go back to an original source to easily produce the correct Cyrillic form, something that is not currently available in the traditional Library of Congress system. In bibliographic references, the name of the city where the item was published is not transliterated but is simply translated into its common English name; the name of the publishing house is transliterated. All measurement units are metric unless otherwise noted.

PART ONE

The Overall Framework

CHAPTER ONE

Dependency on Russian Energy: Threat or Opportunity?

EVER SINCE 2010, when the giant Russian energy firm Gazprom started building the Nord Stream gas pipeline connecting Russia directly with Germany—and especially since the unveiling of plans for parallel Nord Stream 2, which would double the pipeline's capacity and likely significantly reduce the transit of Russian gas through Ukraine—Ukraine has been pursuing an all-out campaign to prevent the construction of this pipeline and to preserve the country's role as the key transit provider for Russian natural gas exports to the European Union's member states. At the same time, Ukraine found itself at war against Russian aggression—having over 7 percent of its territory either outright occupied by Russia or controlled by Russian-backed separatists—while seeking to minimize its imports of Russian energy. Taking these events at face value, why would Ukraine, given Russian aggression, want to continue both its transit relationship and also the related deep entanglement of its economy with Russia's? Would not this continue to make Ukraine vulnerable to Russian energy blackmail, especially in a situation of open conflict?

This story, and many similar stories I have encountered in the course of more than two decades working on energy issues in the countries of the former Soviet Union (FSU), exemplifies some of the thorniest issues with which I have grappled in my professional life. Throughout all these years—which included spending three years conducting field research in Russia, Ukraine, Belarus, Lithuania, Moldova, and Hungary, and writing three books on energy politics in the region—I have asked myself repeatedly: How have Russia's energy-poor neighbors dealt with Russia's energy prowess?[1] How have they dealt with the threat of Russia's use of its energy power against them, most obviously through possible supply suspensions? I sought to answer these questions by looking at them from many different angles. I talked with politicians and analysts of all stripes in all the countries involved, and attended countless academic, think tank, and industry meetings. I pored over thousands of pages of industry analyses in Russian, Ukrainian, Hungarian, and German. With the help of a translator, I unveiled key insights from Lithuanian intelligence reports exposing major gas scandals. As I worked on this, increasingly sharp press and academic coverage started to unfold about the Russian energy weapon and the threat implied by it for Russia's energy-dependent neighbors.

Yet the more I looked at this issue, the more I understood that the *threat* Russian energy represented for these states could not be understood without also understanding the opportunity, even the *temptation*, represented by Russian energy.[2] I realize that this sounds highly controversial. Do I mean that these countries actually *wanted* to be dependent on Russian energy? Temptation and opportunity—in what sense? The temptation has been, most obviously, one of corrupt gains that could be made by well-connected groups able to tap into the large energy rents that could be accrued even in a situation of energy dependency.[3] Indeed, the post-Soviet period presents many examples of energy policy being hijacked by corrupt interests, as we often saw in the case of Ukraine—I wrote an entire book on the subject.[4] But the more deeply I delved into the issue, the more I came to understand that there was something even deeper and more complex than corruption at play here: how risk and opportunity, threat and temptation, were but two faces of the same phenomenon—these states' participation in the value and supply chains (i.e., the entire process, from the discovery of an energy commodity to its delivery to final consumers) associated with the exporting of Russia's energy riches. The rewards of this participation came most prominently not from sales to end consumers at the physical end of the value chain, but mainly from transit and other midstream activities facilitating access to profits, subsidies, and rents.

Even in those situations where elite corruption in energy-dependent countries did *not* get in the way of the state initiating a proactive energy policy, there was often a tension between two goals: establishing infrastructure to diversify supplies, and strengthening the country's role in the energy value chain of its main supplier, Russia. This took place in a variety of ways, for example, through a country's role in Russian oil and gas exports (e.g., Ukraine's role in gas transit, Latvia's role in oil transhipment through the Ventspils port, or Lithuania's and Belarus's roles in oil refining) as a way to both maintain a degree of leverage vis-à-vis its largest supplier and as a means of accessing spillover profits from Russian exports. But behind both threat and opportunity was something even more basic: demand for fossil fuels and their by-products, a key hallmark of twentieth-century economic development generally and especially so in FSU states whose resource use was shaped by energy-intensive Soviet patterns of economic development. Because of the way energy technical systems work (see chapters 3 through 6), being part of an energy exporter's value chains often locks in dependency on its supplies. And continued participation in these chains was also the result of strong path dependencies inherited from the Soviet period.

So, on one hand, participation in these chains helped keep countries such as Ukraine dependent on Russia; on the other hand, participation brought significant income to the country and actors within it. Similar tensions could also be found in the cases of Belarus and the Baltic states.[5] In some cases, this participation was mainly elite-based; in others, it was part of an economic development strategy in which the benefits of integration into Russian energy value chains could trickle down to the entire population; for example, in the case of Belarus in the early 2000s, this became the key to the survival of an otherwise economically unviable regime.[6] Although Ukraine and Belarus may offer the most obvious examples, a similar tension has characterized relations with states and other actors well west of their borders, including EU states and companies involved in Nord Stream and other Russian energy export projects.

These two aspects of the role of Russian energy supplies in the broad region from Vladivostok to Brussels create the puzzle this book seeks to answer—a puzzle that cannot be understood without paying attention to the technical and commercial aspects of energy, which are crucial for understanding the transit and other midstream activities at the book's core.

Some may ask: given the momentous changes taking place in global energy markets, are Russian fossil fuels still an issue?[7] As I write these lines in 2020, the economic power of Russian oil and gas companies seems to be declining as a result of developments such as the rise in liquefied natural gas supplies, the fracking revolution and resulting U.S. exports and oversupply of oil and gas, the sharp decline in world oil prices—which in the spring of 2020, as a result of the COVID-19 pandemic crisis, fell to their lowest point in two decades—and the EU Commission's measures weakening Gazprom's monopoly on natural gas supplies to the region. The rapid technological advances in energy storage driving the renewables revolution through rapidly declining costs, as well as international agreements such as the December 2015 Paris Agreements, promised the dawn of a (hydro)carbon-free energy future. However, though a bright, carbon-free energy future may be in the making, the transition to it has continued to be paved with fossil fuels, at least through the second decade of the twenty-first century— and thus the use of coal, the most environmentally problematic fossil fuel, reached world records in 2014. In two of the three scenarios drawn up by the International Energy Agency for 2040, the role of fossil fuels in global energy changes only modestly—from the current 81 percent, as of 2016, to 79 percent, under the agency's Current Policies Scenario, or to 75 percent under its New Policies Scenario. Only under its more radical Sustainable Development Scenario would fossil fuel use decline to 61 percent by 2040.[8] Thus fossil fuels are still very much worthy of our attention.

Most important, whatever the future prospects of fossil fuels, they remain central for understanding a key formative period for former Soviet states: the first twenty-odd years of their post-Soviet statehood, from 1991 to the Russian annexation of Crimea in 2014. During this period, in post-Soviet country after post-Soviet country, specific ways of navigating the balance between the threat and opportunity of Russian energy left a strong imprint on their political systems;[9] the rampant corruption that characterized the sector in many of these states led to a weakening of democratic governance, often hijacking the hopes unleashed by the 1989–91 democratic revolutions.[10]

So far, scholars have been asking: how has Russia used energy as a weapon against these states? An even more important question, however, is: how has that influence been able to penetrate so deeply into these states' domestic political fabrics? If energy power had been simply about Russia's external power (threat), its consequences would not have been so devastating. But the way this power interfaced with the interests of a variety of actors along the entire value chain (opportunity)—in Russia, other FSU states, and the EU—affected these states' social relations in a much more fundamental way, creating a number of coalitions and alliances that deeply affected both each state's domestic politics and its foreign relations. In the case of Ukraine, for example, energy-sector-driven corruption helped destroy the hopes associated with independence in 1991 and the Orange Revolution in 2004; access to resources that could have been used to build a successful and efficient independent state was bogged down by corruption.

Therefore, the central questions this book seeks to answer are: How have the specificities of these energy value chains affected power relations in the region, and how have these been different for different types of energy? How have these specificities constrained or amplified Russia's ability to use energy supplies as leverage?

To answer these questions, the book brings into dialogue insights from economics, sociology, and critical geography, in addition to political science. From political science, I take power as a central organizing concept, yet understood not only in relational terms of power as influence but also as a dynamic social force (Foucault) and as constitutive power empowering actors to be and do—that is, the power *to*.[11] Such constitutive power interacts with "power as influence"—sometimes potentiating, sometimes constraining an energy supplier's ability to use energy as a means of leverage, which forces us to rethink our assumptions about the directionality of "energy power." From economics, I take the importance of commodities, of analyzing their trade in terms of their whole value chain life cycle and not simply the supply of ready products (Gereffi et al.), within the context of the fragmentation, internationalization, and reintegration of production on a global scale (Wallerstein).[12]

This book also builds upon previous work in cultural theory, anthropology, sociology, and geography that reflects on the value of commodities above and beyond their exchange value (Braudillard), on how inanimate objects operate in social life and affect human–material interactions (Appadurai, Latour), on the importance of materiality for understanding the role of energy resources in political life (Mitchell, Barry, Rogers), and on how energy infrastructures help shape relationships between individuals, the state, and industrial enterprises (Collier).[13] Anthropological perspectives on the various extra-economic "uses" of economic exchange (Gregory, Carrier), as well as on the identity-shaping power of industrial sites (Burawoy) also provide important insights for understanding power issues in the local-space critical nodes analyzed in this book, many of which (e.g., refineries) are also industrial sites.[14] The book builds on these insights to create a new understanding of the value and power chains linking Russian energy sources to their end consumers in the EU and beyond.

CONVENTIONAL CONCEPTIONS OF ENERGY AND POWER—AND THEIR LIMITATIONS

Until now, our views of energy have been too one-dimensional to do justice to the realities outlined above, in at least three ways. First and foremost, energy relations in the region have been viewed largely through the Russian *state energy power* dimension. Second, more generally, we have tended to look at energy issues without paying much attention to the differences between different energy types, and largely *through the prism of oil*, contemporary societies' most-talked-about fossil fuel. And third, we have reduced complex energy issues to a *focus on energy supply*. Focusing on these three dimensions has made it harder to understand the true impact of Russian energy on the social and political life of countries related to Russia's energy value chains—from Latvia, with its lucrative transshipment of Russian oil until the mid-2000s, to Italy's unique role in the value chain of Russian coal exports, to EU-state energy companies' active participation in Russian energy projects.

These three traditional ways of looking at energy—focusing on energy as state power, exports/supplies, and oil—share the fact that each has exacerbated the neglect of the technical and commercial aspects of energy's value and supply chains—how the processes needed to transform primary energy supplies to end-use energy affect power relations. The concept of technopolitics enters the scene here, because—as in the work of scholars such as Gabrielle Hecht and Timothy Mitchell—it brings to the fore both how power may be exerted through certain technologies (i.e., the use of technology for political purposes) and how technical requirements shape political questions, with the implication of technology's ability to empower actors—different actors in different circumstances.[15] Let us take a brief look at each of the these traditional ways of thinking about energy.

Russia's "State Energy Weapon" and Its Discontents

Given Russia's major role as oil, natural gas, and coal supplier to the EU and—especially—to energy-dependent former Soviet states, much attention has focused on the Russian state's use of energy as a means of exerting power over other states—Russia's energy weapon.[16] Given Russia's significant energy resources—at the time of its annexation of Crimea in 2014, it was the world's largest exporter of natural gas, second-largest exporter of crude oil (the largest, if one includes both crude oil and refined oil product exports), and third-largest exporter of coal—such views are not surprising.[17] In much of the existing literature, images of weak neighboring states and the EU with its weak common energy policy are juxtaposed with a picture of the strong Russian state, with its centralized control of the energy sector able to use "energy power" as a political weapon vis-à-vis its energy-dependent neighbors and other consumers. Thus, the focus has been on Russia's state power and exports, and on the share of these in the energy imports of consumer states.[18] This emphasis can be seen as a delayed reflection of approaches developed in the shadow of the 1973 oil crisis and 1973–74 oil embargo by the Organization of the Petroleum Exporting Countries (OPEC) and the Organization of Arab Petroleum Exporting Countries (OAPEC),[19] which awoke scholars to the power of energy and helped shape the way we think about energy actors and energy power.[20] Even though the embargo was from an association of states, OAPEC, and not individual states, it was perceived by many through the lens of the attempt to use state-owned companies to influence other states' policies (i.e., Western states' support of Israel), contributing to an overwhelming focus on energy as *state* power.

This experience fostered thinking about energy power in terms of one particular type of power: power to get another state *to do something* desired by another state; in other words, power *over someone*. In this Dahlian conception of power, power is influence, or "power over," "an attribute that an actor possesses and may use knowingly as a resource to shape the actions or conditions of action of others," for example, by withholding or threatening to withhold energy supplies.[21] This type of thinking has had a long-term impact on the field, fostering speculation about energy as a "weapon." Geopolitical and neorealist approaches highlighting states' use of strategic commodities as a means to exercise power vis-à-vis other states have dominated these debates,[22] which gained new strength in the 1990s with discussions of Russia's use of energy in its relations with energy-poor post-Soviet states, and, potentially, EU energy importers; such relations have largely been analyzed in terms of "power, security, and zero-sum geopolitical competition."[23]

However, it is not enough to simply talk about the use of energy as a weapon without understanding the entire set of actors and processes in the energy value chains. Once the full array of actors is brought into the analysis, a more complex picture emerges. The traditional approach has failed to offer satisfactory explanations for other key post-Soviet and European energy dynamics, from Ukraine's lack of resolve in breaking its energy dependence on Russia (until massive price increases, starting in 2010[24]), despite the heavy political costs created by this dependency; to EU companies' wavering support for infrastructure projects (e.g., the Nabucco gas pipeline), intended to reduce the Union's dependence on Russian energy and, conversely, support for projects such as the Nord Stream pipeline, solidifying this dependency. State-centered approaches are not able to fully explain these situations because they neglect a key piece in the puzzle: the role of multiple actors above and beyond the central state, *located all along the value chains extending between production in Russia and use by end consumers in the EU*, and whose behavior is also constrained by the technical requirements of these chains.

In particular, energy analyses privileging the role of the Russian state have underestimated the impact of three types of actors. First, some actors are not involved directly in energy extraction ("upstream") but in its further processing and trading ("midstream" and "downstream"); these include not only transit operators but also refineries, operators of storage facilities, and domestic gas and electricity suppliers. Second are domestic energy actors in energy-dependent post-Soviet states such as Ukraine and Belarus, which have been understudied due to general perceptions of these states as objects of Russian designs with little agency of their own. In reality, however, these energy-dependent states have had more agency than is commonly attributed them, with Russia's ability to exert energy power having often been conditioned by domestic political processes in the energy-dependent states themselves, including the fact that in some cases important elite groups have found it advantageous to continue a situation of energy dependency as a means of extracting rents for themselves.[25] And third are Russian actors that do not fit neatly within the re-statization narrative commonly used to describe the country's energy processes under Vladimir Putin's leadership (2000–) and Yukos's nationalization in 2004: formally private energy actors—such as Gunvor and others working behind the headlines dominated by the state-controlled, giant producers Gazprom and Rosneft, as well as individual actors that, despite working formally as executives of state-owned companies or state institutions, may de facto be pursuing their own private interests.[26] The fact that some of these actors may be at the very top of the state apparatus does not invalidate this point.[27]

The emphasis on energy as a Russian state weapon is also related to two longer-term trends in conventional approaches to energy: the focus on oil, and the overwhelming emphasis on supply and export issues, to the detriment of other aspects of the energy process. I turn to these briefly before presenting this book's alternative perspective.

Still Hostages to Oil?

Since the 1973–74 OPEC/OAPEC oil embargo, oil has dominated Western discussions of energy and power.[28] Although there is no shortage of good research on other types of energy, such as natural gas, attempts at theorizing the role of energy in domestic politics and international relations have largely focused on oil, fostering the implicit assumption that other fossil fuels, such as natural gas, work in the same way as oil does.[29] Other types of energy, such as nuclear power and renewables, have received much less attention; coal has been largely ignored. The fact that two of the most prominent bodies of literature linking energy with political development, those on the "oil curse" and "rentier state," are based specifically on the experience of *oil-rich* states also contributed to this trend.[30] Yet it is not necessary to look very far to see that for many states, and in international trade, other hydrocarbons are as important as oil. Although oil is the largest internationally traded commodity, and in 2015 it played the most important role in the global total primary energy supply, at 31.7 percent, followed by coal (28.1 percent) and natural gas (21.6 percent), coal was the most important source (at 39.3 percent) for electricity generation world-wide.[31] Coal use in particular has seen an increase in the transition period between the unconventional hydrocarbons boom and a possible decarbonized future.[32] New coal-fired generation capacities were being built worldwide—hardly a sign of coal going away from the global energy mix. The EU imports about one-third each of its oil, gas, and coal from Russia, making the virtual lack of research on coal as a component of these states' energy imports from Russia especially puzzling.

The overwhelming emphasis on oil not only has prevented us from thinking seriously about the differences between various energy types (see chapter 3) but also has fundamentally limited our ability to understand how energy really works throughout the entire value chain—the key focus of this book. When we make a serious effort to understand the differences between different types of energy, we not only see how different they are in terms of issues such as how each requires different means of transportation and processing before they can be used by end consumers but we also gain a better understanding of how they may have an impact on power relations. Thus, as is discussed in chapter 3, the *degree of processing needed* before an energy commodity is brought to market, and *whether this processing is best done directly at the production site* (as in the case of natural gas) or can be done in a variety of locations (as in the case of oil), will affect the relative power of midstream players in various geographical locations.[33] So the ways in which the uneasy balance between opportunity and risk plays itself out will be different for different types of energy.

The Tyranny of an Overconcentration on Supply

The emphasis on energy as a weapon has also led us to think mainly in terms of its most obvious use: through intentional supply disruptions. This emphasis reflects conventional approaches to energy security, which have largely been from a consumers' perspective. Defining energy security as mainly security of *supply* has exacerbated the neglect of key aspects such as security of *demand* (i.e., the impact of stability of demand on energy exporters) and the technical hurdles involved in getting energy to be usable by final consumers.[34] Similarly, much of the emphasis on energy supply has been based on the idea of energy as a security concern, not as a good that needs to be paid for. In reality, as a private good with the characteristics of a public good—that is, as a privately provided public good—energy is both, given its strategic and social welfare importance for concrete societies.[35] Despite recent publications arguing that the increase in unconventional oil and natural gas exports from the United States may lead to a heyday of U.S. influence (along with a decline in Russian influence in European markets[36]), the idea that access to energy supplies may provide a security blanket regardless of price considerations is problematic, though it was perhaps accurate in a militarized setting such as World War II, when the United States' abundant access to oil compared with that of Nazi Germany played a key role in the war's outcome.[37] Such an approach to energy security and energy power focusing on supply/exports exhibits both empirical and conceptual limitations.

At an empirical level, a focus on exports/supplies does not do justice to the complex nature of energy trade in broader Europe. Russia depends significantly on Western technology for oil and natural gas extraction. To reach consumers in the EU and other nearby markets, oil, gas, and coal from Russia must not only travel thousands of kilometers from their production sites and transit through states with diverse political and economic relations with Russia. They must also go through a series of complex production and postproduction processes. These technical processes affect not only actors' profits but also their engagement with further sets of actors that are key for completing specific steps in these value chains, such as transit, storage, and refining services.

At a conceptual level, a focus on exports/supplies limits our perspective, because it draws on only one aspect of power: power as "power over" another person or state. Yet energy is power not only because it (i.e., its supply/withholding) can provide a state with influence or power over other states, but also because of its constitutive elements—that is, how the energy process affects "what capacities and practices" various actors are "socially empowered to undertake" ("power to").[38] In an energy context, such a constitutive perspective pays attention to how control over energy may both help constitute actors at a variety of levels (e.g., domestic-level political groups, firms, states, cartels, other international organizations) and affect relationships between them.

This constitutive process often takes shape through the prospect of accessing and sharing profits *through* and *throughout* the value chain—*through* the value chain in the sense of the value chain being used for the constitution of energy power; and *throughout* the value chain in the sense of processes taking place at each stage in the chain, not just its supply/export component. So to understand the influence aspects of energy power, it is also necessary to understand its constitutive elements and how they help shape social actors—for example, which energy-related actors are able to develop political salience in a political community as a whole, not only within their sector.

UNDERSTANDING POWER RELATIONSHIPS THROUGH A VALUE CHAIN PERSPECTIVE

Following a specific good through its entire supply chain from conception to final use—as shown by groundbreaking studies such as Rivoli's *The Travels of a T-Shirt in the Global Economy*—can provide insights that may elude approaches based on large *N* studies. Although this is a book about energy, much inspiration for it came from research on commodity and supply chains outside the energy field.[39] And though inspired by these books' reader-friendly narratives, this book also explicitly incorporates a rigorous academic methodology (see chapter 2). Moreover, in contrast to most research in the supply chain narrative tradition—which has largely focused on single-commodity studies of global resource flows, from beef to shea butter to oil—this book explicitly seeks to *compare* the distinctive value chains of three fossil fuels.

In order to understand the balance of opportunity and risk, of threat and temptation, in Russia's energy relations with post-Soviet states and broader Europe, in the chapters below we follow Russia's three key fossil fuel exports—natural gas, oil, and coal—from production in Siberia through final use in Germany, revealing, as the journey unfolds, the types of "power over" and "power to" that are unveiled—energy as an instrument of Russian power over other states, but also the role of Russian energy in helping to constitute domestic and transnational actors from the farthest corners of Russia to Brussels, which is the political center of the European Union—with myriad political implications.

The book is divided into three parts. Part I presents the overall framework (this chapter and chapter 2), as well as the necessary background on how the material characteristics ("materiality") of each of the fossil fuels followed in the book—natural gas, oil, and coal—affect the typical features of each of their markets, as well as power relations along their value chains (chapter 3).

Part II of the book focuses on hydrocarbon chains and political power. It takes the discussion from the theoretical to the empirical by following Russia's top three fossil fuels (natural gas, oil, coal) and the actors related to each of their value chains, from production and export through end use. Chapters 4 through 6 are devoted to the analysis of exemplary value chains of specific Russian hydrocarbons: natural gas (chapter 4), oil (chapter 5), and coal (chapter 6). These exemplary chains all run along the same basic spatial path: extraction in Russia, transit/processing in Ukraine (and other states), and final use in Germany. The chapters analyze the main characteristics and challenges of the respective value chain as experienced in the geographical area covered by its path.

Part III focuses on new types of energy and new political chains. Chapter 7 revisits the question of the impact of energy materiality and value chains in shaping post-Soviet politics in the crucial years leading up to Russia's annexation of Crimea in 2014. Chapter 8 analyzes how the market and political disruptions since 2014 have been changing the balance between energy threat and opportunity, given the global challenge of decarbonization.

CHAPTER TWO

Is Energy a Weapon or a Constituent Part of Disaggregated Power Relations?

CHAINS CAN connect, but they can also constrain, and even enslave. This book seeks to shed light on these two aspects of the role of energy in domestic and international power relationships.

This book thus seeks to answer a key question: How has the participation of consumer states' actors in the value chains of Russian energy exports affected social and political power relationships in each of the involved states, but also at the European level? In seeking answers to this question, the book also explores whether these patterns are similar or different for the various energy commodities exported by Russia, such as oil, natural gas, and coal. What energy-type-specific incentives have affected relationships in the area? How these questions are answered will ultimately help us better understand a key policy question: How have these processes constrained or amplified Russia's ability to use energy supplies as a means of leverage?

AN ALTERNATIVE VIEW OF ENERGY AND POWER AS UNFOLDING ALONG THE ENTIRE VALUE CHAIN

In chapter 1, I presented some of the limits to a state-power, imports-based view of energy politics. This is not meant to imply that the

Russian leadership has not used energy supplies as a means of political influence. Undoubtedly, it has repeatedly sought to do so.[1] This book does not deny this reality, but it seeks to deconstruct energy power into a much more complex engagement—an engagement between actors having various types of power, and taking into account the entire energy process from production to end use, including its technical aspects. Considering how significant energy issues have been for shaping relations both between Russia and the post-Soviet states, and between Russia and the European Union, it is highly surprising that so far no comprehensive analysis of these relations along the complete chain from producer to end user has been conducted.

The political, economic, and security implications of energy trade from the 1990s to today set the context for the importance of understanding its value chains. From the European experience, we also know the power of value chains as a basis for reconciliation and political integration, as seen in the case of the European Coal and Steel Community (established in 1952) as an instrument of postwar reconciliation and, as it came to pass, the European Union's predecessor.[2] Energy trade and access to transit were key in security issues, such as the United States' and the EU's relations with Iran. At the political level, energy trade was key in terms of propping the political power of leaders such as Vladimir Putin and Hugo Chávez. At the economic level, energy trade was the basis for the fast growth of the Kazakh and Azerbaijani economies after 1991, whereas the example of China tells us much about how crucial access to energy imports has been to maintaining its high levels of economic growth.

These chains include not only production and transportation but also the multiple technical steps without which this energy would be useless to final users. Spatially, these chains go through Russia, transit states (e.g., Ukraine and Belarus, themselves also large consumers), and consumer states. Functionally, the vertical value chain involves the production ("upstream"), processing, transportation ("midstream"), and distribution ("downstream") tasks required for primary energy to be usable by end users. Upstream activities usually relate to the actual production (i.e., extraction) of a primary energy resource, midstream activities relate to its transportation between markets and further processing into usable goods, and downstream activities relate to the marketing and distribution of ready products.[3] (Processing can take place in producing, transit, or consumer states.)

The upstream sector involves the prospecting for and production of crude oil, natural gas, and coal. It includes searching for potential fields, drilling exploratory wells, and subsequently operating the wells or mines to bring the crude oil, raw natural gas, or coal to the surface. The midstream sector processes, stores, markets, and transports these commodities. It is not limited to transportation but also involves adding value in the form of processing; the good delivered at the end of the chain is never the same unprocessed raw material that entered the value chain in the production field, but is altered by processing, whether visible or invisible. In some cases (e.g., the export of crude oil), this processing is related to physical change (refining). In the case of natural gas, the midstream contribution is less visible but no less important, because its main role is preventing undesirable changes to the good as to safeguard the characteristics necessary for it to be used by the end consumer (e.g., protecting natural gas from exploding or being dissipated into the atmosphere). The downstream sector refers to the distribution and selling of final products to consumers, such as natural gas, refined oil products, and coal, and the coke and metallurgical products produced from them.

At the same time, these vertical chains intersect horizontally with other important, nonenergy industries; these industries may be energy-intensive and/or use fossil fuels or their derivatives as direct industrial feedstock, as in the case of coking-coal-dependent metallurgy and the natural-gas-dependent production of chemical fertilizers.[4] In countries such as Russia, Ukraine, Lithuania, and Belarus, these industries constitute some of the largest sources of export revenue and have consistently produced some of the wealthiest and most influential business actors ("oligarchs")—from Russia's metals magnate Oleg Deripaska, now known worldwide because of his possible connection with Russian collusion in the 2016 U.S. elections, to Rinat Akhmetov, whose coal and steel empire spans from Ukraine to the United States.[5]

What does this all mean for understanding Russian energy power in the post-Soviet region and beyond? Understanding energy power as unfolding along the entire value chain allows us to identify key physical as well as commercial nodes that may act as gateways and gatekeepers, enabling or constraining Russian power. Understanding energy power as both constitutive ("power to") and relational ("power over") helps us better understand the development of and the motivations for such gatekeepers acting as gate openers or closers to Russian influence under particular circumstances.

What Are Value Chains, and Why Do They Matter?

Value chains (often also referred to by the related concept of "supply chains"[6]) are at the very center of the story told in this book. Although the term "value chains" is hardly a household one, such chains became part of our lives in the spring of 2020, as the COVID-19 pandemic started to disrupt supply chains of household products we had long taken for granted.

These chains are all around us, embodied in most of the goods we use in our daily lives—from the refined oil (gasoline) that runs our cars, to the sugar we use to sweeten our coffee, to the salt that seasons our fries. Indeed, household items like these embody key issues central for the energy story told in this book: they include fungible goods (i.e., goods sufficiently standardized in quality between various producers as to be easily tradable), and continental or global transit journeys.[7] They bring to the fore issues of tradability (often discussed as "commodificability") and value addition (or subtraction) often through global processing and technical chains, issues that are at the core of this book's inquiry.

In analyzing value chains, insights from the literature on global value chains (GVCs) can be helpful, because it focuses attention on the *entire cycle* of "economic activities that are required to bring a good or service from conception, through the different phases of production (involving a combination of physical transformation and the input of various producer services), to delivery to final consumers."[8] Although the concept of value chains is closely related to the more widely used term "supply chains," as well as to network analysis, it goes beyond them in that it emphasizes not only the actors in the network and the movement of goods and their requisite materials in a supply chain but also the value addition or subtraction that takes place as a good moves through this chain, as is discussed below. Thus the concept of value is key for understanding the redistributive implications of various chains.[9] Although usually taken for granted, payment and financing chains, and the financial flows associated with them, are also crucial for the functioning of value chains. Value chains can also be used to hide profits from governments, for example, through "transfer pricing," whereby companies use reduced prices for sales between their own entities as a way to hide profits and minimize taxes, in the context of a weak global regulatory framework controlling these chains.

This book uses important insights from the GVC literature, but also goes beyond it in four important ways. First, though this literature has tended to focus on value chains as abstract systems in themselves, I add a decidedly spatial dimension to their analysis. Taking the spatial element seriously also means fully taking into account the local political environment of the areas crossed by concrete value chains. Second, the GVC literature has focused largely on manufacturing industries and the relocation of their low-value-adding activities to lower-cost locations in the Global South, a model not easily applicable to the fossil fuel sector, where relocation opportunities are more limited, and where there is often high value added (and destroyed) through ancillary production processes that are highly dependent on the ups and downs of global markets.[10]

Third, in contrast to the GVC literature, this book's approach acknowledges that in the energy industries, there is not only value *creation* but also *possible value subtraction and value destruction*; these issues have important power implications for the communities and actors involved.[11] Although one may intuitively think of a chain where each further production step adds value to a product, the situation for commodities such as oil may be different, given the wide price swings characteristic of this industry, as was seen in April of 2020, when oil futures went from $20 to –$37 in just a week, and largely swung back a few days later.[12] Fourth and finally, I address the political aspects of these value chains in a more explicit way. Though the GVC literature looks at governance as involving "the ability of one firm in the chain to influence or determine the activities of other firms in the chain," focusing almost exclusively on *firms* as actors in value chains and neglecting the role of states and political governance, I pay much more attention to the political and regulatory environment.[13] For instance, Gereffi and colleagues note that the power of lead firms, which in their framework is key for the governance of value chains, is closely related to barriers to entry.[14] Yet factors such as corruption and a lack of transparency also affect such barriers to market entry, and thus warrant adding a more explicit political and regulatory dimension to the analysis of value chains.

A value chains perspective provides a different and more accurate lens for understanding power relations, because it allows us to see actors and relationships to which we may not otherwise have paid attention. For example, using a value chain perspective for the coal sector enables us to link the upstream (production) with key industries using coal supplies, allowing us to see the key connections between energy policies; the rise of Ukraine's richest and most influential oligarch of the postindependence period, the metallurgy magnate Rinal Akhmetov; and the development of unsustainable policies in the Donbas region, which would ultimately facilitate Russian-instigated separatist elements there.

Bringing Technology and Process Back In: Rediscovering the Power of the Midstream

Processing activities constitute a key but hitherto largely neglected part of value chains. Studies of energy and politics have traditionally focused on the transit aspect of the midstream (i.e., the transportation of an energy commodity between one market to another). Although the 2006 and 2009 Russian gas cutoffs to Ukraine also affected transit supplies to the EU and brought much-needed increased interest to transit states, conceptualizing the midstream largely in terms of transit limits our ability to understand energy processes. Thus, a first step for bringing the midstream back in requires understanding "midstream" in its full meaning: not simply as transit, but as also including other key activities between initial production and sale to end consumers, such as refining and storage. Though long neglected in general understandings of the oil value chain, storage issues made headlines in April 2020, when, as discussed above, oil futures prices briefly went into the negative as excess production and a lack of storage made some producers willing to pay buyers to get the oil off their hands. Despite this key role, there has been little theoretical conceptualization of other midstream activities besides transit, which has an established research tradition.[15]

Primary energy sources such as natural gas, oil, and coal are useless to final consumers in unprocessed form. Thus the story of how energy is reconstituted as political power cannot be told without telling the story of process—how primary energy sources are reconstituted as end-use (electric/heat/transportation fuel) power, whereby the political power impact does not take place only at the end of the physical chain with the end use of energy but also as a by-product of processes taking place at each stage. Each of these processing/handling steps is thus crucial, can produce or destroy value for a variety of players, and has important distributive and power implications.

The role of midstream processing and its actors is different for each energy type. (For example, natural gas can normally only be processed at the production site, whereas crude oil may be refined thousands of miles away.) These processing differences will also affect the possible roles played by related actors and also the possible coalitions that may emerge between them—including between local energy actors in consumer and producing states. In fact, such coalitions may in some cases seriously constrain the ability of a supplier state to implement its desired policies in the consumer state.

Bringing back the midstream and in particular processing is an important contribution of this book, because processes and processing are often overlooked in discussions of energy and power. The literature on the political economy of conflict—in particular, analyses of the role of natural resources in civil conflict situations (see below)[16]—while discussing how the characteristics of various natural resources can affect the availability of financial resources to the parties to a conflict, does not explore these goods' technological and value chains, and their social effects. Similarly, the literature on the resource curse (discussed in more detail below) has focused on energy exports as a source of a state's *revenue*, but not on the processes through which the energy commodities generating these revenues are produced or brought to market.

Looking seriously at process also makes possible a serious examination of some of the secondary "goods" produced by energy systems—not only the ready-to-use electricity, heat, and motor fuel at the end of the chain but also the by-products of various energy systems at various stages of the value chain—rents, income as "currency" for domestic bargaining among groups, employment, and systems of social provisioning associated with these systems (e.g., the enterprise-based provision of many social services in the USSR). In the same way as economic anthropologists such as Gregory and Carrier have shown that the social *functions* performed by a particular exchange may be as important as the goods exchanged, the secondary functions performed by various uses and exchanges of energy goods may be as important as the supply itself.[17] At each stage in the energy transformation process, a portion of the energy is transformed into electricity, heat, or movement, but the rest of the energy is not—it may dissipate as heat or simply be lost. We can think of the "uses" of energy in broader social processes in a similar way (see figure 2.1).

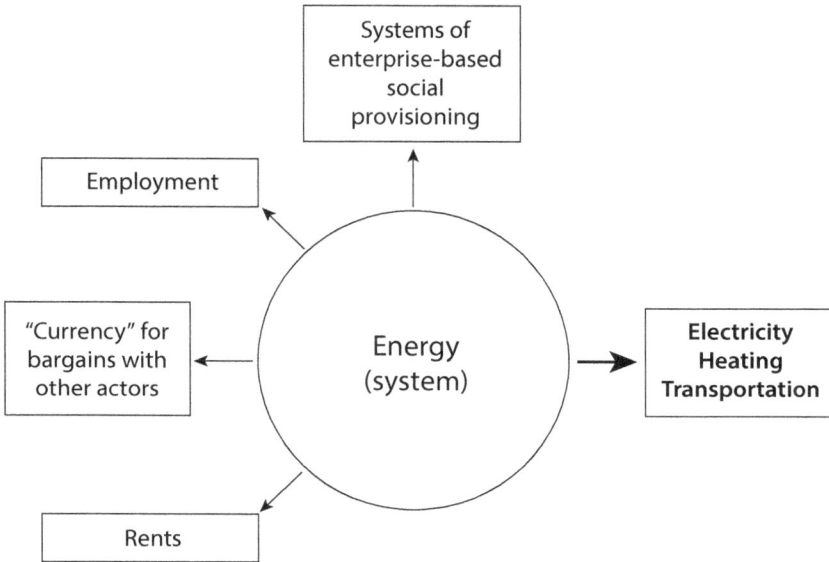

Figure 2.1 Goods produced by energy systems as processes

This, in turn, has implications for our understanding of "energy as a weapon": energy can be used for a variety of domestic and external purposes whose intended and unintended consequences will also affect a state's ability to use energy as a means of external political leverage. So the various domestically and externally oriented uses of energy also can act as constraints on a state's ability to use energy for political pressure. This is in addition to other, more commonly discussed constraints, such as corruption, penetration of the state by private interests, state capacity, and principal/agent issues.[18]

Materiality Matters

This book proposes a new way of looking at energy actors and their interests—starting from the physical nature of the material resources available to them ("materiality"), and analyzing how their concrete characteristics affect their value chains and, through them, power relationships. Here, I take as a key starting point materiality as *both enabling and constraining* human choices, as explored in the literature on human–material interactions best known through the work of

Arjun Appadurai and Bruno Latour.[19] We cannot find a full answer to the question of how human actors use material goods such as energy to pursue certain goals—including its use of energy for external political leverage—unless, following Collier, we also ask "how nonhuman actors" and conditions "structure the choices of human actors."[20] As shown by Bakker in her study of water privatization in the United Kingdom, the material qualities of a resource may complicate attempts by stakeholders to use it for their own goals.[21]

The material differences between different energy types play a key role in our analysis (see table 2.1). As is discussed in more detail in chapter 3, a key difference concerns whether the base good is solid, liquid, or gaseous in its original state, which will affect (1) the way each lends itself to storage, transportation, and trade as uniform units (i.e., the degree to which it can be turned into a commodity); and (2) the type and shape of markets emerging around each. As is discussed in chapter 3, each energy type also exhibits important differences in terms of the type of processing necessary before it can be utilized by end users. Processing will also affect actors' engagement with further sets of actors key for completing specific steps in their specific value chains, such as in refining and transit. These materiality-related processing differences create opportunities and constraints for relationships between actors, and thus can facilitate a variety of domestic and transborder coalitions.

What is the difference between a materiality perspective and a more general one paying attention to the technical aspects of energy production? They are not the same; rather, materiality has to do with the essential physical characteristics of a good, whereas technology plays the role

TABLE 2.1

Natural Gas, Oil, and Coal and Their Main Differences at a Glance

Energy type	Natural gas	Oil	Coal
Physical state	Gaseous	Liquid	Solid
Value-to-volume ratio	Low	High	Low (higher for metallurgical coking coal)
Typical means of transportation	Pipeline	Pipeline, tanker; also rail	Rail, ship
Substitutability	High	Low	Medium

Note: "Substitutability" is defined as the ability of a type of energy to be substituted by other types of energy at the end-use level.

of mediator—the state of technology helps determine what is physically doable and economically feasible to do with a good at any given point in time. Thus, for example, the liquefaction of natural gas into liquefied natural gas (LNG) and its subsequent seaborne transportation were only made possible with the development of this technology.

The take on materiality proposed by this book represents a new approach to the issue, in two ways. First, though some authors have discussed the materiality aspects of energy *infrastructure*, I take these insights further, using materiality to understand not only the role of energy infrastructure but also the role of each *type of energy* itself.[22] Second, previous attempts at looking at the impact of the physical characteristics of energy goods on social relations—scattered among a number of bodies of literature—all show an overwhelming preoccupation with the end-result, direct-outcome elements of energy power: *power over others, export revenue*, and *supply*. Two interesting—though indirect—attempts at tackling the question of the impact of differences between types of natural resources on political relationships have taken place in the area of conflict studies[23] and, closer to the energy area, the literature on the resource curse and rentier states.[24] In general terms, the rentier state literature has argued that an abundance of exportable energy resources (and the resulting abundance of revenue) makes a state prone to a number of problems that may hinder democratic governance. Because these rents make it possible for the state to access significant income without needing to tax its population, the state evolves from a "production" to an "allocation" stance, weakening both crucial links to its citizens and governance.[25] Its focus is more on the effects of the entrance of large, export-related rents on the political system and not so much on the *processes* related to the creation of these rents. Thus, both bodies of literature—on resources and conflict, and on rentier states—share a common limitation with those that emphasize energy's use as a weapon: an almost teleological interest in the end results (revenue, degree of dependence, influence over concrete actions by another state) but much less in the *process*. The approach proposed here also contrasts with the resource-rent emphasis on value extraction; though this literature focuses on value *extraction* from natural resources, a process-centered approach pays attention to processes of value *creation* (as well as destruction) around the resources and their associated technical processes, and to their social consequences.

Another way of tackling the impact of differences between different types of energy would focus on what dependency on various types of energy means. There has been some discussion (albeit seldom in a systematic manner) of how differences in a state's energy imports and consumption mix (i.e., the relative roles of oil, natural gas, coal, nuclear energy, and renewables) affect its ability to withstand a supplier's intentional stoppage of supplies.[26] We also know that the means whereby an energy commodity is best transported (i.e., by pipeline only—natural gas—or also by ship, truck, or rail—oil, coal, LNG) will affect how easy it will be for a supplier to turn off supplies, and also how easy it will be for the affected state to replace such supplies on short notice. However, we know very little about how differences between various energy resources affect power and power relations at a variety of other levels that are *not directly related to supply and supply disruptions.*

This book explores how, within the post-Soviet context, different types of energy and their different value chains led to different ways of incorporating local actors into related transborder coalitions, affecting power relations and a state's ability to use energy as a means of external leverage. Thus, we build on existing knowledge on how the characteristics of a commodity affect its ability to be used for foreign policy pressure (discussed above), but take the inquiry a step further, analyzing how such characteristics affect a commodity's ability to be used for the empowerment of concrete local actors, and as a focal point for a variety of activities—including rent-seeking and corruption—facilitating transborder cooperation between actors with the goal of exploiting these opportunities.[27]

LOOKING AT ENERGY POWER FROM THE BOTTOM UP: HOW THIS BOOK TACKLES IT

This book's argument, in a nutshell, is that the material characteristics of an energy good—in interaction with its main related actors and their "uses" of energy, and the governance environment (see figure 2.2)—will affect the technological and value chains for that good, in turn affecting power relations. How do these three elements interact? This book is first and foremost about value chains and their actors. Materiality, choices, and the governance environment are constraints affecting actors' behavior and interactions within that value chain.

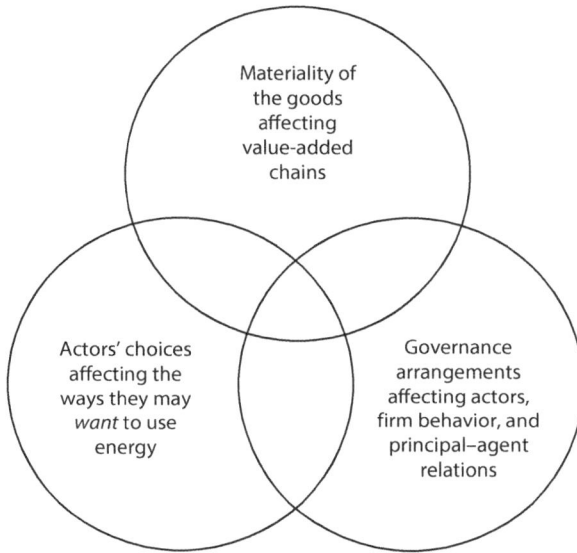

Figure 2.2 Factors affecting power interactions involving energy actors

How do these differences between energy types make an impact on power relations? The impact will take place through two main pathways. The first pathway works through the ways in which the nature of the value chain and its technical constraints will affect distinct distributive openings and distinct typical value chain challenges. In doing so, it endows some actors within the chain with more or less power, often bestowing it in unexpected locations in the value chain affecting various actors' counterpower vis-à-vis supplier states. For example, despite Belarus's high energy (and, arguably, political) dependency on Russia, throughout the 2000s Belarus, having established itself as a key refining center for Russian oil, was able to ignore key oil refining-and-export revenue-sharing agreements with Russia that were intended for the benefit of the central Russian state budget, thanks to a situational coalition between powerful Russian and Belarusian oil actors, a process that cannot be fully explained by a state-centered framework.[28]

The second pathway through which materiality has an impact on power relationships is by affecting (constraining or supporting) an energy producer's ability to use energy for external political goals. The nature of the value chains will matter here, because their requirements create not only different possibilities for intentionally disrupting supplies (as discussed above), but also different framing conditions for the establishment of situational coalitions between energy players within or across borders, at times leading to otherwise unexpected outcomes possibly trumping official policy. Thus this approach shares an interest in subnational actors with interest-group-based perspectives on trade in the tradition of Baldwin, Milner, and Moravcsik.[29] It does, however, go significantly beyond these because it looks not only at interest groups and their interests but also at how the particularities of the specific value chains they inhabit constrain and condition the realization of those interests.

Methodology: Focusing on the "Calm Before the Storm" Period, 2011–14

The "calm before the storm" period, October 2011–March 2014, was chosen as the focus period for this book. This does not mean that the periods before or after it remain outside the field of interest. Rather, this means that I take this period as exemplary, providing a snapshot of these value chains as they existed at a key period representative of broader trends between 1991 and 2014. The specific focus period was chosen because it represents a period of relative stability concerning both prices and energy-related governance in each of the three sectors and key countries covered by this book. It opens with the commissioning of the Nord Stream natural gas pipeline in October 2011, and it ends with the Russian annexation of Crimea in March 2014. This also represents the last period of price stability and relative calm in international energy markets before the large-scale disruption caused by the mid-2014 collapse in oil prices resulting from the unconventional oil and gas revolution—as well as the last period of calm before the Russian military intervention in Ukraine.[30] Because I am comparing three different value chains, having a stable focus period, rather than covering a longer period of changes, helps limit the number of moving parts, allowing us to focus on the differences between natural gas, oil, and coal.

Why the focus on oil, gas, and coal? To understand how the material characteristics of various energy goods affect their value chains and the interrelationship of actors within them, it makes sense to compare the value chains of various types of energy. But what types of energy to focus on? Although Russia's energy relationships with neighboring states include a range of types of energy, from nuclear power to electricity, this book focuses on Russia's top three fossil fuel exports: natural gas, oil, and coal. They were chosen from the larger universe of Russian-produced energy and energy technology (including renewables, nuclear power, and electricity generated from primary energy sources) because they are *primary energy sources* and *commodities*, as well as the most significant ones in trade with the countries of the former Soviet Union and the European Union.

How to carry out this comparison? This can be done at an abstract level, analyzing the typical value chains for oil, natural gas, and coal and how each creates distinct framing conditions for actors' interactions. This task is tackled in chapter 3. To go beyond this, the book subsequently follows—in the case study chapters 4, 5, and 6, respectively—the concrete physical chains of Russia's natural gas, oil, and coal exported (as raw materials or as refined or semiprocessed industrial products) to the European Union.

Case study selection: choosing exemplary value chains. Each of the case studies in this book follows a *concrete, exemplary physical value chain* for natural gas, oil, or coal.[31] It does not attempt to cover all existing value chains related to the export of that type of energy from Russia to the EU. This would be physically and methodologically impossible; oil, natural gas, and coal are produced in various parts of Russia, and then they are exported to the EU through multiple transportation means and ports or border crossings, and through various transit states, creating dozens if not hundreds of physical value chains that could be followed. Rather, the book examines one *exemplary* value chain each for oil, natural gas, and coal, through which the typical characteristics of value chains involving that commodity can be assessed.

However, from the multitude of possible chains, how best to choose the concrete physical value chains to be followed as exemplary cases? Indeed, it would be tempting to choose the target chains on the basis of sheer volume (i.e., one particular physical chain's contribution to all of Russia's exports of a particular commodity), or of the interesting nature of actors' political links all along the chain. But because the book's focus is on the impact of the materiality of the energy goods at hand, choosing concrete value chains according to the *similar conditions principle* makes most sense. This principle means holding other conditions constant while varying the energy commodity on which we are focusing, so the impact of its material characteristics can be best assessed. Keeping these conditions as constant as possible means first and foremost keeping the spatial aspect (in particular, the countries through which the physical chain is going) as constant as possible for the chains that are being compared, allowing for a better comparison because related conditions (e.g., governance systems) will remain constant.[32]

On the basis of these criteria, the value chains to be compared were chosen so as to hold constant key points on their spatial path: extraction in Russia, transit/processing in Ukraine, and end use in Germany. A specific country within the EU—Germany—and not the EU as a whole was chosen as the spatial end point of all the chains. This is so because having the chains end in various EU states would not have preserved the same governance conditions—despite the growing role of EU-level legislation and initiatives, there continued to be significant differences in national-level energy policies, legislation, and competitive environment among EU states (e.g., on nuclear power plants and support for renewables-generated electricity) to warrant having all the exemplary value chains end in a single EU state, so as to keep the conditions as constant as possible between the three chains. On this basis, the chains shown in table 2.2 and in figure 2.3 were chosen.

Each of these value chains starts with a raw material unit (i.e., a "molecule" of natural gas, crude oil, or coal), which, as it moves westward toward EU markets, is subject to either physical transformation processing (cleaning/refining/transformation into feedstock for other industries), or other, less visible technical processes necessary for the good to remain usable as it reaches its destination (e.g., via pipeline). The natural gas, oil, and coal chains chosen as exemplary case studies (again, in chapters 4 through 6—see table 2.2) reflect this diversity. The natural gas value chain (chapter 4) involves the exporting of natural gas to Germany, where it is used for electricity generation. The oil value chain (chapter 5) involves German imports of diesel refined in the Czech Republic of Russian oil transited through Ukraine. The coal value chain (chapter 6) involves the export of coking coal to Ukraine, its use as feedstock for the metallurgical industry, and the exporting of the resulting products to Germany.

TABLE 2.2
This Book's Value Chain Case Studies

Book Chapter and Commodity Value Chain	Description	Countries Involved
Chapter 4: Natural Gas: From Western Siberia to Franken I Power Plant in Nürnberg	Export of "raw" Russian natural gas to Germany and use for electricity generation	Russia–Ukraine–Slovak Republic–Czech Republic–Germany
Chapter 5: Oil from Siberian Fields to German Gasoline Stations	German imports of diesel refined in Czech Republic from Russian oil transited through Ukraine	Russia–Ukraine–Slovak Republic–Czech Republic–Germany
Chapter 6: Coal from Kuzbass to Ukraine's Metallurgical Complex in the Donbas to Germany	Export of Russian coking coal to Ukraine, use as feedstock for metallurgical industry, export of resulting products to Germany	Russia–Ukraine–Italy–Germany

When we think about value-adding in energy, the first examples that come to mind involve the physical transformation of a good into another good—for example, the transformation of crude oil into gasoline through the refining process and within a clearly delimited spatial location such as a refinery. Yet in addition to this more visible type of value adding, there are also less obvious types of value adding, such as what takes place throughout the process of transit/transportation of natural gas from production to end user and throughout an entire pipeline system. This is because in some cases the value-adding process involves the good's physical transformation into another good (as in oil refining), but in other cases the contribution consists exactly of preventing undesirable changes to the good to safeguard the characteristics necessary for it to be used by the end consumer (e.g., in the case of gas pipeline systems, which, when functioning properly, protect natural gas from exploding or being dissipated into the atmosphere[33]). This, however, does not affect the comparability of the chains studied in this book—both types, visible and invisible value added, are part of legitimate value chains.

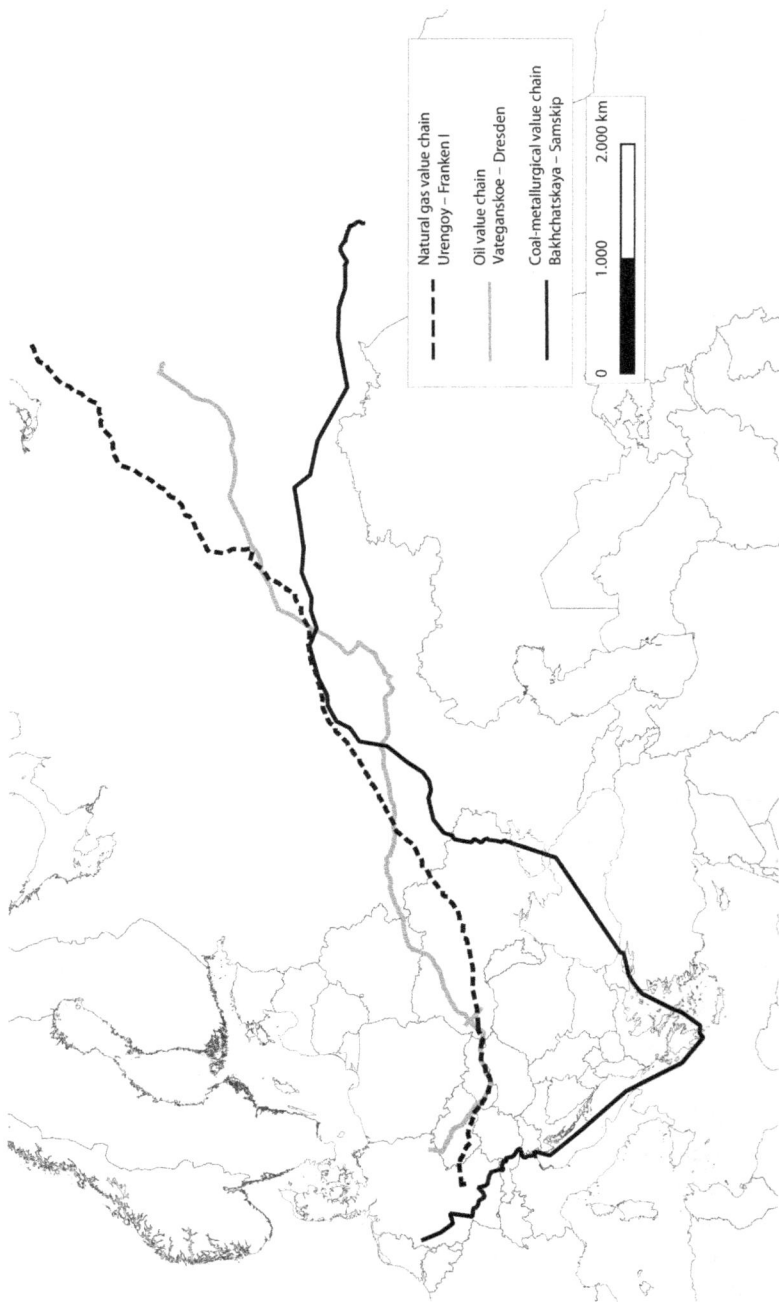

Figure 2.3 The natural gas, oil, and coal value chains followed in this book at a glance

Source: Map created by Matthias Neumann using QGIS and GIS data from Natural Earth (free vector and raster map data at naturalearthdata.com), OpenStreetMap (https://www.openstreetmap.org), and Wikipedia; further editing in Adobe Illustrator.

Although the direct comparison of these three exemplary value chains passing through Ukraine and ending in Germany forms the core of the book, each case study chapter, as needed, also refers to other relevant physical value chains for the same good. Moreover, as counterpoint to the conventional fossil fuel value chains analyzed in chapters 4 through 6, chapter 8 analyzes the market and political disruptions and reconfigurations created by the "creative destruction" (Schumpeter) implied by the entrance of unconventional oil and gas, as well as LNG, into former Soviet Union and EU markets.

This book thus uses the following of a concrete physical unit (again, a "molecule," in shorthand) as a narrative device, but it also addresses processes such as the existence of virtual (i.e., nonphysical) oil and gas swaps, and the fact that molecules mix when entering a closed network, making it impossible to track "single" molecules (as in the case of oil and natural gas molecules), or that a coal molecule itself undergoes an important transformation during the metallurgical production process. I discuss these important nuances in the respective case study chapters.[34]

Analyzing exemplary value chains. Each of these exemplary value chains is analyzed utilizing a similar methodology that focuses on these issues:

- The good, its technical production processes from extraction to end consumer, and the corresponding value chains.
- Vertical linkages in this value chain (linking upstream, midstream, downstream, and sale to end-consumer operations).
- Horizontal linkages in this value chain linking various energy and nonenergy processes, and the trees and subtrees of the relationships created. (For example, for the post-Soviet natural gas industry, vertical linkages include the supply of natural gas for electricity generation; key horizontal linkages take place with industries dependent on specific by-products of the natural gas industry, such as ethane, through which ethylene, a key component in plastic, is produced.)
- Soviet political economy/infrastructure legacies affecting value chain processes.
- How has the nature of each chain affected the key relationships with domestic actors? How have the technical requirements of each chain bestowed power to different actors in various spatial

locations? For example, the relatively compact and labor-intensive production necessary for coal production, and the way such production tends to monopolize economic activity in an area, were preconditions for the political impact of coal workers as compared with those in less labor-intensive sectors that were also characterized by more spatially extensive production patterns, such as oil.[35] As is seen in the discussion of the coal industry in chapter 6, this role, both direct and as manipulated by other actors, can have crucial political implications.

- What has been the role of concrete business and political actors along each chain (e.g., Dmytro Firtash for natural gas, Ihor Kolomoyskyi for oil, and Rinat Akhmetov for coal in the case of Ukrainian oligarchs)?

In addition to looking at value chains as whole systems, the analysis pays special attention to critical physical points (nodes) where either key processing takes place or where "value is created, destroyed, or otherwise regulated."[36] Some examples involve the preprocessing of primary energy before it can be traded, refining crude oil into higher-value products such as gasoline, transit from a lower-price market to a higher-priced one, points where export duties and taxes are levied onto a product, gas pipeline intake points, oil import terminals, and gas trading hubs where natural gas is further distributed. These nodes are important because they are spaces where opportunities for profit making and profit sharing created by specific value chains are displayed, and they are also spaces for competition for these profits and rents, which makes them spaces for negotiation and sites of alternative governance, often sidestepping formal institutions.[37] It is at these points where key actors seek to deploy their insider knowledge and connections.

These nodes are also key points where administrative regulations come into play (e.g., regarding export and import duties and taxes), making them focal points for lobbying activities. They are also potential *chokepoints*, where gatekeepers with the power to set administrative regulations may have an interest in creating artificial scarcities and barriers to entry (e.g., limiting access to export pipelines) for their private enrichment.[38] And last but not least, they are key points where the further course of the value and supply process may be blocked by interested actors—the producer, transit states, or other participants in midstream and downstream processes. Because each of these nodes is key for both energy supply security (as potential chokepoints) *and* profit making, the decisions made at and about them will be key.

So far, we have been referring to these nodes as physical locations. Yet *commercial* and *regulatory* nodes are as important for the big picture as physical nodes. Although the physical energy units ("molecules") moved along physical chains and through physical nodes, this movement was affected by decisions made at important commercial nodes, nodes that were not always coterminous with the physical ones and whose impact had a nonlinear spatial footprint. Thus, for example, the conditions and profitability of a particular oil refining operation are not only determined by the refinery as a physical node but also are affected by the contractual conditions and price of the oil purchased, something determined at a separate commercial node, for example the room where the contractual conditions for a specific party of oil are set, or even a virtual place (platform) used for oil pricing.[39] Similarly, regulatory nodes such as the EU Commission in Brussels are locations where key regulatory decisions affecting a value chain (e.g., rules for access to transportation infrastructure, or environmental standards) are made (see figure 2.4).

Analysis of the specific nodes will seek to answer these questions:

- Who are the main local, transborder, and international actors (including international investors and the EU as a regulatory framework) affecting a particular node? How do they make an impact on social relations at the local, regional, and national levels?

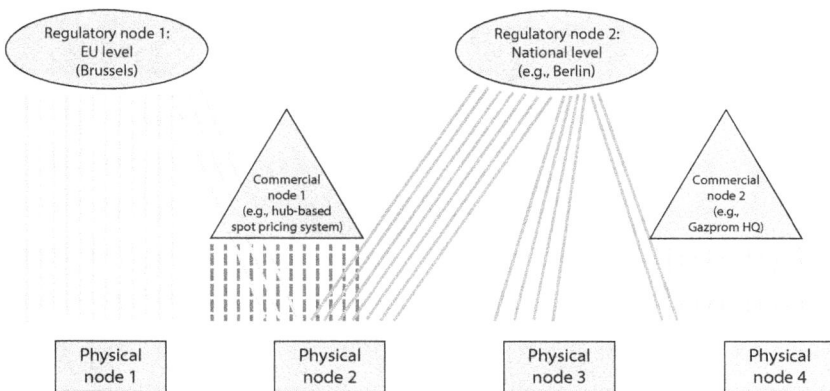

Figure 2.4 Physical, commercial, and regulatory nodes and their interaction

- How are these actors related to the vertical and horizontal value chains of the energy commodity in question?
- What factors may be present affecting possible coalitions between local actors (providing value-added services) and actors from the producer states? What are the implications for the use of energy as external power?

How does understanding the role of value chain nodes help us answer questions about post-Soviet Russia's reach and influence? The discussion above tells us that the various nodes in a value chain will also be critical as gateways, and that the actors at them are key gate-keepers able to act as gate openers or closers, with the location and role of these nodes largely determined by the energy type in question.

Conceptualizing and studying value chains: methodological chal-lenges. Following concrete physical value chains, as is done in this book, is not without methodological and empirical challenges. At the empirical level, information on these chains must be accrued in a piece-meal fashion, because there is no unified system of access to informa-tion on each of these chains, a problem magnified by the confidential nature of many commercial contracts and prices, and by a lack of trans-parency among some of the key players involved (see figure 2.5).[40]

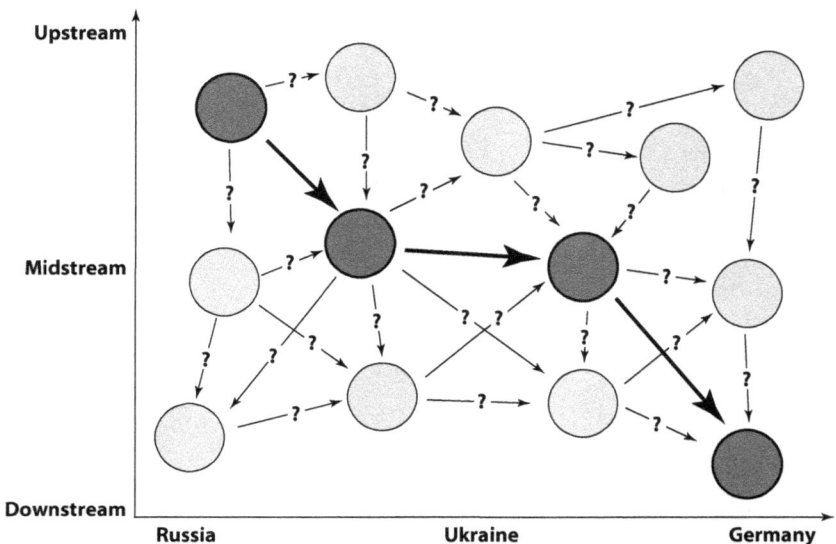

Figure 2.5 The challenge of finding hidden value and supply chains

Nevertheless, information available in companies' yearly reports, sectoral statistics, and press reports make it possible to piece together verifiable physical supply chains. (In the few exceptions where specific segments of the chain may not be verifiable from factory to factory per se, but are highly plausible given broader verified sectoral material flows, the situation is noted accordingly.) Despite these challenges, the information available is sufficient for the purposes of this inquiry, which focuses on *patterns*.

The Three Key States Crossed by the Chains

As noted above, a key criterion for choosing the exemplary chains was the desire to keep constant the countries through which the physical chain is going through for the chains that are being compared, allowing for a better comparison by keeping related conditions (e.g., governance systems) constant. Three countries are key: Russia as the start of the chain, Ukraine as a key transit state, and Germany as the end point; other states were present in the oil and gas (Czech Republic and Slovak Republic) and coal (Italy) chains. What were the key governance and economic conditions prevalent during the book's focus period in the three key states giving shape to our chains?

Russia. The beginning of our focus period found Russia at the tail end of Dmitry Medvedev's in-between presidency and the beginning of Vladimir Putin's second term in office, which started in May 2012. It also witnessed the strongest period of popular protests since the early 1990s, which crystallized in December 2011 around the slogan "for fair elections" and against Putin's decision to run for president in 2012. The protest movement, which was at its height between 2011 and 2013, came in the wake of the 2008 economic downturn, and before that of 2014, both related to significant declines in the price of oil, Russia's largest export. In terms of governance, it was a period of increased repression and control of the media, which was also projected externally and in 2014 was accompanied by increasingly open destabilization activities in Ukraine, culminating in military intervention and the annexation of Crimea in March 2014. More specifically, in terms of energy governance, the key issue during this period was the further consolidation of Rosneft as the Kremlin-favored oil and gas company after its takeover of TNK-BP in 2013, making Rosneft the world's largest publicly traded oil producer.

Ukraine. This book's reference period largely coincided with Viktor Yanukovich's presidency (January 2010–February 2014), which was marked by his increased centralization of power, especially vis-à-vis the opposition led by former prime minister Yulia Tymoshenko. In terms of governance, despite increased closeness to the EU, exemplified by negotiations toward a deep and comprehensive trade agreement with the EU and the joining of the Energy Community in 2012, few positive trends could be seen; on the contrary, the Yanukovich presidency was marked by increased corruption and the president's attempt to bring his close associates into long-standing rent-seeking schemes. In terms of the economy, during this period Ukraine was experiencing strong pressure on its trade balances as the bill for natural gas imports increased, while income from exports went down with the decline in global prices of Ukrainian key exports such as steel. The period ends with Yanukovich's ouster from the presidency as a result of the Euromaidan Revolution and the start of Russian armed intervention in Crimea and Eastern Ukraine.

Germany. During the reference period, Germany—where Angela Merkel was in the middle of her second term as chancellor—was both experiencing an economic upturn and undergoing rapid change in its energy sector. It was in the middle of an export boom that started in 2009, which brought with it growing trade surpluses and record low unemployment, making it one of the healthiest economies in the EU while a recession and debt crisis were engulfing other EU states such as Greece, Ireland, Spain, and Portugal. Despite the economic upturn, Germany during this period was in the midst of rapid and not always smooth change in the energy sector. These changes had to do with the further implementation of ambitious renewable energy goals under the Renewable Energy Sources Act (the basic law was passed in 2000, and key extensions were added in 2012) as well as the not always smooth dismantling of an electricity generation and natural gas imports system based on large, established market leaders—firms such as Ruhrgas, E.ON, and RWE—and its replacement by a variety of smaller players, a process made more complicated by the sudden decision made by the German government in the spring of 2011, after the Fukushima nuclear accident, to immediately close eight nuclear power plants, plus the remaining nine by 2022.

In addition to the specific governance systems prevalent within national borders, the chains also intersected with broader regulatory spaces represented by the reach of the nodes discussed above (see figure 2.4), for example, those delimited by the reach of EU policies (not only to member states but also to others agreeing to these as part of broader initiatives affecting the regulatory environment, such as association agreements or EU-compliant contractual arrangements). This also meant that natural gas, oil, and coal were often subject to different governance and regulatory systems. Although, for all three goods, nation-states retained a degree of regulatory jurisdiction, the degree of regulatory fragmentation—as well as the location of borders between different regulatory programs/regulatory competencies— was different for each of these goods. In the case of coal, the degree of national as opposed to supranational regulation was the highest. In the case of oil, the EU constituted a weak regulatory space, concerning first and foremost issues such as fuel environmental standards. In the case of natural gas, the EU's regulatory space was not only the deepest but also the broadest in geographical scope, encompassing not only EU member states but also non-EU states to which the EU had sought to export its regulatory regime, such as the contracting parties of the Energy Community (which by 2011 included, along with the EU member states, Albania, Bosnia and Herzegovina, the former Yugoslav republic of Macedonia, Kosovo, Moldova, Montenegro, Serbia, and Ukraine). The attempt to bind Russia to a compatible gas transit regulatory program through the Energy Charter Treaty process met with limited success.[41] Although related to the governance characteristics and key objectives of each jurisdiction, these governance arrangements were also related to the nature of the goods involved.[42]

THIS BOOK'S ACADEMIC AND BROADER CONTRIBUTION

The issues addressed in this book have key policy implications. The first is self-evident: understanding how different types of energy lend themselves differently for various power uses can help us understand the factors supporting or, alternatively, constraining Russia's ability to use energy supplies as a means of leverage. The approach provides powerful tools for understanding key policy issues, such as the possible interest of various Russian energy actors in cooperation with specific actors in the importing states with access to important infrastructure for the completion of particular value chains. Similarly, looking at these processes can provide a much better understanding of how some local actors in the EU (e.g., the energy companies RWE and E.ON) would come to support specific Russian initiatives such as the South Stream (and, later, Nord Stream) pipelines, even when such initiatives were not supported by the European Union. Understanding actor coalitions as unfolding *through and throughout* specific value chains has direct implications for key EU policy issues, such as the separation (unbundling) of energy production, transportation, and retail in EU states required by the EU's Third Energy Package (2009), as well as Russian companies' responses to these, such as attempts at gaining control over regional gas distributing companies in EU states. It is impossible to understand Russia's energy power—and the constraints to it—without understanding these value chains and how they deeply permeate local politics and business in each state through which this chain goes. Energy power does not end at the border, and it is only by understanding these value chains, how deeply they go into the affected countries, and how they tie in with domestic players, that we can understand the true extent of this power. Thus, following the physical, material chain is not just a means for bringing the reader along on this journey; it is also central to the story as looking at energy power through a materiality and value chain lens takes you to a different place than when not looking at materiality.

Looking at resource politics more globally, an "entire value chain" approach to energy can make an important contribution to our understanding of energy security. By looking at the full spectrum of midstream activities, we gain a new perspective on the role of consumer states that are also providing infrastructure and refining services important for the producer, such as Singapore, the Netherlands, Belgium, and Malaysia.[43] And last but not least, the book makes an important contribution by bringing coal—largely ignored in the literature on energy and security—squarely to the center of the political economy of energy discussion.

But before getting to the book's concrete value chains spanning from Siberia to Germany, let us review the connection between the materiality characteristics of the three goods traversing these chains—natural gas, oil, and coal—and the sets of market and power relations taking shape around them. We tackle this in chapter 3.

CHAPTER THREE

Energy: Materiality and Power

AS PREVIEWED in the last chapter, understanding actors' interactions *through and throughout* energy value chains offers a more powerful lens for explaining post-Soviet energy interactions than does a simple focus on energy as state power.[1] These relationships are best understood in terms of the interaction between three key sets of factors: the material characteristics of an energy good, the way involved actors "use" energy, and the governance environment. This book deals with the governance environment as well as actors' various uses of energy in chapters 4 through 6 as we follow concrete physical value chains for oil, natural gas, and coal from Russia to Germany via Ukraine. This chapter introduces the materiality side of the issue—that is, how the material characteristics of different energy goods can affect the constitution of power relations around them.

Our starting point is the fact that various types of energy—such as oil, natural gas, and coal, fossil fuels that have dominated Russia's energy relations with both post-Soviet neighbors and more distant partners—are not analytically interchangeable; rather, the characteristics of each specific type have important implications for their further use.[2]

Thus, this book aims to analyze energy interactions by starting from the very nature of the specific energy resources in question and how their concrete characteristics ("materiality") affect their value chains, and, through them, power relationships. The physical characteristics of (various) energy goods are taken as a starting point, in the sense that materiality is both *enabling* and *constraining* human choices.[3]

WHAT WE ALREADY KNOW ABOUT MATERIALITY, ENERGY, AND POWER

But before we dig deeper, let me briefly recapitulate what we already know about how the characteristics of different types of energy affect power relations. At a general level, the literature on sustainability has discussed the environmental and other implications of reliance on broad categories of energy, for example, fossil fuels as opposed to renewables. By necessity, however, this literature has missed the insights that can be gained from comparing various types of fossil fuels. Specifically concerning fossil fuels, research has examined how reliance on imports of specific types of energy—as reflected in different import energy-mix profiles—can make an impact on an energy-dependent state's ability to fend for itself against a supplier's intentional stoppage of supplies.[4] We know, for example, that the means by which an energy resource is most efficiently transported (e.g., by pipeline for natural gas, as compared with a variety of options for oil) will affect how easy it will be for a supplier to turn off supplies, along with how easy it will be for the affected state to replace such supplies at short notice and, thus, withstand an interruption in supplies (see table 3.1). (For example, Lithuania shifted to oil supplied by tanker after Russia interrupted oil supplies via the Druzhba pipeline in 2006.)

However, such a framework, focusing on the impact of energy import mixes on the importing state's ability to cope with supply disruptions, still looks at differences between types of energy solely in terms of their external impact. We still know little about how these differences affect power relations at the intersection between their domestic and external dimensions.

This chapter develops what such an analysis would look like, unpacking the various power implications of differences between different types of energy (materiality). It tackles the issue in several steps. The first step sets the scene by contextualizing the impact of materiality

TABLE 3.1

Differences between Oil, Natural Gas, and Coal, and Their Impact on Importing States' Ability to Withstand an Interruption in Supplies

Aspect	Oil	Natural Gas	Coal
Transportation options	A variety of options available: tanker, pipeline, rail	Shipped almost exclusively by pipeline (not including liquefied natural gas technology, which is currently significantly more costly).	Due to its high weigh-to-energy ratio and high cost of transportation in proportion to value, usually shipped by tanker and rail.
Importers' ability to respond to blockades / supply suspensions by switching to other suppliers?	Switching to other suppliers can take place relatively quickly; can also be supplied by tanker or rail.	Switching to other suppliers is more difficult due to infrastructure issues (whether fixed pipelines or liquefied natural gas facilities).	Switching to other suppliers is more difficult due to long transportation times.
Capacity to be easily substituted by other energy sources?	Relatively low (especially in transportation sector)	Relatively high	Medium for electricity generation; medium to low for industrial uses

and discussing its interaction with other important factors. In the second step, I compare oil, natural gas, and coal, the three fossil fuels at the center of this book, on the basis of key physical characteristics and their secondary manifestations. I then analyze the main mechanisms through which these materiality differences come to affect power at the international and domestic levels.

MATERIALITY UNBOUND, MATERIALITY CONSTRAINED: CONTEXTUALIZING ENERGY MATERIALITY

Understanding its contextualizing factors is essential for applying the materiality framework proposed in this book. These factors have to do, first and foremost, with nature as a human co-creation, the role of technology, legacies, and politico-economic systems. These factors mediate how the primary physical characteristics of an energy good manifest themselves in secondary characteristics and, further, in power relations at both the international and domestic levels.[5]

Materiality cannot be seen as a purely external or "objective" force;[6] rather, its impact needs to be seen in the context of the mutual production of society–nature relations,[7] and, more generally, of how humans and inanimate objects ("things") co-constitute each other.[8] What this means is that humans as observers, measurers, and users of nature not only experience it as an external factor but also co-create it. Concerning natural resources, including energy resources, De Gregori reminds us that "resources are not; they become," in the sense that they are not so much an objective that is given but are related to human actors' perceived needs and technical capabilities to use different nature-given objects to fulfill these—all of which are changeable rather than given.[9]

At the same time, the impact of a good's key physical characteristics is not absolute but is mediated by the state of technology used on it. Indeed, though some of the differences between types of energy are unambiguously given by nature, others lie at the intersection of what is given by nature and what is physically doable given available technology. Thus, for example, the very viability of liquefied natural gas (LNG) as an internationally traded substitute for gaseous natural gas is predicated on the existence of natural gas liquefaction technology— before it became available, it was impossible to think about natural gas as being anything but a gaseous substance.[10] Another example concerns the way we look at natural gas and oil. Natural gas is often— though not always—extracted from the same fields as oil; even in those cases, their value chains depart at the wells themselves, solidifying separate identities for both energy sources.

Similarly, the impact of materiality is mediated by the choices made by involved actors, including societal choices. It is intertwined with human knowledge structures and the socially contextualized priorities of various politico-economic systems, including each system's understandings of the preferred uses of energy within it. Even widely used energy concepts, such as the distinction between recoverable and proven oil and gas reserves, are not based on objective criteria but are related to actors' subjective and socially contextualized understandings of acceptable risk and profit margins. A standard definition of proven reserves is what is proven to be "economically producible" using current technology.[11] Thus what gets counted as a proven reserve is related to actors' understanding of what can be recovered economically using current technology as well as the current understanding of what constitutes an appropriate economic return.[12] (Technically recoverable resources, conversely, are resources that "can be recovered with current technology, but whose recovery is not economical under current conditions."[13]) Thus what constitutes proven reserves is not an objective given but also depends on social conceptions of what constitutes an economically sensible investment and acceptable profit, and to what extent energy investments should be guided by profit motives as opposed to other goals (see below). We should not assume that a profit-based capitalist logic of value and priorities is always at play. Rather, we can see a situation where a profit imperative may be the priority, situations where the use of energy supplies for social welfare and populist goals may be the priority, or situations where reducing the CO_2 footprint of energy use may be the priority.[14]

In Soviet-style socialism, for example, profitability and economic efficiency considerations played a very limited role; they were secondary to the supply considerations that were key for Soviet-style material planning and the use of energy supplies as means of fostering cohesion in the system.[15] Similarly, we need to acknowledge that "corrupt energy," the use of energy for corrupt rent-seeking (which is not necessarily innate to socialism or capitalism but whose growth can benefit from the inconsistencies of a transition period), has its own rules of the game that do not necessarily align with efficiency or company profitability criteria. Similarly, the decarbonization initiatives unveiled by the European Union in the 2010s also imply a certain hierarchy of priorities. That is, different politico-economic systems have different priorities in making choices about energy production and use. The hierarchy of priorities also involves substate-level actors' preference rankings concerning the various uses of energy. Thus, for example, an actor's choice to use energy for external pressure may preclude actions based on economic profitability criteria.[16] All this mediates the direct impact of materiality.

Returning to the example of LNG, we see that its ability to function as an internationally traded substitute for pipeline natural gas is predicated not only on the existence of the necessary technology (which was first patented in 1915) but also on LNG fetching sufficiently high prices (and an "appropriate economic return") to justify the high cost of liquefaction and further regasification.[17]

Last but not least, the impact of the materiality characteristics of various energy goods is also mediated by the regulatory and governance environment in which choices are made—highlighting the importance of materiality does not imply arguing that forms of ownership, regulatory, and governance issues do not matter. Rather, I am arguing that if we were to assume equal regulatory framework conditions, the materiality characteristics of the energy good under consideration would make a difference. Regulations, moreover, do not arise in a vacuum; rather, regulations affecting a particular energy good arise out of a dialogue between the technical nature of the good and the goals of those defining policy. In analyzing the development of Europe's natural gas infrastructure, for example, Högselius and colleagues have shown how the governance and political imperative of building separate capitalist and socialist gas supply networks could not be sustained in the face of economic and materiality-related geographic realities, leading to the impetus for the creation of a single, pan-European system.[18]

The impact of materiality is also mediated by legacies, including socially sedimented technological infrastructures. Because of their high cost and difficulty of replacement, infrastructures may continue to embody outlived technologies even when newer ones may be available, as if freezing them in time. In the cases discussed in this book, this is seen most clearly through the issue of transportation infrastructures inherited from the Soviet period, which have continued to affect the management of post-Soviet oil and gas by, for example, limiting the import and export options open to countries in the region.[19] I am not arguing, thus, that post-Soviet oil, natural gas, and coal functioned in the same way they did in the Soviet period but that the legacies of the Soviet ways of dealing with these issues deeply affected the infrastructural setup through which post-Soviet energy would work and flow. Although a supply-centered system like that of the USSR is no longer fully present in Russia or the other post-Soviet states, the *legacies* of those priorities are still relevant, intermingling with profit motivations and the governance environment. We may also see conflicts between priorities, such as when profit or foreign policy considerations coexist with the use of energy for social welfare or populist policies.

PRIMARY PHYSICAL CRITERIA FOR UNDERSTANDING FOSSIL FUEL MATERIALITY

These caveats notwithstanding, the physical differences between different types of energy do matter, making a structured comparison essential.[20] Before presenting a structured comparison of oil, natural gas, and coal, it is important to clarify its scope—a particular subset of the universe of all possible energy sources. Our inquiry focuses on *primary energy sources*, that is, raw energy before conversion or processing (in contrast to *final energy and energy services* consumed by end users, e.g., electricity, gasoline, or heating). Within primary energy sources, I focus on those types of energy that are easily tradable (i.e., "commodifable"), in contrast to local-use, nonstorable, and nontradable types. At the same time, we are comparing fossil fuels, a subcategory of nonrenewable resources.[21] Although this book focuses on the nonrenewable energy commodities oil, natural gas, and coal, I recognize that a community's reliance on local renewable energy resources creates a totally different set of political power dynamics between them and central institutions.

Different types of energy can be compared on the basis of innumerable criteria, referring back to different types of qualities. Including all possible factors, however, would be an insurmountable task. Thus, the list of criteria to be compared may be best tailored to the specific purpose that is being pursued in analyzing such characteristics. Scholars interested in the cultural representation of energy, for example, have paid attention to qualities such as the depth of its underground deposits (as in the case of Rogers's study of oil and culture in the Perm region of Russia[22]), smell, and color. In contrast, my own list focuses on those characteristics that are acknowledged by the energy industry as central and are key for shedding light on the main area of interest here: how various types of energy function as part of supply and value chains. Even with this narrowing of focus, this kind of enquiry requires comparing energy types across multiple criteria, which does not lend itself easily to the kind of parsimonious (e.g., a 2 × 2 table) presentation popular with political scientists; this may be a reason for the scarcity of work analyzing the impact of materiality in political science.

I first compare natural gas, oil, and coal according to primary physical criteria, and then on the basis of secondary features related to these primary characteristics. Primary physical criteria refers to basic characteristics of an energy good, before it is further processed or distributed. The secondary criteria we compare go back to these essential differences in physical characteristics, because they affect further sets of characteristics in the supply and value chains.

Primary Criterion 1: Physical State

The most obvious physical difference between oil, natural gas, and coal concerns their *basic physical state*. Although they are all fossil fuels—that is, energy sources formed from decayed organic materials through millions of years—the basic physical state of each at ambient temperature differs: gaseous for natural gas, liquid for oil, and solid for coal. (The discussion here concerns physical state at reference ambient pressure and temperature points;[23] natural gas can be turned into a more compact and energy-dense energy carrier, LNG, when processed at extremely low temperatures.) We will be coming back to these distinctions once and again, because they form the basis for a number of other differences. Differences in physical state have significant implications for differences in the secondary characteristics discussed below, such as transportation options, the typical size of markets, value chain–specific challenges, and the potential autonomy or networkness of users.

Primary Criterion 2: Degree of Homogeneity within the Good

A second key differentiating factor concerns the degree of homogeneity within the good, that is, the degree of difference between subtypes of the same good, in particular those concerning caloric value and other characteristics affecting their use, fungibility (i.e., the mutual replaceabilty of units), and marketing as commodities. This is a complex issue to tackle, given the fact that no fossil fuel is totally uniform and that human-made categorizations and classification blueprints (e.g., branding and blending into brands) have been introduced as a means of managing this internal diversity so as to make possible the marketing of these goods as commodities.[24] Branding and sale as different types is an integral part of the coal and oil business, with different brands (oil) and benchmarks (coal) being marketed and priced separately. However, these intra-energy type differences are smaller than the differences between different types of energy, with the range of observable within-good variation being very different for natural gas, oil, and coal.

Coal is highly heterogeneous. The caloric (heating) value per weight of different coal types differs widely—from about 14 megajoules per kilogram for brown coal / lignite to 24 for bituminous coal to 32.5

for anthracite coal.[25] This wide diversity also makes it hard to achieve transparency in pricing. In addition, different types of coal also differ widely in terms of the level of humidity, ash, and sulfur content, which are key for determining their potential uses. These differences can take place even within relatively small geographical areas; even neighboring coal mines may produce different types of coal; these different types and their main uses are discussed in more detail chapter 6. The key point here is that, even more than in the case of oil, different types of coal are more narrowly specified for use in specific infrastructures (e.g., specific electricity-generation plants) than in the case of natural gas or oil. This means that high dependence on both coal and legacy infrastructures can be mutually reinforcing. (This is in addition to the distinction between coal used for electricity generation and as feedstock for the metallurgical industry, which is discussed separately.)

This situation has implications for all coal industry players, but in particular for importers, because imports sourced from a particular area or mine may be extremely hard to replace in case of a supply suspension. Legacy infrastructures may exacerbate this situation, as in the case of Ukraine: especially in its eastern regions, where key infrastructure was specifically developed to operate with the type of coal supplied by geographically nearby mines in Russia while both were constituent republics of a single and energy-centralized state. Such mines later became part of the separate state of Russia, which since 2014 has been involved in military aggression against Ukraine. (After independence in 1991, Ukraine continued large-scale imports of coal from mines located on the Russian side of the border.) Moreover, Ukraine's dependency continued to be reproduced by the infrastructures inherited from the Soviet Union: not only the often-discussed oil and natural gas pipelines directly tying Ukraine to supplies from Russia but also less visible but no less important electricity generation and industrial infrastructure specified to work with specific types of Russian-sourced coal. This is also a reason why, despite Russia's military aggression since 2014, it has been very difficult for Ukraine to replace coal imported from Russia, even as it has made important strides in replacing oil and natural gas supplies.

Although, as noted, the substitutability of coal in general for electricity generation can be considered medium, the substitutability of specific types of coal in closely coupled generation plants, such as many built during the Soviet period, is low. And though hardly homogeneous in absolute terms, *oil* is relatively homogeneous compared with coal. Crude oil from various sources differs in terms of density (with less dense oil actually containing "higher quantities of hydrocarbons that can be converted to gasoline"[26]), as well as sulfur content, which is more popularly understood in terms of their role in producing "sour" or "sweet" (lower-sulfur) oil. These different source oils are then blended to produce separately marketed brands. Although there are dozens of officially certified brands of crude oil worldwide, three are used as main price benchmarks: West Texas Intermediate (WTI), Brent, and Dubai/Oman.[27] In contrast to coal, which can differ significantly from mine to mine, crude oil from relatively broad regions tends to share certain general characteristics, to the point that geographic denominations (e.g., WTI and Brent, a combination of oils from fifteen North Sea fields) are often used to refer to the major subtypes. In addition to the inherent homogeneity or heterogeneity of oil as a good, the oil denominations (brand) system's ability to capture crude oil's existing heterogeneity within well-defined brands is also of interest. The technical possibility of batching—transporting oil via pipeline in batches separated by a buffer fluid so different types of oil may travel on the same pipeline without mixing—helps strengthen such branding and differentiation between brands. A key consequence for consumers is that oil has widely quotable prices (with about two-thirds of world contracts using Brent prices as a benchmark reference[28]), which, together with the existence of a global market, should aid in promoting transparency in pricing.

Natural gas is relatively more homogeneous than oil or, especially, coal. Small differences do exist—which are related to the level of natural gas liquids (NGLs) and calorie content, in turn related to the relative methane content—but these are dealt with in the cleaning processing that usually takes place immediately after production before natural gas is brought into a pipeline (i.e., "bringing up to pipeline specification"). Despite these differences, of the three fuels discussed here, only natural gas is widely traded as a relatively uniform "good" with no widely used benchmark brands.[29] This lack of widely used benchmarking is compounded by the technical impossibility of batching, that is, transporting natural gas via pipeline in batches of different qualities, in contrast to the case of oil, where such a possibility helps strengthen the branding of different oil qualities.

One of the main implications of natural gas's relative homoge-neity is that it has made possible the development of a technically smooth-functioning (albeit expensive) pipeline infrastructure, with a number of further implications. It allowed for the concept of natural gas as a swappable energy carrier to develop—one molecule of Rus-sian methane (the main component of natural gas) in the pipeline is chemically undistinguishable from one molecule of, say, Norwegian methane, although one may be contractually Russian and the other Norwegian. The relative homogeneity of the good makes technically possible extensive virtual swaps (taking place in Europe already from the 1960s[30]) as well as the development of gas trading hubs, where natural gas from various sources is available and can be sold at spot prices. (The limitation here is not so much the interchangeability of the gas but—as is discussed in chapter 4—the governance setup and the ability of pipelines feeding from these hubs to maintain the nec-essary pressure if not fully used.[31]) Although the sale of natural gas at spot prices is a relatively recent phenomena related to the move away from long-term contracts, such spot sales—and competition by LNG—could not work as well with a less homogeneous good.

Primary Criterion 3: Energy Density of the Good

A third important difference concerns an energy good's energy density, which is defined as the amount of useful (extractable) energy per unit, usually measured in megajoules per kilogram.[32] Whereas crude oil and coal are measured by weight, natural gas is usually measured by vol-ume (in cubic meters),[33] making it difficult to compare both directly. In terms of energy density per weight,[34] however, natural gas is the most energy-dense energy carrier (at 47.2 megajoules per kilogram), followed by crude oil (41.9 megajoules per kilogram) and coal (which varies from about 10.0 to 31.4 megajoules per kilogram).[35] Volumet-ric density—that is, the energy density per unit of volume—produces a different ranking, with crude oil by far the most energy dense, at about 37,000 megajoules per cubic meter, compared with natural gas, at about 34 to 39 megajoules per cubic meter (i.e., a thousandfold difference).[36] Thus it is reasonable to say that for most practical pur-poses, oil can be considered the most energy-dense of the three fossil fuels.[37] This also means higher revenue per unit for energy-dense types of energy. Energy density becomes important for value chains because energy-dense types of energy are less expensive to transport globally relative to total value; this also makes oil more suitable for global, non-pipeline shipment than natural gas.

Primary Criterion 4: CO_2 Profile and Other Ecologically Problematic Emissions per Unit of Energy

A fourth criterion concerns each type of energy's carbon intensity (i.e., the grams of CO_2 emitted per kilowatt-hour generated as electricity), along with its level of negative environmental impact.[38] Of the three main fossil fuels, given current technology, natural gas produces the least ecological damage per unit of energy produced, followed by oil and coal. This becomes important for the value chain because decisions on energy investments, transportation means, and infrastructure will also be made on the basis of their ecological consequences. (At the same time, as seen with the boom in worldwide coal use for electricity generation in 2015, in the absence of clear legal regulations or a mean-ingful CO_2 emissions trading system, price considerations often trump ecological ones.) These differences in CO_2 intensity will also affect other secondary differences discussed below, such as substitutability (one energy commodity's ability to be substituted by another), given that decisions on substituting one energy source with another may need to be reconsidered in the context of growing carbon constraints and actors' relative prioritization of decarbonization as a policy goal.

Primary Criterion 5: Ubiquity and Spatial Footprint

Finally, an important difference in terms of an energy good's physical characteristics and footprint concerns natural differences in ubiquity and natural distribution (as well as related differences in the quality and ease of access of deposits). One aspect of this concerns whether con-crete resources are only available in a geographically concentrated area, or are more evenly distributed worldwide. Although coal reserves are available in almost every country (and there is a relatively globalized market with several strong suppliers, including Australia, Colombia, Indonesia, and Russia), oil and natural gas reserves are predominantly concentrated in a narrower area (mainly North Africa, the Middle East, and some areas of North America and Eurasia). Differences in quality and ease of accessibility compound these, leading to widely different production costs, which have traditionally been significantly lower in the Middle East (unchallenged even by recent "low-cost" shale gas production in the United States), leading to differential rents between producers endowed with varied natural advantages.[39] Such differential rents have key implications for power issues through the issue of the profitability of the industry in a concrete location and low-cost producers' ability to drive out other, higher-cost producers, affecting the relative bargaining power of specific producers.

Access to capital-intensive exploration technology becomes even more important in the case of resources that are less uniformly distributed and harder to access (oil and natural gas, as opposed to coal), exacerbating differences in various producers' access to differential rents and ability to capture economies of scale.[40] So in the case of less ubiquitous energy types such as oil and natural gas, we see more potential for inequality between states, inequalities that will also be exacerbated by differences in access to know-how, technology, and financing. Another aspect concerns whether a resource is "diffuse"—that is, scattered widely, and at least in theory amenable to be extracted by a large number of small operators; or is a "point resource"—that is, concentrated in small areas and more likely to be extracted by a few producers.[41]

MAIN DIFFERENCES BETWEEN OIL, NATURAL GAS, AND COAL: SECONDARY FEATURES

The differences in primary physical characteristics discussed in the last section also lead to differences in secondary features related to the marketing and use of various energy resources (see table 3.2).This section describes these differences and their impact on power relations.

Secondary Feature 1: Transportability

The physical state of an energy commodity at ambient temperature and pressure is the most important characteristic affecting its *transportability*. Differences in transportability, in turn, bring a variety of ripple effects for exporters, importers, midstream processors, and all actors involved in that good's value chain, from producer to end user.

TABLE 3.2

Natural Gas, Oil, Coal, and Their Main Differences at a Glance

Energy Type	Natural Gas	Oil	Coal
Primary physical criteria			
Physical state	Gaseous	Liquid	Solid
Homogeneity	High	Medium-high	Low
Energy density/value-to-volume ratio	Low	High	Low
CO_2 intensity	Medium	High	Very high
Ubiquity and spatial footprint	Less ubiquitous	Less ubiquitous	More ubiquitous
Secondary features			
Transportability/best transportation options	Pipeline	Pipeline, tanker, rail, truck	Rail, ship, truck
Size of typical markets	Regional	Global	Regional/global
Processing needed	Near production site	Variable	Mainly near production site
Exporter states' ability for unified action (cartel)	Lower	Higher	Lower
Substitutability	High	Low	Medium
Role in nonenergy value chains: Where in value chain does additional revenue from participation in nonenergy industries come in?	At start of value chain, immediately after production	At midstream level—as products of refining process	At downstream level—already processed coal is used as industrial feedstock (coking coal) or heating source (steam coal)
Networkness	High	Medium	Low

At the level of producers (and exporters), transportability affects producers' choices on how to bring a product to market. Here I have in mind not only the theoretical possibility of using one or another means of transportation but also their cost and other issues affecting exporters' choices. From an exporter's perspective, alternative transportation choices—including decisions on the upkeep and repairing of existing pipelines, building new pipeline routes, transport by tanker, and/or (for natural gas) liquefaction into LNG for shipment via tankers—also mean different profit structures, different possibilities for obstructability of these shipments, and different patterns of relations with other actors involved. They may also affect whether a producer decides to prioritize sales to domestic or foreign markets, decisions that may synergize—or not—with state-level decisions about using energy as an externally directed influence resource. At the level of midstream players, alternative transportation means imply different patterns of relations with other actors involved along the supply and export route (i.e., pipelines, ports, and transshipment infrastructure crossing multiple borders) and different degrees of replaceability of services provided by a transit state. At the level of consumers, the means by which an energy commodity is best transported will affect the ease with which supplies may be stopped, and the ease with which an importer may be able to tap into alternative supplies. (This is also related to how various means of transporting energy may make a route more flexible or, on the contrary, predetermined. Thus, e.g., shipment via tanker has a high degree of flexibility, whereas pipelines follow a fixed route.)

In the case of crude oil, the liquid nature of the good at ambient temperature means maximum flexibility in the means by which it can be transported. Although, for most continental routes, the most economical (and for landlocked areas the only) means of transportation is through pipelines, it is also possible to transport the good on seaborne tankers and by rail as well as—in extreme cases—by truck. (For longer distances, transportation by tanker is more economical.) The availability of these two other means of transportation in addition to pipelines means more flexible options for both exporters and importers, but also means that oil pipeline operators need to contractually disincentivize the possibility of empty pipelines through flight to other transportation means (the sunk costs problem).

In the case of natural gas, its gaseous physical state at ambient temperature makes for a high-volume product that is best transported via pipeline. But movement within the pipeline is far from automatic: being lighter than air, natural gas easily dissipates if not contained, and it also needs to be under a certain minimum amount of pressure in order to move through the pipeline. This has two further implications: first, gas pipelines are expensive to build; and second, the need to maintain a certain pressure in the pipeline means using a pipeline at half-capacity is not an option, because certain minimum volumes need to be maintained for the pipeline to be functional. This means that high pipeline utilization rates are needed not only because of the need to amortize the significant investment already made but also because of the technical requirements for pipeline transportation, adding an important technical component to the sunk costs issue (discussed below). Similarly, natural gas needs to be stored under pressure (or under cooling, in the case of LNG), making the cost of storage much higher than that of oil.[42]

Yet LNG transportation involves its own sunk cost challenges: though in theory the reexporting of imported volumes is possible, in reality this is often not possible due to contractual clauses requiring that the LNG must first be unloaded and then reloaded—something not all regasification terminals are able to do. Moreover, if the utilization rate is low, the relative cost of keeping the temperature low enough to prevent vaporization (i.e., to keep LNG liquid) increases; any gas that evaporates in the tank needs to be flared because it cannot be injected into the grid.[43] In this sense, references to LNG behaving in ways that are more similar to oil than to pipeline natural gas are only partially correct, due to the need for expensive and technically demanding cooling systems to prevent evaporation. On the contrary, for LNG to remain in a liquid state in order to "behave as oil," an expensive, sunk-cost-intensive, and technologically demanding process needs to be guaranteed.[44]

In the case of coal, the solid physical nature of the good means that it cannot be transported by pipeline;[45] it is shipped primarily by rail and ship, the latter being the less expensive option but not one available to all producers; sea and rail transportation are often combined, making for a less "fluid" and uninterrupted process than that associated with oil transportation.[46] For exporters, this means more direct human intervention (workers) is needed to transport the coal, making it relatively more susceptible than natural gas or oil to potential disruptions created by workers themselves, as compared with the case of oil—one of the reasons for coal miners' prominent role in social democracy's rise in twentieth-century Europe.[47] For importers, this situation means more theoretical supply options (because coal supply is not tied to pipelines), but also having to deal with a variety of midstream actors each able to block supply, adding to the difficulty of accessing alternative supplies. Moreover, coal's low energy content per weight means higher transportation costs per unit of energy, making it less economically justifiable to transport for long distances. In the case of Russia's domestic coal supplies, for example, transportation costs made up about 50 to 60 percent of the final cost of steam coal and about 30 to 40 percent of the final cost of coking coal, compared with less than 10 percent for oil.[48]

Secondary Feature 2: Size and Location of Typical Markets

Transportation issues related to the physical characteristics of a commodity, such as its physical state and energy density, also affect the size and location of its typical markets. Given the current costs of various transportation technologies (i.e., high-cost LNG processing and transportation costs relative to the price of natural gas), this means that whereas the oil market is largely global, gas markets continue to be largely regional.[49] One further implication is that whereas there is a widely quoted price for oil (most often the Brent quotation), there is no such "world" price for gas, with additional implications for issues of transparency and multiple pricing—as seen, for example, in mid-2014, when average natural gas prices in Asian markets were more than twice those in the United States.[50] The degree to which a market is global as opposed to regional can have important implications; in global highly integrated markets where participants have multiple supply options, intended coercion by means of suspension of supplies may be felt first and foremost in the form of higher prices and adjustment costs, in contrast to less integrated markets (and, consequently, less supply options), where the attempted coercion may be experienced by the target state as an actual shortfall in supply.[51]

Secondary Feature 3: Type and Degree of Processing Needed

The *degree of processing needed* before the good is brought to market, and whether this processing is best done directly at the production site or in a variety of locations, will affect the role of various actors in the value chain, both in terms of their location in the chain and their spatial location, also affecting their ability to access value-added profits. This will also affect actors' engagement with further sets of actors key for completing specific steps in the chain, such as in refining and transit.

In the case of coal, processing is relatively limited and is mainly related to the washing and sorting taking place in close proximity to production; the possibility of "refining" into much-higher-value products is limited. (The processing of coking coal into coke for metallurgical use refers to a separate process.) Although such processing is often done near the production site, it may also be done elsewhere, with the main reason for near-production-site processing being the economic inefficiency of transporting unprocessed coal containing significant amounts of stones and other low-value materials over long distances.

In the case of natural gas, processing usually takes place near the production site, leading to significantly less flexibility in how other players may become involved in the process. Most processing takes place in proximity to the wellhead, not only because of economic and marketing issues (bringing that gas to pipeline standard for a particular pipeline, extracting higher-value NGLs for separate processing) but also to make it possible for natural gas to be transported safely and efficiently in the first place—if allowed to enter a transit pipeline as raw gas, natural gas may damage the pipeline. Even more crucially, raw natural gas that is straight from the well contains hydrogen sulfide—a highly toxic and corrosive sulfur-bearing compound—which must be removed at the well to prevent damages to humans, pipelines, and other equipment.[52] If in the case of coal the main reason for near-production-site processing is financial (the economic inefficiency of transporting raw coal over long distances), in the case of natural gas this is first and foremost due to technical constraints.

In the case of oil, there are no overwhelming economic or technical reasons requiring this processing to take place at the wellhead. In fact, because oil is easily transported in crude form, refining often takes place close to the location of final sale, reflecting the needs of those end markets.[53] This creates more flexibility in terms of where refining can take place, opening new opportunities for midstream players. At the same time, refineries are usually specified to process one particular type or brand of oil (e.g., light oil or Urals).

This spatial spectrum of processing possibilities also has an impact farther down the road, because different grades of oil have different refined product mix profiles, which has an impact on refining profits and also affects the distributional impact on upstream, midstream, and downstream players alike.[54] A good illustration of how the issue can also affect transborder actors and relations between states is provided by the case of Belarus in the period 1996–2007, when local refineries and the country's budget agency were able to make significant profits from the refining of Russian crude oil.[55]

These differences between energy types concerning the type and degree of processing also mean that the degree of dependency on primary energy imports needs to be contextualized differently in situations where domestic processing for further export may take place (as in the case of crude oil), as compared with situations where this is not usual. For example, because natural gas is only seldom reexported as gas-generated electricity but is usually used domestically for electricity and heating, a 90 percent dependency on natural gas imports can mean something different than a 90 percent dependency in the case of crude oil—in the later case, a significant portion of the oil imported may be used for refining and the subsequent exporting of the refined products. Similarly, a low degree of dependence on crude oil imports means little if dependency on oil products remains high. This is important so as not to misunderstand situations such as that of Ukraine after 2011, when crude oil imports were drastically reduced, only to be replaced by oil product imports.

Secondary Feature 4: Typical Investment Patterns, Challenges, and Opportunities

Various types of energy also differ in their investment requirements, which will also affect how actors in their value chains interact. The comparative *capital intensity* (how much capital is needed to get the energy off the ground and into final use) along with *sunk costs* (large investments that once made cannot be easily recouped) of an energy commodity's production, processing, and delivery will play an important role in relations between various participants in that good's value chain. At a minimum, the capital intensity of a good's production will affect actors' readiness to invest in one or another type of energy. Such capital intensity is especially high in the case of natural gas infrastructure, because the need to keep natural gas under high pressure for it to be able to move at all places high demands on the pipeline walls, requiring specially strong—and expensive—steel alloys. Also, even if oil pipelines are similar to natural gas ones in that both require pumping stations to help move the good along the pipeline, moving natural gas is much more technically challenging, making the compressors used for natural gas transportation much more expensive than those used for oil transportation.

Although all energy value chains present challenges concerning issues of coordination and sharing risk between participants (e.g., buyers and sellers), these challenges will be more acute in the case of those types of energy characterized by higher sunk costs. In particular, the level of transportation investments/sunk costs relative to the actual revenue or expected profits tells us much about the likely challenges in the relationship between suppliers and consumers. In the case of natural gas, for example, due to the higher levels of risk and sunk cost investments involved in its typical pipeline transportation, contracts have traditionally included provisions allocating risk between seller and buyer, such as long-term contracts and take-or-pay provisions committing the buyer to a certain level of yearly purchases for the duration of the contract.[56] Despite the recent rise in one-time, no-further-commitment natural gas spot purchases in a growing number of trading hubs in the EU, the need for risk-sharing between seller and buyer remains. Sunk costs related to dedicated infrastructure—which, having been specifically built for a very particular purpose, cannot be used for any other purpose—may also affect the intensity of related actors' lobbying, because the less portable investments in a particular project are, the more incentives investors will have to lobby to maintain a project's profitability.[57]

Secondary Feature 5: Impact on Exporters' Ability to Engage in Unified Action

Issues such as the degree of homogeneity of a good, its related fungibility, and whether it commands a global (as opposed to regional or local) market play an important role in determining whether a cartel including a significant number of producers will be possible. This is so because such conditions make it easier for cartel members to agree on a cartel price.[58] In addition, technical issues affecting how an energy good is produced and whether output can be reduced at will to manipulate prices will affect its exporters' ability to establish an effective (formal or informal) cartel. This explains why it has been easier for oil exporters to develop a cartel than for gas exporters because, despite is high degree of homogeneity, natural gas still lacks a truly global market.[59] Moreover, natural gas extraction techniques make it extremely hard to quickly stop production at will, something that is very important for a cartel to be able to agree on effective joint measures to decrease or increase supply as a means of managing prices. Although the issue requires additional research, it is also possible that these or other relevant characteristics may also have an impact on importers' ability to engage in unified action.

Secondary Feature 6: Substitutability by Other Energy Resources

Whether a type of energy can be easily substituted by another will affect the elasticity of demand for it. This also has an impact on power—an importer state can limit the negative consequences of a cutoff in supplies by switching, not simply to another supplier of the same type of energy (which may not always be possible), but to other types of energy that are either domestically produced or are more easily accessible as imports. Conversely, if a state's demand for a good is inelastic, that reduces its counterpower vis-à-vis a supplier. Seen in terms of the four main uses of primary energy (for electricity generation and for commercial/residential, transportation, and industrial use), the most substitutable types of energy are those whose use in one or more of these areas can be easily substituted by another energy type. In purely technical terms, natural gas is the most substitutable, because its main use in electricity generation and heating can be substituted by oil and coal—and, increasingly, renewables. Oil and coal are less easily substitutable, particularly in the transportation sector (oil) and some industrial uses (e.g., coking coal use in the metallurgical industry). Thus, for example, oil—which is used for transportation, industrial uses, and to a lesser extent in heating and electricity generation—is a flexible type of energy but is not easily substitutable, because only limited commercial alternatives currently exist for its use, for example, as fuel for truck freight.

It must be kept in mind, however, that substitutability is a function not simply of the technical characteristics of the energy good itself but also of the characteristics of the economy using that energy good (e.g., the relative weight of the service sector or heavy industry) as well as its infrastructure legacies; the specifics of interfuel substitution will depend on the specific structure of the economy.[60] Of particular interest is the case of many post-Soviet states, which inherited infrastructures fine-tuned for the use of specific types of energy that were easily available in the context of a centralized, energy-rich state but that—as in the case of Russian coal in Ukraine—were not necessarily so after 1991. Thus we can only gain a full picture of how an importing state's energy mix affects its ability to counter external supply disruptions when we also include in the picture the structure of its economy and the degree to which economic sectors within it can substitute various types of energy. In other words, even if an energy-dependent state could refocus its entire energy imports strategy on oil in response to a gas supply cutoff, this would be of very limited effectiveness if the country's infrastructure would not be able to actually use those oil imports for uses previously associated with natural gas, for example.

Substitutability issues can also have an impact on domestic relationships. As shown in the case of coal in Ukraine (see chapter 6), a lack of viable substitutes for the specific types of coal needed for highly specified uses (power plants and metallurgical factories) strengthened the bargaining power of those able to supply the exact type of coal needed, and also strengthened the incentives for control of the entire coal-to-metallurgy and coal-to-electricity value chains. The results are not insignificant—in an example of energy's role as constitutive power, and as evidenced by the power of Rinat Akhmetov, Ukraine's richest and most influential oligarch of the post-Soviet period.

Secondary Feature 7: Role in Production Chains of Nonenergy Industries

An additional criterion for comparing crude oil, natural gas, and coal concerns each of these fuels' ability to tie in with other industries not directly associated with energy. The different ways in which oil, natural gas, and coal-related feedstocks interact with the value chains of nonenergy products have important implications for relationships between players. All three fossil fuels at the center of this book play an important role in nonenergy industries also affecting the ways different actors will be related within the chain. Two such ways involve the use of fossil-fuel-related feedstocks as *direct feedstock in other production processes* (as in the case of NGLs and oil derivates) and the use of a specific type of energy as heating sources in situations where, due to technical reasons, the type of energy source matters in the production process because its specific properties may play a needed role for that specific production process (as in the use of coal in kilns to calcinate limestone in cement production or the use of coal coke in metallurgy). In addition, price, availability, and environmental considerations may make a particular fuel a key source of electricity generation in very energy-intensive production, such as chemical fertilizer and cement production.

These various feedstocks also differ in terms of where in the value chain of the source fuel they start to be marketed separately. So, for example these may be substances separated immediately after production (e.g., NGLs[61]) or refined from a fossil fuel (as in the case of ethylene derived from oil) in a midstream production process. In other words, both natural gas and oil provide important feedstocks for other industries, but in the case of natural gas this role is played mainly by substances separated immediately after production, such as NGLs, though in the case of oil these are refined products resulting from the refining process. So, for example, in the case of natural gas only actors involved (physically but also through ownership relations) in immediate proximity to production can reap the gains involved in the separation of NGLs, though in the case of oil, actors spatially located in various midstream locations can reap the gains related to the role of oil derivates as feedstocks for other industries. This has to do with spatial constraints but also with the fact that the natural-gas-derived feedstock used for other industries is derived mainly by means of separation at the start of the value chain, though in the case of oil the feedstocks are refined derivates.

Another way in which energy industries interface with nonenergy ones has to do with the requirements that the transportation and processing of that type of energy entail for other industries. Thus, for example, the high pressure that the steel used for natural gas pipelines needs to withstand means unique demands—and also business opportunities—for metallurgical producers. This, as noted by Högselius, set the basis for unique situations, such as specific metallurgical companies lobbying for certain natural gas supply routes and related pipeline projects because they would create demand for their industries; it was also these requirements (i.e., Soviet requirements for some specific types of steel alloys for the kind of large-diameter pipelines they were seeking to build) that in the first place paved the way for the East–West trade in steel pipes during the Cold War.[62]

Crude oil's role in other industries takes place mainly in the form of its refined products or derivates such as ethylene, propylene, and "aromatics" such as benzene and toluene used as key feedstock for the chemical industry.[63] Coal, in the form of coke, plays a key role as a heating element in the metallurgical industry as well as—as discussed above—in some types of cement production.[64] Natural gas plays an important role in the production of fertilizers and cement; one of the most widespread technologies used in cement manufacturing uses natural gas to fire the kiln at the heart of the production process.[65] Natural gas is also used for co-firing and melting of glass, as well as for drying and dehumidification in the food industry.[66] In the post-Soviet region, it has also played an important role as a source of electricity generation in all energy-intensive industries, such as metallurgy and cement production.

Secondary Feature 8: Effects on Autonomy/Networkness

Energy networkness has to do with the degree to which users depend on a network as opposed to autonomous supplies (e.g., from non-networked residential solar panels). More crucially, it is related to the degree to which the overall functioning of the system may be dependent on the network working properly *as a network*. Although all energy types work in one way or another as part of a network, in the case of natural gas, this networkness is especially crucial, because it has to do with the system being physically balanced as a system—that is, not overloaded or underloaded in its connecting parts.[67] For natural gas, such network balancing is also crucial in a very basic physical way: if the load and pressure in the pipeline system are not right, the entire system may not work properly, possibly leading to a standstill or other accidents, which is a real danger in the case of natural gas, where pipeline connections go all the way to individual residential consumers—as seen in the case of Andover in suburban Boston in 2018, when a failure to properly monitor pressure during a repair operation led to dozens of homes in three cities exploding and catching fire within minutes.[68] In this sense, natural gas is closely related to electricity where, due to storage issues, production and use also need to be closely coupled.

This networkness element (which is also related to the way different types of energy can be produced, stored, transported, distributed, and used) will also have an effect on the autonomy/networkness of users, with potential political implications. One side of this issue concerns a state's ability to successfully adjust to import supply disruptions, which may wreak havoc in a highly networked system (with the additional complication that networks are not necessarily coterminous with national borders and may also be the legacies of previous politico-economic configurations). Another side of the issue concerns domestic political relations, whereby communities with access to more autonomous sources of energy and energy services will have a better chance to withstand pressure from central providers (including the state through state-directed companies) than those without such access.

MATERIALITY DIFFERENCES AND THEIR IMPACT ON ACTORS' RELATIONSHIPS WITHIN THE VALUE CHAIN

The last section discussed how oil, natural gas, and coal compare in terms of a number of key criteria. So how do all these differences affect power relations? I argue that they will affect power relations through the way in which they affect value chains and actors' relationships within these.

In order to do this, let us first clarify how we look at power. As discussed in chapter 2, this book conceptualizes energy-related power as involving not only relational ("power over") but also constitutive ("power to") elements. A constitutive view of power emphasizes "how social relations define who the actors are and what capacities and practices they are socially empowered to undertake" ("power to");[69] in an energy context, such a perspective pays attention to ways in which control over energy may both help constitute actors at a variety of levels (e.g., domestic-level political groups, firms, states, cartels, other international organizations) and relationships between them. Concerning relational "power over" someone, this book understands energy power as not only economic but also political, and understands that it may be manifested in ways that go beyond coercion. This view of power builds upon the work of international political economy theorists such as Susan Strange, which have considered power as going beyond coercion and also including elements of bargaining.

How does power work within the context of value chains? How do power and value chains intersect? Economists working on value chain issues—and, in particular, the global value chain (GVC) perspective popularized by Gereffi and colleagues—have dealt with the issue by looking at "the ability of one firm in the chain to influence or determine the activities of other firms in the chain" and the variety of patterns that this may take.[70] This is in turn related to the governance of value chains, which they define as "systems of governance that link firms together in a variety of sourcing and contracting arrangements."[71] For example, they discuss "market," "modular," "relational," "captive," and "hierarchical vertical integration" as alternative patterns of organizing these relationships.[72] Each of these types of global value chain governance has pluses and minuses and may lead to different incentives for various actors. For example, whereas vertical integration, where a firm directly controls all steps in the production of a good ("hierarchical value chain," in Gereffi's terms), may appear as the most desirable option for producers facing sunk cost and stranded assets risks, a vertical integration strategy also involves significant costs and risks: a loss of flexibility, the opportunity costs associated with the significant investments required by such a strategy, and the need for political agreement (and related risks) in case of foreign acquisitions.[73]

The GVC literature focuses almost exclusively on *firms* as actors in value chains, neglecting the impact of political governance and regulatory nodes such as states.[74] Yet in order to make a value chain–centered approach more useful, it needs to be enriched with a recognition of the importance of political governance also including the role of states as regulatory nodes, a dimension often neglected by the GVC literature.[75] Here it is useful to keep in mind the fact that this literature itself has undergone a transformation, from its Wallersteinian world-systems-analysis roots focusing on how a "general capitalist or systemic logic drives commodity chains," a tradition that afforded more space for a view of governance including the role of the state, to a much narrower focus on firms.[76]

Thus, though largely neglected in the GVC approach, political governance—as opposed to governance by firms within the value chain—also matters. This includes two elements. First, we need to take into consideration the role of political governance—such as regulations affecting taxation, duties, and market entry—in affecting the way firms are connected in value chains (i.e., whether we will see hierarchical chain vertical integration, a captive relationship, etc.). For example, the specific governance situation in Ukraine's coal sector in the 1991–2014 period (when there was high political pressure for continued subsidies to the mining sector, which, together with lack of transparency, made it possible for metallurgical producers to accrue high subsidies through artificially low coal prices) made it possible for metallurgical producers to establish "captive" value chains involving domestic coal mines. Second, we need to recognize the role of legacies in helping shape regional value chains.

Understanding Typical Energy Value Chains and Their Challenges

To understand how materiality issues affect power relations in the value chain, let us first take a look at how energy value chains work in general and how the typical value chains of various energy commodities can create different framing conditions for actors' interactions. This sub-section discusses only the general characteristics of energy value chains as a whole; chapters 4 through 6 discuss in more detail the specificities of the oil, natural gas, and coal value chains.

In their most general sense, fossil fuel value chains are composed of upstream, midstream, and downstream activities. The upstream sector refers to the prospecting for and production ("recovery") of crude oil, natural gas, and coal. It includes searching for potential fields, drilling exploratory wells, and subsequently operating the wells or mines to bring the crude oil, raw natural gas, or coal to the surface. The midstream sector processes, stores, markets, and transports these commodities. In the natural gas industry, the midstream includes gas treatment, separation of NGLs, LNG production and regasification plants, storage, and gas pipeline systems. In the oil industry, the midstream typically includes refining, transportation, and storage. In the coal sector, the midstream is more limited, referring mainly to cleaning, transportation, and (in the case of coking coal) processing into coke. The midstream is not limited to transportation but also involves value adding in the form of processing; the good delivered at the end of the value chain is never the same unprocessed raw material that entered the chain in the production field but is altered by processing, whether visible or invisible. In some cases (e.g., crude oil), this processing will be related to a physical transformation (refining). In the case of natural gas, the midstream contribution is less visible but is no less important, because its main role is preventing undesirable changes to the good so as to safeguard its necessary characteristics to be used by the end consumer (e.g., protecting natural gas from exploding or being dissipated into the atmosphere). The downstream sector involves the distribution and selling of final products to consumers; these products include, among others, natural gas and its derivatives, refined products from crude oil (e.g., gasoline, diesel, and chemical industry feedstock), and coal and coke. Related infrastructures include local gas distributors and gasoline stations.

Having established the importance of looking at energy relations through the prism of their entire value chain, let us look at the role of these value chains in shaping relations between actors—something that is deeply fraught with power implications. In contrast to the GVC perspective, this book sees power as closely related to the materiality in the value chain. At the same time, as discussed in chapter 2, the approach used here differs from more extreme understandings of materiality; in my approach, agency and actorness remain firmly with human subjects, but the materiality characteristics of the goods with which these actors deal will help shape the constraints and options open to them. Materiality (in its broader sense, having to do primarily with infrastructures) may also play a very different role: through human actors using it discursively to support specific perspectives or policies. In their discussion of the use and misuse of the concept of natural monopolies in the United States and Russia, respectively, Malkholm and Wengle show how materiality characteristics may be discursively recruited to support various policy options, such as giving a national champion like Gazprom special privileges as a result of the purported natural monopoly stemming from materiality-related characteristics such as natural-gas-specific economies of scale.[77]

Value Chains and Relationships between Actors: Three Mechanisms

Based on the differences between natural gas, oil, and coal discussed above, this section analyzes three main mechanisms whereby the material characteristics of energy goods make an impact on value chains and actors' relationships within them. Each of these mechanisms highlights one important element of how the distinct, materiality-related constraints of a chain affect power relations within it—through the distributive openings they create, through the differential power they may bestow upon actors at different locations in the chain, and through how their distinct challenges lead to distinct responses affecting power relations. These are not necessarily mutually exclusive; we may see more than one of these mechanisms at play in the value chain of a particular energy good. Let us look at these mechanisms in more detail.

In a first mechanism, the materiality characteristics of specific energy goods help set in motion processes that create *distinct distributive openings*. At the production/upstream level, this can take place through issues such as profit sharing with the inhabitants of a producing region, a sector's workers' ability to press for a higher share of profits,[78] or the general societal impact of types of production such as diffuse versus point production—that is, whether they are produced in a spatially spread-out or concentrated manner. At the processing/ midstream level, these openings involve the way in which the technical requirements for specific value chains create constraints on the location of processing actors, allowing (or not) actors located in specific locations to capture a portion of the profits. At the end-distribution/downstream level, these distributive openings may take place through the issue of possible arbitrage gains (including illicit gains) related to price differentials created by various subsidization plans for end users, or patterns of control created by specific energy distribution forms, such as those discussed by Collier in his study of Soviet-era heating networks.[79] Such openings can also affect the constitution of transborder coalitions—for example, a commodity's ability to be used as a focal point for rent-seeking and corruption can serve to facilitate transborder cooperation between actors sharing the goal of exploiting these opportunities and, arguably, as a means for a foreign state to weaken another state through corruption.[80]

In a second mechanism, the technical constraints of distinct value chains (e.g., in terms of processing, storage, and transit services) can *endow actors at various levels of (upstream, midstream, downstream), and spatial locations in the chain with more or less power.* The technical processes necessary to make energy available to its users often bestows power in unexpected spatial locations, affecting actors' relationships. The spatial constraints on the processing of different types of energy, for example, affect not only actors' profits but also their engagement with further sets of actors that are key for completing specific steps (at key nodes) in these commodity-specific value chains. Thus, whether the processing of an energy good can take place at a variety of locations or only close to production will affect the relative power of actors in various spatial locations. For example, oil processing (refining) can take place in a wide range of spatial locations, though in the case of natural gas, this is largely limited to locations close to the wellhead, limiting the role of spatially distant actors. As discussed in chapter 2, these actors are not simply producer, transit, and consumer states as unified actors, but they are a variety of actors spatially located in or between these. For example, the material characteristics of natural gas as a type of energy most efficiently transported overland via pipelines, along with the high sunk costs associated with such infrastructure, increased the importance of midstream actors, especially those able to provide the shortest route between producer and export markets, and set the basis for Ukraine's key role as transit state for exporting Russian natural gas to Western Europe, creating unique opportunities for a variety of Ukrainian actors able to benefit from both legitimate and corrupt business opportunities around transit operations. (This also means that technological breakthroughs affecting how a good can be processed also have the potential to affect the role and power of various actors in the chain, as seen in the case of LNG, discussed in chapter 8.)

The third mechanism may be the most interesting. In this mechanism, the material characteristics of an energy good affect the *typical challenges* affecting its particular value chain and, through these challenges and possible ways of dealing with them, also affect relationships between actors. All value-added chains present challenges—among others, those related to coordination, efficiency, and, most prominently, the management of investment risks.[81] With respect to investment risks, prominent types of risk are those related to sunk costs (costs that, once made, cannot be recovered) and, in particular, stranded assets (costly assets that may become economically obsolete before the end of their expected economic life[82]).

These challenges, however, do not affect all value-added chains equally—the value chains of various goods, due to their materiality characteristics, present various unique challenges, which influence the means used to deal with them (e.g., contractual forms allocating risk between buyers and sellers), creating specific framing conditions affecting actor relations within the chain. Challenges related to how to share risks between supplier and buyer when the infrastructure needed for such supplies is very costly (the issue of sunk costs) and inflexible (the issue of "asset specificity" and potentially stranded assets) are seen most clearly in those industries requiring high and unmovable investments due to their technical needs, as in natural gas and oil delivery by pipeline.[83] In particular, types of energy characterized by being both high volume but low value per volume and gaseous in form (e.g., natural gas) tend to have high transportation and storage infrastructure costs relative to the value of the goods, making them especially prone to risks related to stranded assets and sunk costs, in turn leading to producers' needs to share these risks with buyers, for example, through specific contractual forms such as take-or-pay clauses.[84]

In each of these three mechanisms, the materiality-related transit and processing differences and their resulting value chains create challenges, opportunities, and constraints for relationships between actors (see table 3.3). These can, in turn, translate into transborder coalitions able to trump officially declared state energy policies.

TABLE 3.3

Distinct Energy Value Chains, Distinct Challenges: Effects on Actors' Behavior Through Typical Ways of Dealing with These Challenges

Type of Energy	Typical Characteristics	Materiality Issues Affecting Typical Value Chain Challenges	Typical Challenges (from Producers' Perspective)	Typical Ways of Dealing with These Challenges
Natural gas	Low value per unit of volume, gaseous, limited transportation options	Gaseous form requires more technology and energy for pipeline transportation; leads to higher transportation and infrastructure costs as compared with oil	Sunk costs related to high-cost, dedicated transportation infrastructure	Contractual: long-term contracts; destination clauses; take-or-pay clauses
	Gaseous substance requiring active pressure management to keep system in physical balance	High networkness requires high investments, close coordination to maintain working pressure	Risk of stranded assets (in case a different route or source of energy is chosen)	Contractual: long-term contracts
		Risks higher than in the case of oil due to higher cost of infrastructure	Sunk costs	
Oil	High value per unit of volume, liquid, many transportation options	Due to its physical characteristics, can be refined almost anywhere, adding to issue of coordination with processing actors	Coordination of midstream processing	Vertical integration and control of midstream (processing) and downstream distribution to keep more value added within producer firm
			Risks due to price volatility	Outsourcing
			Risk of stranded assets due to importers' ability to access crude oil via multiple transportation options	Risk-hedging through diversified economic activities and futures trading

TABLE 3.3
(*continued*)

Coal	Low value per unit of volume, solid "bulk cargo," relatively limited transportation options	Solid nature requires more human involvement and transshipment coordination	Coordination between large numbers of stakeholders	Vertical integration
		Typical low value per volume leads to less resources available for weatherproof storage	Risk of physical loss of the coal mass, or energy value loss from degradation in transit	
		Wide variety in thermal value and other qualities	Difficult standardization due to wide variety in thermal value and other qualities	(Multiple submarkets for different grades)

CONCLUSION

This chapter's discussion has shown how the physical features of various types of energy (e.g., physical state, homogeneity, energy density, CO_2 profile, and ubiquity) come to affect further characteristics of their typical supply and value chains (e.g., transportability, type of markets and processing, ability for cartelization, investment patterns, substitutability, role in nonenergy value chains, and networkness), all of which, in turn, will affect relationships between actors.

We have also seen how these materiality differences affect both external and domestic relationships. Thus, for example, issues such as an energy good's physical state, along with its degree of within-good homogeneity and related commodificability will affect its transportability and marketability, in turn affecting external energy relations. These characteristics will also affect transparency (or the lack thereof) in pricing, affecting possible arbitrage gains. We also saw how the different ways in which natural gas, oil, and coal value chains interact with the value chains of nonenergy products have important implications for the ability of specific players to gain power, not only or not necessarily in terms of their "power over" others, but first and foremost by becoming socially constituted and empowered to take on increasingly prominent roles ("power to") at a variety of levels, ranging from informal economic groups to firms to political actors. These roles become especially important because, for example, coking coal-dependent metallurgy in Ukraine and Russia constitutes one of the largest sources of export revenue for these countries and has consistently produced some of their wealthiest and most influential business actors. Energy-good-specific rents contributed to the emergence of important political players and groupings, to their increased power, and to their ability to influence policymaking.

Paying attention to materiality also helps us better understand the relationship between the external and domestic levels: by creating opportunities and constraints for relationships between actors, materiality characteristics can also affect the nature of transborder coalitions, to the point that these may be able to trump officially declared state energy policies or challenge the applicability of otherwise seemingly reasonable policies. To give but a preview, let us consider the long-standing issue of the Nord Stream pipeline bringing Russian natural gas to Germany directly, and the issue of compliance with the European Union's regulations requiring gas pipelines in EU territory to offer third-party access (and to have the spare capacity to back it) to other suppliers and banning pipeline owners from also being the providers of the gas carried by the pipeline.[85] In the case of the OPAL pipeline—connecting Nord Stream's end point, Lubmin, with Olbernhau on the German-Czech border—it is not possible to offer this capacity, because there is no other possible source of natural gas for this pipeline, which was built specifically to transport natural gas imported via Nord Stream. At the same time, the materiality characteristics of natural gas as a physical substance create important constraints: being lighter than air, natural gas easily dissipates if not contained, and thus must be under a certain minimum amount of pressure in order to travel through the pipeline. What this means in practice is that certain minimum volumes need to be maintained for the pipeline to be functional, making use of the pipeline at low capacity not an option. In this way, introducing materiality considerations into our analysis makes us look at issues such as the European Union's spare capacity requirements in a new light.

Looking at materiality and at the physical, material chain linking the various stages of energy production and use provides a different perspective compared with the one you would get by just looking at energy as an abstract concept and a political instrument. The subsequent case study chapters illustrate how such an approach can be used to understand long-standing issues in a new way.

PART TWO

Hydrocarbon Chains and Political Power

CHAPTER FOUR

Natural Gas: Managing Pressure from Western Siberia to the Nürnberg Power Plant

THIS CHAPTER begins the case study portion of the book comparing the value chains of three key fossil fuels produced by Russia, transited via Ukraine, and delivered to end consumers in Germany: natural gas, oil, and (coking) coal. This chapter analyzes the natural gas chain, going from production in Urengoy, Russia, to end users in Nürnberg, Germany (see figure 4.1). This value chain has constituted a key element of Russia's energy relations with both the European Union (which in 2012 imported 32 percent of its natural gas from Russia[1]) and the post-Soviet transit and consumer states.

The key chemical constituent of natural gas is methane; natural gas, as delivered to end users, is almost totally composed of methane. Thus, our natural gas molecule is, first and foremost, a methane molecule—the simplest and smallest hydrocarbon molecule and "the lightest stable organic molecule."[2] In contrast to the cases of oil and coal analyzed, respectively, in chapters 5 and 6, the physical transformation that the natural gas (methane) molecule went through from production in Russia to final consumers in Germany was, at first glance, rather simple—"just transit" to final users—with no intermediate

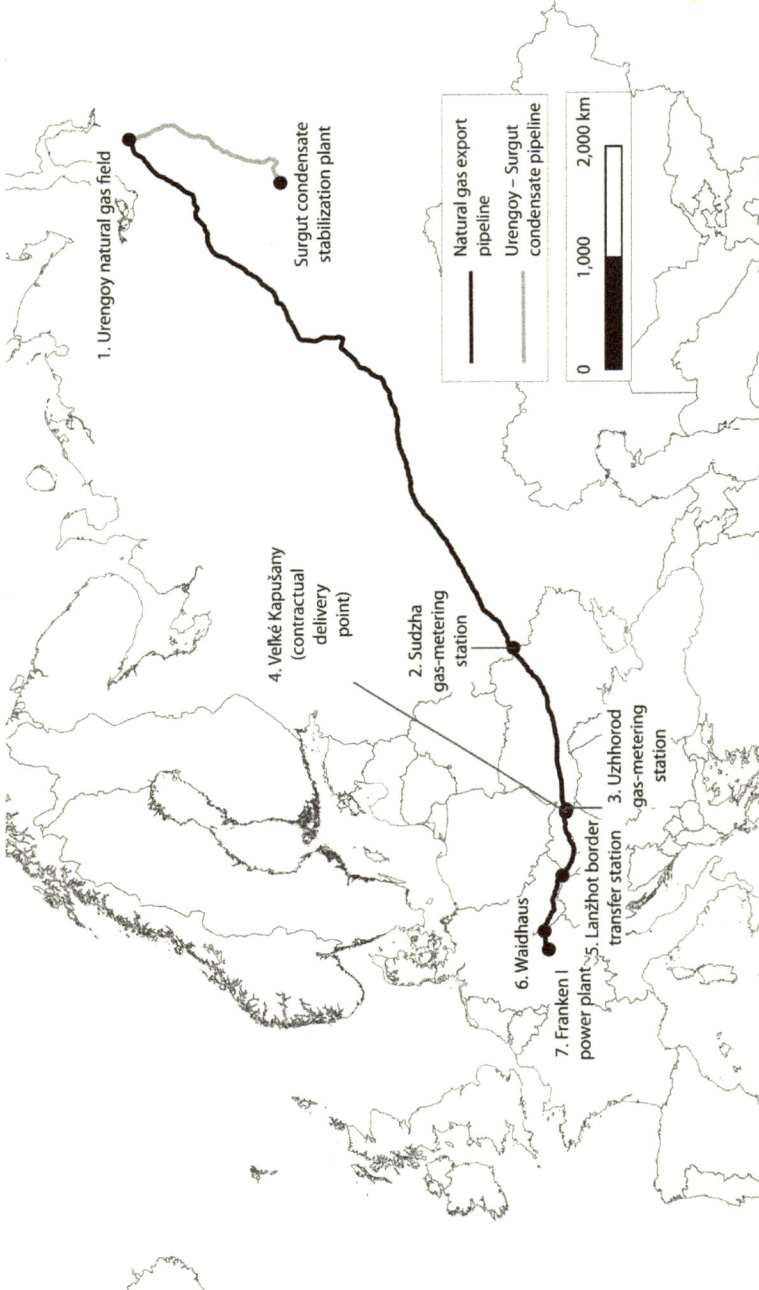

Figure 4.1 Overview of the natural gas chain followed in this chapter

Source: Map created by Matthias Neumann using QGIS and GIS data from Natural Earth (free vector and raster map data at naturalearthdata.com), OpenStreetMap (https://www.openstreetmap.org), and Wikipedia; further editing in Adobe Illustrator.

physical transformation (i.e., as in the case of oil refining) involved.[3] This image, however, is deceiving. Behind this apparent simplicity, behind this "just transit" journey, lies a complex infrastructure put in place exactly to make sure that natural gas's characteristics would remain *unchanged* through this journey and would be safeguarded so as to guarantee its ability to be used effectively by end consumers. This complex and capital-intensive infrastructure ranged from processing units, to pipelines purpose-built to protect natural gas from exploding or dispersing into the atmosphere, to compressor stations to nudge natural gas onward on its journey, to pressure-reducing units to brake natural gas's pressure before going into small-diameter pipelines at city networks, to gas storage facilities to help balance temporary ups and downs in demand.

Although some of the differences between the natural gas value chain and those of the other fossil fuels discussed in this book had to do with differences in sectoral governance, important differences also go back to variations in the physical characteristics of the goods themselves. These differences, as discussed in chapter 3, also affect key characteristics of the value chain as a system, for example, through the ways in which they affect the transportation process.

In this sense, three elements of natural gas's materiality are especially significant. First, as discussed in chapter 3, though natural gas from different fields may differ slightly in composition, it was relatively homogeneous compared with oil and coal, and was typically not marketed separately as different goods,[4] facilitating physical as well as virtual swap operations.[5] A second key characteristic concerns natural gas's gaseous state at ambient temperature, which deeply affects its transportation options, by requiring specialized and very costly infrastructure. One aspect of this situation is well known: in gaseous form, natural gas can only be transported efficiently via pipeline (see chapter 3, on an exception, liquefied natural gas, LNG). A less known but crucial aspect has to do with the demands that this gaseous state and related pressure issues place on infrastructure. Weighing less than air, natural gas has a tendency to dissipate in the air and needs to be under pressure in order to move in the pipeline, which, in turn, makes necessary a highly specialized infrastructure and places unique demands on the pipelines transporting this gas. Due to the very high pressure that pipeline walls need to withstand, the steel alloy in gas pipelines needs to be much stronger than that used for oil pipelines—most large-diameter gas pipelines function at over 70 bar pressure, that is, seventy times conventional pressure, while most oil pipelines usually function at 50 bar or less.[6]

Last but not least, natural gas, together with electricity (with whose markets it is closely connected because gas is widely used for electricity generation), is a deeply networked type of energy, also in comparison with oil. This requires a tightly coupled system and highly specialized, purpose-built infrastructure. Although both oil and gas are most effectively transported to mid-distance continental locations by pipeline, the gas grid is more complex to keep in balance, due to the direct integration with end consumers, which also makes gas pipeline infrastructure more expensive than equivalent oil infrastructure.[7]

These materiality elements affect both natural gas value chains as a whole and policy and regulatory attitudes toward them. These key characteristics have had an impact on consumers through the existence of largely regional markets, as well as through the unique challenges faced by the natural gas value chain. In interaction with the governance and other features of the spatial area encompassed by the Urengoy-Nürnberg chain, these characteristics affected the chain's course, as well as the kinds of relationships that could—or could not—emerge within it.

THE GLOBAL AND REGIONAL MARKET CONTEXT

From among all the routes taking Russian natural gas to Germany, the natural gas value chain analyzed in this chapter uses as an *exemplary chain* the journey of natural gas from production in Russia to final consumers of electricity in Germany via the physical infrastructure of the Brotherhood pipeline system passing through the Ukrainian, Slovak, and Czech gas transit systems, as well as regional pipelines and the electricity generation system in Germany—interacting, at each spatial stage, both with infrastructure nodes and the interests of important local actors, and with decisions made at supranational commercial and regulatory nodes.[8] The main steps in this chain were production; cleaning; bringing to pipeline standard; transportation within Russia; entrance into the export pipeline system; interaction with Russia's natural gas export system; transit through Ukraine, the Slovak Republic, and the Czech Republic; and transformation into electricity in Germany.

Although representative of natural gas value chains as a whole, the journey discussed in this chapter took place in a concrete space and at a particular time. The particular time was that of this book's focus period, October 2011 to March 2014.[9] The concrete space was the political/regulatory space created by institutions that were in force in the countries and regulatory spaces (i.e., the EU) covered by the chain, discussed in chapter 2. At the same time, this chain unfolded in the context of global and regional natural gas market trends. During the period 2011–14, three such trends were key. First, during this period, natural gas prices continued to differ significantly between various regional markets. In contrast with the United States, where reference prices for natural gas had been going down since 2008, in Europe this was a period of relatively stable prices before the start of a downward trend in mid-2014. Second, this was also a period of generally sluggish global demand for natural gas, due to low growth rates in countries belonging to the Organization for Economic Cooperation and Development and growing use of coal and renewables. This was especially clear in the EU, where demand for natural gas fell to record lows in 2011–12; the impact on prices was not immediate, in part as a result of the still-prevalent long-term contracts.[10] By 2011, EU production had also declined significantly, by nearly 30 percent from its 1996–2004 levels, leading to increased reliance on imports from outside the EU, especially Russia.[11] Third, by this point unconventional oil and gas production was already affecting EU markets, but this had more to do with the indirect effects of growing production in the United States than with increased production in the EU, where several states had banned shale gas production.[12] LNG use remained limited, at about 15 percent of imports, playing a significant role only in the few areas of the EU that were still only peripherally linked to long-distance natural gas pipelines, such as Spain and Portugal.[13]

The EU market environment in 2011–14 was also changing because of regulatory issues. Some of these changes were related to new energy security measures taken by the EU in response to the 2009 Ukrainian-Russian gas crisis—such as support for expanded reverse flows, LNG imports, and gas storage capacity—but these were not yet fully implemented in Central Europe and the Baltic states.[14] No less important were new renewables requirements, and ownership unbundling policies requiring the separation of energy production, transportation, and distribution, which had been reshaping the EU market since 2007 with the aim of transforming pipelines from a private good to a common carrier open to multiple users. This was also a period of transition concerning contractual modalities in the gas market, spurred by EU measures undermining—or downright outlawing—typical features of Gazprom gas contracts, such as oil-price-indexed pricing, destination clauses, and long-term contracts; this period also saw a decline in long-term contracts and a rise in hub-based deliveries.[15] (Gazprom, however, seemed unwilling to wake up to these trends, insisting on maintaining its traditional contract model, a stance that made it lose market share vis-à-vis more flexible competitors such as Norway's Statoil.[16]) At the level of the countries of the former Soviet Union (FSU), the 2011–14 period was characterized by relatively stable production in Russia, as well as strong decreases in gas demand in Ukraine, especially in 2014.

RUSSIA UPSTREAM

The first leg of our gas molecule's journey took it from Urengoy in Siberia to the start of Gazprom's Brotherhood pipeline. This section describes the technical and regulatory hurdles our molecule had to face in this first part of its journey.

Urengoy

Our gas journey starts in the Urengoy field, the beginning of the pipeline system, which, through several largely parallel lines and sublines, would each year bring over 100 billion cubic meters of natural gas to users in the European part of Russia, the FSU countries, and the EU.[17] The history of Urengoy, located in the Yamal-Nenets Autonomous Region, as a field and as a population center is impossible to separate from the history of the pipeline system. (Some excellent studies have come out in recent years on the history of the pipeline; I touch on that history only as necessary.[18]) The Urengoy field, discovered in 1966, brought new life to the near-forgotten city Novo-Urengoy, where the headquarters of Gazprom's 100 percent subsidiary Gazprom Dobycha Urengoy were built shortly thereafter, in charge of production in the entire Nadym-Pur gas region, including twenty-two gas and oil fields.[19] Novo-Urengoy became Russia's unofficial "gas capital," quickly overcoming Yamal-Nenets's official capital Salekhard in population (about 110,000 vs. 42,000 in about 2012) and economic significance.[20] Some of the effects had to do with increased salaries relative to other areas of

Russia—in 2012, for example, the average monthly salary in the Novo-Urengoy region was significantly higher than the Russian average; even considering higher costs of living, this is a significant difference.[21]

This economic significance also meant an overwhelming dependence of the entire city and region on Gazprom. Novo-Urengoy had from its very inception been a monotown, albeit one not only specializing in hydrocarbon extraction but also incorporating exploration and processing activities. As such, it became a magnet for gas specialists from the entire USSR. The articles in *Gaz Urengoya*, Gazprom Dobycha Urengoy's corporate newspaper, provide a glimpse into some of the ways in which this mobility along uniquely Soviet natural gas career paths, from Grozny to Baku to Kazan to Western Siberia, had both made and remade the region.[22] A glimpse at regular air routes from Novo-Urengoy's airport tells us of these links as well—prominent destinations included not just Moscow, Tyumen, and Salekhard but also Ufa and Kazan.

The Urengoy field is the Earth's second-largest known gas deposit and was for many years believed to be the largest.[23] Together with Yamburg and Medvezhye, Urengoy is one of Russia's three super-giant fields, which by 2012 accounted for about 45 percent of Russia's total reserves and the lion's share of its natural gas production.[24] From a production economics perspective, two things were key about Urengoy. First, despite the sheer size of its reserves, Urengoy, like Yamburg and Medvezhye, was also an aging "legacy" field.[25] By 2001 its gas deposits had been depleted by 62 percent, with a number of effects on production.[26] The field's early exploitation had focused in its shallow sediment layers, which were easier and more economical to exploit and to process due to their lower concentration of contaminants;[27] with this easy production stage over, production became more challenging, reflecting the broader trend of the end of inexpensive natural gas production in the Russian Federation as a whole. Second, the substance coming out of the Urengoy fields (unstable gas condensate, a mixture of various hydrocarbons—gas, light hydrocarbons, crude oil—water, sand, and contaminants such as hydrogen sulfide and carbon dioxide[28]) was still a long way from being the lighter-than-air dry gas that we associate with the clean, blue-burning gas on which Gazprom had built its reputation. In particular, Urengoy condensate was characterized by having a significant level of natural gas liquids (NGLs) and contaminants such as sulfur.[29]

Processing Gas to Create a Standard Product: Making Gas Worthy of Brotherhood

These characteristics are important for understanding the next step in our gas molecule's life in Urengoy: (pre)processing.[30] This processing requires several steps, first separating natural gas from oil (if needed); then from water and contaminants; and, finally, NGLs. This is in addition to any precleaning that may take place as part of the process of gathering gas supplies from the specific well for further processing. Although the substance we normally call "gas" is composed of nearly 100 percent methane, as discussed above, the substance extracted from the wellhead also contains other hydrocarbon molecules. Urengoy-produced natural gas in particular was rich in liquid hydrocarbons, which required immediate processing not only in order to separate higher-value NGLs and sulfur to be marketed separately, but also because of their corrosive properties.

There are a number of reasons why this processing needed to start in close proximity to the production area. First, if not removed, some of these other hydrocarbons found in "wet" natural gas can form ice-like compounds that can block, corrode, and rupture a pipeline.[31] So "wet" gas, before it is pumped into the pipe, must be artificially "dried." This affects spatial patterns as follows: though in principle it is possible to install gas-processing plants away from production areas, doing so is highly uneconomical, because in order to do this it is necessary to build special pipelines there able to transport "wet" gas.[32] The second reason for close-to-the-field processing is that natural gas "becomes" a product within a specific pipeline (where it mixes with natural gas from other production locations) and, as such, it needs to be processed to be brought to pipeline standard. This usually means being free of contaminants and water, and within specified ranges for caloric value. In the case of the Brotherhood pipeline system, this caloric value was the standard for Russian H-gas—the gas with the highest known methane content and caloric-value per weight, and thus the gas that is "usually used by engine designers as a reference gas."[33] The third reason is that, because NGLs fetch a much higher price than "dry" natural gas, by removing them, they can be put in the path of further commercialization as feedstock for the chemical industry.[34]

In the case of our natural gas molecule, the raw mixture (unstable gas condensate) produced at Gazprom's Urengoy field was sent to the

Deethanization Unit, the key unit at the Novy Urengoy Condensate Treatment Plant.[35] This plant is worthy of our attention as it exemplifies the close connection between the material characteristics of a good, the spatial location of infrastructure, and the further impact on value chains. It is here, immediately after production, that the very unique interaction between the natural gas value chain and compressor technology—one of the factors making natural gas transportation more costly than that for oil—starts. Gas comes out of the field at very high pressure, up to nearly 350 times atmospheric pressure (i.e., 350 bar).[36] Because it is extremely difficult to handle natural gas at such high pressure, the first step involves using technology to reduce pressure at this point, so that this initial processing can take place. This drop in pressure is also what makes condensates (i.e., NGLs) drop out of the mixture in processing plants such as the Novy Urengoy Condensate Treatment Plant. This plant was not only a major investment but also a major technological feat at the time of its construction (it was completed in 1984).[37] Because of the physical qualities of the condensate produced at Urengoy (its high sulfur content), exploitation of the field would have been unthinkable without the Condensate Treatment Plant; spatially, the unit needed to be located in close proximity to the field. After passing through the Condensate Treatment Plant, part of the de-ethanized gas condensate was transported by a special condensate pipeline to Surgut, where a special unit (the Condensate Stabilization Plant, named after V. S. Chernomyrdin)[38] would further process it as NGLs and stable gas condensate; part of the latter would be further processed into motor oils such as diesel and gasoline.[39] Of the de-ethanized gas condensate gas not sent to Surgut, a portion was sent to the Tyumen region for local use, and the bulk of it went to the trunk pipeline that would eventually become the Brotherhood pipeline going to Europe.[40] It is this last stream that we follow in this chapter.

The three-way fork road open to Gazprom's condensate upon arriving at the Condensate Treatment Plant—regional use, processing as higher-value products, and/or export—was representative of the choices open to Gazprom as a corporation, concerning each field but also corporate strategy as a whole. These choices involved what portion of the gas to use for domestic supplies (in a situation where average export prices to Western Europe were nearly four times higher than domestic ones[41]), which to export (and to where), as well as which portion to further process as higher-value motor fuel and chemical industry feedstock from NLGs—the most profitable subsegment of the natural gas value chain.[42]

But before decisions were made concerning what percentage of production would go to where, these were filtered through three sets of circumstances. First, there was the long-standing bargain whereby Gazprom (of which, by 2004, the Russian state had acquired a majority of shares) traditionally fulfilled certain domestic (as well as external) tasks for the state (e.g., helping maintain social stability through low domestic prices) in exchange for certain privileges, such as a continued monopoly on pipeline-bound exports. This bargaining role was also tied to the issue of whether Gazprom would sell natural gas domestically or abroad, which was also related to the issue of its sales for domestic power (electricity) generation, nearly half of which was based on natural gas and which constituted about 40 percent Russian natural gas consumption in 2012.[43] Traditionally, Gazprom sold its gas to power generators at a price much lower than the export price, and this was used as means to keep end-user prices low; in international comparison, Russian end-user electricity prices for both industries and households were the lowest of all major countries.[44] Thus, the early 2000s saw Gazprom involved in a long dispute with parastatal monopoly electricity utility RAO UES on the need to move to coal for power generation in order to free more natural gas for export.[45] The issue was also intermingled with the unbundling and privatization of RAO UES, which was liquidated in 2008. RAO UES's restructuring and partial privatization was ongoing since 2003; by 2012 Gazprom owned over 30 percent of generation installed capacity in European Russia (and 21 percent of Russia's total capacity).[46] With power generation in European Russia largely based on gas, Gazprom's entry into the power generation market also raised questions of competition, given the company's role in gas supply and the "risk that this position could be used to penalize competitors in the electricity-production market,"[47] in the sense that it could use its dominant position as a natural gas supplier to prevent market access by competitors. If in the past Gazprom had been expected to supply gas to RAO UES at prices much lower than export parity, by 2006 repeated discussions of domestic gas prices reaching European netback levels by 2011 (and, later, 2014) likely opened for Gazprom the prospect of capturing profits and/or state subsidies in its electricity business.

Second, Gazprom's behavior is best understood as a complex interaction between its managers, simultaneously acting on behalf of the state (as main shareholder and having multiple other means of exerting pressure on the company), on behalf of the company's corporate interests, and on behalf of their own private interests, including through side dealings not in the company's interests.[48] Third, there was the fact that these strategies and pacts had to be regionally specific, given the size of the Russian Federation and wide differences in natural resource endowment between regions.[49] The implication is that, whatever export strategies Gazprom would implement, these would also have regional-level implications that would need to be taken into account.

RUSSIA MIDSTREAM

This section describes our molecule's journey from its entry into the Brotherhood pipeline to its reaching the Ukrainian border. This journey included both a 3,000 kilometer–plus travel through the pipeline and through Russia's complex regulatory landscape, at this time grappling with the issue of Gazprom's role as a monopolist, as well as challenges to it.

From Urengoy to the Rest of the World through a Changing Regulatory Landscape

After going through the Novy Urengoy Condensate Treatment Plant, the substance produced at the Urengoy field, which was now dry gas, would begin its 3,291-kilometer journey through the Gazprom/ Brotherhood pipeline system up to the Ukrainian border. In the course of this journey, it would come into contact with a Russian gas market and regulatory system (with Moscow as the single regulatory node) in the midst of major changes concerning Gazprom's role in production, domestic supplies, and exports.

Exports and the issue of Gazprom's export monopoly. In a nutshell, the situation at the start of the focus period was as follows: Gazprom exported nearly 45 percent of its annual production,[50] almost exclusively to the Commonwealth of Independent States, Eastern Europe, the EU, and Turkey; about 80 percent of these exports (accounting for about 56 percent of Gazprom's profits[51]) transited through Ukraine, mainly through the Brotherhood pipeline. Although the focus period was one of intense discussion of possible exports to Asian markets as alternatives to the EU (partly as a means to impress on European buyers the risks involved in diversifying away from Russian gas, as Russia could also turn to other markets[52]), most of these Asia-bound exports would not have originated in Urengoy but in gas fields thousands of kilometers to the east.[53] So, though Gazprom as a corporation and its Board of Directors faced significant decisions about what to do with its gas, Urengoy gas was, for the moment, firmly looking west.

In reaching its lucrative Western European markets, Gazprom had long benefited from monopoly export rights, which were enshrined in law in 2006.[54] This monopoly was further supported by preferential access to domestic pipelines and related infrastructure. Such preferential access was key, if only because of the long distances between the gas fields and consumers and related sunk-cost investments; Gazprom gas had to travel, on average, over 2,500 kilometers to reach domestic markets—and almost 3,300 kilometers to reach foreign ones.[55] Given the continental geography involved, transportation by pipeline was largely unavoidable, because rail and road transportation are highly uneconomical and technically nearly impossible, given natural gas's extremely low energy density per volume and gaseous state. Although processing into LNG would have created more transportation options, and by 2009 Russia had opened a liquefaction plant (Sakhalin), this was not a viable alternative for Urengoy gas. Leaving aside the 7,000 kilometers from Urengoy to Sakhalin, LNG makes most sense for tanker shipments to overseas locations, not for (relatively) nearby landlocked markets already served by a well-developed pipeline system, where significant unrecoverable (sunk) cost investments have been already made. In this case, the physical characteristics of natural gas affected Gazprom's options through the issue of sunk costs related to already-existing transport infrastructure.

A key issue was under what conditions gas produced by other, "independent," producers would be allowed to be transported in Gazprom pipelines and even exported—in other words, issues of third-party access to Gazprom's pipelines. This concerned first and foremost the Unified Gas Supply System (UGSS) high-pressure system of long-distance and export pipelines, one of the three levels of gas pipelines existing in Russia (the other two being the intraregional gas network and local distribution grids, where Gazprom had no monopoly rights).[56] This high-pressure system is intrinsically related to our journey not only because of its importance in bringing gas from Urengoy to Western European markets but also because the UGSS itself had been established with the goal of bringing gas from the Urengoy, Medvezhye, and Yamburg fields to markets in European Russia and further points west.[57]Although other companies were allowed to produce natural gas and non-Gazprom producers' share in total gas production had been increasing rapidly since 2000, the lack of capacity in the Russian pipeline system made it difficult for these companies to commercialize this gas, even domestically. Although third-party access (i.e., for independent producers) to UGSS trunk pipelines existed de jure, a lack of clarity in the legislation, along with uncertainty concerning transportation tariffs (set by the Federal Tariff Service) complicated actual access.[58] Independent producers also complained of difficulties accessing gas storage facilities (see below).

Infrastructure and the impulse for change. If, through 2008, Gazprom seemed to be sitting firmly on both domestic and export pipelines, its domestic monopoly started to weaken after that year. This was partially a result of declining domestic demand, which, together with the expansion of the pipeline network, reduced transportation bottlenecks—long used as justification for denying access to the pipeline—thus allowing for more gas produced by independent producers to be shipped and reach consumers.[59] It is at this point that some aspects of Gazprom's special status start to actually benefit independent producers. Although Gazprom received considerable preferential treatment, in contrast with other producers, it was subject to state regulation concerning both prices charged for domestic sales and—especially until 2006—exports to members of the Commonwealth of Independent States.[60] It was required to sell its gas domestically at prices set by the Federal Tariff Service, though independent producers were not. Having to supply gas domestically at low regulated prices was often a burden to Gazprom as compared with much higher export prices to Western European markets, but the equation changed in the wake of the 2008 economic downturn. With supply (driven by production by independents) going up but demand stagnant, being subject to regulated domestic prices proved a problem in a different way: Gazprom was not allowed to offer discounts to industrial users, as independent producers could. Having been given greater pricing flexibility, independent producers such as Novatek (as well as oil companies producing associated petroleum gas—"associated gas"—as part of their oil-producing process, e.g., Rosneft) were able to offer prices 10 percent lower than Gazprom and were able to increase their sales, especially to industrial users. As a result, between 2011 and mid-2014, Gazprom's share in domestic gas production declined from 83.6 percent in 2011 to

69.7 percent.[61] In addition, the Gas Exports Law amendment of December 2013 gave some non-Gazprom producers (de facto, Novatek and Rosneft) the right to export LNG, but not pipeline gas.[62]

The changes in export regulations discussed above tell us that infrastructure, however important, does not in and of itself determine outcomes. Moreover, though the image of (Soviet/Russian) pipelines as "veins of steel" is a powerful one, concrete infrastructure objects such as pipeline systems are not unchangeable physical givens—they also age and decay. Despite an upgrade program started in 2011, the legacy of serious underinvestment in the 1991–2002 period continued to be felt.[63] This affected reliability as well as the costs of transmission.[64] The technical state of transit pipelines within Russia itself also affected supplies to the FSU countries and beyond.

Not by Pipelines Alone? Managing the Flow of a Networked Bounty

As evocative as the image of high Russian officials demonstratively turning off the valve for Russian gas supplies (e.g., to Ukraine in 2009) may be, the technological processes involving transboundary gas flows are much more technically complex than that image would convey. Thus, for example, because natural gas production cannot simply be turned off at short notice, in the absence of accessible storage (and one technically able to perform intake/offtake at the necessary speed), a producer may have little option but to let it escape or flare (in the case of petroleum associated gas).

As discussed in chapter 3 and at the beginning of this chapter, natural gas is, together with electricity, highly networked energy, both in the sense of its being a closely coupled system infrastructure-wise and in the sense that the various parts of the system need to be in physical balance for it to function safely and efficiently. In the case of natural gas transportation, where maintaining the proper pipeline pressure is essential for the gas to move at all, *and* where proper interconnection between pipelines of different diameters and pressure levels is key, such "networkness" issues are essential. They are also related to the physical characteristics of natural gas as a substance, as, being lighter than air, it needs to be under pressure; it also needs to be physically contained—pressure increases its capacity to dissipate. As we will see below, this would affect the technical needs of the system and, through them, actors' relationships in the value chain. The required natural gas network balancing took place both at the level of regional/domestic gas deliveries and at the level of international transit. At the level of regional supplies within Russia, this was done mainly through Gazprom's dispatch control—that is, the system adjusting pipelines' volumes and pressure levels as the gas moves from large, high-pressure trunk systems to low-pressure, small-diameter city network pipelines.[65] Although in this case only small variations were usually at issue, in the case of high-pressure long-distance pipelines such as Brotherhood, larger, seasonal variations made the availability of gas storage facilities a key technical necessity for the functioning of the system as a whole.

After leaving Urengoy, our gas molecule had to travel over 3,000 kilometers—nearly a week—and through twenty-two compressor stations to reach the Ukrainian border. What flowed out of Urengoy was not one pipeline but a network of pipelines, most often a parallel formation of ten large-diameter (1,420 millimeters / 56 inches) pipelines, an arrangement that was not only technically necessary (it would be extremely hard to move natural gas through even larger pipelines) but also facilitated supplies to nearby cities such as Salekhard and Ekaterimburg. Thus the Brotherhood pipeline, even if built for export purposes, also fulfilled a variety of other domestic roles.

ENTERING UKRAINE

The Urengoy gas molecule we are following in this chapter entered Ukraine at a unique moment in its energy history: in 2011, the last year before the entrance in 2012 into full operation of the Nord Stream pipeline, which was completed in 2011 to bring Russian gas to Germany through a direct link under the Baltic Sea instead of transit via Ukraine, thus threatening to take significant transit volumes and revenue (about $2.2 billion in 2011) away from the country.[66]

In 2011, Ukraine imported 44.8 billion cubic meters of gas from Gazprom, which represented 67 percent of its gas needs and about 21 percent of Gazprom's exports.[67] So as of early 2011 (i.e., before the opening of the Nord Stream pipeline), the country was not only the largest transit country for Gazprom gas (and the largest hydrocarbon transit country in the world) but also its largest importer.

Ukraine as Importer: Political and Governance Aspects

Formally, Urengoy gas "entered" Ukraine before crossing the border into Ukraine—it was counted as entering Ukraine once it was accounted for at the Sudzha gas-metering station (GMS) in Russia, as there was no metering station on the Ukrainian side (see the discussion of GMSs below). What was the political and energy-political context into which this gas—both destined for transit and in-country use—came? The focus period largely coincided with Viktor Yanukovich's presidency (January 2010–February 2014), which was marked by his increased centralization of power, along with his attempts to position his family and close associates at the center of rent-seeking schemes.

This period was also deeply marked by the aftermath of the January 2009 contract (with Gazprom's headquarters in Moscow as a commercial node) signed between then–prime minister Yulia Tymoshenko and Gazprom in the wake of the 2009 gas crisis.[68] (On January 1, 2009, arguing unpaid debts, Gazprom cut gas supplies destined for Ukraine; a week later, as a means of exerting additional pressure, it cut all gas supplies through Ukraine, which were restarted only ten days later. For the first time in memory, this led to a total stoppage of Russian gas supplies to EU states Bulgaria and Romania, and also to Moldova, the Former Yugoslav Republic of Macedonia, Serbia, Bosnia-Herzegovina, and Croatia.) The contract had positive aspects from a medium- and long-term perspective. First and most important, it did away with RosUkrEnergo's intermediary role, establishing a ten-year direct contract between Gazprom and NAK Naftohaz Ukraini, which was a significant improvement given the highly corrupt role intermediary companies had played in the past.[69] Second, marking a clear break from previous contractual arrangements, it ended the cross-subsidization of transit and gas prices and established a clear differentiation between imports and transit services.[70] It also included a transparent price formula based, for the first time in Ukrainian-Russian gas relations, on the European netback principle, which was a major improvement over the "negotiated prices" contracts that dominated Ukrainian-Russian gas relations between 1991 and 2009.[71]

However, most immediately, the 2009 contract had brought significant gas price hikes (the new formula stipulated that Ukraine would pay 80 percent of the European price in 2009, and 100 percent of the European prices from 2010 to 2019, with quarterly adjustments; the base price, however, appeared to be artificially high[72]) that would deeply affect Ukraine's energy situation during our focus period. Despite a discount negotiated by Yanukovich (the "Kharkiv agreements" of April 2010) in exchange for an extension of the lease to Russia of military facilities in Crimea,[73] during most of the period 2011–14 Ukraine was paying prices not only twice as high as those it paid before 2009 but also some of the highest in Europe—by April 2014, $485 per 1,000 cubic meters.[74]

Although some European importers were able to negotiate lower prices with Gazprom (in part because of the pressure of new gas volumes from the United States; see chapter 8), Ukraine was not able to do so. Although the burden of earlier price increases had been softened by Ukraine's booming steel exports during 2008's period of record prices, by 2009 steel prices had plummeted (see chapter 6), making price increases especially painful. The proportion of Ukraine's gross domestic product spent on gas imports nearly doubled between 2005 (4.5 percent) and 2011 (8.6 percent). The price increase was made worse by the take-or-pay clauses in the contract and its strong penalties for late payment; if NAK Naftohaz were to be unable to make those payments on time, it would be automatically moved to 100 percent yearly prepayment for the reminder of the ten-year contract. These take-or-pay clauses were seen by many as Gazprom's attempt to compensate for weaker gas demand in the EU by holding Ukraine responsible for large imports at high prices.[75] Moreover, the 2009 agreements had given Gazprom the right to market 25 percent of the imported gas directly to Ukrainian industrial users, undermining national oil and gas company's NAK Naftohaz's few sources of profit.[76] And gas transit fees paid Ukraine would remain unchanged at a much lower price than the European average and, relative to the price of gas, even lower than their 2008 levels.[77] Similarly, though the contract guaranteed a minimum transit of 110 billion cubic meters a year for 2009–19, it did not include ship-or-pay penalties if Gazprom were not to comply with the agreements, and the guaranteed minimum was violated as early as 2011.

These factors compromised NAK Naftohaz's ability to pay Gazprom on time, creating a constant situation of near-crises. At the same time, the contract cast a long political shadow. Dissatisfaction with the agreements and the sharp price increases played a crucial role in the run-up to the February 2010 presidential elections, leading to conflicts within President Viktor Yushchenko's Orange coalition and propelling Viktor Yanukovich's successful bid for the presidency in February 2010.[78] The contract was denounced by Yanukovich as state treason and misuse of power by former prime minister Yulia Tymoshenko, serving as an excuse for a criminal case against her (she ended up in jail between October 2011 and the February 2014 Euromaidan events), and also for his increasingly authoritarian measures. The larger point here is that, despite Yanukovich's pro-Russian reputation (and his clearly pro-Russian choices in late 2013 and 2014), the 2009 gas contracts set the stage for tense relations with Russia during the focus period. Yanukovich's attempts to renegotiate the contracts, despite his pro-Russian reputation, found little sympathy on the Gazprom side; prices paid by Ukraine only started to go down in 2014 in the wake of the global hydrocarbon price slump.

This period was also marked by contradictory tendencies concerning Ukraine's gas market governance, which was affected both by country-level developments and by the impact of the EU's energy governance initiatives (with Brussels as the single regulatory node) "exported" to its neighborhood through new institutions (e.g., the EU-promoted Energy Community) as well as through broader developments related to the Eastern Partnership process and the promise of closer relations with the EU in the form of a possible association agreement and/or a deep and comprehensive free trade agreement. On one hand, as part of the process of Ukraine's joining of the Energy Community (effective February 2012) and in order to fulfill its requirements, laws were passed formally opening the way for third-party access to the Ukrainian gas transportation system[79] and the unbundling (i.e., the separation of its production, transportation, storage, and distribution activities) and reform of NAK Naftohaz. On the other hand, few real changes took place, with the above-noted laws not fully implemented.[80] Reform of NAK Naftohaz was an especially complex issue given the company's history of corruption and lack of transparency.[81] Moreover, the Yanukovich period was itself marked by unprecedented levels of corruption going all the way up to the highest echelons of power, clearly contradicting the transparency goals of the Energy Community; real reform of the gas market would only start in 2015, after Yanukovich's ouster. Although unbundling was a key pillar of the Energy Community, during 2011–14 NAK Naftohaz retained its monopoly on the transportation and distribution of natural gas. Although, in March 2011, the government cancelled the company's monopoly on gas imports, which at first glance seemed a liberalization measure, in reality the measure was used discretionally to benefit a major Yanukovich supporter at the expense of NAK Naftohaz's long-term sustainability (see below).[82]

THE LEGACIES OF UKRAINE'S ROLE IN SOVIET GAS EXPORTS: THE IMPACT ON VERTICAL AND HORIZONTAL VALUE CHAINS

This section analyzes how the legacies of Ukraine's key role in the building of the USSR's natural gas export system would continue to have an impact on the situation decades later. These legacies would also shape our molecule's journey through Ukraine.

Infrastructural Legacies Related to Vertical Links in the Value Chain of Russian Natural Gas Exports via Ukraine

Several unique features of Ukraine's gas transportation system—largely inherited from its role in Soviet gas export value chains—shaped the course of our molecule's journey through Ukrainian territory. Key among these was Ukraine's high density of capital-intensive, dedicated gas transit infrastructure: 22,000 kilometers of high-pressure trunk pipelines (including seventy-two compressor stations), part of a 37,000-kilometer network of primary and secondary pipelines and major storage facilities.[83] This infrastructure was key for the technical management of Soviet exports, because it made possible not only the transit of supplies from Siberian fields such a Urengoy but also the management of the risk inherent in highly networked systems by enabling the "diversion of gas flows through other pipelines should an accident or failure occur," as well as bringing into the pipeline supplies from Central Asia when other sources faltered.[84] This thick infrastructure was also key for supplies to Ukrainian users, and it helped consolidate Ukraine's economy as one highly dependent on natural gas.

Gas-metering stations. Ukraine also inherited something that shone through its absence: GMSs to measure incoming flows, located within its territory. Being part of a single Soviet energy and political system (and one with only limited pricing mechanisms) had downplayed the importance of counting and accounting for gas volumes and the need for metering stations within Ukrainian territory. As of 2011, twenty years after Ukraine's independence, all metering stations for gas coming from Russia were located in Russian territory, a legacy of the trust between technical professionals who had been working together for decades, but also a result of the high cost (about $50 million to $76 million per unit) of building GMSs.[85] Lacking these, the Ukrainian side had to rely on information gathered on the Russian side.[86] Such a lack of clarity concerning how much gas had come in, and when, would be crucial not only for Ukraine's transit and supply disputes with Gazprom but also for the distributive impact of such trade—the lack of transparency and accountability raised by this situation made it easier for gas to disappear or be miscounted, affecting the rent-seeking opportunities open to involved players.[87] Moreover, without such GMSs, some policy alternatives, such as the idea of modifying the Western European gas purchase contracts with Gazprom to have a delivery point at the Ukrainian-Russian border and not the conventionally used Ukrainian-EU border—a key goal, because it could help guarantee transit through Ukraine even after the expiration of the current transit contract in 2019—remained merely hypothetical.[88] This also touches upon "obsolescent bargain" discussions of the changing role of infrastructure as a result of political changes: many of (Min) Gazprom's pre-1991 contracts had delivery points in areas that, as a result of the EU's expansion in 2004, became part of the EU, and thus were subject to its regulatory framework.[89]

Pushing the gas through the pipeline: compressor stations and their often-unaccounted-for gas. Natural gas can travel at up to 40 kilometers per hour in some pipelines. But it cannot do this by itself—while natural gas initially emerges from underground reservoirs with significant natural pressure, movement along the pipeline is a different matter. Given the best technology available at the beginning of the twenty-first century, every 200 kilometers or so, it needs the help of compressor stations to move in the pipeline; compressors are almost always powered by gas drawn from the pipelines themselves—in some cases, as much as 10 percent of the total gas transited.[90] Ukraine inherited a mighty system of such expensive compressor stations.[91] The need for compressor stations is part of a broader technical challenge inherent in natural gas transportation and distribution to end consumers: the need for pressure management. So the enterprise—the entire supply chain of transporting, distributing, and bringing natural gas to users—becomes an *enterprise in managing pressure*: from reducing pressure when natural gas comes out of the reservoir so that it can be handled, to significantly increasing pressure to make it possible for gas to move forward in the pipeline, to reducing pressure again as it reaches smaller-diameter city pipelines so that it can be safely distributed. As natural gas reaches power plants and residential end users, pressure needs to be reduced again to progressively lower levels for each of these respective users. This makes compressor stations exemplary of the one of the distinctive challenges found in the natural gas value chain: the high cost of transportation infrastructure. This high cost was also in comparison with oil; though oil pipelines also use pumping stations to help move oil forward, gas compressors are much more expensive and technologically demanding, with links to military technology, such as that used in jet engines.

The compressors' reliance on gas from the pipeline itself often led to confusion as to the ownership of the technical gas used to operate the turbines. This was a key cause of conflict during the January 2009 Ukrainian-Russian crisis, when NAK Naftohaz argued that some of the gas Gazprom considered as stolen was simply technical gas needed for the operation of the pipeline, so part of the dispute was about whether Naftohaz should have provided this technical gas "from its own stocks."[92] Previous to the January 2009 contract, the issue of technical gas had not been dealt with explicitly in Ukrainian-Russian gas contracts. This lack of transparency also made it easier for those wanting to engage in theft and corruption, because, at least through the late 2000s, NAK Naftohaz did not differentiate publicly between technical gas itself (i.e., that used to power compressor stations), leakage, volumes unaccounted for due to metering errors, and gas stolen from the system.[93] With technical gas amounting to about 10 percent of Ukraine's total natural gas consumption, the amounts involved were significant, as were the possibilities for mislabeling theft as another type of loss.[94]

Underground gas storage. Another important legacy of Ukraine's key role in Soviet export value chains was its extensive system of underground gas storage facilities, which was the largest in Europe.[95] These facilities were a legacy not only of Western Ukraine's importance as the last domestic station of the Soviet natural gas exports chain but also of Ukraine's own history as the USSR's main gas producer in the 1950s and 1960s—many of the areas developed as underground gas storage facilities starting in the 1960s used to be major gas fields, but were transformed to serve as storage after their depletion—the very fields from which the first Soviet (future Brotherhood pipeline) exports to Czechoslovakia had started in the 1960s, long before the Urengoy field came online.[96]

The materiality of natural gas makes storage facilities, in combination with the transportation system and access to it, key for exports. Earlier in this chapter, I discussed the need to manage pressure variations associated with deliveries to city systems. In long-distance pipelines such as Brotherhood, such variations in pressure and load, which were related to shifts in seasonal demand, would be much larger—unless properly managed, they could bring the system to a standstill. Careful decisionmaking regarding pressure and supply volumes, though necessary, is not enough to deal with these large fluctuations, making gas storage facilities, as well as the technical equipment needed to maintain needed pressure within the storage facility and to pump natural gas to and from them, crucial for managing peak-use demand ("peak shaving"), for reducing end-user vulnerability, and for optimizing the use of existing pipelines. This is so because it is technically very difficult to reduce or stop production when demand is low; the need for gas storage is especially keen in areas with large seasonal temperature variation, as in the case of continental Europe.[97]

Although the Russian Federation had significant storage capacities elsewhere, none were located adjacent to the Brotherhood pipeline in the Russian Federation. In contrast, six underground gas storage facilities were located relatively adjacent to the pipeline in Western Ukraine in the area between Ivano-Frankovsk and Uzhhorod (see figure 4.2). In other words, in its journey from Urengoy to Germany, our gas molecule only had available gas storage facilities in Ukraine and in the Czech Republic.[98] Their location immediately before entry into the EU market, a distinct market with distinct prices, is hardly surprising, because these facilities were used not only to balance gas flows and maintain adequate working pressure in the pipelines but also to temporarily store natural gas to take advantage of seasonal and weather-related demand and price variations.[99] This balancing functioned as follows: Ukraine's gas transmission system received gas through "many large entry points on the Russian-Ukrainian border, allowing both Russian transit gas and gas shipped for domestic consumption to be dispatched to Ukraine's eastern regions."[100] Gas was then added to the transit pipelines from Ukraine's underground storage facilities (which held both domestically produced gas and gas imported from Russia) to the remaining gas to "make up for the gas taken out for domestic supply." Gas, both

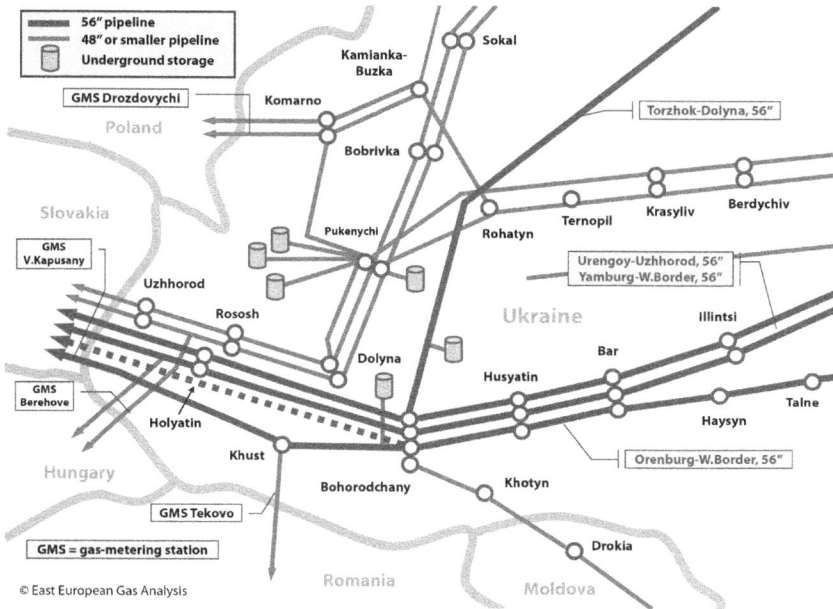

Figure 4.2 Uzhhorod area gas infrastructure map

Source: East European Gas Analysis, http://www.eegas.com/uzhgorod.htm; adapted by Matthias Newman.

Note: The Uzhhorod gas-metering station is not labeled on the map. The map is also not to exact scale; about 1 centimeter = 100 kilometers.

domestic and imported, was injected into Ukraine's storage facilities between about April 15 and October 15 and was withdrawn during the winter. During winter peak times, for example, gas pumped from Ukraine's underground gas storage sites near its Western border could supply "up to 40 percent of daily transit volumes" to EU markets.[101]

In addition to its use in managing networkness and Gazprom's exports to Western Europe, underground storage could also be used in more domestically related ways. Ukraine reportedly used supplies from storage—but shipped in reverse of the usual route—to supply its own population during the January 2009 gas cutoff.[102] Their technical characteristics also made stored volumes hard to secure and account for, facilitating their misappropriation and helping create distinct distributive openings. Thus, in the pre-2011 period there were several instances of NAK Naftohaz gas "disappearing" from underground storage areas, involving sector players such as Dmytro Firtash and his company RosUkrEnergo.[103]

The larger point to be made about this inherited, natural-gas-specific infrastructure in Ukraine is that, on one hand, it created the necessary conditions for large-scale supplies, though on the other hand it also facilitated rent-seeking. At the same time, the case of Ukraine brings to the fore the question of how the same infrastructure, in different political/governance situations, may play very different roles. Indeed, bargains and agreements set around concrete infrastructures may obsolesce once political realities change as a result of developments such as states gaining independence.[104] The most obvious example comes from the changed role of natural gas transit infrastructure before and after 1991—upon achieving independence, countries such as Ukraine "changed, virtually overnight, from constituents of a single energy-rich state" to being separate, energy-poor entities that were heavily dependent on Russian energy, and to also being politically independent transit states.[105] But a look at the governance of the natural gas sector during our focus period 2011–14 (which can be seen as representative of the postindependence period as a whole) also shows how infrastructure that could in theory bring both income and some counterpower vis-à-vis suppliers may see this possible role squandered if misused for other purposes. I am referring to Ukraine's declining role in natural gas transit, which was the result not only of external decisions by Gazprom but also of domestic Ukrainian dynamics that affected the use of the infrastructure as well as Ukraine's reputational capital as a transit state (which is discussed later in the chapter).

At the same time, Ukraine's high density of natural-gas-related infrastructure also meant that if the country would be left out of the transit value chain, it would not be able to use this infrastructure—going well beyond pipelines—and would lose not only jobs but also the sunk costs of the investments made in its modernization since the 2000s.

Infrastructural Legacies Related to Horizontal Links in the Value Chain of Russian Natural Gas Exports via Ukraine

The legacies of Ukraine's role in Soviet gas export value chains were felt not only in transportation infrastructure but also in "softer" structures—the energy-intensive economic system developed during the Soviet period of low-cost energy supplies and its horizontal impact on various domestic industries. On its way from the Sudzha Gas Measuring Station just east of the Ukrainian border to Uzhhorod on its western border, natural gas had many opportunities to get involved in a variety of other, horizontally linked industries, and in the rent-seeking of those who controlled them. This was also facilitated by the structure of the inherited pipeline system, where some enterprises had direct intake access to the trunk (export) pipeline.[106] One of the horizontally linked sectors was metallurgy, which I discuss in chapter 6. Another was the production of nitrogen fertilizers, which uses natural gas as its key feedstock; this industrial sector became a central part of not only the Ukrainian but also the Belarusian and Lithuanian economies—and a power basis for some of their most important oligarchs.[107] Through these horizontal links, Russian gas had many opportunities to become part of what at first glance may appear as purely domestic Ukrainian rent-seeking situations but were certainly not.[108]

Thus, a small excursus is warranted for the case of Ostchem Holding, a conglomerate of chemical industry and fertilizer companies, as an example of horizontal value chains related to natural gas. By March 2011, Dmytro Firtash—already known as the central player in RosUkrenergo-related corrupt deals in the 2000s as a result of which Ukraine lost hundreds of millions of dollars to intermediary companies—had acquired control of Ukraine's major chemical plants, thus controlling 76 percent of Ukraine's (and 2.28 percent of global production) of nitrogen fertilizers. In 2011, at the beginning of the focus period, Ukraine's chemical industry, which was largely controlled by Firtash, was responsible for about 10 percent of Ukraine's total natural gas consumption. This was an industry whose very existence had been made possible by low natural gas prices—nitrogen fertilizers are a type of chemical fertilizer whose production not only depends heavily on gas as a source of energy but also as a raw material through its use of gas-intensive ammonia; natural gas constitutes about 80 percent of nitrogen fertilizers' production costs. During most of the post-1991 period, the sector had been able to make significant profits from the difference between low feedstock prices (natural gas) and much higher world prices for ammonia and fertilizers. With 80 percent of production being exported, large profits were possible, but the competitiveness of these exports was predicated on Firtash's factories having access to low-cost natural gas supplies.[109] The sharp gas price increases starting in 2009 threatened these profits, especially as world prices for ammonia and fertilizer started to go down. Thus, it is not surprising that sector actors such as Firtash would seek to find new ways to maintain their advantages—such as through direct purchases from Gazprom.[110] They are relevant for our larger story because by engaging in these direct purchases, Ostchem deprived the national gas company, NAK Naftohaz, of a significant portion of its sales to industrial users, one of its few sources of profit and key to balancing its chronically loss-making (but mandated by law) supplies to residential consumers, further weakening the company, and making it harder to invest in transit infrastructure.

Such an arrangement would not have been possible without Yanukovich's direct support through the March 2011 abolition of NAK Naftohaz's monopoly on gas imports. This was happening at the same time as Yanukovich's increased centralization of rent-seeking opportunities in his own "family" under coordination by his son Oleksandr.[111] Rather than seeking a confrontation over this new actor seeking a piece of the rents, Firtash found a way of synergizing with this increased centralization: by sharing some of the profits of his Gazprom arrangement with Yanukovich associates. This was done by reselling, at a discounted price, some of this gas to a key Yanukovich associate (Serhii Kurchenko), who in turn sold it (at much higher prices) to other users, reportedly including a subsidiary of NAK Naftohaz itself.[112] All in all, Ostchem is reported to have imported about 20 billion cubic meters of gas at below-market prices, at a profit of over $3 billion, some of which was "recycled" to Yanukovich through Kurchenko as well as through contributions to the Party of Regions.[113] This also opened the door to a specific type of Russian influence: weakening the political system through corruption.

At the same time, and despite the general perception of Yanukovich as pro-Kremlin (in hindsight, this is strengthened by his escape to Russia in February 2014), relations with Russia were far from cloudless during his presidency. This was first and foremost related to Gazprom's (and the Russian leadership's) unwillingness to revisit the 2009 gas contracts and fast-moving plans to move gas transit away from Ukraine, but also to broader trends, such as the declining importance of Ukraine and Russia as markets for each other's exports (including Ukraine as a consumer of Russian oil and gas).[114] Thus, either by design (most likely) or as a result of other factors, Ukraine was becoming less important for Russian natural gas value chains. Looking specifically

TABLE 4.1

Gas Transit Through the Ukrainian Segment of the Brotherhood Pipeline in the Direction of the Slovak Republic in the Context of Ukraine's Total Gas Transit, 2011–14 (in Billion Cubic Meters)

Transit Flow	Project Capacity	2011	2012	2013	2014	2014 as Percentage of 2011
Brotherhood pipeline (gas out at GMS Uzhhorod)	92.6	70.6	51.8	53.5	31.4	44.47
Total transit	146	104.2	84.3	86.1	62.2	59.69

Source: Calculated by the author on the basis of data from the Office of the Prime Minister of Ukraine, "Report for 2015 Following the Results of Monitoring the Security of Natural Gas Supplies," September 2015, submitted to the Secretariat of the Energy Community, 12, https://www.energy-community.org/portal/page/portal/ENC_HOME/DOCS/3842350/2198FDD2CC031492E053C92FA8C0BE17.PDF.

at the amount of gas transited through Ukraine via the Brotherhood pipeline, the decline was significant: from 70.6 billion cubic meters in 2011, to 53.5 in 2013, to 31.4 in 2014 (see table 4.1). Overall gas transit through Ukraine also experienced a decline, although not as strong.[115] If in its heyday, transit via Ukraine accounted for about 80 percent of Germany's gas imports from Russia and about 20 percent of its gas total imports, by 2014 this amount had been drastically reduced, to less than 10 percent of the total.[116] As is discussed in more detail in chapters 7 and 8, this trend represents nothing less than a cataclysmic event for Ukraine, and not only because of the loss of revenue.

During the reference period, Ukraine was also becoming less important to Gazprom as a market.[117] Ukraine's gas imports already started to decline significantly in 2009, largely as a result of the higher prices resulting from the new contract, and declined even more rapidly from 2011 (44.8 billion cubic meters) to 2014 (19.6 billion cubic meters).[118] This reduction, however, was not mainly due to a more efficient use of available resources but to other factors, such as the fall in industrial activity and not including the statistics for territories temporarily occupied by Russia (Crimea and the so-called Luhansk and Donetsk People's Republics).[119] Nevertheless, it is important to understand that the reduction of imports from Russia (along with reverse supplies from EU states, discussed below) started already in the Yanukovich period—small-scale (0.06 billion cubic meter) imports from the German company RWE, via reverse flows through Poland and at a lower price than gas imported from Gazprom, which started in November 2012.[120]

After passing through Ukraine's complex domestic landscape, that part of Urengoy gas destined for further transit got ready to leave Ukraine at Uzhhorod, through the 25-kilometer pipeline segment connecting it with Velké Kapušany in the Slovak Republic.

What would happen in this 25-kilometer segment was representative of much broader challenges: starting in 2011, Ukraine had sought to organize "reverse" gas supplies (i.e., the possibility of importing gas, which, even if physically coming from Gazprom fields in Russia, would not be Gazprom's in a contractual sense), as a way to diversify given increased prices and (starting in February 2014) open Russian aggression. If the possible use of reverse flows to reduce Ukraine's contractual dependency on Gazprom had been discussed since 2011, the events of 2014 brought new urgency to the issue. In April—that is, immediately after the Russian military takeover of Crimea—Gazprom announced an 81 percent increase in gas prices to Ukraine; after a dispute over payments, it ceased supplies for six months that year.[121] This provided a significant impetus for pushing for large-scale reverse supplies from Ukraine's neighbors, especially the Slovak Republic.[122]

THE SLOVAK REPUBLIC: ENTERING THE EU'S PHYSICAL AND REGULATORY SPACE

Upon crossing the Ukrainian-Slovak border, Brotherhood gas entered a new contractual, governance, and regulatory space. This is meant in two ways: first, long-term contracts between Western European importers and Gazprom were traditionally specified for delivery to the Ukrainian-EU border (i.e., Velké Kapušany). After delivery, the molecule ceased being under Gazprom ownership.[123] With the 2004 expansion of the EU, delivery points that were previously outside the EU (e.g., Velké Kapušany) suddenly came to be located inside the EU, with the implication that "Gazprom found itself in a situation in which its gas was now flowing in EU pipelines which were now subject to EU regulation," which complicated issues related to Gazprom's long-term contracts.[124]

Second, and most important, upon crossing into the Slovak Republic and, thus the European Union, Brotherhood gas entered fully into the EU regulatory space (with Brussels as regulatory node)—a regulatory space where energy liberalization measures were, exactly at this moment, challenging the basic tenets of the Gazprom business model based on long-term contracts and fixed delivery points. Rather, it entered a regulatory space where gas trade spaces were also gradually being reconceptualized in spatial terms: from points of delivery to hubs understood as large spaces, within which distance would be contractually inconsequential and within which a gas/methane molecule would be freely replaceable by another. Although the goal was to create a unified EU market with interconnected, entry/exit zones spanning the borders of several states, the space in question was not yet that of the EU as a whole but somewhat smaller spaces, each defined by and constrained within the framework of an entry/exit system.[125] As of 2014, most of the Central European countries' gas markets were organized as single "entry/exit zones."[126]

This regulatory system concerned first and foremost long-standing EU competition and single market policies, which gradually came to affect the energy field as well.[127] Additional energy security regulations, especially those concerning natural gas, had been implemented as responses to the January 2009 crisis and the related interruption of gas supplies through Ukraine, which, having seriously affected supplies to several EU states, had woken up the EU as to the consequences of Gazprom's market power given some EU states' lack of alternative connections and need for coordinated response to energy challenges.[128]

Natural Gas as "Networked Energy" and Its Meaning for EU Governance

When Brotherhood gas crossed into EU territory at Velké Kapušany, it was entering into a natural gas trade space that the EU was increasingly conceptualizing as a networked space, and into a regulatory environment and infrastructure development program that paid special attention to energy networkness and networked energy. EU energy initiatives during this period prioritized networked types of energy as a focus of priority investment to connect markets and break the infrastructural dependency of some EU states on a single supplier. Specifically, natural gas (together with electricity) was seen by the EU as "networked energy" par excellence and as the most networked of all primary energy sources, ahead of oil and coal.[129]

Materiality considerations were key here: networked energy has to do with things such as the degree to which users depend on a network as opposed to autonomous supplies (e.g., from nonnetworked residential solar panels). But much more crucially, it relates to the degree to which the overall functioning of the system may be dependent on the network working properly *as a network*. Although all energy types work in one way or another as part of a network, in the case of natural gas as well as closely related electricity, this networkness has to do with the system being physically balanced as a system, an especially important consideration in synchronous systems where, due to difficulties or the cost of storage, the energy source needs to be produced and used in close synchrony.[130] And though it took as much as two weeks for Urengoy gas to reach end consumers in Germany, the chain can be considered synchronous due to the cost and limited availability of storage.

For natural gas and electricity, such network balancing is also crucial in a very basic, physical way: if the wattage load to the electricity grid, or the load and pressure in the system of natural gas pipelines, are not right, the entire system may not work properly, possibly leading to collapse (blackouts), a standstill (gas not moving, due to insufficient pressure in the pipeline), or other accidents, especially in the case of natural gas, where pipeline connections go all the way to individual residential consumers (i.e., the "burner tip"). The networkness element of EU thinking, together with natural gas's limited ability to be transported efficiently overland by means other than pipelines, gave natural gas a special role in EU policy; Ukraine appealed to the concept to make the case for EU support for reverse supplies and against Gazprom-Slovak contracts it saw as in violation of EU regulations (see below).

We return to this issue below, but here it is important to note that the regulatory aspects of energy (and, in this case, natural gas) networkness found themselves in an interesting interplay with its material aspects. As this networkness became increasingly dense with new connections and supplies, EU officials in charge of energy issues, influenced by transatlantic intellectual trends about the desirability of unbundling other network-related industries such as telecommunications,[131] started to use this very density as a justification to change the regulatory system in a way further emphasizing networkness and the policy choices they saw as emanating from it (i.e., the need for a special status and policies related to networked types of energy), providing an example of how the materiality characteristics of a good or system may be discursively recruited to support policies that reinforce this very characteristic.[132]

REVERSAL: WHO WOULD CONTROL
UZHHOROD–VELKÉ KAPUŠANY?

At Velké Kapušany, however, Brotherhood gas was entering not simply the EU but also the Slovak Republic. This is significant because, as many EU-wide energy regulations were gaining ground, state-level legal prerogatives—as well as the role of local-level actors—continued to be important. Like Ukraine, the Slovak Republic was both an important transit state for Gazprom and highly dependent on its natural gas supplies; in 2012, it imported 97.9 percent of its gas needs (5.5 billion cubic meters) from Gazprom, one of the highest levels in the EU and comparable with FSU states such as Lithuania and Moldova.[133] The Slovak Republic's long-term contract with Gazprom (signed in 2008, and in effect through 2028), despite lower prices negotiated in 2012, included a reexport ban provision, and the Slovak leadership was uneasy about risking problems with its near-monopoly supplier Gazprom.[134] Thus, in responding to Ukraine's request, key Slovak actors (e.g., the country's transit system operator [TSO], Eustream) had to weight their own balance between threat and temptation, risk, and profits.

If in the case of oil (see chapter 5), the Slovak Republic's role in the transit of Russian energy was mainly straightforward, in the case of natural gas during the focus period, the Slovak Republic's TSO Eustream was faced with the opportunity and the challenge of responding to Ukraine's request for reverse supplies while balancing this with its role as participant in Gazprom value chains. In this case, we also saw a situation where the commercial and regulatory nodes are not coterminous with the physical ones, and where there may also be an overlap, with Bratislava and Brussels as the regulatory nodes, and Gazprom's headquarters as the commercial node, simultaneously exerting influence on Velké Kapušany and its operator Eurostream. Subject to the impact of the regulatory nodes, the threat of sole dependency on Gazprom supplies, and the temptation of transit payments, Eustream sought to balance these. This was the context within which discussions about possible reverse supplies to Ukraine in 2011–14 took place. On April 28, 2014, Ukraine and the Slovak Republic (represented by the gas transit TSOs Eustream and Ukrtransgaz) signed a memorandum on the introduction of reverse gas flows; the reverse flow was officially launched in September 2014. Yet the way there was anything but easy.

Infrastructure, Reversal, and the Gas Molecule: Technical and Contractual Issues

The issue of reverse flows brought up the larger question of hubs—in the sense of a space where gas volumes coming from different sources and going in different directions meet—and, in particular, of whether Velké Kapušany and Uzhhorod would work together as a hub, or simply as a one-way door or even chokepoint. As in the case of networkness discussed above, "hubness" depended on both technical and contractual/regulatory issues, yet the latter could not trump the former.

At first glance, Uzhhorod, in connection with Velké Kapušany, seemed predetermined to be a hub. If Ukraine was thickly populated by gas infrastructure, this was even more the case for its western border region. Three major trunk pipelines met in Uzhhorod: the TransBalkan pipeline toward Hungary and Romania, the Soyuz pipeline bringing gas from the Orenburg field in the Volga-Urals region, and the Brotherhood pipeline. A glimpse at a detailed map of gas transit-related objects in this border area reveals a thick and complex infrastructure, including extra-wide-diameter (1,420 millimeters / 56 inches) trunk and transit pipelines; smaller-diameter pipelines moving gas from and to urban centers and industries; large-volume underground gas storage facilities, some of them directly adjacent to the trunk pipelines; and four exit gas measuring stations near entry points to Poland, Hungary, and Romania (see figure 4.2).[135] Although some Brotherhood gas went to Hungary and Romania, the five main large-diameter lines crossed into the Slovak Republic through the 25-kilometer journey from the Uzhhorod GMS to Velké Kapušany, the largest gas interconnector point in Europe, through which about 37 percent of all Russian gas exports entered the EU.[136]

Yet, despite this thick infrastructure, Uzhhorod–Velké Kapušany's technical design was not fully that of a hub but rather that of a key export gateway for Soviet exports to Central and Western European markets (see figure 4.2).[137] Moreover, as important as technical solutions may have been, technical changes in and of themselves do not create a hub. Rather, a hub requires a number of contractual, regulatory, and technical steps, such as the existence of fully liberalized industrial, commercial, and residential gas markets, third-party access to infrastructure, and transparency of information on volumes and prices.[138] Whether Uzhhorod–Velké Kapušany could function as a hub for the purposes of reverse supplies to Ukraine would depend not only on the technical constraints embedded in the existing infrastructure but also on Eustream as a decisionmaking node, and on Gazprom's ability to make Eustream comply with legacy contractual arrangements barring reexports.

How could the different parts of this thick infrastructure be connected so as to allow reverse supplies to Ukraine? Three options eventually emerged. A first solution would not have required a physical reversal: rather, a virtual reverse flow whereupon the physical gas from Russia would not go all the way to Germany, but the last compression station in Ukraine would receive a message ("network code") confirming that a certain amount of gas had changed ownership, and that it should be redirected for Ukrainian use—officially making this German gas sold to Ukraine, although technically this gas would never get to Germany.[139] However, because the Russian side refused to provide the network codes necessary for this virtual operation to happen, the reverse flow had to take place physically.[140] The second most obvious solution would then come into play: reversing the flow through one or more of the five parallel trunk lines connecting Velké Kapušany and Uzhhorod, a solution that was technically possible, considering there was sufficient unused capacity in the pipeline, and also a solution that the European Commission sought to mediate between Eustream and Ukrtranshaz.[141] This ingenious possibility was made possible by the constraints of natural pipeline transportation itself: due to the need to keep a certain pressure in the pipe, and the strain this pressure puts on the pipe, it is technically very difficult to ship very large volumes of gas through a single, very large-diameter pipe; major pipelines need to have several lines.[142] This technical requirement related to natural gas's materiality, in turn, meant it would have been possible for one line of the pipeline to be reversed without affecting the bulk of the transit, helping to shape the political question as well—as the technopolitics tradition would remind us.

After the EU supported this second option in 2013 with the argument that the Uzhhorod–Velké Kapušany trunk pipeline was able to operate bidirectionally because there was sufficient capacity in the main pipeline to use one of its lines in reverse mode, Gazpromeksport (together with Russian authorities) claimed this would constitute a breach of existing contract provisions with Eustream banning reexports.[143] Such contractual provisions had developed historically together with long-term gas contracts as a means to deal with challenges specific to typical natural gas value chains—at least as they existed up to 2011—such as sunk costs and the need for large, long-term investments in expensive dedicated infrastructure, all related to natural gas's materiality characteristics (see chapter 3).

Gazpromeksport's contractual provisions, however, were not in line with the networkness perspective promoted by the EU; when the Slovak Republic's TSO Eustream made reference to its contract with Gazpromeksport to refuse to use one of the five lines of the main pipeline from Velké Kapušany to Uzhhorod for reverse gas supplies, Ukrainian prime minister Arseniy Yatseniuk appealed to the EU, arguing that contract violated EU law.[144] This took place in the context of a then-ongoing EU investigation, on whether Gazprom had abused its dominant position in Central and Eastern Europe by building artificial barriers to free gas flows.[145] The Ukrainian government also denounced the contract as giving Gazprom control over the Uzhhorod–Velké Kapušany segment, which, according to EU regulations, should be controlled by the TSOs of the two countries involved—that is, Ukrtranshaz and Eustream.[146] The Ukrainian government also accused Gazprom of hindering Ukrtransgaz's function as a TSO by refusing to provide it with the network codes necessary to operate transit on the segment.[147]

"Big reverse" versus "small reverse." In the final analysis, decisions needed to be made by Eustream, which, as the Slovak TSO, was the key governance and technical player on the issue.[148] Two other key actors involved in the process were the Slovak government and the Economics Ministry, the owner of Eustream but with no formal managerial control over it. The Slovak government was generally wary of a reversal, "fearing it would provoke its own dispute with Gazprom."[149] Thus, its position concerning a "big reverse" versus a "small reverse."

As discussed above, the original idea was to facilitate the reverse by reversing one of the five lines going from Uzhhorod to Velké Kapušany ("big reverse"). Yet this solution could not be implemented, because Gazprom considered it a breach of contract; Slovak prime minister

Robert Fico also supported this position.[150] Fico, who had a solid pro-Russian reputation,[151] was uneasy about the reverse flows, and insisted that the EU Commission's explicit support would be necessary for the reverse to happen.[152] Thus his many comments on the issue, such as that the Slovak Republic was being pressed by "two huge boulders from right and left" (i.e., Ukraine and the EU),[153] and criticizing Ukraine for alleged nonpayment of delivered gas.[154]

So a third option came into play: reverse supplies would take place, but indirectly, through a bypass solution—a smaller (700 millimeters in diameter, as compared with 1,420 millimeters for the trunk line) and at the time inactive pipeline from the Vojany coal and gas power plant (a coal-/gas-fired power plant located a few kilometers away from Velké Kapušany) to Uzhhorod ("small reverse").[155] After the pipeline was upgraded to increase its volume and use a compressor station, by 2014 Ukraine was already able to import about 18 percent of its total gas imports from the Slovak Republic.[156] Although Ukraine had freed itself from "Gazprom-contracted gas," it did not necessarily free itself from Gazprom gas in a physical sense, because the provenance of the molecule physically or virtually being supplied to Ukraine through reverse agreements could not be determined (but was most likely Russian, as no other gas reached the Velké Kapušany hub). Yet the point is that this gas was *contractually* not Russian, which made an important difference in price and supply conditions.[157]

After this convoluted journey of uncertainty between Velké Kapušany, Vojany, and Uzhhorod—all within the first kilometers after entering the Slovak Republic—Brotherhood's gas journey toward the Czech Republic would be much calmer from that point on, with only one interruption: about 30 kilometers from the border, a branch pipeline would take some of the Brotherhood gas across the border with Austria, to be traded at the Central European Gas Hub at Baumgarten, the key natural gas trading hub in Central Europe, where physical supplies from Norway and Russia's Brotherhood met, and to which a bidirectional connection had been built in 2013.[158] After this branching, Brotherhood gas saw no more interruptions before crossing into Czech territory at the Lanžhot Border Transfer Station.

Our molecule went through the Czech Republic without many issues, but, in contrast to the situation in the Slovak Republic, it started to face significant competition in the Czech market. Since 2011, the Czech Republic had been receiving natural gas from several pipeline systems: German pipelines entering the country at Hora Svaté Kateriny (bringing gas from Norway); Nord Stream Russian gas supplies via the OPAL pipeline entering the country at Brandov; and Brotherhood Russian supplies through Ukraine and the Slovak Republic, entering the country at Lanžhot. Yet though physical access to gas supplies promised geographical diversification, this did not happen in the short term; during our focus period, 2011 to 2014, between 97 and 100 percent of the Czech Republic's gas imports were sourced from Russia.[159]

About 40 kilometers into Czech territory, near Malešovice, the pipeline divided, with a somewhat smaller pipeline veering northwest in the direction of Olbernhau and Germany's OPAL system. The main trunk pipeline, carrying 75 percent of the gas volume, would continue to Waidhaus in Germany. It is through this pipeline that our molecule's journey continues.

DOWNSTREAM GERMANY

This section describes the last stage of our molecule's journey. In this stage, it crosses into Germany, a country in the midst of deeply rethinking its energy system.

Entering Waidhaus—a Russian-German Tradition

In entering Germany at Waidhaus, Bavaria, Brotherhood gas was not only entering a traditions-rich set of infrastructures and relationships dating back to the very start of Soviet gas exports to Germany but also the complex reorganization of domestic gas supplies in Germany as a result of EU and national-level regulatory changes as well as the increased use of renewables.

First, let us look at the tradition. In 2010, before the opening of the Nord Stream pipeline, Germany imported 35 billion cubic meters of gas from Gazprom, of which the largest share transited through Ukraine and entered through Waidhaus.[160] At Waidhaus, Brotherhood gas entered into an infrastructure that, although in German territory, had developed as part and parcel of the great Soviet push for gas exports in the 1970s, co-built by Soviet and Western "system builders."[161] In 1970, Germany had become the second Western European state to sign a contract to import natural gas from the USSR (the so-called gas-for-pipes agreement, as part of Chancellor Willi Brandt's Ostpolitik[162]), and, since then, an impressive infrastructure had been built for this purpose. The infrastructure involved concerned not only that used to transit gas from Western Siberia to Germany, but, within the heart of Europe itself, the MEGAL pipeline, to further transport that gas from Waidhaus to Southern Germany and France. In the 1970s, these contracts and jointly built and financed infrastructure had also helped consolidate a situational coalition and cartel division of the market between Ruhrgas and Gaz de France, its partner in building MEGAL; at the time the pipeline was built, both companies agreed not to sell gas transported over this pipeline in each other's home markets.[163] This infrastructure had also established Ruhrgas as Mingazprom's main partner, and the Ruhrgas/MEGAL network as the backbone of German gas supply for more than three decades.

At the same time, though the Ruhrgas-(Min)Gazprom's Long-Term contracts had set the standard, by the 1990s they had also turned into a limitation. This was so because setting deliveries to—but no further than—the West German border blocked Gazprom's ability to benefit from the added profit of downstream supplies to end consumers. It sought to override this hurdle through proposing to its long-standing partner Ruhrgas the establishment of a joint venture—JV—to market Soviet gas in the domestic German market. After Ruhrgas refused, it turned to a BASF subsidiary, Wintershall, which accepted the offer but could not gain access to existing pipelines; subsequently, in the early 1990s, the JV set out to build its own infrastructure, including three pipelines and an underground gas storage facility. Despite Gazprom's attempts to capture the added value of downstream sales in Western European states, the JV with Wintershall remained an exception rather than the rule.[164]

Through that jointly built infrastructure, Soviet natural gas and its materiality characteristics, in particular its high caloric value, had set new standards for natural gas used in Germany and Europe as a whole (H-gas, which nevertheless coexisted with local and Dutch L-gas).[165] It also set the standards for what would become typical gas contracts between Western European importers and the Soviet Union for over three decades, such as their typical duration (twenty to thirty years), oil price indexation, and typical take-or-pay commitments for 75 to 85 percent of the nominal quantities.[166] Thus, in this sense, decisions made at the commercial node of Gazprom's headquarters in Moscow had an impact going well beyond the Soviet—and later, Russian—border.

However, by 2011, this tradition found itself under great stress. Nearly forty years after Soviet gas first arrived at Waidhaus, supplies continued, but the system they had helped create had fallen apart. Two key aspects of this were what some have called "the destruction of the midstream," and the crisis of large gas-fired power plants. As it transited through the MEGAL pipeline and waited to be converted into electricity at the Franken I power plant near Nürnberg, our gas molecule experienced and was affected by these processes.

The "Destruction of the Midstream"

The term "destruction of the midstream" is often used in the sense of "destruction" of the role of "old incumbent" gas transportation and trading companies such as Ruhrgas (as well as, later, E.ON, Verbundnetz Gas, Wingas, RWE, and Gasunie), which had played key roles related to Soviet and then Russian gas in Europe since the 1970s. In that system, which had largely come into existence as a by-product of the setting up of large-scale imports of Soviet natural gas in the mid-1970s, these companies, through a demarcation agreements system, acted as regional monopolists, buying gas from Gazprom via long-term contracts, receiving it at the border, and selling it to regional and local distributors within specifically demarcated areas.[167] With direct contacts with the largest foreign suppliers but not end consumers, these companies can be seen as "midstream utilities."[168]

This dismantling process was facilitated by factors coming from the top, from the side, and from below.[169] From the top, EU regulations (emanating from Brussels, in its role as a regulatory node) called for liberalization (and demonopolization) of national energy markets from the early 2000s and reached a key threshold with the Third Internal Energy Market Package in 2009. These laws reduced the privileged role of key midstream players such as Ruhrgas. Rather than facing a single voice on gas matters, Gazprom now had as interlocutor a multitude of smaller actors in a highly fragmented system. Moreover, with many former midstream utilities now taken over by electricity companies, the German gas industry came to be managed "through the lens of electricity industry interests."[170] As the contractual system started to change in the direction of increased spot- and hub-based gas trading, companies such as Ruhrgas came under pressure and, still subject to the provisions of long-term contracts signed years ago, could not react with the same flexibility as smaller companies buying gas in the spot market could.[171] Moreover, once more gas started to be spot-traded, the role of wholesalers and intermediaries started to become obsolete. This increased market flexibility, and the increasing price convergence between different markets also helped disrupt a business model that was to a certain extent based on price differentials and the arbitrage between them to assure returns on investments in a situation of sunk costs as a key challenge in the natural gas value chain. From the side, the process was aided by the various battles for corporate takeover between the embattled companies, in which, for example, Ruhrgas was taken over by E.ON.

Finally, from below, the process was also aided by the "renewables revolution" (see below), which was related to growing law-mandated support for renewables-generated electricity, as well as by local governments reclaiming more power vis-à-vis the former large utilities through, for example, the acquisition of their power plants by local *Stadtwerke* (municipal utilities) and the attempt to make local electricity supplies increasingly independent from traditional suppliers.

In addition to these pressures, by late 2011 large-scale gas supplies to Central and Western Europe through Ukraine—the physical stream from which the incumbent companies derived their volumes and profits—were facing a new challenge: Nord Stream gas. This also affected Brotherhood supplies to the Czech Republic and other points south through the issue of the OPAL pipeline, which was commissioned in 2011 to bring Nord Stream gas from its Lubmin terminal to Hora Svaté Kateřiny at the northern part of the Czech-German border and (together with the connecting Gazelle pipeline, commissioned in early 2013) also to Waidhaus at the southern part of the Czech-German border—both points where Brotherhood gas was coming into Germany. This also affected future supplies of Ukraine-transited Brotherhood gas to the Czech Republic, as it made it possible for the Czech Republic to receive Russian gas via Nord Stream and Germany rather than via Ukraine.[172] During the focus period, up to 2014, due to EU regulations (i.e., the Third Internal Energy Market Package of 2009) requiring third-party access and prohibiting energy suppliers from simultaneously owning the distribution network, Gazprom was allowed to use only half of OPAL's capacity.[173]

Although, at the time of writing in 2020, it was not clear how much natural gas Gazprom would ultimately be allowed to transit via OPAL, the wide support OPAL and Nord Stream found in German and other Western European gas companies as well as governments speaks of the continued weight of the profit motive for how European actors with influence in Brussels—such as Gazprom's partners in the Nord Stream project Wintershall and Ruhrgas (Germany), Gasunie (Netherlands), and GDF Suez (France)—would react to offers to participate in Gazprom's export value chains, as defined and redefined by the company.[174] And though Nord Stream has been characterized as a political project making little economic sense as compared with the existing route through Ukraine, it is important to distinguish between Russia and its Western European project partners: regardless of the projects' lack of economic sense, Gazprom has gone out of the way—especially concerning Nord Stream II—to offer these companies low-risk profit conditions.

The Crisis of Gas-Fired Power Plants: Waiting for a Cold, Cloudy, and Windless Day at Franken I

After traveling 124 kilometers east from Waidhaus, our gas molecule arrived at the Franken I power plant in the Gebersdorf area of Nürnberg, Bavaria, which was owned by E.ON, one of the "big four" utilities (together with RWE, EnBW, and Vattenfall Europe) that still controlled a significant part of German power plants in 2011. Although originally built in 1913, Franken I had been refurbished in 1973 and 1976, exactly as Soviet gas was arriving in the region. In addition to electricity, it also produced district heating (*Fernwärme*) for Nürnberg.[175]

Given the fact that in 2011 about 28.5 percent of natural gas used in Germany was gas transited through Ukraine, and that 13.9 percent of electricity was generated by gas, we can calculate that about 4 percent of electricity in Germany at this point was generated from Ukraine-transited natural gas.[176] In addition to being used for thermal (electricity and heat) generation, a significant part (39 percent) of natural gas in Germany was used by industry, in particular by the chemical and petrochemical sector, with about 10 percent of total use.[177]

Seen from the perspective of the *Stadtwerke*, however, the situation looked quite different. By October 2011, Franken I was seldom being used—only as a reserve power generator at times of peak electricity demand and when wind-powered turbines and photovoltaic installations could not deliver enough electricity due to cloudy and windless conditions.[178] The reason behind this was the relatively high price of natural gas and oil as feedstock for power generation, as well as measures in support of renewables. As the shale gas and fracking revolution swamped U.S. markets with natural gas and its price went down, much of the coal pushed out of the U.S. market by natural gas supplies was exported to Europe, where—in an example of the still overwhelmingly regional nature of gas markets—gas prices were significantly higher and U.S. coal found significant demand. As this inexpensive coal became available, and in the absence of meaningful CO_2 prices forcing coal-based generating companies to think twice about their high emissions, coal power plants experienced a renaissance from about 2011 to 2014.[179]

But it was not only American coal that was pushing Western Siberian gas out of Nürnberg. Since the entrance into force of a number of laws guaranteeing a minimum price for renewables-generated electricity, gas-fired power plants in particular had been under stress.[180] The trend was strengthened as the partial closure of nuclear power plants in the wake of the March 2011 Fukushima accident created a gap in production; these closings also affected gas-fired electricity production, because some of the key players in gas-fired electricity generation (e.g., Franken I's owner E.ON) also had significant nuclear power plant assets, and the need to close these early seriously affected their bottom line.[181] In this sense, Franken I's situation was similar to that being experienced at this time by dozens of gas-fired power plants across Germany. These plants were being used only sporadically, but this significant infrastructure needed to be kept up, manned, and at the ready. Thus, gas-fired power plants were becoming a liability for their owners, the "big four"—E.ON, RWE, EnBW, and Vattenfall.

This was also the case for Franken I. In May 2012, E.ON announced it would close several power plants in Southern Germany over the next two years, including Franken I. However, making reference to the "system relevance" (i.e., networkness importance) of such power plants even if they were not used constantly, the German Federal Network Agency (Bundesnetzagentur) in charge of regulating electricity, gas, telecommunications, postal, and railways networks denied the request.[182] The argument for this denial went back to the concept of networkness—and thus to the logic of maintaining the working capacity of gas-fired power plants for backup use at times when renewables-generated electricity would not be available.[183] With generation from networked windparks and solar collectors heavily dependent on the weather, natural gas at Franken I was kept waiting for a cold, cloudy, and windless day for a chance to shine through.

Meanwhile, how did this affect the power relationships between the various actors involved? The taking over of important positions in gas and electricity supply by municipal utilities (*Stadtwerke*) as opposed to the legacy incumbents (e.g., E.ON and Ruhrgas) had local but also international implications. If, at the local level, this represented an increase in local power, at the international level the growing imbalance between increasingly fragmented German gas/electricity players and an increasingly centralized and powerful Gazprom created a worrisome asymmetry.

CONCLUSION: MATERIALITY, ACTORS' CHOICES, AND THE NATURAL GAS VALUE CHAIN

What were the key characteristics of the natural gas chain extending from Urengoy to Nürnberg analyzed in this chapter? One important characteristic was that key value-adding activities took place at the spatial start (Novo-Urengoy) and end of the chain (generation into electricity in Nürnberg) rather than in the spatial middle sector of the chain. This does not mean, however, that there was no value or price added along the chain as natural gas moved from the lower-price Russian market to higher-priced Western European ones—without transit services, Urengoy gas could never be monetized as services to end users. Rather, natural gas's key physical characteristic, its gaseous state, made necessary capital-intensive infrastructure, which affected relations with actors at various spatial locations throughout the midstream and downstream portions of the chain. The size of the investments needed heightened the question of sunk costs and fostered specific contractual clauses. The specific need to place complex and expensive infrastructure such as underground storage facilities just before entrance into a new market meant specific areas such as Western Ukraine, in a twist to the "obsolescent bargain" argument, inherited key infrastructure, making it—now as an independent state—a key player in the producers' export value chain. This would hold true unless the producer sought and was able—through other alliances and coalitions, such as those that grew around the Nord Stream project—to start removing that transit player from its value chain altogether, but leaving it with significant social sunk costs.

Another key element is that, despite trying, during the reference period Gazprom was not able to turn this natural gas chain into a vertically integrated one: despite repeated attempts to gain a stake or JV status with the Ukrainian, Slovak, and Czech transit systems, it was not able to do so. Thus, *in this exemplary chain*, key technical and value-adding nodes were not formally under Gazprom's ownership (see table 4.2).

Although Gazprom was not able to reach the vertical integration of the Urengoy-Nürnberg gas chain, it was able to achieve control of important segments of parallel chains, such as through the purchase of Belarus's Beltransgas in 2011, related to gas deliveries to Germany via

TABLE 4.2
Natural Gas Value-Added Chain: Spatial and Technological Processes, 2011–14

Spatial Stage	Technological Process	"Stage" in Value Chain	Main Actors
Russian Federation	Extraction	Upstream	Gazprom
	Separation	Midstream	Gazprom
	Transportation by trunk pipeline		Federal Tariffs Commission
Ukraine	Transportation by trunk pipeline	Midstream	Ukrtranshaz
	Underground storage		NAK Naftohaz
Slovak Republic	Transportation by trunk pipeline	Midstream	Eustream
Czech Republic	Transportation by trunk pipeline	Midstream	RWE Transgas
Germany	Transportation by MEGAL diameter pipeline	Midstream	Open Grid Europe
	Delivery to power plant Use for electricity generation	Downstream	E.ON*

* E.ON Gastransport was sold to the Macauarie Group and other institutional investors in 2012.

the Yamal pipeline through Belarus and Poland. At the downstream segment of the chain, Gazprom's participation in the storage and marketing of natural gas in Germany was made possible through its Wingas joint venture with Wintershall, inaugurated in 1993.[184]

So, barring direct vertical integration and control of JVs, which means did Gazprom have at its disposal to influence markets and politics at midstream and downstream market locations along our chain? Some of this was related to constitutive power, through supporting specific actors linked to the chain either vertically (intermediary companies, e.g., RosUkrenergo) or horizontally (actors related to businesses dependent on low natural gas prices for their profits, such as Firtash's Ostchem chemical fertilizer empire) to develop the resources to become socially empowered to develop political salience in the polity as a whole, not only within their sector. This could be achieved through the granting of preferential prices for some users (as in the example of Ostchem) or help to some nontransparent players to develop their business (RosUkrEnergo, where Gazprom was majority co-owner). Similarly, some of the ways in which natural gas could be used for rent-seeking (e.g., within Ukraine) were directly related to Ukraine's role in the value chains of Gazprom, especially contracts and accounting practices which did not appropriately distinguish between various components (e.g., transit and gas payments in pre-2009 contracts, and technical use gas from losses and stolen gas in Ukrtransgaz's own accounting).

The de facto limitation to pipeline deliveries—with their inflexible, largely point-to-point infrastructure—during our focus period implied constraints both for Gazprom as a supplier and the importing companies and states. At the same time, the larger point to be made about inherited, natural gas-specific infrastructure is that, on one hand, it created certain framing conditions for supply possibilities as well as rent-seeking. Conversely, the case of Ukraine brings to the fore the question of how the same infrastructure, in different political/governance situations, may play very different roles. Indeed, bargains and agreements set around concrete infrastructures may obsolesce once political realities change.

CHAPTER FIVE

Oil: Managing Value Swings from Siberian Fields to Gasoline Stations in Germany

THE LAST chapter analyzed the natural gas value chain, going from production in Siberia to end users in Germany. This chapter continues the case study portion of the book by analyzing the oil value chain—a key element in Russian energy relations with both the European Union (which in the last decade imported about 30 percent of its oil from Russia) and post-Soviet transit states.

In contrast to natural gas, the physical transformation that our oil molecule went through from production in Russia to final consumers in Germany was relatively complex. In contrast with natural gas's transit journey, where a complex infrastructure was put in place exactly to make sure that natural gas's characteristics would remain unchanged through this journey, in the case of oil, a physical transformation (refining into motor fuels, e.g., gasoline and diesel) was key to the value chain. Although some of the differences between the natural gas and oil value chains had to do with differences in the sectoral governance environment (e.g., the fact that a multitude of companies exported crude oil from Russia, whereas a single company—Gazprom—held a monopoly over pipeline gas exports, or the higher priority given by the

European Union to natural gas security of supply), important differences also go back to differences in the physical characteristics of the goods themselves. These differences, as discussed in chapter 3, also affect key characteristics of the value chain as a system, for example, through the ways in which they affect the transportation process.

As discussed in chapter 3, oil distinguishes itself by its relative heterogeneity; given relatively broad variations in key characteristics (e.g., viscosity and sulfur content), crude oil is usually blended to produce a number of standardized "brands" marketed as such; such blending and branding allow actors to manage oil's heterogeneity by channeling it into a smaller number of widely marketed benchmark brands.[1] Key effects on actors down the value chain are price differentials between brands, as well as widely quotable prices (with nearly two-thirds of world contracts using Brent crude oil prices as benchmark reference[2]) and the existence of a global market. As is analyzed in this chapter, these characteristics, in interaction with governance and other features of the spatial area encompassed by the chain, affected its course, as well as the kinds of relationships that could—or could not—emerge in the chain.

THE GLOBAL AND REGIONAL MARKET CONTEXT

The oil value chain analyzed in this case study uses as an *exemplary chain* the journey of oil from production in Russia, to final consumers of diesel in Germany via the physical infrastructure of the Southern branch of the Druzhba pipeline (which divides in Belarus into northern and southern branches, with the northern branch going through Belarus and Poland), and refining in the Czech Republic, interacting at each spatial stage with infrastructure nodes and the interests of important local actors, while being affected by decisions made at relevant commercial and regulatory nodes. The main steps in this chain were production; transportation within Russia through the Transneft system; interaction with Russia's export regulation system; transit through Belarus, Ukraine, and the Slovak Republic; refining in the Czech Republic; and sale as diesel in Germany (figure 5.1).

Although representative of oil value chains as a whole, the journey discussed in this chapter took place in a concrete space and at a particular time. One concrete space was the political/regulatory space; in chapter 2, I provided an overview of the governance and economic

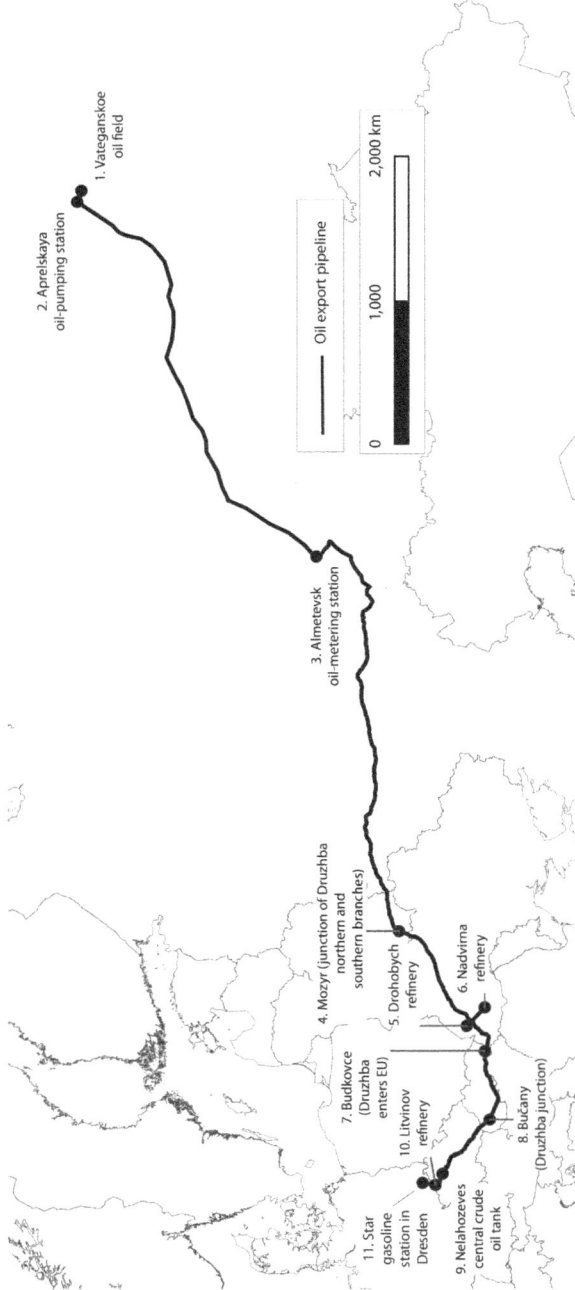

Figure 5.1 Overview of the oil chain followed in this chapter

Source: Map created by Matthias Neumann using QGIS and GIS data from Natural Earth (free vector and raster map data, at naturalearthdata.com), OpenStreetMap (https://www.openstreetmap.org), and Wikipedia; further editing in Adobe Illustrator.

conditions prevalent during the focus period in each of the key national states crossed by the chain. At the same time, the journey discussed in this chapter took place in the context of global and regional oil market trends. During the period 2011–14, these were characterized by four key trends at the European, post-Soviet, and global levels.

First, this was a period of relative price stability between two sharp swings: the rapid increase in prices between early 2009 and early 2011, and the even sharper decline starting in June 2014; during this period, benchmark Brent crude oil prices remained largely stable at about $100 to $110 per barrel.[3] This period could be characterized as one of calm before the storm unleashed by the significant growth in U.S. unconventional oil production and the associated sharp fall in oil prices starting in mid-2014. Second, in terms of the global refining sector, 2011–14 saw a continuation of global shifts in oil demand from the states belonging to the Organization for Economic Cooperation and Development (OECD) to non-OECD states,[4] as well as increased competition for European refiners from oil products refined in non-OECD and U.S. refineries with lower operating costs due to less strict environmental requirements and access to lower-priced raw materials.[5] Third, at the level of the European Union, crude oil production continued the decline starting in 2000; in its motor fuels (gasoline and diesel) refining sector, the EU continued to be a net importer of diesel and a net exporter of gasoline, a structural trend related to the tax advantages received by diesel engine vehicles;[6] by 2013, the EU was the largest exporter of gasoline and largest importer of diesel in the world, which prompted many to start rethinking EU oil security of supply not so much in terms of crude oil but of access to high-demand oil products such as diesel.[7] (Here, the picture was starkly different than in the case of gasoline; even after prices stabilized in late 2011, concerns about declining demand and gasoline oversupply related to reduced exports to the United States and resulting excess capacity continued.) This was reflected in fierce competition between the main refining groups in the area, especially PKN Orlen, OMV, Slovnaft, Shell, ENI, and MOL. All these factors were putting pressure on refinery margins, which declined continuously until early 2014.[8] One result was the closing of over twenty EU refineries between 2010 and 2014 and the loss of over 10 percent of its refining capacity.[9]

This, in turn, further reduced EU diesel production, an oil product for which a strong imbalance between production and demand had

developed in the last decades and which the EU was already importing in large quantities (see the discussion below of diesel vs. gasoline
demand). Although also the result of regulatory decisions (tax preferences for diesel fuel and vehicles leading to higher demand), this was an
issue because of the technical characteristics of the good limited actors'
range of options. Because of oil's material characteristics and the structure of its molecules, a refinery cannot produce only diesel or gasoline
but must produce both as part of a broader slate of oil products and has
only limited leeway in terms of the proportion of each to produce.[10]
Fourth, at the level of the former Soviet Union (FSU), the main trends
were increases in refining in Russia (plus 15 percent, between 2011
and 2014) and Belarus (plus 9 percent), while the Ukrainian refining
sector showed steep declines, compensated for by nearly equally strong
increases in oil product imports. (These trends in Russian and Ukrainian refining are discussed in more detail later in the chapter.)

FOLLOWING THE VALUE CHAIN: UPSTREAM

This section describes the start of our oil molecule's journey. After
observing its movement in the upstream segment of the oil value
chain, it examines its path from the production field to becoming part
of LUKoil's export portfolio.

Vateganskoe, Khanty-Mansiysk Autonomous Okrug–Yurga

The oil value chain starts in the Vateganskoe field, 30 kilometers
from the town of Kogalym, and part of the LUKoil–Western Siberia (LUKoil-WS) operations headquartered there.[11] LUKoil-WS was
the largest of LUKoil's subsidiaries; it was responsible for nearly half
of its production in the 2010s.[12] Its operation area covered the Tyumen Region, the Khanty-Mansi Autonomous Region–Yurga, and the
Yamal-Nenets Autonomous Region—areas that, taken together, create an area larger than Kazakhstan, the ninth-largest country in the
world. LUKoil, one of the private oil companies created out of the
chaos of the early 1990s, was established on the basis of geographically proximate territorial production units (production associations)
led by seasoned "oil generals" with deep roots in the Soviet oil bureau-
cracy. One of them was Vagit Alekperov, who rose from head of the

Kogalym oil production association to founder and longtime president of LUKoil.[13]

It is hard to underestimate the importance of LUKoil in the local economy of towns such as Kogalym and in the Khanty-Mansi Autonomous Region as a whole. Vateganskoe is part of a triangle of intense petroleum production—with axes in the LUKoil fields of Langepas, Urai, and Kogalym—in the company's area of origin (the name LUKoil comes from the initials L-U-K, after these cities). Vateganskoe was put into production in 1984, its development taking place in parallel with the development of Kogalym, the nearest city, as a livable city—and thus it was in 1984, one year after production started at Vateganskoe, that basic infrastructure (i.e., "a medical point, a bank, a police station, and a children's club," in addition to various food stores and a bookstore[14]) was established in Kogalym. By 2011, Kogalym had transformed itself from an oil "Wild West" location into a reasonably prosperous oil town boasting a multinational, multiconfessional population, an image that the company later saw as its mission and interest to promote.[15] Vagit Alekperov's career in Russia—which started in Kogalym—and his rise to president of LUKoil were in many ways representative of the broader trend of the Western Siberian oil cities as "multiethnic melting pots," where oilmen from all parts of the USSR, including the oil-producing areas of the North Caucasus and Azerbaijan (as in the case of Alekperov), were able to rise high in the industry.[16] The dominant role of LUKoil and the petroleum industry in the region was not without pitfalls, however, and there were repeated concerns about the local economy's lack of diversification.[17]

Vateganskoe was one of LUKoil's largest fields—its second-largest in terms of production, and the largest in terms of proven reserves.[18] It produces light, low-sulfur oil that is highly valued for its refining-friendly qualities; it also produces associated gas as part of the oil production process. (Oil and natural gas may be found in the same field but are produced differently.) As a result of Gazprom's monopoly on exports and price caps on natural gas sold domestically, gas produced by oil companies as a by-product of oil production was often commercially unutilized and was discarded by being flared into the atmosphere, releasing significant amounts of CO_2 in the process. (Although LUKoil did not commercialize this associated gas as pipeline natural gas, part was used as fuel for local power stations, and part was processed into propane and natural gas liquids for use in LUKoil's own [and other] chemical plants.[19])

Yet despite its large production, Vateganskoe was also an aging giant, a mature field whose output was declining and where it was progressively getting harder and more expensive to produce.[20] As such, Vateganskoe was representative of many aging "brownfields" in LUKoil's portfolio. The "browning" of Western Siberia was, in turn, part of a broader trend in Soviet and Russian oil and gas production, whereby—as a result of natural factors, outdated technology, and poor management of fields—production had to move progressively east—from the Ukrainian fields near the Carpathian mountains to the Urals in the 1950s, to Western Siberia in the 1970s and 1980s, to areas further east in Eastern Siberia as well as the Arctic offshore in the 2010s. This was also representative of LUKoil's challenges, because the company had significant exposure to such aging brownfields. More generally, brownfields and the policies needed to deal with their challenges represented a move from low- to high-production cost resources, one of the reasons—together with the fragmentation of the sector among multiple small producers—for the decline in Russia's oil production in the first post-1991 decade.[21]

Out of Vateganskoe and into the world. A small fraction of the oil produced at Vateganskoe did not become part of LUKoil's regular portfolio but was refined locally at LUKoil's technically outdated mini-refinery in Kogalym and used for the local needs of LUKoil's local motor vehicle fleet.[22] Thus, most of the oil produced at Vateganskoe became part of LUKoil's regular portfolio and, as such, related to important decisions needed to be made by the firm. What to do with this oil: Sell it as crude oil in Russia? As crude oil abroad? Refine it within LUKoil's own network in Russia, or abroad, in one of LUKoil's refineries in Ukraine and the EU? (In our case, this meant anywhere between LUKoil's closest full-size refinery in Perm and the Zeeland refinery in the Netherlands, where LUKoil had a 45 percent ownership share; it also owned refineries in Italy, Bulgaria, Romania, and Ukraine.[23]) Maximize the output of gasoline or diesel? (During our reference period, Russian refineries were producing slightly more diesel than gasoline[24] (and LUKoil refineries nearly twice as much[25]) but, capitalizing on strong EU demand, exporting 55 percent of diesel production but only 20 percent of gasoline production.[26] In terms of domestic consumption, diesel consumption was about 80 percent of the level of gasoline, a clear contrast to the situation in EU, where diesel demand was more than twice as high as that for gasoline.[27] (Let us remember, however, that a refinery's manager does not have full control over the slate of oil products produced, because it depends on the specific interface between the qualities of the crude oil feedstock and the refinery's technology.)

But in the background, LUKoil also faced issues such as how much to invest in aging fields with declining production, and how much in new ones. To what extent should it pursue vertical integration?[28] Although LUKoil prided itself in being one of Russia's largest vertically integrated oil companies, from the literature on oil economics we know there may be reasons why vertical integration may not always be preferred, because other types of relationships, like pay-for-refining agreements, may give oil producers more flexibility. Where to invest? In production? In refinery modernization? Needless to say, these are extremely complex questions for any multinational oil company, and as such also for LUKoil, which already by 2005 had become Russia's most internationally active oil company. These were also very complex questions, given LUKoil's relationship with the Russian state and political elites, a relationship characterized by careful treading on political issues, especially after the dismantling of Yukos in 2004. Such careful treading, together with a degree of trading in mutual favors and preferential treatment, had allowed the company to, by 2013, remain as Russia's second-largest oil company despite the growing concentration of state assets in the sector.[29] It is also in this context that decisions concerning exports as well as the acquisition of refining activities in EU locations such as the Czech Republic were made, a topic discussed in more detail later in the chapter.

In making these decisions, LUKoil executives (with LUKoil's headquarters in Moscow as a commercial node) had to pay attention to long-term strategic development issues, but also to short- and medium-term factors (e.g., price developments and maintenance schedules for specific refineries). The breadth of possible choices was also limited by regulatory constraints (e.g., the Russian taxation system and EU fuel quality standards), by relationships with the state and the political leadership, and, last but not least, by oil's materiality characteristics as a good.

In terms of the constraints imposed by the Russian tax and duty system, companies such LUKoil had to deal with a unique feature of Russian oil sector governance seldom used by other states—its system of oil export duties (often referred to as "export taxes"). With about 40 percent of Russia's crude oil production being exported in the 2010s, this was a significant instrument of state policy and also a key area of contention between players.[30] In addition to their role in revenue collection, export duties were also intended to fulfill a domestic purpose: at least in theory, to provide incentives for companies to supply oil domestically rather than export.

So the first regulatory node oil encountered was the Russian oil taxation and duties system.

An Excursus on the Russian Oil Taxation and Duties System

A small excursus is in order concerning the Russian duty and taxation system during the focus period, 2011–14. This system is and was a highly complex one, within which I focus only on two key elements, which constituted the bulk (90 percent) of tax payments: the Mineral Extraction Tax, and export duties.[31] The year 2011 represents a turning point in both. Now that the process of consolidation of oil activities in the hands of state-owned companies such as Rosneft after the 2004 dismantling of Yukos was largely completed, and that oil production had recovered after the 1990s slump, 2011 brought a reconsideration of whether existing fiscal instruments were being used in the most effective manner.

A look back at the tax and duties system in place for the previous decade helps us understand the system that, replacing it in 2011, was in place during our focus period. During the Soviet period, revenue from state-owned oil enterprises was extracted administratively rather than through taxation, so Russia inherited little in the form of a comprehensive oil tax system. Its first post-1991 attempts at oil taxation were fragmentary and haphazard, and it took a decade for a comprehensive oil taxation system to take shape.[32] Starting in 2000, rising oil prices synergized with growing dissatisfaction with oil companies' ability to shelter profits in the free-for-all 1990s. Thus, the system inaugurated by Finance Minister Alexei Kudrin in 2001 focused on revenue extraction efficiency, targeting companies' gross revenues rather than profits and paying little attention to the specificities of various production areas.[33] The result was a system that was extremely effective in transferring oil rents to the state, but that disincentivized production, especially in marginal fields with high production costs. A second state goal, fully rolled out only in 2005, was to promote the export of purportedly "higher value added" refined oil products as opposed to crude oil; with this aim, the export duty for heavy refined products such as fuel oil was set at only 38 percent of the export duty on crude oil.[34] (Although all refined oil products were taxed at a lower rate than crude oil, the export duty for light oil products such as gasoline was higher than that on fuel oil, so as to make sure not too much gasoline was exported, because this could also lead to domestic shortages.) Thus the export duty system in place in the 2000s tried to simultaneously fulfill several goals—not always smoothly.

The goal of exporting "higher value added" refined oil products as opposed to crude oil was both a response to domestic criticism that Russia was becoming little more than a raw materials supplier for the West, as well as an embodiment of Soviet-Marxist perceptions of value added. According to this view, more processing equals more value added, and the more processing a good would have undergone in Russian Federation territory, the more value-added profits would the Russian state be able to accrue.[35] Although this view synergized with the modernization rhetoric of the early Vladimir Putin (2000–2004) and Dmitry Medvedev (2004–2008) presidencies, there were two problems with this reasoning. First, the oil industry as a whole is characterized by price volatility and swings in demand, which can lead to both rapid value increases *and* decreases; as a result, refineries are a low-margin, high-volume business. The relative profitability of the upstream and the downstream is very much a product of relative prices at any given time, so that "value added" through processing is not always reflected in increased profits.[36]

Second, because of the legacy of the Soviet system (outdated refineries, a system focused on domestic supplies rather than economic efficiency), refining in the post-Soviet environment was often a value-*destroying*, not value-adding, process. Thus as noted by Gustafson, it was not unusual that a ton of Russian crude oil traded in, say, Rotterdam would fetch a price higher than that of the same barrel when sold as products, due to the large share of low-value refined products (e.g., fuel oil, *mazut*) in an average ton of refined products.[37] As a result, the 2001 Tax Code had ended up supporting not high-value-added refining, but the export of low-value-added heavy oil products while disincentivizing the first.[38] Instead, often illegal mini-refineries ("*samovar* refineries") continued to be used, and investments in refinery modernization took a back seat.[39] By 2011, the level of modernization of Russian refineries, as captured by Nelson's Complexity Index, was significantly behind that of European and U.S. refineries.[40] Thus the purported goal of increasing higher-"valued-added" exports often competed with the goal of maximizing export revenues.[41] With reduced income, oil companies reduced investments, leading to the prospect of sharply reduced production. The incentives for refined products' exports was also backfiring; with world oil prices increasing, producers had an increased incentive to export high-price oil products, leading to shortages at home.

The system of export duties also affected Russian companies' relationships with post-Soviet transit states by providing incentives for engaging in refining and reexporting through some states, as shipments to certain Commonwealth of Independent States (CIS) or Customs Union countries, most notably Belarus (as well as, during limited periods, Ukraine), did not count as "exports" during much of the 1991–2014 period.[42] Indeed, the issue of which countries should be exempted from these export duties was a constant issue of debate and was also used by the Russian side for political pressure; whether oil and gas deliveries would be duty free has been one of the major issues of debate concerning the Russia-Belarus-Kazakhstan Customs Union since before it entered into force in July 2010.[43]

Largely as a reaction to the trends described above, a new taxation system was established in October 2011 (the so-called 60-66-90-100 system[44]), representing a key change in oil export duties. The new system lowered the tax on crude exports, making these much more attractive for Russian oil companies. It also equalized the export tax rate on most refined products (except gasoline, which was taxed at a much higher rate, of 90 percent of the crude oil rate, as a means of promoting domestic sales), reducing the incentive to export heavy oil products such as fuel oil. (Although, in general, diesel is considered to be in the same refined products category as gasoline—"light products"—during the focus period, the levels of excise taxes on diesel were about 60 percent of those for gasoline, while export taxes were about 75 percent of those on gasoline.[45])

The new tax legislation reversed the virtual subsidization of the refining sector that had taken place in the last decade at the expense of the upstream sector (which also meant that the new policies had a negative impact on companies with significant refining assets, including LUKoil but, especially, Bashneft).[46] This was the first type of signal a company like LUKoil was facing during the focus period. At the same time, export duty exceptions that had traditionally been granted on a field-by-field basis continued.

The second signal LUKoil was facing concerned the Mineral Extraction Tax (MET). The system in place since 2001 had emphasized taxing revenues (as opposed to profits), with a multitude of often poorly codified exceptions for specific fields. Instead, the MET guidelines put in place in 2011 used a detailed coefficients system to calculate tax breaks to economically neglected areas and priority-development fields, which, nevertheless, did not fully eliminate haggling. Despite these changes, post-2011 oil taxation policy continued to fulfill multiple goals for the state: budget revenue, "value adding," and securing domestic access to oil products as a means of preventing social tensions that could arise in situations of shortages were important considerations. These also reflected the interests of multiple players active in the sector, starting with the ministries of energy, finance, transportation, and natural resources—the last of which was in charge of two key agencies: the Federal Agency for Subsoil Use (Rosnedra), in charge of subsoil licenses; and the Federal Service for the Supervision of the Use of Natural Resources (Rosprirodnadzor). In particular, the finance and energy ministries often found themselves at odds concerning the taxation question. Thus, in the context of a growing budget crisis, the Finance Ministry's goal of maintaining the significant contribution of the oil sector to the Russian budget—just oil-related tax revenues constituted 41.8 percent of overall tax revenues in 2013—often clashed with the Energy Ministry's goal of protecting production targets and investment levels.[47] In addition to these two basic interests, taxation and duty policies also reflected other domestic-level goals, such as the desire to prevent politically sensitive gasoline shortages, especially just before an important election such as the presidential contest in 2012; chronic deficits and regional-level shortages in mid-2011 had been attributed to oil companies' increasing their gasoline exports to benefit from the price difference between increasing export prices and low, regulated domestic ones.[48]

More generally, the situation must be understood within the broader context of the various "goods" produced by energy systems (see chapter 2), and where companies such as LUKoil had to pay attention to the way their actions as a multinational company affected their roles within Russia, whether at the local level (through its dominant role in many local economies) or regionally (as supplier of key oil products), all of which also affected its relationship with federal authorities.[49] This was the tax environment in which a multinational company characterized as having both aging and new fields and significant refining capacity, such as LUKoil, found itself. At the same time, it is important to keep in mind that though some taxes such as export taxes had an immediate effect on company choices, others (e.g., the MET) had a delayed effect, given the seven- to ten-year time frame needed to develop new oil fields.

FOLLOWING THE VALUE CHAIN: MIDSTREAM

This section describes our oil molecule's journey from Vateganskoe to Transneft's system of export pipelines. Given the difficulties involved in gaining access to this system, this journey involves navigating both physical space and a complex maze of rules and regulations.

Transneft and the Oil Export Quotas and Allocations System

It was still a long way from the Vateganskoe field to the Druzhba pipeline, which starts nearly 2,000 kilometers to the southwest, in Almetyevsk, Tatarstan. The oil produced at Vateganskoe first had to be collected and transported to the Aprelskaya oil-pumping station, located just 8 kilometers north of Kogalym. From here, a trunk pipeline would transport the oil to the start of the Druzhba pipeline in Almetyevsk.[50] These trunk pipelines, controlled by monopolist Transneft, moved 93 percent of Russian crude oil;[51] during the focus period about 85 percent of LUKoil's oil exports went through Transneft export routes.[52] (Although, in contrast to the case of natural gas, Russian legislation did not prohibit the construction of privately owned oil pipelines,[53] and starting in 2003 some private companies had sought to build their own pipelines to reach export terminals, those that succeeded were more the exception rather than the rule.) Thus, oil produced at Vateganskoe entered the Transneft oil pipeline system, the largest in the world, and one incorporating both technical (transportation) and regulatory oversight roles. Although Russia abolished formal oil export quotas in 1995, indirect quotas continued in the form of regulations concerning access to Transneft pipelines, including its export pipelines.[54] And though the duties and taxes discussed above affected companies' priorities and decisions about whether to export the oil produced, these decisions would not be implementable without an export allocation and access to the main export pipelines; sometimes, companies held over their export allocations "in expectation of a lower crude duty the following month."[55] Except in those few cases where an oil company itself owned the infrastructure, crude oil transportation within Russia was regulated by yearly transportation services agreements between oil suppliers and Transneft, on the basis of an application by the oil company. For exports, this concerned quotas for export capacity to specific destination points. Although, in theory, these quotas could not be swapped between companies, in practice they sometimes were, including the swapping of quotas for destination points in one geographical direction for points in another.[56] Similarly, in numerous situations oil companies were allocated additional or "special" export allocations, for example, in exchange for work in domestically disadvantaged areas.[57] Access to export pipeline capacity was granted quarterly by Transneft on the basis of offering capacity proportional to each company's declared production plans. Each company was allowed to flow this oil to Transneft's system, each of whose export pipelines functioned as a "giant reservoir" for oil from different fields and companies; at specific delivery points, oil companies could take equivalent oil amounts "for them to export according to the schedule and allocated volumes."[58]

Reaching distant export markets first requires reaching gateway ports or export pipelines, in turn depending on the technical possibility of moving oil around Russia so that no bottlenecks ensue, especially in terms of supplies to regional refineries. The technical state of export pipelines played a key role, leading to a situation of chronic deficit of export capacity, which continued through the mid-2000s.[59] This reality, coupled with the system of quotas for the use of export pipeline capacity, meant that domestic supply coordination issues could also create problems for supplies to concrete export markets. Thus, for example, after Rosneft's acquisition of TNK-BP in 2013, when seeking additional volumes to export to China, it began to revoke contracts previously signed by TNK to supply crude oil to refineries belonging to other Russian oil companies (e.g., Gazprom Neft's refinery in Omsk). As a result, these other companies, facing problems with supplies to their own refineries in Russia, had little option but to redirect these volumes to supply their own refineries, which affected their exports and created problems for importers along the Druzhba pipeline.

Such a system of allocations and regulations around a highly profitable commodity such as oil perforce mobilized a variety of interests. In the case of Transneft as a physical, commercial, and regulatory node, the main actors involved have been Transneft's management itself (either representing the company's corporate interests or their own personal ones, in addition to state directives[60]), the oil companies, and the Federal Tariff Service, with the main conflicts concerning transportation tariffs (proposed by Transneft for approval by the Federal Tariff Service) and the financing of additional infrastructure.[61] Their relationship was also influenced by Transneft's status as a state-owned company with oversight over oil transportation. Thus, the way from production field to export was affected by regulatory (export quotas) and technical issues (how to physically get the oil to the export pipelines or terminals), which also came to influence each other.

Joining Druzhba at Almetevsk, Tatarstan

After transiting nearly 2,000 kilometers on Transneft pipelines, the oil produced at Vateganskoe arrived at the start of the Druzhba pipeline in Almetevsk, Tatarstan; by now, this oil had been over two weeks on the road from Kogalym.[62] In addition to oil from Western Siberia, oil from the nearby Urals as well as the Caspian entered the pipeline at the Almetevsk oil-metering station. In entering the Transneft pipeline, Vateganskoe oil entered Transneft's reservoir-like system discussed above, where oil from different fields and qualities would mix. At this point, Transneft's inability or unwillingness (see below) to transport oil "in batches" as a way to keep oil of different qualities separate and distinct, protecting their characteristics and brand market price, becomes an important issue. As discussed in chapter 3, in contrast to the case of natural gas, the differences between particular brands of oil are still very significant, as their unique characteristics, especially sulfur level, have an important impact on the type of processing infrastructure that can be used with them, as refineries are specified to work with specific types of oil (e.g., high-sulfur and low-sulfur oil). Although Vateganskoe produced the light, low-sulfur oil that is typical of the Western Siberian oil region, it lost many of its unique, refining-friendly characteristics once it mixed, in Transneft pipelines, with other grades of oil. And though in OECD countries oil transported by pipeline is often shipped in batches—which means that different types of oil may travel on the same pipeline without mixing, separated by a buffer, often a technical hydrocarbon[63]—this was not the case in the Transneft system feeding the Druzhba pipeline, with the implication that the oil exported through Druzhba was not the low-sulfur oil characteristic of Western Siberia but a blend—Urals (also traded as REBCO, Russian Export Blend Crude Oil), combining low-sulfur, "sweet" oil from Western Siberia with heavy, high-sulfur "sour" oil from the Volga-Urals region.[64]

It has been argued that the decision not to use batching was more a political decision than one dictated by technical necessity, and that Transneft's refusal to segregate flows so as to maximize the value of the light oil portion was a result of political influence from the leadership of Tatarstan and Bashkortostan, whose flagship oil companies Tatneft and Bashneft have provided income crucial for the leadership's political projects. Given the fact that these regions produce lower-priced, heavy, high-sulfur oil, if this oil would be sold separately, the income received by these companies would decline; with Volga-Urals oil mixed in, the resulting blend, REBCO, fetches more per ton than Volga-Urals oil would, benefiting Tatneft, Bashneft, and other Volga producers at the expense of companies producing lighter Western Siberian oil such as LUKoil, because their oil could no longer be marketed separately at full price.[65] If technopolitics reminds us that power may be exerted through the use of certain technologies, as we can see in this case, the decision to use—or not use—specific technologies depends on the political power of concrete actors in the chain, in this case the Tatarstan and Bashkortostan leadership, within its own intricate relationships, both with the federal center in Moscow and with oil companies and Transneft.

Thus, the oil exported via Druzhba was actually a mix of two very different oils—"sweet," low-sulfur oil from Western Siberia and high-sulfur oil from the Volga-Urals region, providing an example of how infrastructure may not simply transport a good but also "make" it as well. Once sweet Western Siberian oil was mixed with high-sulfur Urals oil, it lost the characteristics that made it easier to refine, as well as value.[66] (This does not mean, however, that the oil transited via Druzhba would be indistinct in a contractual sense. Rather, within the same pipeline coexisted various contractual arrangements affecting oil exported by specific companies—during the focus period, Bashneft, Rosneft, Gazprom Neft, LUKoil, Slavneft, and Russneft—and oil contractually tied to specific destinations. In other words, even if these molecules would be undistinguishable and untraceable, still, a certain portion of the total could be governed by one contractual system, and others by a different contractual arrangement.)

Yet it was by no means self-evident that oil from LUKoil's Western Siberian fields would flow at all in the direction of Druzhba. By 2012, several trends were coinciding to make transit via the Druzhba pipeline (as well as sales to the markets located along it) less attractive. First came the opening of the Eastern Siberia–Pacific Ocean (ESPO) pipeline in 2009, which linked the Eastern Siberian oil fields with the Pacific port of Kozmino, and the resulting growth of exports to Asian destinations, affecting oil companies' thinking about where to direct oil produced in Western Siberian fields. With increased pipeline capacity easing export bottlenecks and giving producers the chance to decide whether to export eastward or westward on the basis of expected netback revenue, the decision to ship oil west to European markets was slowly ceasing to be self-evident for Western Siberian oil producers. Although Western Siberia remained the center of the Russian oil industry and during the focus period nearly two-thirds of Russia's crude oil exports went to EU markets, exports to Asian markets nearly doubled between 2011 and 2014, mainly at the expense of supplies to FSU markets, with the trend continuing after that year.[67]

Second, the Russian government itself was in the middle of a campaign to circumvent Ukraine and the Baltic states as oil export routes, reducing their participation in the value chain of Russian oil exports. Key examples are measures such as the building of the Baltic Pipeline System (BPS) I and II, and the cessation of exports through Latvia's Ventspils port (in 2004) and of indirect exports via refining in Lithuania's Mazeikiu Nafta (2006), noted in Russia's Energy Strategy to 2020 and Russia's Energy Strategy to 2030.[68] Thus some oil previously being exported to the EU via Druzhba moved to seaborne exports via the Primorsk and Ost-Luga ports in the Russian Baltic.[69]

Third, the developments discussed above were taking place within the context of the material state of the Druzhba pipeline itself. Although much research on energy relations and path dependencies in Central and Eastern Europe tends to refer to infrastructure as a largely immutable given, infrastructure such as the Druzhba pipeline was by no means immutable—it is changeable, if only because it decays over time and has an exploitation limit. When Druzhba turned fifty years old in 2014, it was reaching that limit. And though few seemed to be paying much attention to the issue then, a number of technical and maintenance problems had started to already emerge by the mid-2000s, issues that, though important in their own right, could also be used as justification to reduce supplies (as in 2006, when a rupture in the Druzhba pipeline transiting oil to the Mazeikiu Nafta refinery in Lithuania was left unfixed and used as justification for a permanent suspension of supplies).[70] As a result of these last two factors, as early as 2007 some were talking about "the end of Druzhba";[71] and there was discussion of how importers along the Druzhba pipeline would need to brace for possible reductions in supplies.[72]

Indeed, the volume of exports via Druzhba as a whole (including both its northern and southern branches) decreased about 25 percent from October 2011 to January 2014,[73] as well as in terms of its proportion of Russia's total exports (from 39 percent in 2011 to 33.3 percent in 2013[74]). These trends were even sharper in the case of LUKoil, which went from shipping 37.2 percent of its crude oil exports via Druzhba in 2011 to 28.5 percent in 2014.[75] Thus, seen in the larger context of Russian oil exports, how important was our exemplary chain, that related to oil shipments through Druzhba's southern branch? (As noted above, the Druzhba pipeline divides in Mozyr, Belarus, into northern and southern branches, with the southern branch going through Ukraine and the Slovak Republic and ending in the Czech Republic.[76]) In 2011, most Russian oil exports (61 percent) went by tanker, and a smaller part was carried by the Druzhba pipeline (39 percent), of which less than half (i.e., less than 17.5 percent of total Russian exports) went through its southern branch.[77]

After transiting through the Russian segment of the pipeline, Druzhba crossed into Belarus, where, at Mozyr, it divided into northern and southern branches, the latter going through Ukraine (the exemplary chain we are following). Although we are not specifically following Druzhba's northern branch reaching Germany through Poland, it is worthwhile noting that its first stop at the Mozyr refinery, and further supplies to Belarus and its second refinery, Novopolotsk/Naftan, became from the mid-1990s to about 2014 the basis for Belarus's economic survival as well as the political survival of its president Alexandr Lukashenka (1996–).[78]

Ukraine: The Oil Midstream Between Old and New Oligarchs

After the pipeline divided into northern and southern branches at Mozyr, Druzhba oil entered Ukraine. In its course from Brody near the Belarusian border to the pipeline exit point in Uzhhorod at the

Slovak border, Druzhba-transported oil entered a complex political economy and governance environment where crude oil and its derivates imported from Russia played a key role, in terms of potential income to the state, rent-seeking, and the political and economic power of specific Ukrainian actors, in the process touching on some of the most problematic confrontations between interest groups in postindependence Ukraine.

Druzhba oil in Ukraine before 2011: traditional roles and rents. Druzhba oil's journey in Ukraine included both its transit to further points in the pipeline and supplies to Ukrainian refineries, both of which were midstream operations potentially associated with significant revenues. Although best known for its role in gas transit, for many years up to 2000, about 43 percent of Russian crude oil exports transited through Ukraine via Druzhba, two additional transit pipelines, and the Prydniprovsky pipeline system transporting Russian (and Kazakh) oil for export through the Odesa port.[79] Revenues from this transit role were subject to fluctuations in transit volumes and recurrent disputes with Russia concerning transit fees, but in the 2011–14 period these went progressively down, from $200.6 million to $160.8 million a year.[80] This income helps explain some of the indecisiveness shown by the Ukrainian state concerning oil diversification projects (an important issue, because by 2013 Ukraine depended on Russian oil for 63 percent of its crude oil imports[81]). Because of the role of refineries in the oil midstream, our understanding of the size and degree of dependency on oil imports needs to be contextualized differently than in the case of natural gas, given that a significant portion of the oil imported may be used for refining and the subsequent exporting of the refined products. Also, there may be situations—as in Ukraine after 2011—where crude oil imports were drastically reduced, only to be replaced by imported oil products. Starting in 2014, a significant part of crude oil imports from Russia was replaced by imported refined oil products from Belarus, produced on the basis of Russian oil.[82]

In fact, the case of oil transit through Ukraine in the first two decades of Ukrainian independence is a prime example of the tension between the "threat" and "opportunity" aspects of participation in the value chains of Russian exporters. If for many years the diversification of oil supplies remained a stated goal of Ukrainian policy, the actual pursuit of these goals was much less decisive, in part because of the weight of inherited infrastructure (e.g., existing export pipelines crossing its territory, and the fact that Ukrainian refineries had been specified to work with the semi-heavy crude oil typical of Russian blends), but also because of the profits both private actors and the state were receiving from participation in these chains. This was especially clear in the period between 1991 and 2011, with our focus period (2011–14) acting as a transition between this and a later period, when Druzhba's significance would be reduced sharply. Thus it makes sense to first take a look at the role of Druzhba oil before 2011, before returning to the focus period.

In the two decades before 2011, the income related to the value chain of exports of Russian oil associated with the Druzhba pipeline was so strong as to largely derail two key Ukrainian oil energy imports diversification initiatives: the Odesa-Brody pipeline and the adjacent Odesa oil terminal able to receive and transship tanker-transported oil.[83] Having been many years in the making, the Odesa-Brody pipeline was intended to diversify Ukrainian oil imports from exclusive dependence on Russian pipeline supplies by facilitating the importing of oil from a variety of suppliers—which would arrive by tanker to the new oil terminal—and bringing it to Brody, where it would connect with the Druzhba pipeline flowing westward. The Odesa-Brody pipeline was also connected with Druzhba in a conceptual way: by becoming a player in the transit of Caspian oil to Western Europe (by having Caspian oil transited from Odesa join the existing westbound pipeline at Brody), Odesa-Brody was intended to make Ukraine a key player in a new, non-Russian-centered value chain.

The actual turn of events around these two key objects (the Odesa-Brody pipeline and the adjacent Odesa oil terminal) in the decade after their completion in 2002, however, speaks of the power of existing value chains (both formal or informal) and the income related to them. In the case of the Odesa oil terminal, arguably as a result of corrupt practices, control of its operations was ceded by its state operator Ukrtransnafta to an offshore company,[84] taking away from Ukraine the ability to manage the terminal, and, instead, allowing it to be managed in a way that was inconsistent with the diversification goal, preventing potential Caspian suppliers from shipping their oil via the Odesa port to Europe.[85] This is an example of a situational coalition, whereby corrupt groups within Ukraine (often in coordination with Russian ones) benefited from maintaining Ukraine's participation in the value chains of Russian oil exports.[86] Although this coordination was focused on increasing rent-seeking for these groups, it also had strong geopolitical and geo-economic effects. At the same time, serious questions arose as to the commercial viability of the project—the Odesa-Brody pipeline project was completed without guarantees that Caspian oil would be available for it.[87]

If the example given above is telling of how corrupt groups within Ukraine manipulated and benefited from maintaining Ukraine's participation in the value chains of Russian oil exports, the example of the Odesa-Brody pipeline additionally tells us how state-level benefits accrued by participation in the value chains of Russian oil exporters also helped derail diversification initiatives. If Odesa-Brody was intended to help Ukraine diversify its oil imports, once it was completed, it quickly changed its direction—to be used in reverse, that is, to transit Russian oil from Brody to Odesa for its further export by tanker.[88] Although there is much evidence of rent-seeking by specific Ukrainian groups as related to the Odesa-Brody reversal decision,[89] the transit fee income accruing to the central Ukrainian budget as a result of the reversal was significant enough to create a short-term incentive.[90]

The case of the Odesa-Brody pipeline also relates to the refining dimension of Ukraine's participation in the value chains of Russian oil producers. If the idea behind Odesa-Brody was not only to make Ukraine a player in the transit of Caspian oil to the EU but also to reduce the country's dependency on Russian oil, attention would need to be paid to the issue of refineries—crude oil in and of itself is useless; it first needs to be refined into usable oil products. Thus Odesa-Brody's much-announced diversification game-changer role could not work without significant refinery modernization, so that Ukrainian refineries would be able to process the light Caspian oil set to come through Odesa-Brody, whose refining characteristics differed significantly from their traditional raw material, Urals/REBCO higher-sulfur oil.[91] Similarly, without a refinery policy designed to promote diversified ownership of Ukraine's refineries and, thus, less of an exclusive emphasis on Russian oil supplies, domestic demand for Caspian oil supplied through Odesa-Brody would be limited.

This took place in a context where, between 1991 and 2011, a significant portion of Druzhba oil volumes went to supply outdated refineries inherited from the Soviet period (which, in addition to Druzhba oil, also used some domestically produced oil and Russian oil supplied via the other three pipelines serving Ukraine). (As in the case of Belarus and Lithuania, Ukraine inherited an oversized oil refinery system originally built as part of a Soviet-Union-wide system, yet which, remaining on its territory after the demise of the USSR, became part of the energy infrastructure of a much smaller country—in 2011 its total refining capacity, including refineries currently not in use, was more than three times larger than the country's oil products market.[92]) Even leaving aside other issues, this brought significant challenges, given the fact that these refineries were able to work profitably only as part of a larger network guaranteeing regular crude oil supplies and access to sale markets. Even when our oil molecule traveling from Vateganskoe did not enter any of these refineries, these are significant for the story because they helped create a certain environment that affected the very role of the molecule's route along the Druzhba South pipeline through Ukraine.

Two of Ukraine's eight refineries active in the early 2000s were located close to the Druzhba pipeline: the Drohobych and Nadvirna–Neftekhimik Prikarpatya refineries in Western Ukraine, in addition to the Odesa refinery adjacent to the Odesa-Brody pipeline connecting to Druzhba. By 2002, Ukraine's six largest refineries had been purchased or had their control acquired by Russian companies (of which, TNK acquired the Lysychansk refinery, LUKoil acquired the Odesa refinery, and the Russian-Ukrainian company Ukrtatneft acquired the Kremenchug refinery[93]). In the short term, the vertical integration implied by these purchases assured stable crude oil supplies from the mother company; together with increased import tariffs for oil products, this led to a sharp but temporary increase in refining between 2000 and 2004, which, nevertheless, did not reach 1991 levels.[94] Such ownership relationships were not always characterized by stability, however—as shown by the case of the Kremenchug refinery (discussed below), serious conflicts could arise between Ukrainian and Russian co-owners. Moreover, ownership relationships could not assure stable crude oil supplies or full use of these refineries.

The sale of these refineries to Russian oil companies is also significant for the story because, despite Ukraine having officially moved to oil purchases at market prices already in 1994 (in contrast to the case of gas, where special-for-Ukraine prices continued for much longer), Ukrainian refineries often imported crude oil from their Russian mother companies at lower-than-world prices due to intracorporate pricing.[95] This created price differentials and arbitrage opportunities that made it attractive to engage in activities such as the illegal reexporting, at higher prices, of oil earmarked for these refineries. A related scheme involved relabeling and reexporting Russian (Druzhba) oil as Ukrainian-produced oil for the purposes of avoiding value-added taxes.[96] Although the fact that such activities most often went unpunished had to do first and foremost with corruption and the overall governance environment, they were also facilitated by the price differentials and arbitrage possibilities made possible by Ukraine's participation in the value chain of Russian oil exporters.

At the same time—even accounting for short-term recovery periods, as in 2002–4—the decline of Ukraine's refinery sector from its Soviet-period high took place gradually but inexorably after independence. If the wave of refinery purchases by Russian companies in the early and mid-2000s discussed above promised badly needed new investments, these—with the exception of the Lysychansk refinery—did not take place, "and the Ukrainian government did not insist" that the new owners do so.[97] Yet the Ukrainian government was also to blame for creating an unfavorable climate for Ukrainian refineries. Key here was the elimination of import duties for oil products in 2005, a measure taken by the newly inaugurated post–Orange Revolution Yuschenko presidency that was intended to solve a fuel crisis and maintain low prices as a means of preventing social discontent (the crisis had started when, after a governmental attempt to introduce regulated prices, Russian-owned refineries withheld supplies). Although the measure introduced competition, it made imported oil products cheaper than Ukraine-produced ones, depriving Ukrainian refineries of their market and reducing incentives for investments. Dragged down by cheap imports and outdated Soviet-era technology unable to fulfill increasingly stringent EU fuel standards, three refineries (Nadvirna, Drohobych, and Kherson) had already stopped production in the years 2005–7.[98] The Odesa refinery closed down in 2011, and Lysychansk in 2013. By 2013, Ukraine's refineries were using less than 8 percent of their total design capacity of nearly 52 million tons, a sharp decline from 2007 (33.3 percent) and even 2011 (21.7 percent).[99] By 2014, only one refinery, Kremenchug, was working on a permanent basis, using domestically produced oil. As a result, crude oil imports plummeted between 2011 and 2014, reaching nearly zero by the end of the focus period. Although this also meant a steep decline in imports from Russia, it also reflected the end of any significant refining in Ukraine, with the vast majority of oil products used in the country being imported. By 2014 Ukraine was importing 90 percent of the diesel used in the country, the highest level in broader Europe.[100]

Druzhba oil in Ukraine, 2011–14. In the first two decades after 1991, Druzhba was used actively and as such became the center of key rent-seeking manipulations; but the story of the Druzhba-related value chain in Ukraine during the years 2011–14 is one of decline, which first and foremost was associated with two factors. The first factor had to do with changes in Russia's export routing policies attempting to sideline Ukraine, discussed above, and their impact on Ukraine's transit role. The second factor had to do with a reduction in Ukraine's role in oil refining, leading to less oil going to Ukrainian refineries through Druzhba. This was in turn related to both domestic policies and changes in the external environment. Domestically, the duty-free system for oil product imports starting in 2005, and corruption (first and foremost, illegal imports of oil products; see also the separate discussion below), were key. Externally, key factors were the changes in Russia's oil export taxation system introduced in 2011 (which led to significant growth in Russia's overall oil product exports between 2011 and 2014[101]) and the establishment of the Eurasian Customs Union in 2010, including Russia, Kazakhstan, and Belarus (which helped Belarus access Russian oil under preferential conditions, making its exports to Ukraine even more competitive compared with domestic production[102]). These changes took place within the general constraints placed by materiality and infrastructure on actors' choices. Thus, for example, the Soviet-era legacy of oil products pipelines linking Belarus's Mozyr and Novopolotsk refineries with Ukraine as well as the physical possibility itself of transporting such products via pipeline made possible large-scale oil product imports from Belarus.[103]

Ukraine: Oligarchs, Refining, and the Fall of the Druzhba South Pipeline

Refining and transportation issues put Druzhba oil in close contact with the interests of key Ukrainian economic players, both traditional oligarchs and representatives of a new political-economic group gaining ground after Viktor Yanukovich's access to the presidency in 2010. The case of one of these traditional oligarchs, Ihor Kolomoyskyi, and his Privat Group, the main players in Ukraine's oil market for many years, provides an especially telling example of the impact of domestic rent-seeking on Druzhba's role in Ukraine.[104] Although not the only Ukrainian oligarch involved in the oil business, Kolomoyskyi's control of key oil assets during 2011–14 makes for an especially relevant case. By 2014, Privat controlled key assets in the value chain's segments: production (Ukrnafta), transportation (Ukrtransnaftna), storage and refining (the Kremenchug, Nadvirna, and Drohobych refineries), and retail (about 1,500 gasoline stations, and about 30 percent of the gasoline and diesel retail market).[105] This raises the question: why did Ukrainian refiners and Kolomoskyi in particular, one of the most politically influential persons in Ukraine, not use their political influence to complain about competition from the duty-free imports situation and change it? Even if some of Kolomoskyi's refining assets stood idle for part of the time (as in the case of the Nadvirna and Drohobych refineries), such ownership was advantageous for Kolomoyskyi, because it gave him a special status as "domestic fuel processor," and preferential conditions for oil products imports.[106] In addition, their own involvement in the illegal importing of oil products and tax-dodging on gasoline sales cannot be excluded.[107] Kolomoyskyi's lack of interest in the long-term health of Ukraine's refining sector has also been explained in terms of his overwhelming interest in "the fast collection of rent from the oil industry" and Ukrnafta, "without considering the future of the company"—in other words, his inability to transform from a "roving" to a "stationary bandit," in Olson's terms.[108]

Privat's informal control over the state oil transportation monopoly Ukrtransnafta was especially important. Despite the fact that Privat only owned a minority of the company's shares, it used a regulatory loophole to place a close associate, Oleksandr Lazorko, as Ukrtransnafta's CEO in 2009. The impact of this control should not be underestimated, as well as the fact that Lazorko (who was CEO of Ukrtransnafta from 2009 to 2015) remained in his position through three very different presidencies: that of Orange Revolution "father" Viktor Yuschenko (2005–10), that of Viktor Yanukovich (2010–14), and the first year of the Poroshenko presidency after 2014's Euromaidan Revolution, despite formal state control over Ukrtransnafta.[109] This was representative of how Privat's "too big to touch" status increased its power and helped shield it from state control, despite changing coalitions being in power.[110] The fact that from the early days of Ukraine's independence the group had taken control of Ukraine's largest commercial bank, Privatbank, counting as its clients nearly half the population and through whose electronic system most salary and pension payments were made, basically meant it was impossible to attack Privat without risking bringing the entire system to a standstill.[111]

The rent-seeking activities of local actors such as (but not limited to) Kolomoyskyi affected the fate of Druzhba oil in Ukraine in two main ways. First, they exacerbated the decline of Ukrainian refining and, thus, the decline in shipments through Druzhba as well as other pipelines, affecting the load level of the transit pipeline, which was important for its proper functioning.[112] Key here was the widespread smuggling of oil products, which by 2012 accounted for nearly 15 percent of oil products consumed in Ukraine, and became especially prominent during the years 2012–14, when, under President Yanukovich's protection, his close associates set up record-size smuggling operations.[113] Thus, companies such as Vetek, led by Yanukovich protégé Serhii Kurchenko, easily pushed both legal importers and local refiners out of the market.[114] In addition, the proliferation of small illegal refineries (there were over a hundred in 2012), which were producing low-quality fuels and avoiding taxes, also undermined the role of established refineries.[115] More generally, the tax legislation still in place, which made the importing of oil products profitable, provided few economic incentives for owners to invest in refinery modernization.[116] This applied to both Ukrainian-owned refineries and to those purchased by Russian companies in the mid-2000s.

Raiding activities involving refinery assets also affected refining volumes. A prime example concerns the conflict around Ukrtatnafta (owner of the Kremenchug refinery) between Kolomoyskyi's structures and his Russian partners (the Tatarstan oil company Tatneft). After a corporate raid as a result of which Tatneft was de facto removed from the management of the company, in 2007 Tatneft stopped supplies of oil to the refinery, with consequences going well beyond it.[117] This was one of the factors leading to Kolomoyskyi's attempt to seek access to non-Russian supplies for Kremenchug, and his ability to reshuffle pipeline flows to the detriment of other refineries, which I discuss below.

The second way in which domestic actors' rent-seeking activities affected Druzhba was through the misuse, for private gain, of state-owned enterprises. Private control over formally state-owned companies was a pattern seen repeatedly in Ukraine (and also in other FSU states) during the postindependence period; in the area of oil transit, such issues were most clearly evident in the case of Ukrtransnafta, discussed above, which was responsible for the operation of Druzhba's Ukrainian segment. With Kolomoyskyi in control of Ukrtransnafta, the company's regulatory powers (with its headquarters in Kyiv as the regulatory node) were used in two main ways that would have a long-term impact on Druzhba in Ukraine.

First, as discussed above, Ukrtransnafta's operational control over Ukrainian trunk pipelines and their oil flows was used to favor Kolomoyskyi's refineries, to the detriment of competing refineries and refining as a whole. This was especially important because the company was in charge of the Odesa-Brody and Druzhba South pipelines, as well as the Pidvenyi/Yuzhny transshipment terminal in Odesa, and used this control to prevent rival refineries from receiving regular oil supplies, making their work unprofitable if not impossible. Kolomoyskyi's attempt to seek access to non-Russian supplies for Kremenchug, and his ability to reshuffle pipeline flows for this end, had a negative influence on other refineries' ability to receive needed supplies. The key victim was LUKoil's Odesa refinery; in 2009 Ukrtransnafta reversed the Odesa-Kremenchug pipeline to allow Kremenchug to receive (non-Russian) oil from the Odesa (Pidvenyi/Yuzhny) terminal, allowing the refinery to access oil by pipeline instead of much more expensive rail. Because of the routing and technical requirements of the pipeline, the Odesa refinery could only work with Russian oil if Kremenchug did as well.[118] As a result, LUKoil's Odesa refinery was unable to access its contracted supplies. Faced with a much higher oil bill, related to the need to import oil by tanker and having it transshipped at high cost by the Privat-controlled oil terminal, the Odesa refinery was shut down in 2011.[119]

That the oil carried to Kolomoyskyi's refinery by this pipeline reshuffling came from Azerbaijan instead of Russia speaks of the complex, often Janus-sided role played by actors such as Kolomoyskyi: occasionally presenting themselves as champions of Ukrainian national interests (energy diversification), while weakening Ukrainian statehood from inside through corrupt behavior.[120] This tension and this contradiction would come to a climax two years later, after the Euromaidan Revolution: on the night of March 19, 2015, when, in the wake of a law approved by the Verkhovna Rada reforming Ukraine's state-owned joint stock companies, the Ukrainian government sought to dismiss Kolomoyskyi associate Lazorko and regain control of Ukrtransnafta's management. After learning of the decision, Kolomoyskyi sent a private armed security group—in fatigues and face masks—part of the private militias he had been funding to support the Kyiv government against pro-Russian separatist forces in Eastern Ukraine, to raid the company's headquarters in Kyiv. While the raid was going on, Kolomoyskyi could be heard screaming in the background, accusing, in Ukrainian—a language he seldom used—and among loud expletives aimed at the press, "Russian saboteurs" of trying to storm the company.[121] This raid can be seen as a desperate attempt by Kolomoyskyi to prevent Lazorko's dismissal, but also as a warning that Kolomoyskyi's significant power should not be taken lightly; in fact, despite the ensuing formal change in the company's leadership, Kolomoyskyi's influence continued at an informal level.

Similarly, through his control over Ukrtransnafta (and also Ukrnafta, Ukraine's largest oil and gas producer), Kolomoyskyi was able to purchase Ukrainian-produced oil at below-market prices and to keep other refineries from accessing it, despite the fact that this oil was formally sold at auctions. This manipulation was made possible by Kolomoyskyi's control over Ukrtransnafta and trunk pipelines. Despite the formal existence of oil auctions, these had little meaning as the oil was physically made available in Kremenchug, and—given Kolomoyskyi's control of the pipeline and reshuffling of key routes—could only be transferred to other refineries at great cost, via rail or truck.[122] As in the first example, this damaged other refineries' business and refining in Ukraine as a whole. The price difference between these transportation options can in turn be related to oil's materiality, because they can be traced back to crude oil's liquid physical state, which makes the much more economical transportation by pipeline possible.

The second way concerned Kolomoyskyi's structures taking advantage of their operational control over Ukrtansnafta and Ukrnafta to steal from them, basically bringing them to bankruptcy from within. Kolomoyskyi's structures used this control to sell services to these at overinflated prices, while underpaying for oil.[123] Examples included overcharging for use of storage facilities at Privat-controlled refineries,[124] as well as the illegal removal ("pumping") of technological oil (also known as "technical oil") from several trunk pipelines operated by Ukrtansnafta,[125] including one of Druzhba's reserve lines in Western Ukraine in April 2014. Privat argued that the pumping was necessary in order to protect the oil from Eastern Ukrainian separatists. In addition to taking this oil illegally, Privat overcharged Ukrtansnafta for its storage, while actually not storing it but refining and selling it as oil products.[126] The damage to Ukraine and Druzhba was not only in terms of the financial loss but also in very concrete terms affecting national energy security: having lost its technical oil to Privat, Ukrtransnafta simply did not have the means to purchase it anew.[127] It has been estimated that through such activities, Kolomoyskyi's structures extracted several hundred million dollars from Ukrtransnafta.[128] Similarly, the misuse of the company to limit market access for competing refineries while privileging Kolomoyskyi's helped shrink Ukraine's refining industry and also the utilization level of pipelines such as Druzhba. As a result, if in 2000 Ukraine was transiting (through all pipelines) 56.4 million tons of oil per year, by 2011 this was only 17.7 million tons,[129] which also led to technical problems related to the loading and upkeep of Ukraine's oil transit pipeline system as a whole, as its average utilization was only 25 percent in 2009–11.[130] The discussion above shows the close link between the health of the refining system and that of Druzhba as a transit operation, in the sense that neither the economic profitability of transit supplies through Druzhba nor its optimal technical functioning could be guaranteed.

This was in stark contrast with the situation in Belarus. If the value chain had followed Druzhba North via Belarus, instead of Druzhba South via Ukraine, one would have found a significant amount of value added in the Belarusian spatial segment of the chain, specifically related to oil refining and reexporting. Without denying the importance of the special treatment Belarus received due to its unique relationship with Russia, domestic policies, and in particular a concentrated refinery modernization policy that allowed Belarusian refineries (and in particular, the Mozyr refinery, located about 50 kilometers from the Ukrainian border) to achieve a high output of light oil products from Russian Urals oil, made it possible for Belarus to maximize profits from these.[131]

Why Did the Oil Molecule Avoid Ukraine? Summarizing the Ukrainian Stage of the Physical Value Chain

As explained above, the riddle of why Ukraine's oil refining system collapsed so thoroughly is not so much a riddle as a "perfect storm" of several intermingling factors: external conditions fostering oil refining in nearby Belarus and Russia, a lack of investment, domestic policies decreasing or abolishing import duties that put domestic refineries at a disadvantage, and, last but not least, corruption. This last factor, corruption, made refining in Ukraine especially difficult by increasing transaction costs around it. Economists such as Williamson have used transaction costs to try to understand why some transactions are internalized through vertical integration, while others are given to other actors through contracts such as in outsourcing and pay-for-refining agreements.[132] Such transaction costs can be especially high in situations where a reliable rule-of-law system is not in place—a particularly sore issue for Ukraine where, in the period after independence in 1991, high levels of corruption could be observed. Such high transaction costs within the Ukrainian oil sector help explain the collapse of its refining industry: with refining as a whole being unprofitable due to the influx of lower-price imports, the vertical integration of the refining sector into the broader system of the Russian oil producers was not a realistic possibility. What remained was a system where transactions would occur not so much through anonymous contracts, where each party's obligations are clearly defined, but through relational contracting, where contracts are embedded in a structure of relations, as in the case of the Privat Group's de facto control of key players in Ukraine's oil production and oil transit system.[133] None of this bode well for the oil molecule in Ukraine.

Entering the EU Space at Budkovce in the Slovak Republic

Druzhba oil entered into EU territory at Budkovce in the Slovak Republic, a key point both in contractual and regulatory terms. Contractually, Budkovce is key because when EU firms purchase oil delivered through the Druzhba South pipeline, they purchase it at the Ukrainian-Slovak border at Budkovce. This meant the supplier (a Russian oil company through Transneft) had to deal with and pay for all the transit up to that point, including negotiating transit fees with the countries en route (Belarus and Ukraine), while the importer pays for and arranges transit via the countries west of the transfer point, that is, the Slovak Republic and the Czech Republic.[134] Although, as in the case of natural gas, this meant entry into a new regulatory space, EU regulations concerning oil transit and transportation were not nearly as complex or stringent as in the case of natural gas; until 2013, oil was only marginally included as a priority area in the EU's Trans-European

Networks.[135] (For example, if by 2014 the EU was pressing for an end to calculating natural gas transportation fees on the basis of delivery points in favor of entry/exit systems—see chapter 4—this was not yet the case concerning oil.)

In justifying these differing levels of regulation for natural gas as compared with oil, EU policymakers were going back to some of the materiality differences between oil and natural gas discussed in chapter 3, first and foremost the variety of transportation alternatives available for crude oil due to its liquid state, as compared with natural gas.[136] They were also making reference to oil's less obvious nature as networked energy, in contrast to natural gas and electricity. Thus in the case of oil, the impact of EU governance in our value chain would not be felt so much through direct transit-related regulations as through indirect ones (e.g., those related to environmental standards for fuel) as well as general EU competition rules.[137] The regulatory space crossed by Druzhba oil in the Slovak Republic was first and foremost represented by the regulations governing the Transpetrol pipeline system, which since 2009 had been owned exclusively by the Slovak state through the Ministry of the Economy.[138]

The role of Druzhba oil in the Slovak economy. Nearly 380 kilometers into Slovak territory, upon reaching Bučany, Druzhba divided again, with its main trunk continuing to the Czech Republic and a small, 620-kilometer side line ending at Slovnaft's refinery in Bratislava, the Slovak Republic's sole refinery. Thus Druzhba oil moving via the Slovak Republic constituted both oil destined for transit to the Czech Republic (discussed in the next section) and for use in the Slovak Republic; while physically undistinguishable, both were contractually distinct.[139] During the years 2011–14, the Slovak Republic was receiving oil on the basis of a state-to-state framework agreement that was signed in 1999 and in effect through the end of 2014.[140] This agreement was an exception to the company-to-company agreements most common for Russian oil exports to the Visegrad region by 2010, and may have been related to the unique history of the Slovak-Russian relationship. The Slovak Republic was the only non-CIS country signatory (observer status) to the 1993 Surgut Agreement establishing a joint CIS Commission on the development of the oil and gas fields in the Surgut area of Western Siberia. The Slovak Republic's participation in the agreement led to assumptions that Russia was applying deep discounts on oil and gas prices to the Slovak Republic in order to support the government of the pro-Russian prime minister at the time, Vladimir Meciar.[141] This Russian oil, delivered exclusively through Druzhba, constituted the totality of the Slovak Republic's oil imports as well as the entirety of oil used by the Bratislava refinery.[142]

Although Druzhba's load in its Slovak segment continued to decline in the 2000s (by 2009, being at less than 50 percent of its capacity of 20 million tons[143]), it continued to be important for the local economy. The Slovak Republic received about $50 million yearly in oil transit fees in 2012 and 2013, a figure that was still significant despite having fallen nearly 20 percent since 2008.[144] The Bratislava Slovnaft refinery (purchased in 2004 by Hungary's MOL) processed 5.4 million tons of crude oil (2012) per year, all of it Russian oil supplied via Druzhba. In contrast to the dire situation of Ukrainian refineries, during the reference period, Slovnaft's production capacities were in full use, producing gasoline and diesel for sale through its own 220 station-strong gasoline station network but especially for export—during our focus period, about two-thirds of Slovnaft's revenues came from exports to neighboring states (Poland, Austria, Germany, and the Czech Republic),[145] and they constituted nearly 5 percent of the Slovak Republic's total exports.[146] Although these exports were made possible by the technical modernization of the Bratislava refinery to comply with rising EU fuel standards (with Brussels as the regulatory node), the refinery was not upgraded to be able to use lighter, non-Urals/REBCO oil, and it remained, in a typical lock-in situation, technically tied to Russian supplies.[147] And though the Slovak Republic had the theoretical possibility of upgrading a connection to the Adria pipeline to import tanker oil (including that from non-Russian origin) from Trieste, this was not pursued during our focus period due to both pricing and technical issues—doing this would have made little sense unless the Bratislava refinery would be respecified to work with lighter oil.[148]

Crossing the Morava into the Czech Midstream

Oil not used by the Slovnaft refinery continued its transit journey. In crossing the Morava River at Hodonín, Druzhba oil crossed its last border as crude oil. From this point on, it could have only one destination: the Litvinov refinery, the end point of the Czech-Slovak branch of the Druzhba South pipeline. (Talks about extending the pipeline 160 kilometers up to the Leuna refinery in Germany stalled due to insufficient commercial interest.[149]) It had been nearly 5,500 kilometers and a nearly eight-week journey since Vateganskoe.[150]

The role of the Czech Republic and the Slovak Republic in Russian oil exports as a whole was small. Russian crude oil exports to the Czech Republic (via the Druzhba pipeline, as well as some additional amounts arriving by tanker to Trieste and then via the Ingolstadt–Kralupy nad Vltavou–Litvinov, or IKL, pipeline) constituted less than 2 percent of Russia's total oil exports.[151] Concerning the Slovak Republic, even when the country depended on Russian oil for 99 percent of its use, exports to this country, about 5.5 million tons per year, constituted less than 2.5 percent of Russia's total crude oil exports.[152] This must be seen in the context of the sharp difference in the overall volumes delivered via the Druzhba North and Druzhba South routes, a difference visible well before 2011. During the focus period, Druzhba North carried about 33 to 43 million tons per year (as compared with 15–17 million tons for Druzhba South), with Germany (about 16–23 million tons a year) and Poland (about 17–19 million tons a year) as key recipients, both receiving oil through Druzhba North.[153]

As discussed in the last subsection, the oil arriving in Litvinov was contractually different from the oil delivered to other destinations through Druzhba South. Based on the contract with the buyer (i.e., the company that would be processing this oil in the Litvinov refinery), the Russian exporter would have the oil transported up to the transfer point (Budkovce) on the Slovak-Ukrainian border. From there, the importer would negotiate transportation (including capacity use and transit fees) with the Slovak (Transpetrol) and Czech (MERO ČR) state-owned companies in charge of oil transportation in both countries.[154] These state-owned actors could affect the further course of the oil through the transit fees charged for transit over their territory.

Before arriving at the Litvinov refinery, Druzhba oil passed near one last important physical and energy security node. Although the Druzhba and IKL pipelines do not join, a few kilometers before Kralupy, some Druzhba oil had the chance to, moving through a parallel pipeline, mix with IKL oil at the Nelahozeves Central Crude Oil Tank (known as CCOT), actually a sixteen-tank "farm" covering over 2 square kilometers. This complex, operated by state-owned MERO ČR (which also owned and operated the IKL pipeline and the Czech segment of Druzhba), played two important roles. First, some of its tanks were used to blend Druzhba and IKL oil for particular client specifications. Second and most important, most of the complex was used by the Czech Republic's State Material Reserves Administration for storage of strategic petroleum reserves.[155]

Litvinov as a Destination

The Litvinov refinery as a destination of Druzhba oil is worthy of attention on several counts. It was the only refinery in the Czech Republic using as feedstock almost exclusively Russian (REBCO, Russian Export Blend) crude oil.[156] Although, in theory, Litvinov could operate with sweeter, non-Russian oil, it would make little economic sense given its technical configuration. (The Czech Republic's other oil refinery, Kralupy, had been modernized to work with sweeter, non-Russian oil already in the mid-1990s.) This had to do with the Litvinov refinery's history and technical specifications and the way they created a lock-in with patterns of physical supply. Although originally built under German occupation in the late 1930s to process coal,[157] the refinery's growth, rebuilding, and full switch to oil processing took place in parallel with the building of the Druzhba pipeline's branch via Czechoslovakia and the beginning of supplies in 1965. The factory was rebuilt exactly to capitalize on supplies coming via Druzhba, and it was optimized for the processing of the type of oil coming through it, medium-sulfur Urals/REBCO oil.[158] Such a specification to the typical type of crude to be processed is a common feature of refineries, allowing them to work more efficiently and profitably. And though in principle refineries can accept other types of oil than the one for which they have been specified, the more the crude oil used differs from the one for which the refinery's distillation units have been specified, the higher the refining cost and the lower the production yield, depth of refining, margins, and profitability. What this meant in practice is that Litvinov would not be able to use more than about 10 percent light (Caspian) oil.[159]

The refinery received most of its oil via Druzhba, plus (starting in 2012) a small amount of oil (also Russian REBCO oil) through the IKL pipeline connecting the Czech Republic with the port of Trieste.[160] Although IKL was built in 1996 with the specific goal of giving the Czech Republic and other Central European markets access to non-Russian, seaborne oil, during the focus period it also received Russian REBCO oil delivered by tanker; because of the IKL pipeline's ability to transit oil in batches, it was possible for Litvinov to receive this oil without it mixing with sweeter Caspian oil.[161] This was useful because the refinery and its parent companies could benefit from price differentials between pipeline- and tanker-transported REBCO oil (i.e., from contractual diversification), a situation whereby (in contrast to geographical diversification) the risks of dependency on a single supplier can be managed through the use of a variety of contract types and duration frames.[162]

During our focus period, from October 2011 to March 2014, oil was delivered to Litvinov under two fairly distinct contractual arrangements. The first covered the period through June 2013. Until then, the Litvinov refinery (through its parent company, Unipetrol, and its majority shareholder, the Polish PKN Orlen, Central Europe's largest oil company) was receiving oil from a variety of Russian oil companies on the basis of short-term contracts where prices and volumes were usually negotiated on a quarterly basis, which hindered advance planning for the refineries, because the Russian suppliers would be "within their rights to stop deliveries" in case of contractual disagreements.[163]

It was also during this period, in April 2012 and June 2013, that two key supply disruptions took place in Druzhba's Czech segment. In April 2012, immediately after the Baltic Pipeline System–2 (BPS–2), steering oil exports away from Ukrainian transit and into the Russian Baltic port of Ust-Luga, went online, oil supplies via Druzhba (to the Czech Republic) were reduced to 20 percent of their previous level for ten days. It has also been argued that the needed retooling of Rosneft and LUKoil's oil transit system to work with the new BPS–2 pipeline may have been the source of the problem.[164] This could have been intended as a test of whether refinery owners may be open to paying higher prices.[165]

The June 2013 supply disruption was somewhat more complicated, and it speaks of the complex relationship between the domestic Russian and external aspects of Russian oil trade relationships. In May 2013, after Rosneft's acquisition of Russia's third-largest oil company, TNK-BP (discussed below), and seeking additional volumes to export to China, it began to revoke contracts previously signed by TNK to supply crude oil to refineries belonging to other Russian oil companies (e.g., Gazprom Neft's refinery in Omsk). As a result, these other companies, facing problems with getting supplies to their own refineries in Russia, began to restrict their exports and redirect these volumes to supply their own refineries, creating problems for supplies to the Czech Republic through the Druzhba pipeline.[166] Starting in July 2013, this situation changed, with a new three-year supply contract between Unipetrol's majority shareholder PKN Orlen and Rosneft, which, after becoming Russia's "accidental oil champion" had by 2013 grown to the world's largest publicly traded oil producer.[167] This was the first longer-term contract in recent years affecting the refinery.[168] Its contracted volumes were intended to cover "from 60 percent to 100 percent of Unipetrol's total demand for REBCO crude,"[169] which explains the additional supplies from other Russian companies during this period.[170] This change was also related to domestic changes taking place in Russia during this period, in particular Rosneft's $55 billion acquisition of Russia's third-largest oil company, TNK-BP, finalized in March 2013, which helped consolidate its role as a dominant player in the market and as the world's largest oil producer.[171]

How unique or different was Litvinov from other Czech refineries? Its dependence on Russian grades of oil put it in sharp contrast with the second-largest Czech refinery in Kralupy nad Vltavou, which since its modernization and coupling to IKL in 1996 had been refining exclusively sweet, low-sulfur oil, mainly imported from Kazakhstan, Azerbaijan, and Algeria.[172] All in all, of all the oil supplies used by both Czech refineries in 2012, 63.5 percent were Russian REBCO oil, delivered both via Druzhba and the IKL pipeline.[173]

Litvinov and the rise and fall of LUKoil in the Czech Republic. The Litvinov refinery was at the forefront of the most prominent rise and fall of a single Russian company in the Czech Republic—LUKoil, the producer of the oil we have been following since Vateganskoe-Kogalym. Our focus period, October 2011 to March 2014, represented both a time of great activity by LUKoil in the Czech Republic and a period of intense scrutiny of this activity. LUKoil's interest in Česká Rafinérská (the entity controlling the Litvinov and Kralupy refineries), evident already from the 1990s, was directly related to value chain and value-added issues—a key motivation was the desire to increase the exporting of gasoline and diesel to EU markets, a goal that seemed hard to achieve given the outdated technological state of LUKoil's refineries in Russia, which were not able to refine oil to progressively stricter EU quality standards and EU market requirements. Thus the desire to gain access to refining capacities in the EU or near its borders.[174]

Although the company was able to gain a foothold in the Czech energy economy by achieving control over a large gasoline station network (Jet) in 2007, the products sold there did not come from LUKoil's own refineries.[175] Thus, if by 2011 the company had become one of the largest Russian oil exporters to the Czech Republic (upstream) and also had an important downstream role through the Jet network, it was not able to gain control of the key refining node that would have been crucial for using the Czech Republic as a gateway to EU markets. In 2009–10, LUKoil pressed again for the acquisition of Česká Rafinérská; this period was also rich with discussions about LUKoil's deep connections in Czech political and economic elites, such as LUKoil's use of income from its gas stations to support a foundation led by then–president Vaclav Klaus.[176] This took place at about the same time as other Russian energy companies were also acquiring assets in the Czech Republic and developing connections there.[177] Yet by the time our focus period starts in October 2011, LUKoil had lost its second bid for the Česká Rafinérská and its managers had apparently changed their minds concerning the importance of these assets. In 2011, after it had acquired refineries in Italy and (especially) the Netherlands, LUKoil announced that it no longer had a need for refining capacities in the Czech Republic, whose refining margins (and, thus, profitability) were lower than those of Dutch refineries.[178]

Power outside the spatial chain: PKN Orlen, Central European multinationals, and Płock as a commercial node. Thus, it was not LUKoil that ended up in control of Česká Rafinérská and the Litvinov refinery but a rising Polish oil company, PKN Orlen.[179] Thus the Litvinov refinery during our focus period needs to be seen not only in the context of its spatial location in the Czech Republic but also in the context of the entire system of PKN Orlen, Central Europe's largest oil company and largest company overall, and influenced by PKN Orlen's headquarters in Płock as a commercial node.[180] Czech refining volumes made up about 20 percent of the company's total refining sales, also including its Polish and Lithuanian refineries.[181] In terms of technological complexity, it was a "less complex asset" in PKN Orlen's portfolio, which was "capable of making adequate returns" but was distinctly less advanced than PKN Orlen's prize assets, such as the Płock (Poland) "supersite" refinery with deep conversion capacity and integrated petrochemical operations.[182]

However, it is important to note that during the focus period, the profitability of Czech refineries producing gasoline and diesel declined sharply (touching bottom in 2012–13 and somewhat recovering after that), largely as a result of trends in the international markets such as increased competition from oil products refined in non-OECD states and declining demand for gasoline in the EU.[183] This is especially clear when compared with the profitability (as evidenced by refining margins) of another type of oil product, petrochemicals (olefins and polyolefins, e.g., ethylene, propylene, and benzene used as chemical industry feedstock) produced in the Czech Republic by dedicated refineries (Paramo and Chemopetrol), which were also controlled by Unipetrol and PKN Orlen, whose profitability increased slightly while that for motor oil refining plummeted from 2012 to 2013. This touches directly on value chain issues related to diverse products made from a single feedstock (i.e., crude oil).

PKN Orlen's role as parent company to the Litvinov refinery meant that key decisions about the refinery, including those concerning its crude oil supply and production mix, where not made in the Czech Republic but at PKN Orlen's headquarters in Płock, the commercial node controlling Litvinov. In turn, the Polish state, with 27.52 percent of PKN Orlen's shares, was the largest shareholder.[184] The Czech state did not sign or control oil supply contracts to refineries in the Czech Republic, nor did it have "almost any way to regulate supply," because these contracts were fully under the control of private enterprises.[185] This challenges common perceptions of energy security and energy decisionmaking power as primarily state-level issues. Rather, this example prompts us to look at energy issues in the triangle between national policy, EU policy, and multinational corporation policy, as well as physical, commercial, and regulatory nodes.[186]

Although we are not privy to information about how PKN Orlen's concrete decisions were made, the literature on the factors affecting multinational oil companies' decisions on supplies and output mix at each refinery emphasizes risk management within the context of changing external market conditions, demand, competition, and regulations such as taxes. And though some saw "security considerations" as "rather of minimal impact" after 2014, the fact was that they had been of key significance in the past, and the fact that supplies via Druzhba South were expected to continue declining could not but have affected PKN Orlen's decisions concerning Litvinov.[187] These issues, however, appear to have been bundled by PKN Orlen under the broader category of commodity risks and not explicitly in a "risks from Russia" category. At least from PKN Orlen's perspective, as reflected in its yearly reports, the main issues affecting corporate decisions were related to the macroeconomic situation and the need to ride out risks over which the company does not have control, such as variations in crude oil and oil product prices and exchange rates.[188]

Diesel from Litvinov to Saxony

Litvinov, like the Czech Republic as a whole, produced nearly twice as much diesel as gasoline, which was representative of trends in the EU as a whole and of consumption trends in the country (which used much more diesel than gasoline), trends that had started to solidify after 2010.[189] This was part of a broader process of "dieselization" of the European economy, which was in no small part driven by the power of car and truck manufacturers—as well as refineries—and their ability to secure a much lower taxation level for diesel than for regular gasoline, as well as lower taxes on diesel engine cars, a policy that gained strength in the late 1980s.[190] The argument for lower taxes on diesel was based on the higher efficiency of diesel engines (assumed to be about 20 percent higher than gasoline engines), which was assumed to more than compensate for diesel's CO_2 emissions, which were about 14 percent higher.[191] As a result of these policies, diesel cars as a proportion of the EU's total passenger car fleet increased drastically between 1990 and 2015—from about 11 percent in 1990 to 35 percent in 2010 to over 40 percent in 2015.[192] In Germany, it went from 14 to 26 percent between 1995 and 2010; by 2012 diesel passenger cars outnumbered gasoline ones in terms of new registrations, a trend at odds with developments in other parts of the world.[193] This apparently small difference in the preferred transportation fuel actually had a major impact on the EU's security of supply, also highlighting the importance of oil products and their processing, including global market trends, as opposed to simply crude oil supplies.

Decisions about where to sell the oil refined into diesel at Litvinov were made by PKN Orlen. During our focus period, most of the gasoline and diesel refined by PKN Orlen Group's refineries in the Czech Republic was sold domestically in the Czech Republic,[194] but physical proximity to Germany (the Litvinov refinery was located less than 20 kilometers from the border) also opened new opportunities.[195] PKN Orlen and its refineries had access to German end consumers through their ownership of the Star gas station chain, which had a 6 percent share of the market. Starting in 2013, part of Litvinov's production was sold in Star stations in Saxony, via Unipetrol Deutschland and "direct truck supply from various road terminals."[196] So while Russian oil constituted the totality of oil refined at Litvinov, gasoline and diesel produced there was just a small percentage of German supplies—during the focus period, the Czech Republic exported about 150 milliontons of diesel yearly to Germany (all or most of it from the Litvinov refinery), about 0.5 percent of Germany's total consumption.[197] Our particular diesel fuel ended in the Star station in the Dohnaer Strasse on the outskirts of Dresden, flanked by the Schlosspark and, on the other side, the motor vehicle registration office. Although prices at the pump where slightly higher in Germany than in the Czech Republic (about 10 percent for gasoline and 5 percent for diesel), this was mainly due to the higher level of taxes on gasoline and diesel in Germany as compared with the Czech Republic (with the taxation difference higher for diesel than for gasoline); taxation above a minimum level set by the EU remained largely a matter for state-level competence.[198]

Conclusion: Materiality, Actors' Choices, and the Oil Value Chain

How did materiality issues affect the value chain analyzed in this chapter (see table 5.1)? How did power become manifested in this chain, and how did this manifestation intersect with materiality issues? Concerning power: the impact of Russian oil was not so much in terms of

TABLE 5.1
Oil Value Chain: Spatial and Technological Processes

Spatial Stage	Technological Process	"Stage" in Value Chain	Main Actors
Russian Federation	Extraction	Upstream	LUKoil
	Transportation		Transneft
Ukraine	Transportation	Midstream	Ukrtransnafta (+Privat Group)
Slovak Republic	Transportation	Midstream	Transpetrol
Czech Republic	Transportation	Midstream	MERO ČR
	Refining		PKN Orlen
Germany	Distribution	Downstream	PKN Orlen
	Sale to end users		

its role at the end of the chain or the end consumer in Dresden—after all, diesel refined from Russian oil exported to the Czech Republic via Ukraine constituted only a small fraction of total diesel supplies in Germany—but throughout the chain, through arrangements built around it. And the ways this power could manifest and unfold throughout the chain had a lot to do with oil's materiality characteristics.

As discussed at the start of the chapter, oil distinguishes itself by its relative heterogeneity; despite relatively broad variations in key characteristics (e.g., viscosity and sulfur content), crude oil is usually blended to produce a number of standardized brands marketed as such; this blending and branding allows firms to manage oil's heterogeneity by channeling it into a smaller number of widely marketed benchmark brands.[199] Another key characteristic concerns its liquid state. How did these features affect the value chain at the heart of this chapter? Three points emerge from the analysis of the Vateganskoe-Dresden journey. A first aspect of the impact of materiality that became clear through this case study (especially in comparison with the case of natural gas discussed in the last chapter) concerned the connection between materiality, transportation, and the creation of *distinct redistributive openings* within the chain (i.e., what profits and rents will be available, where, and to whom). Thus, some choices concerning the location of refining itself were made possible by key physical characteristics of oil, for example, the fact that oil could be refined at a variety of spatial locations, which synergized with the (at least theoretical) ability to be transported by a variety of means. This also affected rent-seeking possibilities: though oil, in contrast to natural gas, can be transported by a variety of means, spreading out transit income and both rent-seeking income and opportunities, the difference in costs between different transportation options still matters.[200] In our case, this meant, for example, that Ukraine's role as a major refining center, despite being anchored in an extensive Soviet-legacy infrastructure, could be easily replaced by refining elsewhere, leaving Ukraine out of a major value chain, and leaving behind major sunk costs, which materialized in increased deficits, unemployment, and, indirectly, mass labor migration to, among other countries, Poland and Russia.

Second, oil's less obvious nature as networked energy (i.e., the degree to which the overall functioning of the system may be dependent on the network as a network being balanced, as is most obvious in the case of electricity grids and natural gas, where loads need to be balanced to prevent a dangerous overload), as compared with natural gas, affected the level of regulation on the part of the EU. In this case this meant, for example, less of an interest on the part of the EU to commit to maintaining Ukraine as a transit hub, or EU-guaranteed investments in new supply routes, for example, from the Caspian.

A third and most important element concerns how oil's heterogeneity and the importance of differences between types of oil (in particular, between high- and low-sulfur oil) for the refining process played a key role in our value chain through technological lock-in, in particular the issue of which refineries could process the oil coming through legacy pipelines, and also the options open to upstream actors (producers—e.g., LUKoil) wanting to increase their value-added and associated income by refining closer to (or in) EU markets. On one hand, oil's materiality characteristics made such a strategy possible to start with—as oil, in contrast to natural gas, can be refined anywhere in the spatial realm between producer and consumer, as well as in locations not directly on the spatial supply line, as evidenced by the rise of Aruba, Curaçao, and Singapore as refining centers.[201] On the other hand, the uniquely tight coupling between feedstock product characteristics and the technology that can be used profitably to process it limited the kind of supplies with which a refinery such as Litvinov could work. (In an interesting twist that brings forth key materiality issues, an increase in the average level of sulfur in Urals oil transited via Druzhba South, observable since 2017, has led some refineries along the route to move away from such supplies, exacerbating a further roughly 9 percent decline in supplies via Ukraine to the Slovak Republic and Hungary in the first four months of 2018.[202]) At the same time, we should remember that, though differences in the physical characteristics of oil produced in different fields are real, specific oil blends are not nature-given but are "made" by commercial, technical, and (as seen in the case of Russia's REBCO blend) political considerations.

Thus, as discussed in chapters 2 and 3, the materiality characteristics of the starting good both enabled and constrained the range of choices available to actors in the value chain. In the case analyzed in this chapter, this enabling and constraining took place largely through two of the three mechanisms discussed in chapter 3. First, through the way these materiality characteristics affected the technical constraints of the value chain, in the process endowing (or not) actors at various levels of the chain with (more or less) power (mechanism 2, discussed in chapter 3). Technopolitics reminds us how technical requirements often shape political questions. This can be clearly seen from the example of Ukraine in the 1990s and 2000s, when various Russian actors' acquisitions of Ukrainian refineries were predicated on preexisting supply lines reified by the refineries, having been specified to work with particular types of oil. Although all other Ukrainian refineries had been specified to work with variations of medium-sulfur Urals/REBCO oil, the only refinery that could not work with this feedstock was the Krememchug refinery, which had been specified to process higher-sulfur oil from Tatarstan and Bashkorkostan, from which it received oil via the Michurisk-Kremenchug pipeline.[203] Given the level of regulatory capture and corruption prevalent in Ukraine's oil sector at the time, those in control of the domestic oil pipeline system could manipulate it to bring supplies to one refinery (Kolomoyskyi's Krememchug), but the impact of this manipulation (starving other refineries of needed supplies) was increased by the specification of refineries to work with particular grades of oil. In other words, if there had been less of a technical lock-in between specific refineries and particular types of oil, then Kolomoyskyi's manipulation of oil flows to assure supplies to his refinery would not have had such a significant impact on other refineries, because a single supply stream could have been more easily shared by various refineries.

Second, and most important, we saw how the material characteristics of an energy good had an impact on the typical challenges affecting its particular value chain (mechanism 3, discussed in chapter 3). In the case of oil, this concerned first and foremost the risk of price volatility and the need to adapt to swings in demand as well as to changing regulations. With motor fuel markets highly tied to end-consumer demand and the need to comply with specific EU regulations to be able to tap into this demand, oil producers faced both a risk and a challenge, to which they sought to partially adapt through refinery location and acquisition decisions, which would also affect relationships between actors.

CHAPTER SIX

Coal: Managing Subsidies from Kuzbass to Ukraine's Metallurgical Complex in the Donbas to Germany

THE LAST two chapters analyzed the natural gas and oil value chains, going from production in Siberia to end users in Germany. This chapter concludes the case study portion of the book by analyzing the coal value chain.

As discussed in chapter 3, coal distinguishes itself by its heterogeneity and wide variety of types available, with lignite coal (brown), hard coal (used along with lignite for power generation), and coking coal often used as broad subcategories. Our coal value-added chain concerns one particular type of coal: coking coal (also known as metallurgical coal), which is an essential component of metallurgical production and its transformation into specialized steel products. One of these specialized products, *quarto plates*, which is widely used in shipbuilding and energy infrastructure such as wind turbine towers, is the concrete product at the end of our value chain.[1] Among the wide variety of steel products, quarto plates were chosen due to the high-value-added nature of their business segment, coupled with their use in a variety of engineering and energy applications. Our value chain follows the coking coal molecule from Siberia to Germany (see figure 6.1).

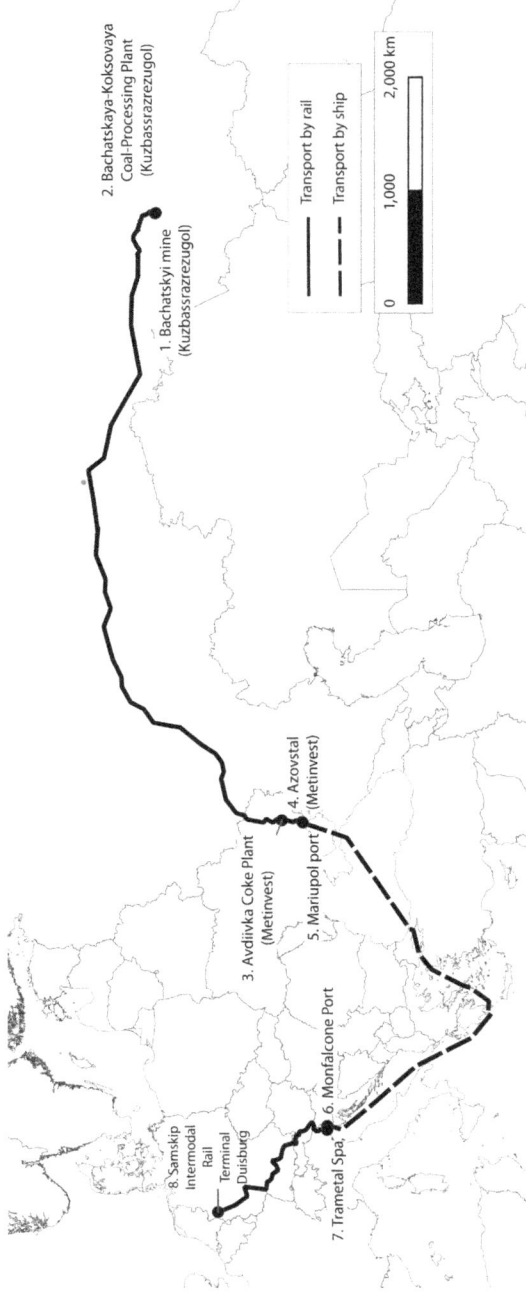

Figure 6.1 Overview of the coal-steel value chain followed in this chapter

Source: Map created by Matthias Neumann using QGIS and GIS data from Natural Earth (free vector and raster map data at naturalearthdata.com), OpenStreetMap (https://www.openstreetmap.org), and Wikipedia; further editing in Adobe Illustrator.

But before there was steel, there was coal. Our coal-steel value chain starts in Kemerovo, Russia. For coal from southern Siberia to end up as steel in Germany, it would need to undergo a complex journey—not simply in terms of transportation but also processing.[2] This processing often took place through politically and economically perilous territory—indeed, few other sectors of the post-Soviet and EU economies have been as contested as the coal sector.

As discussed in chapter 2, in contrast to natural gas or even oil, the physical transformations our coal molecule went through from production in Russia to final steel consumers in Germany were quite complex. In contrast to natural gas's transit journey, where a complex infrastructure was put in place exactly to make sure that natural gas's characteristics would remain *unchanged* through this journey, and also in contrast to the case of our oil value chain, where physical transformation (refining) took place at the end of the pipeline nearly 4,000 kilometers from the start of the transit journey, coal's journey from production in Russia to final use as steel in Germany was a tortuous and complicated one, marked not only by multiple transshipment points but also by several physical transformations: from coking coal to coke used in metallurgical production, and from coke to steel and its specialized products. Although some of the differences between the natural gas, oil, and coal journeys had to do with the specifics of the sectoral governance environment (e.g., corruption levels in specific sectors and countries) at each spatial component of the supply and value chains, important differences also go back to differences in the physical characteristics of the goods themselves. These differences, as discussed in chapter 2, also affect key characteristics of the value chain as a system—for example, through the ways in which they affect the transportation process.

Some readers may be surprised to see coal receive full treatment in this book alongside natural gas and oil. (See chapter 2 for a discussion of the book's case selection methodology.) Coal is apparently not sexy. On one hand, being plentiful, low-priced, and largely ubiquitous by being found in most countries rather than concentrated in a few, it has long been taken for granted, in contrast to scarcer and more "strategic" oil and natural gas. Moreover, coal is often presented as on a fast track to be eliminated from our planet's energy mix as a result of de-carbonization initiatives restricting CO_2 emissions, and thus coal often seems as if it had fallen off our radar. However, as noted by the International Energy Agency, despite the outcry about its negative environmental effects, in the decade between 2004 and 2014, coal's role as a source of primary energy was nearly as significant as "the rest of the fuels— fossil, nuclear, and renewable—combined."[3] During this period and in subsequent years, new coal-fired generation capacities were being built worldwide, making coal far from marginal to global energy issues.

During this same decade, nearly 30 percent of the European Union's coal imports came from Russia, a level roughly similar to that of oil or natural gas. And though coal's multiple transportation options make the danger of a high-stakes cutoff much less likely than in the case of pipeline-transported natural gas (e.g., Russia's gas cutoffs to Ukraine in 2006 and 2009), it was coal that proved to be Ukraine's specially painful Achilles' heel after the Crimean annexation and the start of Russian-supported separatism in Luhansk and Donetsk in 2014, when it found supplies from territories no longer controlled by Kyiv extremely hard to replace.

The coal value chain analyzed in this case study uses as an *exemplary chain* the journey of coking coal from production in Kemerovo, Russia, through final use as quarto plates in Germany's renewable energy infrastructure. Our journey follows this chain largely via the production and marketing chain of Metinvest, the metallurgical arm of System Capital Management (SCM), Ukraine's largest financial and industrial group (SCM's other key company, DTEK, is Ukraine's largest coal producer),[4] which is controlled by Ukraine's richest oligarch business actor, Rinat Akhmetov.[5] In following this chain, this coal went through the very heart of Ukraine's energy-political system as it existed from 1991 to 2014, and through the interests and strategies of its most important economic and political actors.[6]

Let us first outline the technical process that accompanies the coal-to-steel (coking coal to steel quarto plates used in wind turbine towers) chain followed in this chapter (see figure 6.2).[7] The first stage in the process involves producing coal of the necessary grade to produce coke (coking coal); master-blending, sorting, and cleaning this coal; and transporting it to coke-making facilities (coking plants), where, through a complex and energy-intensive process, coking coal is turned into coke (which is almost pure carbon) by heating the coal in special airless ovens to drive out impurities. From there, coke is transported to a metallurgical plant, where its is combined with a second key feedstock, iron ore, and small amounts of scrap metal to produce pig iron in a blast furnace. At this stage, coke is used both as fuel in the smelting process and/or as a reducing agent in driving off the impurities of the product in the blast furnace. This process

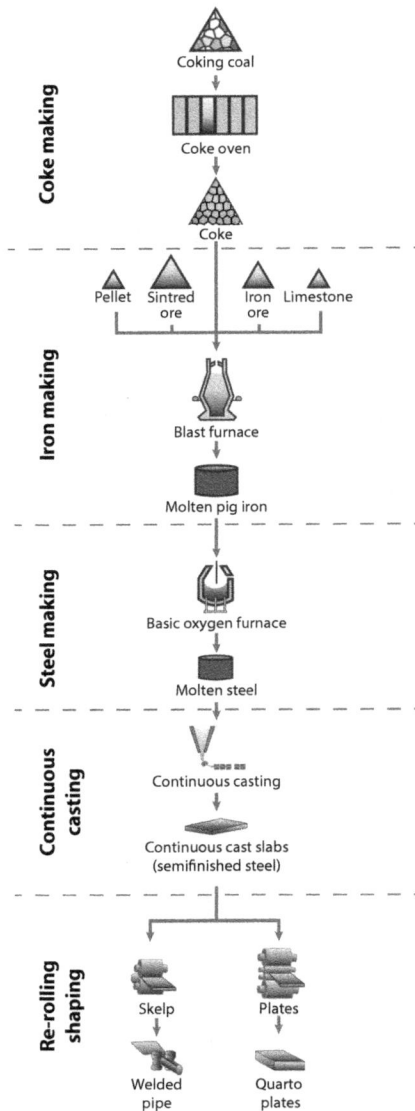

Figure 6.2 From coking coal to steel quarto plates using the BOF process

Source: Figure by Tamian Wood (Beyond Design International, *tamianwood.com*), based on information in this chapter.

yields pig iron (crude iron produced in a blast furnace) containing high levels of impurities, which need to be removed (through "refining") to make steel.[8] This "refining" takes place as follows: pig iron (in ingot or liquid form[9]) is transferred to a furnace, where oxygen is blown into the iron to remove the carbon and other impurities; slag is also produced, which absorbs the impurities, keeping them separate from the steel.[10]

The crude steel produced by this step is not yet usable by end consumers. First, various alloys may be added to create specific steel grades. Second, what is produced with crude steel are not final products but a variety of intermediate castings, including "flat products" such as large-format steel slabs. These castings require additional processing to produce the shapes and qualities needed by end consumers. This necessitates re-rolling (i.e., the shaping of larger pieces of steel into thinner sheets of a specific thickness by passing them through two rolls). This technically demanding re-rolling process may take place in-house or in separate factories (i.e., steel re-rollers, also known as secondary steel producers). After this, the resulting products are most often galvanized (coated with zinc) to improve corrosion resistance. A particularity of this process is the dependence of each stage in the chain on the availability of highly specified feedstock materials.

THE GLOBAL AND REGIONAL MARKET CONTEXT

Although this chapter focuses specifically on coking coal and not steam coal, understanding the context of the coal sector as a whole is key to understanding the factors affecting the export of coking coal (from Russia), as well as the demand for imports of Russian coking coal (in Ukraine) and for finished steel products (in the EU).

What were some of the key global trends affecting the coal value chain during the focus period? In an interesting intersection with the gas and oil chains discussed in chapters 4 and 5, the prices for steam coal fell by more than 50 percent between 2008 and 2014, reflecting its global surplus after new shale gas production in the United States freed large volumes for export.[11] This impact was especially sharp in the EU, particularly in comparison with natural gas prices. One impact on Russia was that while during our focus period coal exports remained competitive, profit margins were "squeezed dramatically" as a result of the additional competition from coal pushed out of the U.S. market due to new supplies of unconventional oil and gas.[12]

On the coking coal side of the question, after a spike in 2011, prices declined by nearly 50 percent between then and 2014, reflecting less demand for steel.[13] In turn, world prices for steel, while showing an upward trend, did not recover from their sharp fall in mid-2008 as a result of the global economic crisis. A key global trend was China's consolidation of its position as the world's largest steel producer and exporter (between 1998 and 2007, it increased its crude steel production by nearly 500 percent).[14] Steel markets during this period were characterized by an increase in excess production capacity. Such overcapacity was triggered by factors such as China's offering of steel at dumping prices, and, more generally, politicians' (in various countries) unwillingness to close large steel mills due to the potential political impact of massive job losses. At a regional level encompassing the former USSR and the EU, 2011–14 was a period of further pressure on the EU steel industry, as competition from cheaper steel (especially from China) increased, while production remained largely stable (also in the former Soviet Union) and consumption declined.[15]

FOLLOWING THE VALUE CHAIN: UPSTREAM

This section describes our coking coal molecule's journey from the mining process to the beginning of its transportation by rail. Although in this part of its journey it would move little in terms of distance, it is a segment rich in the impact of Soviet and Russian technopolitical choices.

Kemerovo

The coking coal exemplary chain starts in the Kuznestskii Basin (better known as Kuzbass), in the Kemerovo region, which is part of the Siberian Federal District in southwestern Siberia. With the closest large cities hundreds of kilometers away, the region is not exactly what would come to mind as a "central location."[16] Yet though geographically peripheral, the region was central both to the coal industry and to the symbolic production of coal mining as a symbol of Soviet prowess and of coal miners as Soviet labor heroes. It is here where 60 percent of Russia's coking coal production originates. Although other areas such as Vorkuta were also important producers, it was here in the Kuzbass that the Soviet celebration and mythification of coal miners was at its highest.

Although organized coal production had existed in the region since the mid–nineteenth century, it was in the high Stalinist period in the late 1940s when large-scale mining infrastructure started to develop, setting the basis for even larger, open-pit operations in the 1950s and 1960s. One of them was the Bachatsky open-pit mine, part of the Kuzbassrazrezugol company. It is in Bachatsky, first established in 1949, that our coal journey properly begins. Bachastsky does not fit the conventional image of coal mining as presented in the Soviet iconography of miners going underground to the pit in elevators, lamps on their foreheads and miners' axes in their hands. Rather, Bachatsky is a *razrez*, an open-pit mine and (according to Kuzbassrazrezugol) the first place in the world where coking coal started to be mined using the open-pit method, in 1966.[17] The open-pit mine area is located 20 kilometers from its administrative headquarters in the town of Belovo, and occupies three large fields, an area much larger than the town itself, fields where the earth has been turned around and a shallow, crater-like space characterizes the landscape. If Bachatsky was a pioneer in the open-pit mining of coking coal, by the start of our focus period, this was no longer exceptional, with 72 percent of Russia's coal coming from open-pit operations in 2012.[18]

Bachatsky's mother company, Kuzbassrazrezugol, was Russia's largest company specializing in open-pit mining.[19] The word *razrez* rightly conveys the idea of a cut in the ground. Explosives blow open parts of the surface to expose the coal, whereupon giant Belazi trucks come in to take away the pieces. To the extent that any tourists come to the region, a common pastime is to go "hunting for Belazi," not a totally risk-free pastime given the size of the trucks—just their tires are more than 4 meters high. Operating on such a different size dimension than normal passenger vehicles, the gigantic Belazis may easily oversee anyone in a regular-size vehicle.[20]

The specific production process at the Bachatsky mine had a clear impact on workers' health due to the high concentration of chemicals in the air. The cumulative impact of dozens of such mining operations on the area went beyond the miners themselves, because it affected the small indigenous population of the region, the Shor and Teleuts, whose traditional way of life based on hunting and fishing was totally disrupted by large-scale mining.[21] At issue was not only the coal-production activity itself but also the fact that, after an area was stripped of coal, the open pits were usually not rehabilitated but left unattended, creating a spectral, desert-like landscape and contaminating water resources long after production stopped.[22]

While carrying with them legacies of the Soviet era, Bachatsky and its mother company Kuzbassrazrezugol were part of a Russian coal industry that had been significantly restructured since 1993. A first stage of this restructuring involved the closing of uneconomic mines; between 1993 and 2000, loss-making ("unviable") coal companies employing nearly half a million miners were closed down, 105 of them in the Kuzbass area.[23] The social costs were very high; because many of the closures coincided with the 1998 economic crisis, wage arrears and reduced government funding to compensate for the lost jobs led to massive strikes in May of that year, including in Kemerovo. Only after 2000 did the situation begin to improve. A second stage of the restructuring involved the privatization of viable mines and the dissolution of Rossugol, the holding where state mining assets had been concentrated before privatization.

Despite its inherent difficulties and social costs, the reform succeeded in eliminating the vicious circle of coal mining subsidies: if by 1993 they had amounted to about 1.05 percent of Russia's gross domestic product (GDP) and were largely spent on compensating mines' operating losses, by 2000 they were largely eliminated; whatever small support of the sector remained was devoted to ameliorating the social costs of the mine closures, and not to covering mines' operating losses.[24] This transformation of the coal sector was accompanied by deeper and deeper inroads of metallurgical companies into it; by 2005 almost all mining companies had been absorbed by metallurgical operators seeking access to coking coal, iron ore, and other raw materials. This was key to meeting their supply chain needs, because most steel production requires iron ore and coke (most often derived from coal) as important raw materials. Kuzbassrazrezugol's managing company, the Urals Mining and Metallurgical Company (UGMK, the Russian initials for Uralskaya gorno-metallurgicheskaya kompania) was typical of this situation, bringing together over fifty enterprises from the raw materials and metallurgical sectors, allowing it to run a vertically integrated production system. (Metallurgical companies are interested in accessing both coking coal and other types of coal, because steam coal may be used to produce the electricity required to run the metallurgical facility as a whole; see figure 6.3. In addition,

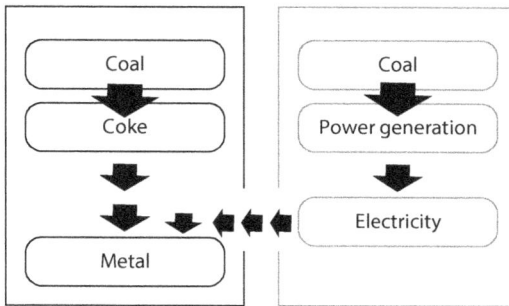

Figure 6.3 The interconnection between the two main coal-related value chains

Source: Figure by Tamian Wood (Beyond Design International, tamianwood.com).

some grades of noncoking coal can be expertly blended to produce the various grades of coke needed for metallurgical production.)

What was the regulatory environment facing a company such as Kuzbassrazrezugol as it made key decisions? Although subsidies had been largely eliminated, the restructured Russian coal market was far from a level playing field, and remained open to political pressure. By 2011 a largely oligopolistic system had developed, with eleven large mining companies accounting for over two-thirds of Russia's coal production (including Kuzbassrazrezugol, as Russia's second-largest coal producer); small producers faced serious profitability problems.[25] Coking coal production in particular was controlled by a handful of vertically integrated metallurgical companies such as Mechel, Evraz, and Severstal.[26] The very emergence of many of these large mining players can be traced back to the early 1990s "nomenklatura privatization" processes, when, in the context of the process of consolidation of state activities under Rossugol (with the goal of further privatization), managers of state mining enterprises carved out their own enterprises' most profitable assets and acquired them through privatization processes that often were not fully transparent. (Although Kuzbassrazrezugol produced mainly steam coal, and coking coal represented only 6 percent of its production, its coking coal production is comparable with that of these better-known companies; during the focus period it also had one of the highest percentages of coking coal exports compared with production.[27])

At the same time, the patronage of mining business by regional political leaders remained high. This also was the case with Kemerovo

Oblast, which was home to Bachatsky and its mother company, Kuzbassrazrezugol. Kemerovo's long-standing governor (1997–2018), Aman Tuleyev, a veteran of the Kemerovo coal industry, was credited with guaranteeing good relations with the main coal companies and supporting their business in the region, while ensuring that some of their profits would trickle down in the form of social programs. Although this role may have required Tuleyev to turn a blind eye to safety regulations with the aim of increasing production (in 2007 the Ulyanovskaya mine in Kemerovo was the site of Russia's worst mining accident since 1991[28]), he managed to maintain stability despite changing economic conditions.[29] He also managed to keep the region a reliable source of electoral support for President Vladimir Putin. Tuleyev's ability to guarantee stability and a high degree of workers' quiescence was all the more remarkable against the background of Kemerovo's history—Kemerovo and Novokuznetsk had been the centers of the 1989 miners' strike that exposed perestroika's weaknesses and complicated Mikhail Gorbachev's attempts at reform, and of further strikes in 1998.[30]

Leaving aside its limitations, Russia's coal market reform was successful at significantly increasing the country's coal production after significant declines in the 1990s. Kemerovo's production grew even faster, doubling between 1996 and 2011. By 2012, it had reached a historical record (201.5 million tons of yearly production), even higher than at any point in the Soviet period. Yet this very increase created new problems: with domestic consumption stagnating, the increase in production created new pressures to export.[31]

FOLLOWING THE VALUE CHAIN: MIDSTREAM

This section follows our coal molecule through the midstream segment. In the case of the coal-steel value chain, midstream operations include sorting, initial processing, transportation, and processing into semifinished products.

Initial Processing

Compared with the processing of natural gas and oil, coal processing before further use is a relatively simple operation, and is mainly related to washing, ash removal, and sorting in coal preparation plants (CPPs) before shipping.[32] In this process, also known as "beneficiation," various common contaminants such as rocks are removed from run-of-the-mine coal, so that the product achieves a degree of homogeneity; the broader term "coal processing" also involves the sizing and sorting of the coal.

Although it is not technically necessary to process/wash coal before transportation, whether this is done or not has a huge impact on the further course of the value chain, with consequences for various actors down the road. Despite its relative simplicity, coal processing makes a significant difference in terms of heating value. Russian run-of-the-mine (unprocessed) steam coal has an average of 4,600 calories of heating value per kilogram, whereas processed coal has about 6,000—a large difference.[33] Similarly, coal with a high humidity content is more likely to freeze during rail transit in the winter months. Thus, low levels of washing of steam coal meant larger volumes of coal would need to be transported in order to fetch the same sales revenue.[34] Here the physical characteristics of coal as a good (e.g., its being a high-volume/low-value good) play a key role by magnifying the further impact down the road of decisions at other levels of the value chain, such as coal preparation.

Despite improvements after 2007, the lack of sufficient coal washing capacity in Russia continued to create problems, both in terms of exports and domestic use of coal. The fact that only a fraction of steam coal was properly washed at a coal-processing plant meant that most often it was untreated, run-of-the-mine coal that was shipped. This also created domestic problems, because most coal used for domestic power generation was unwashed; the high ash content of unwashed coal means less efficient power generation, as well as increased CO_2 emissions and pollution.

Washing at the Bachatskaya-Koksovaya Coal-Processing Plant. Coking coal had a higher chance of being washed than steam coal did—in the focus period, about 90 percent of the coking coal produced in Kemerovo went through a coal-processing plant, a much higher proportion than steam coal's 26 percent.[35] Thus, before entering the railroad system, most of the coking coal produced at the Bachatsky open-pit mine was processed at the Bachatskaya-Koksovaya CPP belonging to Kuzbassrazrezugol near the village of Startobachaty, a shiny and relatively new (2008) CPP built with participation from the American company CETCO and located less than 10 kilometers from the open-pit mine.[36]

The Russian Railways System as a Physical, Commercial, and Regulatory Node

The next technical and regulatory node Bachatsky coal and Kuzbassraz-rezugol had to deal with was the Russian Railways system. The coal trade—and Russian coal exports in particular—is unthinkable without the railroad. The area between the town of Belovo and the villages of Bachatsky and Starobachaty is crisscrossed by railroad tracks, a reminder of the importance of rail freight for regional coal mining. Here coal encountered the next node in its journey: the Russian Railways freight system (which carried about 95 percent of coal transported domestically[37]), as first gatekeeper to transportation to domestic consumers, to other continental points, or to ports for overseas exports. Although generally the production cost of coal in Russia was much lower than in other countries, this was largely offset by high transportation costs. As late as 2013, despite cross-subsidization and lower per-unit freight tariffs for coal than for oil or metal,[38] transportation costs constituted about 50 to 60 percent of the final cost of steam coal and about 30 to 40 percent of the final cost of coking coal, compared with less than 10 percent for oil, and about 20 percent for metallurgical products.[39] To this price element should be added a number of serious logistical challenges, such as insufficient capacity, constant problems with access to freight cars, and coordination with the few, privately owned ports with coal terminals able to service large ships usually used for seaborne coal transportation.[40]

Some of these problems and issues had to do with coal's materiality characteristics. As discussed in chapter 3, as a "bulk dry cargo," coal shipping requires manual intervention to a much larger extent than natural gas or oil. Once at the port, the need for manual transfer from freight cars to ships further complicates exports.[41] As a "dirty cargo" usually leaving a residue in freight cars, it requires dedicated freight cars and cannot simply use a pool of general-use cars on an ad hoc basis. Some of these challenges were unavoidable given the location of Russia's main coal production areas thousands of kilometers away from large urban clusters and export ports—in 2012, coal for domestic use traveled an average of 850 kilometers, and coal for export 4,400 kilometers.[42] The Kuzbass Basin's nearly equidistant location between ports used for exports to Asian markets (Vanino on the Pacific, 5,306 kilometers away) and ports used for shipments to Western markets (e.g.,

Novorossiysk, on the Black Sea, 4,411 kilometers away; Murmansk, 4,732 kilometers away; and the Ukrainian ports used until 2014 for coal shipments, e.g., Pivdennyi/Yuzhny near Odesa, 4,733 kilometers away[43]) should have given coal producers in the region a wide range of choices concerning what to do with their coal: sell it domestically, use it as part of their own firm's cycle of metallurgical production, or export it to Western or Asian markets, or former Soviet Union states such as Ukraine. In reality, however, coal producers' choices were both constrained and enabled by existing infrastructures and the material characteristics of coal as a good which—due to its high volume but low value—can best be transported along long distances by train.

These factors put the Russian Railroads (RZhD) in a unique position as gatekeeper to domestic sales and exports. In turn, the role of rail freight in Russia's coal transporting must be seen within the context of the RZhD's privatization and reorganization since the 1990s. If at first this process took place rather informally (and, after 2003, more formally), one key trend could be discerned: the fact that key changes took place not through the privatization of the railways themselves but, in a "vertical separation" model, through the privatization of freight cars; between 2007 and 2012, nearly 50 percent of RZhDs freight cars came to be controlled by "a network of RZhD subsidiaries and private companies,"[44] at times suspected of having connections with the RZhD leadership, and in particular with Vladimir Yakunin, its longtime president (2005–15).[45] In contrast with the RZhD itself, these subsidiaries were neither subject to tariff regulations nor obliged to serve as a "common carrier" giving full access to all clients, which automatically increased their profit margins.[46] Some also argued that these special privileges granted railcar companies created an artificial deficit of freight cars.[47] Accusations of corruption related to the distribution of scarce goods such as freight cars were repeatedly seen in the press; coal business (occupying the first place, with 25 percent of its total freight[48]) could bring significant gains for RZhD employees involved in corrupt deals.

Although not a node in the conventional image of a geographically constrained location where physical changes in a product happen, the rail system—analogous to the gas transit system, for example—can be considered a technical node in the sense that it should protect the integrity of the product. A key difference, however, concerns the level of networkness: for a pipeline to work properly, a set of physical conditions (e.g., pressure) needs to remain in balance throughout the system, whereas in coal shipments problems such as localized bottlenecks, though at times highly disruptive, cannot abruptly bring down the system as a whole.

In addition, without being a constrained location, the railway freight system can be seen as a node, in the sense that it is a space for the contestation and negotiation of various players' interests: various vertically integrated coal-metallurgical companies, smaller producers, regional administrations, coal-dependent power plants, the tariff-setting Federal Tariffs Commission, and the high-level management of RZhD as representatives of the corporation and/or as individual rent-seeking actors. The role of the RZhD in Russia's coal transportation also involves key governance issues, for example, the coordination of various modes of transportation also involving different ownership structures (e.g., state-monopoly railroads and privately owned railcar companies and port terminals[49]).

In addition, governance issues come up around issues related to the setting of transportation tariffs for coal, and also through the issue of corruption. These transportation bottlenecks exacerbated the processing issues discussed above. Russia's coal transportation challenges were not only technical ones but were also deeply steeped in regulatory issues. This was so in two main ways. First, coal production and use issues in Russia are closely tied with issues of electricity generation and of the choices made by actors in that sector, which underwent a major restructuring after 2005. Second, choices are not only about domestic use versus exports but also, in some cases, between export as raw materials or as generated electricity (an item the Russian government vowed to significantly increase by 2035).[50]

COKING COAL FROM KEMEROVO TO THE DONBAS

In the second part of its journey, coking coal from the Bachatsky open-pit mine, both washed and unwashed, made its way to the Adviivka Coke Plant (Avdiivskyi koksokhimichnyi zavod) belonging to Met-invest in Adviivka in the Donetsk region of Ukraine, 100 kilometers from the Russian border—and over 4,000 kilometers from the coal's origin in Kemerovo.[51] Although, as discussed above, such long overland journeys were a regular feature of Soviet supply chains, they were not considered the ideal either. Thus the Soviet attempt to develop several priority metallurgical areas (e.g., the Kuzbass in the Russian

Federation and the Dnipr, Donetsk, and Azov metallurgical regions in Ukraine), each including, in close proximity, all the basic feedstock needed for metallurgical production—raw materials such as coal for electricity and coke production, iron ore, and water—as well as coking plants and steel and metal factories. Adviivka was located in one of these areas, the Donetsk metallurgical region.

From Exporter to Importer: Pride versus Geological Reality in Ukrainian Coking Coal

The goal of these priority metallurgical areas was to guarantee easy access to needed feedstock (i.e., a high degree of self-sufficiency) in order to minimize the need for long-haul transportation of such high-volume cargo as coal. Yet, despite priding itself on being one of the few large metallurgical companies encompassing each stage in the value chain, by 2011 Metinvest, reflecting broader Ukrainian trends, was covering only half its coking coal needs. Such large imports were interesting, given the Donbas's traditional coal-producing role. Why was the Ukrainian Donbas suddenly importing coking coal?

After all, coal and Ukraine's Donbas were long seen as undistinguishable. Coal had been produced in the region on an industrial scale since the building of a dedicated railroad line in 1874.[52] With coal ubiquitous in the area, common lore had it that "even Donetsk soil" would burn as coal.[53] The region's coal resources were long a point of pride. If in somewhat different ways for Soviet propaganda, local inhabitants, and Ukrainian émigré communities, Donbas coal had become a key element of pride.[54] Mythologized in Soviet propaganda, it was exhalted in endless speeches praising the results of the latest five-year plan. Their anti-Soviet orientation notwhitstanding, it was also a point of pride among (anti-Soviet) Ukrainian émigré communities, from Australia to Argentina. Generations of Ukrainians abroad grew up going to Sunday schools where pride in Ukrainian coal was nourished; coal was seen as a resource on which Ukraine could rely in a postindependence period.

Specifically with regard to coking coal, until World War I, the area was the sole producer of coking coal in the Russian Empire. In the early 1980s, Ukraine produced nearly half the USSR's coking coal exports.[55] Even in 1990, 37 percent of the entire USSR production of coking coal came from Ukraine.[56] It was exactly due to its mineral resources, including coking coal, that the central government—both

Tsarist and Soviet—had decided to invest heavily in the region as a mining-metallurgical center. Yet for all the patriotic fervor associated with Ukrainian coal, both the quality of its coking coal and its production conditions were problematic. At this point, Ukraine's coking coal imports need to be seen within the context of the technical needs of steel production and of coal's materiality characteristics. Although in theory coke used in metallurgical production can be produced from other substances (i.e., oil) besides coal, technological lock-in made coal-derived coke an irreplaceable feedstock for the Soviet metallurgical industry, which used it as a heating and reduction agent.[57] For these characteristics to be obtained, a specific grade of high-quality coal needs to be used as raw material for its transformation, in dedicated coke plants, into metallurgical-grade coke.[58]

Ukrainian coking coal has a high sulfur content, which reduces the calorific value of the resulting coke, increases shipping costs, and may result in brittle and unusable coke and lower-quality pig iron.[59] It is also hard to mine because of its geological conditions—its location at great depth and the extreme thinness of the coal seams make it harder to extract mechanically; it also contaminates it with rock, increasing the ash content.[60] The quality of Ukrainian coking coal has declined since the 1930s and especially the 1950s, when its best and more economically attractive grades started to deplete.[61] Soviet central planners started to shift investments to Siberia and Kazakhstan, where coal, located "in thick seams near the surface," was easier and more economical to produce.[62] This was followed, in the mid-1970s, by a further redirection of metallurgical investments away from the Donbas and toward central Russia and Siberia. Thus many Ukrainian mines started to suffer from underinvestment even before the demise of the USSR.[63] In many ways we can see a parallel between this decline in coal production and that observed in the case of oil and natural gas; where the decline in production from the 1950s to the 1980s was so steep that "no other region or republic has seen its energy position change so rapidly for the worse than Ukraine."[64]

However, the decline in the quality of Ukrainian coking coal—whose easy availability had been one of the main rationales for the development of Ukraine's three integrated coal and metallurgy complexes—did not mean the end of a Soviet policy of support for such complexes. This was so for two reasons. First, despite problems with the quality of coking coal, the regions around Kryvyy Rih, Kremenchug, and Mariupol remained exceptionally rich in iron ore, the other key raw material needed for the production of pig iron and, from it, steel. Second, this has to be seen in the context of the pressure exercised by regional party leaders (in key Ukrainian regions, but also elsewhere in the USSR) for a degree of regional economic autarchy.[65]

Beyond Geology: An Aside into Ukraine's Haphazard Road of Coal Mining (Non)Reform

In addition to these longer-term geological issues, issues relating specifically to the Ukrainian political environment in the early post-Soviet period further reduced the availability of high-quality coking coal. This requires a somewhat longer aside on Ukraine's coal-mining policy in the first postindependence decade.

The Ukrainian Soviet Socialist Republic was a key player in the Soviet economy; gaining independence in 1991 did not erase the dependencies developed over decades of Soviet planning. Yet the disorderly manner in which the partial unmaking of these bonds took place exacted a huge toll on the Ukrainian economy. Purchases of Ukrainian products by Russian partners collapsed; between 1990 and 1994, Ukraine's GDP fell by nearly 50 percent, and was accompanied by hyperinflation and serious liquidity problems.[66] The coal sector quickly became a center of attention, both due to its exacerbation of budget deficits and its political significance (by 1991 the sector employed nearly 1 million people, who depended on the industry for both wages and social services). From the very beginning of their engagement, the international financial institutions to which Ukraine turned for support, such as the World Bank, directed their attention to the coal sector and the economic burden of its subsidization, which by 1993 amounted to 4 percent of the country's GDP.[67]

Ukrainian politicians of the time were also extremely concerned about the mining sector, albeit for partially different reasons. Coal production had declined by nearly 50 percent from 1990 to 1995, which, in the context of growing problems with oil supplies from Russia, prompted security of supply fears.[68] Thus, from the very beginning there were conflicting motivations for coal sector reform, which would have myriad implications in the next two decades. For the international financial institutions, the emphasis was on reducing subsidies and closing unviable mines.[69] For the Ukrainian leadership, the priority was both maintaining production levels and preventing instability in a socially volatile area. That coal issues had a high potential to lead to political instability was well known to Ukrainian politicians—they needed only consider the disruptive potential of any repetition of the miners' strikes of 1993 protesting economic conditions, which had precipitated a political crisis and early elections.[70] These strikes are significant not only as a vivid representation of the social cost of coal sector reform but also as a preview of a trend that was still to come: the instrumental use of coal miners' grievances and fears by actors interested in blocking reform, not because of concern for miners' well-being but because of their own interest in making a profit from the privatization of government subsidies for themselves, while socializing the costs of these subsidies and of nonreform in general. In an example of how technopolitics may enter the scene through the way in which technical requirements help shape political questions, the very possibility of corrupt actors using such a strategy was related to the materiality characteristics of coal as an energy good—to the fact that, as discussed in chapter 3, it requires a high level of human labor relative to the sale price of the good, along with significant human intervention in shipment and transshipment.[71]

Indeed, official policies in the first post-Soviet years were aimed not at reducing subsidies but at keeping all mines in operation.[72] Although many mines (both during and after the Soviet period) lacked investment support for modernization, large sums were spent to maintain employment and meet production targets, a haphazard combination with often "catastrophic economic results."[73] With resources being used to keep mines in operation rather than make investments, unviable mines were allowed to continue to drag down the system, while the viable ones did not have enough investments to function properly.[74] At the same time, a new type of actor was entering the sector, whose emergence was related to the deficits of the transition period and who, once finding a role in it, would turn into one of the biggest hurdles to reforming the sector: the pusher-turned-oligarch. Understanding the further movement of Bachatsky coking coal in the supply and value chain of Ukrainian steel requires a small detour into their role in the 1990s and beyond.

Supply Chains, Pushers-Turned-Oligarchs, and the Ukrainian Coal Sector's (Non)Reform

Although supply chain problems were already evident during the Soviet period despite the façade of central planning, they became even more acute after the demise of the Soviet centrally planned supply relationships between enterprises.[75] Factories were left without the feedstock needed for production and without customers to buy this production. Indeed, how to (re)structure these supply chains and establish each newly independent state's role in the international division of labor was the key challenge facing the post-Soviet economies after the unplanned end of the Soviet planned economy in 1991. These challenges had an especially significant impact on the Ukrainian coal and metallurgical sector because, in an example of a close coupling situation, the technical requirements of the metallurgical supply chain make each stage in the chain highly dependent on the availability of highly specified feedstock materials. Thus a pipe factory cannot produce pipes if it does not have the specific grade of steel needed. The steel factory, in turn, cannot produce steel if it does not have coke, a key agent necessary for the production of steel and pig iron.[76] The coking plant cannot produce coke if it does not have available specific grades of coking coal. And in situations of consumer product shortages such as those seen throughout the former USSR in the early 1990s, the mine may not work if it does not have access to consumer goods with which to—in a barter variation—pay miners.

This was exactly the challenge and the opportunity that a group of young Donetsk managers (e.g., Serhii Taruta) and assorted actors (e.g., Rinat Akhmetov) seized upon in the early 1990s, even before the dissolution of the Soviet Union.[77] Akhmetov, Ukraine's most influential oligarch of the post-Soviet era, whose name will come up repeatedly in this chapter as head of Ukraine's largest coal-and-metal empire, was one of them, but by no means the only one. The prehistory to his becoming Ukraine's wealthiest citizen is shared by other actors, such as Viktor Pinchuk and Serhii Taruta, all originally from Donetsk (thus the common reference to the "Donetsk group" and "Donetsk clan"), and original members of the ISD (Donbas Industrial Union), from which Akhmetov would later part ways to create his own group, System Capital Management (SCM), Metinvest's mother holding company. These individuals, who would later become some of Ukraine's richest oligarchs, started their money-making careers exactly in the supply chain chaos of the early 1990s, in the netherworld between a market that was not yet functioning and a state supply system that was no longer functioning. In this netherworld, they were part of what the Ukrainian historian Volodymyr Holovko has called the "chaotic search" for new forms of industrial organization appropriate for the new conditions.[78] They acted as freelance supply specialist "push-ers" (*tolkachi*)–cum–investors, helping enterprises gain access to criti-cally needed feedstock that otherwise was unavailable, doing the job that state organizations such as Gossnab, the Soviet State Committee for Material and Technical Supply, were no longer fulfilling.[79] These groups' regional basis helped them fulfill the goal of reestablishing links within spatially proximate enterprises.[80] Later in the chapter, we will return to Akhmetov and the rise of his metallurgical empire, but for now it suffices to note how the rise of these groups synergized with Ukraine's lack of coal sector reforms to worsen the country's coking coal deficit situation. In addition to long-standing coal quality issues, this was the second main reason for increased coking fuel imports, which I explain below.

"Gossnab and Gosplan in One"

Key to the rise of these groups was their role in supply chain manage-ment in a situation where needed supplies were simply not available for purchase in the open market.[81] If, in Taruta's words, the supply chain chaos of the 1990s required him to be "both Gossnab and Gos-plan in one," in the sense of not only providing needed supplies to specific enterprises but also arranging for the sale of their products, this profitable role could be made even more profitable by gaining greater control over the involved enterprises—first informally, and later (see below) through formal ownership.[82] As actors such as Taruta and Akhmetov gained inroads into metallurgical industries, gaining vertical control over coal mines and their production became crucial in order to secure access to needed feedstock.[83]

Looking at the same issue through a theoretical lens provides fur-ther insight. As discussed in chapter 5, institutional economists such as Williamson have looked at related questions (why are some transac-tions internalized through vertical integration, while others are given to other actors through contracts and outsourcing?[84]) through the prism of transaction costs. Looking at the same general question, in some of their key work on supply chains, Gereffi and colleagues discuss the various ways in which actors in a supply chain may be coordinated: from market-based coordination, where relations between multiple possible suppliers and multiple possible consumers are decided in a free market through prices, to, on the other extreme, relationships based on vertical integration, where all the steps in the chain take place within the same enterprise. In their framework, one step removed from vertical integration are captive relationships—relationships where one lead firm has "captive suppliers" at its disposal.[85] This characterization is useful for understanding the rise of Donbas coal and metal groups as, given the impossibility of using prices to create and coordinate a market, they set on perfecting and defending other ways of establishing and preserving their role in the Ukrainian coal and steel value chain. They did this exactly through the establishment of captive relationships with suppliers ("capturing" coal mines to supply metallurgical enterprises under their control) and, later, by establishing their own vertically integrated enterprises. During a first period (especially until about 2004), organizations such as ISD and Metinvest held factual management control (which would be close to a "captive" relationship, in Gereffi's terms) over the coal mines (through long-term leases, control of the management, and the provision of machinery at overinflated prices[86]), but without actual ownership. These "captive supplier" mines provided ISD-controlled metal factories with coal at low "indicative prices" (usually below cost), which created a double subsidy for their production.[87] First, low-cost coal lowered these metal factories' production costs, increasing their competitive advantage. Second, they were able to take advantage of state subsidies to the mines, subsidies exactly intended to fill the financial gaps created by their working at a loss. This created incentives to inflate losses, disincentivizing coal sector reform.[88] This combination of factors led to a situation where, by 1995, about 30 percent of Ukrainian coking coal was produced in mines with a unit cost above import parity (i.e., with unit production costs higher than the import costs for equivalent products); to produce this coal, which the mines sold to metallurgical companies at a loss, the wages of 100,000 miners were partially or fully subsidized by the state.[89] So, though some mines were chronically unviable because of their geological situation, others were unprofitable exactly because of the fact that they were forced to sell their production below cost by the metallurgical companies controlling these mines (or, more accurately, intermediary companies controlling both, such as Azovimpeks, which was also controlled by Akhmetov).[90] As noted by the International Energy Agency, average wholesale prices for coking coal lagged behind average production costs by 20 percent or more per ton for most of the 1990–94 period.[91] The situation was slightly better in the steam coal sector, but not by much. For this plan to function, it was actually more advantageous for economic groups to control the coal mines (in a captive supplier relationship) than to own them (in a vertical integration relationship), because this maximized the size of state subsidies.

The absence of a transparent, price-based market coordination between multiple suppliers and consumers was not simply a deficiency to which the new coal and metal entrepreneurs had to adapt—it was what made their rise possible in the first place, and the environment in which they thrived. Thus, their preference for keeping the price of coal supplied to metallurgical industries under their control (and artificially low) is key for understanding why these actors would do everything possible to prevent transparent pricing in the area.[92] This desire to keep prices artificially low applies both to the early period based on captive supplier relationships as well as to a subsequent period marked by direct ownership. It also serves as a reminder that value chain and "value added" are not necessarily interchangeable.

It was only in 2004 that the first coal company was privatized— Pavlohradvukhillia, to Rinat Akhmetov's SCM, followed a few months later by the coking coal mining association Krasnodonvukhillia, moving SCM into the terrain of documented ownership and vertical integration.[93] It could be asked: why move to legal ownership when informal control allowed the best of both worlds, both control and the continuation of state subsidies? The answer has to do with sector newcomers' desire to, in a "winner takes all" scenario, use a second stage of reform (i.e., that characterized by privatization) to secure property rights and consolidate their gains so as to block further reforms.[94] The answer also has to do with the specific political situation of the mid-2000s. After 2004's Orange Revolution brought an end to the Leonid Kuchma regime and to its division of spheres of influence (under the motto "politics is made in Kyiv, business is made in Donetsk"), Akhmetov's and other Donetsk groups were (temporarily) pushed away from the center of power. The need to protect their investments gave Akhmetov's SCM an incentive to restructure its business to become more transparent and also to build modern corporate structures for the two coal-related, value-added chains in which it was active: the coal–power generation–electricity chain (DTEK, established 2005), as well as the coal-coke-steel value chain (Metinvest, established 2006). In addition, an insiders' privatization of iron ore mining and processing enterprises, conducted under President Kuchma's tutelage, led Akhmetov (together with Vadim Novistskii and Kuchma's son-in-law Viktor Pinchuk) to acquire the lion's share of such state property. Assets acquired in this way became an important basis of Metinvest holdings.[95] By 2011, DTEK (SCM's second branch) was by far the largest coal firm in Ukraine, producing half the country's total coal output.[96]

It may be asked: after Akhmetov acquires legal ownership of a number of coal mines, why may he have wanted to continue with artificially low prices for coal, when those low prices would have affected the profitability of his own mines? The answer lies in the fact that further manipulations remained possible, including tax manipulations and the reclassification of metallurgical coal as steam coal so as to lower its price.[97] Moreover, in terms of Akhmetov's interest in both businesses, metallurgical exports clearly had the upper hand as they were much more profitable. Yet due to the decline in domestic supplies, by the 2000s price manipulations alone were no longer able to guarantee Metinvest low-cost access to the amounts of high-quality, low-ash coking coal required to produce coke for its metallurgical operations.

This brings us back to the question posed at the beginning of this section: how did these trends synergize with the issue of availability of high-quality coking coal? The way actors such as Akhmetov and ISD became involved in the market already in the late 1990s affected the coking coal situation we would see in 2011–14 in two main ways. In the short term, the price manipulations and misappropriation of state subsidies in the 1990s created disincentives for transparency and reform, and robbed resources that could have been used for promoting viable mines and their production. Day-to-day decisions made by those controlling these mines in the 1990s also had important medium-term effects. Searching for quick profits, those who took control of mines often pushed production well above the design capacity of the mines, affecting their long-term viability.[98] This combination of factors led to a significant decline in coking coal production—from 35.3 million tons in 2004 to 26.2 tons in 2009 and to 25 tons in 2011.[99]

Metallurgical groups responded to this situation by increasing their imports of higher-quality coking coal from a variety of suppliers (mainly, but not only, Russia). In some cases they also acquired coking coal mines in Russia and the United States to supply these needs (in 2009 Metinvest acquired and started imports of coking coal from the United Coal Company in the United States). Yet these other imports (also including small amounts from Poland and Kazakhstan) remained limited in favor of supplies from Russia, which followed well-known Soviet era supply chains, first and foremost, those originating in the Kuzbass (and, less frequently, Vorkuta).[100]

By 2010, about 90 percent of Ukraine's coking coal imports were coming from Russia, and Ukraine had become one of Russia's largest coking coal importers; between 2010 and 2014, about one-third of Russia's coking coal exports were going to Ukraine.[101] Ukraine was, for these years, the single largest recipient of Russian coking coal exports after Austria, with which it was nearly tied.[102] And, within this period, Ukraine's imports from Russia increased significantly, from 5.579 million tons in 2010 to 6.725 million tons in 2014.[103] This was in addition to purchases of Russian coking coal through trading companies with ties to Russia registered in Cyprus and Switzerland.[104]

The Adviivka Coking Coal Plant

Where did this coking coal imported from Russia go to, and how did it become part of Metinvest's profit structure? The coking coal imported by Metinvest from Kuzbassrazrezugol's Bachatsky open-pit mine (either as run-of-the-mine unwashed coal or as washed, "beneficiated" coal and coking coal concentrate that had gone through the Bachatskaya-Koksovaya coal-processing plant) arrived by rail freight to the Adviivka Coking Plant. At the plant, located in the town of the same name in the outskirts of Donetsk, they became part of the custom blends used in the coke production process, and were added to coal coming from Metinvest's mines in Ukraine and—in a much smaller proportion—the United States. Such coking coal supplies were needed in large quantities—nearly 1.5 tons of metallurgical coal are needed to produce 1 ton of coke.[105]

There was no better place for this coking coal to go than to Metinvest, which accounted for nearly half of Ukraine's overall coke production during our focus period.[106] Of Metinvest's coking facilities, Adviivka was the largest, and one of the largest coke producers in Europe.[107] The history of the plant went hand in hand with the history of Soviet supersized metallurgical dreams in Donbas. It had been established in 1963 to supply coke to the Mariupol Ilyich Iron and Steel Works (Mariupolskii Metallurhinii Kombinat, MMK), part of a Soviet Council of Ministers 1955 decision calling for the replacement of old-technology coke plants in southern Ukraine with more modern ones,[108] and was a Soviet state-of-the-art facility at the time, producing a variety of chemical by-products in addition to coke.[109] The plant was also the first in Ukraine where coal was stored in covered storage instead of in uncovered deposits.[110] In 2006 Adviivka was fully acquired by the Metinvest group, which (through SCM) already had exercised informal control over the company since at least 2004.

An Aside on Metallurgy, Industrial Spatiality, and Identity: "It Was Never Ukraine Here"

If the name "Adviivka" rings a bell for most of those following Ukrainian news after the start of the military conflict in Eastern Ukraine, it is not because of its industrial prowess but because of the tenacity of its workers and managers.[111] Located just a few hundred meters from the front, the plant has been repeatedly under separatist fire. If this in itself was not surprising given the importance of the plant as a key economic asset, it was the loyalty and resilience of plant employees—living in the plant's basement for weeks at a time, and remaining on duty despite significant losses—that was most impressive. If the Adviivka Coking Plant of our focus period was a more run-of-the-mill Soviet-type company with little associated heroism, there was actually one profound continuity between the Soviet and post-Soviet periods: the sense and locus of loyalty. This was not necessarily to Ukraine (or, before 1991, to the Soviet Union), but to the factory itself. Much research on Soviet company towns points to the enterprise itself, not necessarily the town, as an important locus of loyalty, and this was exactly the case with Adviivka.[112] The explanation for such a localization of loyalty on the factory itself also had to do with the legacies of Soviet glorification of metallurgical work and its association with a bright socialist future, as well as with the role played by enterprises as guarantors of personal well-being during the Soviet period in a monotown situation.[113] Thus, for example, the entire city of Adviivka depended on the factory for heating and water supplies. Here, technological considerations also play an important role; because of their need for large amounts of water and energy, coking plants usually have their own water access infrastructure and electricity generation facilities, which may also supply areas around the plant.

For all the heroism attributed to the Adviivka Coking Plant after 2014—when it found itself under constant attack from the separatist territories—during our focus period it was not a particularly Ukrainian or pro-Ukrainian locus of identity. If there was loyalty, it was to the company (after 2006, to Metinvest), and, even more, to the factory as a spatial location itself, as if abstracted from "Ukraine" or "Russia." In the case of Adviivka, this facilitated a certain type of spatial, site-based coalition that trumped broader national allegiances. Through studies of the ethnography of labor process, scholars such as Burawoy have analyzed the importance of the "shop floor" in the constitution of interests and identities;[114] similar links can be observed in other Soviet and post-Soviet factories.[115] Key players such as the director (2012–19) Musa Magomedov—born in a small village in Dagestan, and educated in Donetsk, Kyiv, and Moscow—had biographies that were deeply reminiscent of Soviet value and supply chains. The town's media landscape, like that of much of Donbas, remained tied almost exclusively to Russian-based radio and TV broadcasters. This was largely so even after 2014.[116] And even the most local of news media, the Adviivka Coking Plant newspaper *Zavodchanin* (*Factory Worker*), seemed to have little space for anything Ukrainian—before or after 2014.[117] The particularities of the production process in a location such as the Adviivka Coke Plant facilitated a certain type of site-based coalition that trumped broader national allegiances.

The next stop in the coal-coke-metal chain was the metallurgical giant Azovstal in Mariupol, located 157 kilometers from Adviivka—an almost irrelevant distance when compared with the 4,400 kilometers coking coal from Kemerovo had to travel to reach Adviivka, but still significant considering the fact that coke is much more sensitive to quality losses during transportation than coal is.[118] Coke supplies were key to Azovstal because, for each ton of steel produced, at least 600 kilograms of coke is required.[119] (A second key raw material in the first stages of production is iron ore, the supply of which came from Metinvest's own iron ore deposits.[120])

Azovstal and Mariupol as Exemplary of Soviet-Style Industrialization

In reaching Azovstal, the coke was also reaching Mariupol, a model Soviet industrial city, but in a very different way than Adviivka. If

Adviivka was a model Soviet monotown, Mariupol was, with a population of half a million, a large industrial center with several huge plants
creating the largest industrial center in the Donetsk region—in addition to Azovstal, the MMK Steel Works and Azovmash, Ukraine's largest producer of mining and metallurgical industry machinery.

Although Mariupol's metal industry dated from the Tsarist period
(MMK was established in 1897), Azovstal, inagurated in 1933, was a
quintessentially Stalinist project, one of the largest Stalinist industrialization projects in the region.[121] It was largely as a result of projects
such as Azovstal—as well as Ukraine's other major full-cycle steel producers, MMK, Krivoryzhstal, and Zaporizhstal, and the development
of dedicated mining-metallurgical regions—that Ukraine became the
largest metallurgical producer per capita in the USSR. By the mid-
1980s, Ukraine was producing more than a third of the Soviet Union's
crude steel, ferrous metals, and cast iron.[122]

At Azovstal, coke supplied from Adviivka was combined with iron
ore and small amounts of scrap metal to produce pig iron, and from
it, a variety of steel products, in particular intermediate castings, of
which continuous cast slabs are the best known. By 2010, such continuous cast slabs had come to occupy a prominent place in Azovstal's
production, distinguishing it from other metallurgical factories in the
region, including neighboring MMK. Especially after the opening of
a new continuous caster in 2008, Azovstal became "one of the largest
global producers and exporters" of steel slabs, the most common type
of semifinished steel.[123] What are continuous cast slabs, and why do
they matter? They are not a final product but are the most common
type of semifinished steel. Similar to billets, they are an intermediate
casting requiring further processing before final use.

At this point, a small aside is needed to explain the role of coke and
coking coal in different steel production processes, which require different amounts and grades of coke (and coking coal) to produce steel,
and to place Azovstal's and Metinvest's production in this broader context. The least advanced steel production process, open hearth furnace
(OHF), requires coke as both heating and reducing agent; the basic
oxygen furnace (BOF) process, used at Azovstal, also uses coke in both
roles, but in smaller amounts; and the most advanced electric arc furnace
(EAF), based in the smelting of scrap metal, does not use coke at all.[124]

Azovstal produced steel plates using mainly the BOF system (about
82 percent of its production), as well as (until 2010) the much less

advanced OHF technology (about 10 percent in 2010).[125] These shares were representative of the general picture of steel production in Ukraine around this time, where 74 percent of steel produced was produced using the BOF, and about 20 percent using the OHF process.[126] Although these country-wide figures represented an improvement over 2000 figures, when half of the steel in Ukraine was—in a strong path dependency from Soviet-period OHF-based production technologies—still produced in OHFs, the highest level in the world,[127] Ukraine's use of advanced, energy-efficient steelmaking technology remained limited. Even by 2014, Ukraine's proportion of steel produced using the more advanced EAF systems remained the lowest in Europe. The use of these technologies had implications for Azovstal's energy consumption, for the link between the coal-coke-metal and coal-generation-electricity chains, and for Metinvest's interests in accessing inexpensive energy supplies—the less advanced processes require significantly more coking coal and coal as feedstock. Thus another reason for the high demand of—and need to import— coking coal in Ukraine was the continued prevalence of less advanced and more coke-intensive steel production methods.

Similar to coke production, steelmaking is a very energy-intensive process. In this way, both the coke-making process and the steelmaking processes brought together the two coal-related value chains controlled by Donetsk oligarchs: the coal-power generation–electricity value chain associated with Akhmetov's other key company, DTEK, and the coal-coke-metallurgy chain associated with Metinvest. The synergies between these two value chains noted in figure 6.3 were strong for producers using the OHF and BOF production processes, but nearly null for those using the EAF system, such as Viktor Pinchuk's Interpipe, which has used no coke in the production process since mid-2011.

Azovstal as Key to Donetsk-Based Barter Schemes and Russian Market–Oriented Exports

Azovstal was a key component of the Donetsk energy-political system (discussed below) and, in particular, to the origins of a number of signature Donetsk group barter schemes. These schemes—which were especially prevalent in the early 1990s because of widespread liquidity problems—were used both for payments to workers and exports to

Russia.[128] Barter arrangements had also been key in the establishment of ISD's (and, later, SCM's) control over coal mines and metallurgical companies such as Azovstal.

In this connection, let us recall how Azovstal came under informal and formal Metinvest control. This took place through much of the same process whereby coal mines, coking plants, and other infrastructure in the coal-steel value chain came under the control of ISD and, later, Akhmetov's Metinvest: first, through control of both the feedstock (coke and coal) needed by the factory and of the factory's sales by ISD-affiliated intermediaries (first and foremost Azovimpeks, which made huge profits while bankrupting the company as a means to reduce its price for subsequent purchase); second, through informal control of top management positions through cooptation or intimidation,[129] so as to face no opposition to such policies; and third, through the gradual acquisition of formal share ownership through often flawed privatizations.[130] These steps were completed by 2000, the year Akhmetov decided to separate from ISD. Subsequently, he and ISD's Taruta reached a division-of-assets agreement in which Akhmetov took, among others, Azovstal and the Khartsyzsk Pipe Plant, some of ISD's most profitable assets.[131]

The Coal-Steel Value Chain within the Context of the Donetsk Energy-Political System

More generally, the further stages of this value chain (i.e., the production of exportable steel and other metallurgical products made with the use of coking coal) took place within the context of a broader "energy-political system" in place in the Donetsk—and in Ukraine in general—where the coal sector as a whole was central.

In chapter 2 we discussed how energy is best analyzed not simply as a state-held weapon but also as a resource that may be used by a variety of actors in a variety of ways and with a variety of goals. Taken as a whole, these uses constitute an energy-political system that may be national or regional in character, and reflects broader governance conditions in specific spatial segments of the chain. We speak of a Donetsk energy-political system because of the close concentration of energy-related assets and industries in the region, encompassing energy raw materials, generation, metallurgy, and energy-intensive machine-building and military industries using this metal.[132]

Such a regional system could only exist within the framework of a national governance system that made its continuation possible—for example, the informal "balancing" of powerful business-administrative groups ("clans"), or the unspoken division of responsibilities during the Kuchma period (1994–2004), when Donetsk actors would be given free rein in the region as long as they would not interfere with politics in Kyiv (the "politics are made in Kyiv, money is made in Donetsk" system). Some key elements of this system as it involved relations with Kyiv were the Donetsk group's "service" in terms of helping prevent the rise of a hard-line communist opposition, and rejecting open political regionalism, while instrumentalizing workers' grievances and demands for their own purposes.[133] In the process, a degree of political consensus emerged in the region, shared by all major regional actors, which "culminated in the formation of a regional 'party of power,' the Party of Regions."[134] Rinat Akhmetov was far from an innocent bystander in such processes. His engagement with the Party of Regions took place at several levels. First, his large-scale financing of the party (where he also controlled a group of Rada members directly accountable to him) made him a co-creator of a particular type of Donetsk/Donbas politics. Second, he was able to use his vertically integrated industrial empire for political goals, for example, through the role of the directors of vertically integrated and paternalistically run companies in bringing out the vote for Yanukovich. For example, it was this close political connection with Yanukovich that made it possible for Akhmetov to gain control of a significant share of Ukraine's thermal electricity generation (by 2016, 65 percent—eleven of fourteen plants) and electricity distribution *oblenergos* (40 percent), in addition to coal production (50 percent),[135] and to place his associates in key regulatory positions, such as in the National Commission of Electricity Regulation (NKRE), which allowed key regulations to be changed in his benefit, for example, the regulation prohibiting any single company from controlling more that 25 percent of the electricity generation market.[136] Akhmetov and the Party of Regions also used the Donbas identity issue to stoke fears of regional separatism as a scare tactic to elicit more autonomy (along the "politics is made in Kyiv, money is made in Donetsk" lines discussed above) and subsidies from Kyiv.[137]

This energy-political system was based on key economic players' (oligarchs) interests in the upstream coal sector (i.e., that associated with coal production) not only benefiting heavily from government subsidies but also from convincing coal workers that the continued subsidization of the sector was in their interest, and using sector workers' mobilization for their own goals. An early example of this connection stems from 1993, when miners' strikes to protest declining living conditions had the end effect of placing (for the first time) a representative of the Donetsk group (Yefim Zviagilskiy) as (acting) prime minister, and putting coal mining reforms on ice.[138] In the 2000s, the role of this group grew significantly as export income from the sector grew, boosted by the mid-2000s upswing in the world economy and demand for steel.

By the time of our focus period, 2011–14, such energy-political system was changing in two central ways. First, if until then energy-intensive metallurgical production was subsidized by natural gas prices significantly lower than EU ones, the 2009 gas supply contracts with Gazprom (see chapter 4) opened the door to much higher energy prices for metallurgical operations depending on gas-generated electricity. Second, despite Akhmetov's key role in the financing of Viktor Yanukovich's campaign, with his accession to the presidency in 2010, the existing Kyiv-Donbas compromise came under stress as Yanukovich started to give members of his own inner circle ("family"), such as Serhii Kurchenko, control over key rent-seeking opportunities in the coal and mining sector, which encroached on the now formally established business operations of groups such as Metinvest, and on the de facto balance between key economic/oligarchic groups.[139]

An Aside: Azovstal and Value Chains Eastbound and Westbound

This chapter follows Azovstal's role in a value chain directed westward toward end consumers in the European Union. We should not forget, however, that Azovstal has also been key for a different value chain: that built around supplying steel slabs to the Khartsyzsk Pipe Plant (also controlled by Metinvest) to make large-diameter, electric-welded pipes using a unique anticorrosion technology, and for these to be supplied to Gazprom in exchange for natural gas.[140] (Paradoxically, some of these pipes where used to build the Yamal-Europe gas pipeline that, by rerouting to transit via Belarus part of the Russian natural gas volumes hitherto transited through Ukraine, reduced Ukraine's role in—and income from—this transit.) Indeed, it was exactly around Azovstal—and led by the company's former head of foreign economic relations, Serhii Taruta—that key barter schemes related to exports to Russia were created in the 1990s.

Although the modality of such steel pipe–natural gas exchanges changed starting in the early 2000s as barter sales started to be replaced by cash sales, the main direction of the value chain remained largely unchanged throughout the first two decades of Ukrainian independence: to the east, in the direction of Russian oil and gas companies. This book and chapter focus on the coal-steel value chain going from Russia to Ukraine to Western Europe; however, it is important to note that the original Azovstal-related value chain embraced by ISD and intermediary companies affiliated with it was directed eastward, not westward.

During our focus period (2011–14), both directions in the value chain continued in parallel, with metallurgical-related export income from each direction being nearly equal (thus, e.g., in 2011, 25.6 percent of Ukraine's metallurgical exports went to the Commonwealth of Independent States and 27.5 percent went to Europe; and in 2013, 29.5 percent went to the commonwealth and 26.4 percent went to Europe).[141] The beginnings of Ukraine's 2014 Euromaidan Revolution—with the November 2013 protests sparked by President Yanukovich's sudden decision not to sign a long-sought-after association agreement with the EU—were exactly about what direction should Ukraine focus on in its foreign economic relations: eastward, toward closer relations with Russia; or westward, toward closer relations with the EU. Later, as relations with Russia soured after 2014, these eastbound exports collapsed, and that value chain lost currency and was partially replaced by one based on exports to the West. However, the lost Russian market for large-diameter pipe could not be fully replaced.

Azovstal, Ukraine's Search for Steel Markets, and the Bittersweet Success Story of Ukraine's Steel Exports to the EU

The unplanned demise of the Soviet Union in 1991 affected Ukrainian metallurgical factories—including Azovstal—by severing long-standing links to its major markets in the Russian Federation. Although some of these markets were regained through some of the barter operations organized by Azovimpeks and other intermediary companies discussed earlier in this chapter, the issue remained. One answer was to replace these lost export markets with increased domestic sales. However, domestic demand suffered as a result of the steep declines in GDP. With this economic decline especially affecting traditional steel-consuming sectors—such as machine-building, weapons production, shipbuilding, and construction—domestic demand for Ukrainian-produced steel collapsed, falling by about 80 percent from 1991 to 2002.[142]

Starting in the late 1990s, however, Ukraine's metallurgical exports started to increase. By the 2009–13 period, Ukraine had become one of the largest sources of steel imports to the EU; in 2013, it exported, in absolute terms, more steel than Russia.[143] During the focus period, Azovstal exported about 34 percent of its production.[144] All in all, for almost all the focus period, metallurgical exports constituted the largest category of Ukraine's exports (in 2011, 31.8 percent); they were taken over by unprocessed and low-processed agricultural goods in 2014.[145] In terms of exports specifically to the EU, iron and steel led the ranking, with about 30 percent.

By the beginning of our focus period, 2011, Metinvest had developed an impressive vertically integrated system involving physical assets in five countries and vertical control over the entire production chain, from feedstock to end products. However, if at first glance the story of Metinvest's rise speaks of successful adaptation to new conditions and integration into international markets, further analysis reveals a somewhat different story. Although these increasing metallurgical exports were partly driven by Ukraine's competitive advantages (access to raw materials, e.g., manganese and iron ore; the local availability of a plentiful, low-cost, and specialized labor force; and easy access to export ports, e.g., Mariupol), Ukraine's competitive export prices for steel products could not be sustained without large-scale subsidies. Indeed, Ukraine's "lower production costs" were related to state subsidies, and also to the fact that prices for key feedstocks were kept artificially low through corrupt deals and administrative manipulation.[146] Moreover, the on-the-books lower production costs for Ukrainian steel were at odds with the reality of an outdated and heavily energy-intensive metallurgical infrastructure.[147]

Azovstal's Steel Slab Exports within the Context of Ukraine's Exports of Semifinished Steel and Metallurgical Products

This value chain continues through the exporting of Azovstal-produced steel slabs. Although we focus on this particular product, it must be placed in the context of a broader trend: the boom in Ukrainian exports of intermediate and semifinished metallurgical products. These ranged, in order of complexity and value added, from manganese alloys used to increase strength in steel alloys, to ferronickel used for stainless steel production (Ukraine's largest metallurgical-related export to Germany in 1991–2015), to pig iron (where, for many years, Ukraine was the largest supplier to Southern Europe), to intermediate castings such as blooms and slabs.[148] And though all these products can be distinguished from finished steel products such as pipes and rails, they are not a homogeneous category, as some (e.g., manganese alloys and ferronickel) are intermediary products needed for steel (and other metal) production, whereas others—such as heavy steel slabs, a higher-value-added product—are steel segments ready to be re-rolled into final products of still higher value, such as quarto plates. During the focus period, Azovstal aspired to move from slabs as a key export commodity to higher-value-added finished products, but failed to do so. Heavy steel slabs continued to be central to Ukraine's westbound metallurgical exports.

FOLLOWING THE VALUE CHAIN: DOWNSTREAM

This section describes the last, downstream portion of coking coal's journey along the coal-metallurgy value chain. This segment of the journey is marked by the impact of technology, of regulatory challenges, and of ways of dealing with both of these—leading to unexpected turns in the chain.

Exports to Germany—and an Unexpected Detour

A look at Ukraine's steel export statistics for our focus period reveals Italy as the largest importer of Ukraine's metallurgical production. Although at first surprising, this is explained by value chain considerations. The heavy steel plates and slabs produced by Azovstal went, among other destinations, to Trametal in the Aussa Corno (Aussa Horn) industrial zone in San Giorgio di Nogaro, near Udine in Italy, with shipments mainly taking place through Mariupol's own port adjacent to Azovstal and also controlled by Akhmetov.[149] These were supplies within Metinvest's own vertical chain, because since 2007 Trametal has belonged solely to Metinvest. It was not the only post-Soviet metallurgical outpost in the region—in addition to the few remaining medium-sized, Italian-owned re-rollers in the area such as

Marcegaglia, Aussa Corno was also home to a mill acquired by Russia's Evraz Group.

The slabs arrived typically to the port of Monfalcone (or, occasionally, Trieste) and from there typically moved by truck to San Giorgio di Nogaro.[150] By the beginning of the focus period, the practice of exporting heavy steel plates and slabs to re-rollers in Aussa Corno / San Giorgio di Nogaro for re-rolling and further sale in the EU was so widespread that 65,000 trucks were plying the 33-kilometer road between Monfalcone and Aussa Corno yearly, indelibly affecting the quality of life in the area.[151]

Purchase of Trametal as related to changes in market conditions and dumping investigations against Azovstal exports. Since the mid-2000s, after formalizing ownership of domestic assets previously controlled informally, Ukrainian steel magnates began expanding their assets in the EU. This process involved both moving the formal registration of the key holding companies to the EU (as Metinvest did to the Netherlands), as well as the acquisition of production capacities abroad. With Metinvest having significant—and often unused—production capacity at home, how are these purchases to be explained?

Metinvest's acquisition of Trametal (which started with the purchase of a large package of shares in 2004 and was completed in 2007) was not an isolated move but part of broader trends.[152] These trends included other Metinvest purchases in the EU (e.g., Spartan U.K. Ltd. and Promet Steel in Bulgaria), as well as related purchases by competitor ISD (which acquired Huta Czestochowa in Poland in 2004 and Dunaferr in Hungary in 2005[153]). Specifically concerning the purchase of re-rolling mills in the EU, the trend went beyond Ukraine and included similar purchases by Russia's steel companies, such as Novolipetsk Steel and the Evraz Group.

Such acquisitions had several rationales, all related to Ukraine's own situation in the coal-steel value chain and the tensions between domestic Ukrainian market conditions and EU regulations. Some of these rationales had to do with maximizing value chain synergies, some with avoiding the import restrictions imposed by antidumping measures slapped on certain steel product exports, and some with minimizing taxes.

First, these acquisitions synergized with the strengths of Metinvest's value chain. They did not necessarily duplicate the company's Ukrainian assets, but concentrated on a particular segment: that of steel re-rollers. Steel re-rollers (sometimes also known as secondary steel producers) are factories that specialize in the shaping of larger pieces of steel into thinner sheets by passing them through two rolls. The material used is usually large-format slabs, a "flat product," which is one of several types of intermediate castings produced in a foundry using a simpler technology than that used for the rolling of products of variable thickness, and which require further processing to produce a finished good.[154] In this way, the production of slabs was completed in Ukraine where—as a result of a variety of factors, including subsidies and more lax environmental regulations—they were less expensive to produce, leaving the manufacturing of final products to their factories in the EU, which allowed for these products to be sold as EU-produced.[155]

During our focus period, Ukraine was Italy's largest import source for pig iron, ferromanganese, as well as for ingots and other semifinished products.[156] In contrast to pig iron and ferromanganese, the quarto plates segment is traditionally a high-value-added segment.[157] Thus behind these purchases was an attempt to take advantage of value-added chain synergies (by focusing energy-intensive production in Ukraine, where subsidies and low energy prices made it more profitable, while finishing the products in more technologically advanced factories in the EU), and to come closer to end consumers as a way to optimize logistics. But purchasing re-rolling factories in the EU was also an attempt to limit the damage of a series of antidumping restrictions imposed by the EU and other states on Azovstal. In these investigations, in the decade before 2012, Azovstal was found to be dumping the export price of a number of hot-rolled steel plate products by about 20 percent.[158] This was part of a broader array of antidumping investigations against Ukraine by the EU; of the fifteen dumping investigations opened by the EU against Ukraine between 1998 and 2008, four concerned metals and steel.[159]

If it was clear why Metinvest may have wanted to acquire assets in Italy, what were some of the rationales on the Italian side? How come so many re-rolling companies in Saint Georgio di Nogaro were sold, especially to post-Soviet investors? At the start of this chapter, I noted the global pressures bearing on European steelmakers, in particular excess capacity, increased competition from Chinese production, and the sharp fall in prices in 2008. Although Italy has the second-largest steel industry in the EU (after Germany), these trends and pressures were hitting the Italian metallurgical sector especially hard. (Excess capacity was an issue particularly affecting EU BOF-based producers, a technology that played a larger role in Italy than in the EU as a whole.[160]) Other factors were its weak domestic market and the fact that many Italian steel producers were medium-sized, family-owned companies, which created a highly fragmented landscape and made restructuring and consolidation more difficult, reducing profit margins.[161] Many of the steel companies near San Giorgio di Nogaro fit this family-owned pattern.[162] Another Italian specificity was the existence of "a strong, independent, export-oriented chain of re-rollers, processors, and service centers," which were more prominent than in other countries.[163] This synergized with investments from Ukraine and Russia because such re-rollers constituted a majority of local mills in areas such as Friuli Venezia Giulia, where San Giorgo di Nogaro is located.[164] In turn, these re-rollers required a steady influx of slab as main feedstock. One reason for the concentration of re-rollers in this area is its excellent logistics, having access to rail, road, and port facilities for easy importation of slabs.

Trametal was the most important metallurgical factory in Aussa Corno, and its production consisted exclusively of quarto plates—produced using high-technology reversing mills—used for shipbuilding and construction, including of wind turbines. From Trametal, half its production was exported to Northern Europe, and in particular to Germany (by far the largest importer of Italian-produced quarto plates[165]) by freight train, arriving at the Samskip Intermodal Rail Terminal in Duisburg, and distributed in Germany through Metinvest's dedicated marketing office, Metinvest Trading in nearby Essen, where its office is located a few kilometers from that of Thyssen Krupp, Germany's own metal and steel empire.[166] Although this last stage in the supply chain cannot be verified due to commercial confidentiality rules, it is wholly plausible that Trametal steel plates were used for building wind turbines by Siemens Wind Power, Senvion, and Enercon, because up to 84 percent of a wind turbine, by weight, consists of steel;[167] 85 percent of wind turbines used quarto plates in their construction, and the Metinvest group has a trajectory of supplying steel for wind turbines in Germany.[168] In addition, during the focus period Italy was one of the top three suppliers of such plates to Germany.[169] At the same time, more and more German nongovernmental organizations were raising the question of how ecologically sustainable was the building of wind turbines, given the high amount of steel used in their construction—even raising the question of whether we were moving from "peak oil to peak metal."[170] This alluded to the life cycle of their own quarto plates. If only people knew how much concentrated politics was compressed into each Metinvest Trametal quarto plate.

CONCLUSION

Three main conclusions emerge from this case study, having to do with interest differentiation, incentives for industrial modernization, and the impact of energy materiality. Looking at the coal sector from the perspective of the entire value and technological chain helps us better understand the variety of interests and positions around related issues. Discussions of Ukraine's coal and metallurgical players have often failed to differentiate between their various production subsectors, each sector's connection with the rest of the value chain, and their role in exports. These differences, however, are significant for several reasons. First, different steel-related products have different levels of value added—for example, steel scrap as compared with intermediate products such as pig iron as compared with intermediate castings such as slabs as compared with finished products such as pipes and rail beams.

Similarly, steel produced through different methods has different needs for raw material inputs, not only in terms of direct feedstock but also in terms of the amount of energy (electricity) needed for production. We can also see different interests based on different metal-related value chains, with these interests competing for legislation, as, for example, in the case of the conflict between those interested in exporting scrap metal and those using scrap metal as main feedstock in their steel production chain (first and foremost, Interpipe's EAF-based process).[171] This has also affected broader relations with the EU, as in the mid-2000s one of the reasons the EU kept quotas for rolled steel products' imports from Ukraine low was the fact that it wanted to exert pressure on Ukraine to remove export tariffs on scrap metal that had been introduced in 2003.[172] (See table 6.1.)

More generally, an analysis of the Ukrainian spatial portion of the coal-steel value chain tells us that few key actors in the country had a real interest in modernizing the country's metal production system. This is so because despite incentives for upgrading technology (the growing price of imported coking coal, reduced steel export prices due to the 2008 crisis, and competition from China), weak democratic control structures and the collusion with national authorities allowed steelmakers such as Metinvest to avoid hard financial and energy constraints by making use of generous subsidies and transfers. Moreover, as discussed above, they used miners' grievances instrumentally in this

TABLE 6.1
The Coal-Steel Value Chain: Spatial and Technological Processes, 2011–14

Spatial Stage	Technological Process	Stage in Value Chain	Main Actors
Russian Federation	Extraction Transportation	Upstream Midstream	Kuzbassrazrezugol
Ukraine	Processing into raw material Manufacturing of intermediate products	Midstream	Metinvest
Italy	Manufacturing of final products	Midstream	Trametal (Metinvest daughter)
Germany	Distribution Sale to large users	Downstream	Metinvest Trading Various final users, such as: Siemens Wind Power Senvion Enercon

quest. In this sense, Viktor Pinchuk's facility using more advanced and less energy-intensive EAF technology remained an exception.

Returning to the central theoretical question of this book, how did the materiality-related specificities of coal affect power relations around it? At crucial points in the value chain, the materiality characteristics of coal as a good played a key role in helping to shape the situation. They did this not because coal could have "agency" but because its material characteristics have an impact on the range of choices of the human actors around it. Thus, for example, the nature of coal as a high-volume/low-caloric value energy good requiring significant human labor for its production (as well as transportation) set the stage for the high social costs of coal sector reform and for the ability of Ukrainian oligarchic groups to manipulate and instrumentalize miners' grievances in a way would allow them to continue (mis)appropriating state subsidies as a means to both increase rents and avoid a real adaptation to an increasingly unforgiving international steel market.

Thus, as discussed in chapters 2 and 3, the materiality characteristics of the starting good both enabled and constrained the range of choices available to actors in the chain. In the case analyzed in this chapter, this enabling and constraining took place largely through the three mechanisms discussed in chapter 3. First, it took place through the way these materiality characteristics affected the technical constraints of the value chain, in the process endowing (or not) actors at various levels of the chain with (more or less) power (mechanism 2 discussed in chapter 3). Thus, for example, the high level of close-coupling of the coal-steel value chain, where the technical requirements of the chain make each stage in the chain highly dependent on the availability of highly specified feedstock materials. This bestowed enormous power on anyone able to—such as Akhmetov and Taruta in the 1990s—reconstitute these chains to provide the specified feedstock. Second, we saw how the material characteristics of an energy good affect the typical challenges affecting its particular value chain (mechanism 3 discussed in chapter 3). In the case of coal, this concerned first and foremost the risks and challenges related to physical and energy value loss from degradation in transportation in a situation where its typical low value per volume leads to less resources available for weatherproof storage, and difficult standardization, which synergized with the close-coupling issues discussed above to enhance the power of anyone able to offer a temporary solution. Concerning situations where the value chains of specific energy goods create distinct distributive openings at each level of the chain (mechanism 1 discussed in chapter 3), the case of the coal-steel chain shows us a situation where the need for labor-intensive production and transshipment of a low-value, high-volume good opened the door to the enormous political significance of subsidies, which in turn made possible arbitrage gains (including illicit gains) related to price differentials created by various subsidization schemes for production and wage payments. These kinds of distributive openings made possible Akhmetov's significant power, as well as a peculiar coalition with the coal workers, which in turn were used to directly or indirectly instill fear in the rest of the country concerning Donetsk's power or, alternatively, its potential for separatism.

With respect to this issue, coal's materiality characteristics as a good requiring a high level of human labor relative to the sale price of the good, along with significant human intervention in shipment and transshipment, enhanced the very possibility of corrupt actors using such a strategy based on the instrumentalization of coal miners' grievances—as well as societal fears of miners' political mobilization—as a means to maintain subsidies benefiting not so much the miners themselves but those controlling the coal-metallurgy value chain.

PART THREE

New Types of Energy and New Political Chains

CHAPTER SEVEN

And the Chains Meet Again

IN THIS FINAL CHAPTER, I review the main findings of the three exemplary value chains followed in this book, and discuss their significance for three main areas: our theoretical understanding of value chains and power, the first quarter century of post-Soviet political development, and Russian power in the region.

The three journeys analyzed in this book are in some ways remarkably different, and in some ways remarkably similar. Although each of the three chains involved movement westward across several states, including Russia and Ukraine, the transformation the original good went through was different in each case. In the case of natural gas, the natural gas (methane) molecule remained unchanged; in the case of oil, it was transformed through refining into diesel. And in the case of the coal-steel chain, the original coking coal molecule largely disappeared in order for steel to be produced.

At the same time, in addition to their routing—starting in Russia, transiting through Ukraine, and ending in Germany—all three chains reflected Soviet-period value and supply chains. Path dependencies related to these were manifested through infrastructure, material flows, and patterns of economic development and energy use; tightly coupled technical systems based on these played an important role in all cases well beyond 1991. The impact of the Soviet legacies could also be seen at a very personal level—many of the key players in this book, from Vagit Alekperov to Musa Magomedov, have biographies deeply shaped by Soviet value and supply chains connecting key oil, gas, and coal production areas and educational institutions in the Caucasus, Russia, and Ukraine.

The three chains also met—in more ways than one. Besides meeting in Germany as diesel (oil), steel-produced wind turbines (coal), and electricity (natural gas), our chains met in two other ways. First, they became joined in single persons. In addition to their sectoral specialization, the key players in Ukrainian natural gas (Dmytro Firtash), oil (Ihor Kolomoyskyi), and coal-metallurgy (Rinat Akhmetov) were all also involved in electricity generation. Firtash was connected to electricity through the company RosUkrEnergo (in which he held 45 percent ownership, and which—in addition to acting as an intermediary in gas purchases—in the 2000s was also involved in the export of electricity generated from Russian gas). Kolomoyskyi also had significant assets in the metallurgical and electricity generation sectors. Akhmetov and his DTEK group hold significant assets in electricity generation. The chains also came together through the connections between their secondary supply chains. Wide-diameter steel pipes produced in Ukraine using Russian coking coal as part of the production process were sold to Gazprom to be used in building the Yamal pipeline to partially circumvent transit through Ukraine.[1] Metallurgical production using coking coal also used electricity generated from Russian natural gas. Our molecules also competed; the electricity produced using wind turbines built from steel produced with the coal molecule competed with and displaced Franken I electricity generated by the natural gas molecule.

WHAT WE HAVE LEARNED FROM THE CHAINS: THEIR IMPORTANCE FOR THEORIZING ENERGY, VALUE CHAINS, AND POWER

What have we learned from these chains that helps us better understand value chains and power from a theoretical perspective? The process of following these chains and analyzing their course helps us rethink our assumptions about value added, value chains, and our very understanding of energy space.

Pricing, Value Added, and Value Destruction

The cases analyzed in this book lead us to rethink conventional concepts of pricing, value added, and value destruction in value chains. The natural gas value chain was the closest to the manufacturing industries–based model of a value chain as one where the original good is constantly increasing in value with higher prices the closer the good gets to end consumers.[2] The cases of oil (where, due to significant price volatility, sometimes oil products are sold for less than crude oil) and coal (where sometimes the caloric and economic cost of producing coal was higher than the price or calories produced by it) remind us that "value chain" and "value added" do not necessarily come together. Similarly, from the coal case study we learned that coal-steel oligarchs such as Rinat Akhmetov often had an interest in keeping the price of coal supplied to metallurgical industries artificially low, as a way of reducing both taxes and feedstock costs for their metallurgical companies; manipulations around subsidized prices for specific sub-markets (e.g., residential users and social objects) were also key in the natural gas value chain.

Materiality as Working Through Value Chains

What did we learn about materiality's impact on value chains? Let me first summarize some of the main ways in which this impact took place, as reflected in three main mechanisms (see chapter 3) that link the physical characteristics of various types of energy to constraints on actors' behavior.

In the first mechanism, the materiality characteristics of specific energy goods help set in motion processes that create distinct distributive openings. In the case of natural gas, its gaseous physical state, related transportation constraints and the largely regional scale of its markets, and its lack of a single quotable global price exacerbated less price transparency, which in turn facilitated opportunities for the manipulation of price differentials, arbitrage, and rent-seeking, and corruption based on this arbitrage.[3] In the case of oil, high price volatility in the context of refineries' high-volume/low-unit-profit business model led to high competitive pressure in the industry. In the case of coal, its materiality characteristics (low energy/weight ratio; bulk cargo characteristics requiring extensive human labor in both production and transportation) made possible certain oligarchic manipulations involving the instrumental use of labor (miners') grievances. The use of miners as both an excuse for demanding continued state subsidization of the sector, along with the use of the fear of their political mobilization in a scare tactics campaign vis-à-vis the population as a whole, made possible the appropriation of subsidies intended for workers, subsidies that were key in the type of rent-seeking manipulations observed.[4]

Technopolitics reminds us of how technical requirements help shape political questions. In the second mechanism, the technical constraints of different value chains (e.g., those concerning processing, storage, and transit services) can endow actors at various levels (upstream, midstream, downstream) and spatial locations (see table 7.1), with more or less power, power that can have regulatory and redistributive implications. For example, due to technical issues (e.g., gas liquids' ability to corrode pipeline walls), gas-processing plants involved in natural gas liquid (NGL) extraction need to be located close to production areas. Even before a regulatory framework would come into play, this facilitated the fact of Gazprom itself processing and commercializing the higher-value NGLs. If it had been possible to locate NGL extraction plants anywhere along the spatial trajectory of the chain from producer to consumer, the situation would have been different. Similarly, in a high-networkness energy system such as that of natural gas, due to technical constraints, the de facto transmission system operator (TSO) (e.g., Gazprom, other operators, or, in the post-2010 European Union, independent TSOs in each zone) emerges as a key technical and governance player, because key technical decisions such as whether to allow reverse supplies came to play important governance roles. In the case of oil, the technical possibility of keeping separate different qualities (brands) of oil in a single stream (batching)—something not possible in the case of natural gas—opened the door to situations where what at first glance may appear as purely technical decisions (e.g., on whether to maintain the quality of specific oil types by batching, or not, as we saw in the case of Russian Volga-Urals and Western Siberian Light grades of oil) had important redistributive implications.

Thus, for example, the suppliers of lower-quality Volga-Urals oil (Bashkortostan and Tatarstan) had much to lose from batching as

TABLE 7.1
Spatial Location Considerations for Energy Processing

Energy Type	Potential Processing with Value-Added Implications	Processing Present in Exemplary Chain Followed in This Book	Potential Spatial Location for Processing	Spatial Location for This Processing in Exemplary Chain Followed in This Book
Natural gas	Separation and commercialization of natural gas liquids (NGLs)	Initial processing and NGL extraction	NGLs: spatially close to production	Novy Urengoy, Russia
	Use for electricity generation	Electricity generation		Nürnberg, Germany
	Use as feedstock for chemical fertilizer		Fertilizer feedstock: locations accessible by low-cost transportation (pipeline)	
Oil	Refining as motor oils	Refining into diesel	Anywhere in the chain	Litvinov refinery, Czech Republic
	Refining as chemical industry feedstock			
Coal (coal-steel value chain)	Coke production Metal production Re-rolling	Coke production Metal production Re-rolling	Basically anywhere (subject to high transportation costs)	Adviivka, Ukraine Mariupol, Ukraine San Giorgio di Nogaro, Italy

opposed to mixing this oil in the pipeline as a single brand: if their oil were to be marketed separately from higher-priced Siberian Light oil, the price discount and, consequently, their loses would have been significant. More generally, whether the value chain involved safeguarding the qualities of a good (as in the case of natural gas) or transforming it into an end product through a one-node refining process (as is generally the case in the crude oil–diesel value chain) or transforming it into an end product through a several-node process (as in the case of the coal-steel chain) mattered in terms of the further sets of actors that would become involved in the chains.

In the third mechanism, the material characteristics of various energy goods lead to distinctive value chain challenges; as discussed in chapter 3, these characteristics also help limit the range of possible responses to these. This could be seen, for example, with the issue of how to manage sunk cost risks in natural gas, an industry that traditionally supported a system of risk-sharing between producers and consumers through long-term contracts and take-or-pay clauses. As discussed below, attempts to change the risk management system to a pay-as-you-go basis still need to be fully proven in practice (see chapter 8).

In addition, materiality affected value chains through the ways in which its instrumental use by various actors affected the regulatory environment. This was especially evident in the case of natural gas, where its networkness, as discussed in chapter 4, was not only objectively important in and of itself but also in terms of its uses for Russian and EU energy policy. Russian officials used the concept of natural monopoly—which can be seen as related to networkness—as justification for state-supported monopolies, such as that by Gazprom on pipeline gas exports. In the case of the EU, it was the concept of networkness that provided the initial rationale for the designation of some types of energy (electricity and natural gas) as areas of priority for network development, justifying active intervention in infrastructure development in these sectors. This brings to the fore the constructionist point about infrastructure as not only a material precondition for action but also a justification for it, or, as noted by Wengle, providing a "legitimating narrative" for certain decisions and interests.[5]

Limits on the Impact of Materiality

What have we learned about the limits on the impact of materiality? The three journeys followed in this book tell us about the impact of materiality, but also about the limits to this impact. In chapter 4, we discussed how the need to remove liquid components found in "wet" natural gas constrains the physical location of gas processing and NGL extraction plants because, if such NGLs were to be allowed to remain in the pipeline, they could corrode and rupture it. Chapter 5 discussed how refineries specified for certain types of crude may be difficult to use with other grades of oil. And chapter 6 referred to the tight coupling between Ukrainian electricity generation infrastructure and specific grades of coal only available in selected areas linked to the power generation infrastructure through Soviet-era supply chains. Yet such examples also tell us that the constraints imposed by materiality are not absolute but are mediated by both the state of technology and what is considered to be economically efficient in different social and historical contexts. Thus, for example, though in principle it would be conceivable to locate gas/NGL processing plants away from production fields, in order to do this, it would be necessary to build very high-cost special pipelines able to transport wet gas; decisions on when and where to commercialize various types of NGLs also depend on cost calculations.[6] Thus, materiality-related constraints on the value chain provided the parameters of what *could* be done but did not determine what *would* be done. Here, actors' choices and the governance environment played an important role. Infrastructure can also be used in different ways due to political choices, with the tracing of new pipeline routes such as Nord Stream 1 and 2 (discussed below) being an obvious example.

At the same time, we also saw evidence of the impact of regulatory (including contractual) systems on materiality constraints. Thus, for example, specific contractual forms for natural gas and oil created constraints on materiality through their impact on ways of dealing with specific value chain challenges (see the discussion of mechanism 3 above). Thus, when the EU decided to liberalize the gas market, this meant also seeking to shift one of these value chain challenges, risk related to sunk costs and stranded assets, from something to be dealt with by locking buyers into rigid commitments through contractual conditions, to transforming this risk into pay-as-you-go costs. As seen in the challenge of maintaining standby electricity generation capacity in Germany in the wake of the Renewable Energy Sources Act of 2000 (see chapter 4), the jury is still out on whether this regulatory shifting of risk costs will be effective in guaranteeing needed investments and maintenance costs for backup generation capacity in the long term. This also means that the same infrastructure, in different political/governance situations, can play very different roles. Bargains and agreements set around concrete infrastructures may obsolesce once political realities change as a result of developments such as states gaining independence.[7] The most obvious example comes from the changed role of natural gas transit infrastructure before and after 1991—upon achieving independence, post-Soviet states such as Ukraine "changed, virtually overnight, from constituents of a single energy-rich state" to being separate, energy-poor entities heavily dependent on Russian energy, and also politically independent transit states.[8]

Conceptualizing Energy Space and Value Chain Space

Studying the three value chains at the core of this book has also led to some interesting insights concerning the conceptualization of energy space. For example, we learned that pipelines, key for oil and natural gas value chains, represent a distinct contractual space where various contractual arrangements may coexist. In the case of the Vateganskoe-Litvinov oil value chain, for example, oil exported by different companies (Bashneft, Rosneft, Gazprom Neft, LUKoil, Slavneft, and Russneft exported oil to the Czech Republic during the focus period) and contractually tied to different specific destinations (Litvinov, but also other destinations such as the Bratislava refinery in the Slovak Republic) shared Russian, Ukrainian, Slovak, and the Czech segments of the pipeline. Even with these molecules being untraceable and indistinguishable from one another, a certain portion of the total could be governed by one contractual arrangement, and others by a different arrangement. In the case of natural gas as well, molecules nominally tied to different destinations could also be subject to different contractual arrangements.

Although a pipeline may be a distinct contractual space, it also interacts with the territory it crosses, that is, with national or supranational systems and regulatory nodes governing key issues in that jurisdiction (permission to go through that country's territory, compliance with national-level environmental regulations, etc.). This should be understood in the context of the impact of commercial and regulatory nodes on physical nodes and flows, and of how energy interactions in the broad space encompassing Russia, Ukraine, and the EU should be looked at in the triangle between national, EU, and multinational corporation policy.

Value Chains and Vertical Integration

None of the three value chains followed in this book were fully vertically integrated (in the sense of the producer of the initial good controlling the entire chain). Although examples of vertically integrated natural gas, oil, and coal value chains going from Russia to the EU existed, no vertically integrated chains cold be found going from extraction in Russia *through transit via Ukraine to sale to final users in*

Germany, the key selection criteria for the value chains followed in this book.[9] What at first seemed like a methodological challenge actually reappears as an interesting insight: that these chains were most often not masterminded by the initial producer from extraction to sale to final users, but that the end of the value chain was the result of a series of decisions and transactions throughout the chain; interactions at various stages in the chain, not only its end supply point, turned out to have important power implications.

Specific portions of the exemplary value chains followed in this book were vertically integrated; the degree of vertical integration by a lead actor and the location in the chain of segments controlled by the same actor were different in each of the cases. Although Gazprom was the actor closest to having a fully vertically integrated value chain, its value chain followed in this book was not fully integrated. And though the company played an important downstream role in other value chains (e.g., in the Nord Stream pipeline and the OPAL pipeline connecting to it), it did not in the Urengoy-Nürnberg exemplary chain followed here. Gazprom's failure to develop fully vertically integrated value chains may be ascribed to several factors: the vagaries of its own asset-acquisition policies (discussed below); EU regulations requiring unbundling of production, transportation, and distribution; and the toxicity implied by the name "Gazprom" in post-Soviet states such as Ukraine, making formal ownership of downstream assets highly difficult even before Russia's armed intervention in 2014.[10] However, during the focus period, Gazprom played an important role in gas distribution to end users within Ukraine through a partially owned subsidiary,[11] as well as through its partial ownership of intermediary companies active in gas supplies to Ukraine, such as RosUkrEnergo.

Metinvest, the key actor in the coking coal chain, possessed a vertically integrated production chain starting with coke production in Ukraine through sale in Germany, but did not control raw material production in Russia. LUKoil, the key actor in the oil chain, was, within the focus period and the physical space covered by the exemplary chain, only in control of the Russian portion of this physical chain. In the Czech Republic, it was active as both supplier (one among several) of crude oil and as gasoline station operator (which purchased oil products from unrelated local refineries), but was not active in the refining segment of the chain—although, as discussed in chapter 5, it sought to be through its unsuccessful attempt to buy the Czech Republic's refinery operator.

So, why were some specific *segments* of the value chains vertically integrated, and others not? Why were some transactions internalized by a firm through vertical integration, while others were given to other actors through contracts and outsourcing? Is there something related to materiality that makes it harder to establish vertical value chains around some energy goods than around others? Looking at the issue from a theoretical perspective focusing on institutions and transaction costs (see the discussion of Williamson in chapter 5) may yield further insights. Whether vertical integration encompassed the entire value chain or just some portions of it had partially to do with whether actors wanted to build such a vertically integrated chain—as discussed in chapter 3 (see table 3.3), the value chains for different energy goods exhibit different typical challenges, and vertical integration is not necessarily the best way of dealing with each of these. Although vertical integration is often extolled as a model, in many cases, such as oil refining, it entails significant challenges, such as shifting the risks of refinery margin volatility onto the mother company itself. But the degree of vertical integration also had to do with political and regulatory constraints, such as, starting in the 2010s, the EU's unbundling legislation prohibiting a single company from owning bundled production, transportation, and distribution infrastructure.

At the same time, when looking at value chains, we should think not only about formal but also informal ones, whose very informality could be used to maximize rent-seeking. The case of coal in Ukraine, with its 1990s history of unofficial vertical control and captive supplier relationships in benefit of ISD/Metinvest metallurgical interests (see chapter 6), reminds us of the importance of such informal relationships. Other examples discussed in this book include the illegal importation of gasoline to Ukraine, and illegal mini-refineries in Russia and Ukraine.

RETHINKING ENERGY AND POWER

How has an examination of the three value chains affected the way we conceptualize energy and power? What have we learned about energy and power, both domestic and external?

Domestic Power: Value Chains and Post-Soviet Political Development

What have we learned about the impact of participation in Russian energy chains on the political development of post-Soviet states in their first twenty-five years of post-Soviet political life? In the traditional conception of power most often used in analyses of energy and international politics, power is influence, or "power over." This book's case studies, however, have shown that energy materiality (including energy-type specific ways of producing and processing it) can also bestow power to specific social, economic, and political actors by affecting "what capacities and practices" they would be "socially empowered to undertake"—and, more basically, their very emergence as significant actors.[12] We saw this, for example, in the case of coal actors in Donetsk, whose emergence as key players at the national Ukrainian level took place through the (prospect of) accessing (and sharing) profits through and throughout materiality-constrained value chains.

Although the immediate story and direct comparison presented in this book are about differences between fossil fuels, there is also a meta-story involved. This meta-story, in an ultimate analysis even more powerful than the immediate story told here, is the meta-story of what dependence on, and participation in, the value chains of (Russian) fossil fuels did to the societies and political systems of the former USSR. The examples provided in the case study chapters give us a sense of how entrenched was the connection between the supply of certain energy resources, the actors involved in these supplies, and certain types of political relations, both within each of these societies and across borders. The intermingling between dependency on networked types of fossil fuel energy and the political expectation that this energy and energy services be provided at affordable prices was a key factor in making energy policy decisions that came to have a deep impact on post-Soviet political systems—on both Russia and the other post-Soviet states. The yellow vest protests in France in 2018–19 tell us that this phenomenon is not unique to the countries of the former Soviet Union.

What participation in these value chains meant for the political systems and the remaking of social relations in the first quarter century after the dissolution of the USSR is best understood if we look at the kinds of actors such systems helped constitute, empower, and bring closer to power.[13] Actors able to use the opportunities presented by the loopholes of the transition period—including in relations with Russia as the main energy supplier—and to reestablish value and supply chains sent into disarray by the Soviet dissolution were able to increase their own wealth and power and to use this to establish formal control over production chains at first controlled informally. The various "uses" of energy (systems) above and beyond its direct use helped these actors constitute and strengthen their political power.

Domestically, we saw how the various "uses" of energy above and beyond its direct use helped constitute and empower various actors and strengthen (or reduce) their political power. We saw how domestic political dynamics—for example, the fear of popular protests over mine closings, energy shortages, or price increases—triggered measures in Russia and Ukraine that would have important implications for the value chain and also for the use of energy as an external weapon. In the case of Ukraine, one of the most consequential (and shortsighted) energy policy decisions of the postindependence period, the elimination of import duties on oil products, was largely based on the use of energy systems for domestic purposes. In this case, the policy, introduced in 2005 by Viktor Yuschenko, the newly installed Orange Revolution president, was intended to solve a fuel crisis and maintain low gasoline prices as a means of preventing social discontent, a goal it helped achieve in the short term, but at the cost of exacerbating the collapse of the country's refining and, indirectly, transit role.

Similarly, in the case of the Ukrainian mining industry, the desire to use the energy system to maintain social peace led to the neglect of much-needed reforms, and also set the basis for the instrumentalization of workers' grievances by oligarchs such as Rinat Akhmetov. (This was in the context of a situation where energy policy in the first postindependence decades—at least until 2014—was used more as a means of balancing the power of various interest groups than for actual, proactive policymaking.[14])

The impact of the chains on social relationships was also related to the direction of key value chains and trade relationships. Indeed, much of the fierceness of political confrontations in Ukraine in late 2013 and early 2014 revolved around the choice of what should be the main direction of exports (joining a deep and comprehensive free trade agreement with the EU, or, alternatively, the Russian-led Eurasian Customs Union). After 2014's political changes and Russian military intervention, the choice for westward-oriented chains has solidified, and Ukraine's eastward-bound chains have been largely (but not totally) disrupted. In the case of Russia, the country's main energy export chains went west, while, for most of its independent statehood, important Ukrainian value chains went east to Russia.[15] Thus, for example, in the case of the coal-metal chain, many of the end products produced by Ukraine, such as highly specialized pipes for large-diameter pipeline construction, were exported to Russia.

This must be seen in the broader context of Ukraine's evolving role in the global division of labor encompassing its connection with both Russian and Western markets. During the first two decades of its post-Soviet independence, this role was largely based on the production and exporting of goods—such as steel, ammonia, and fertilizers—whose competitiveness in world markets depended on subsidized energy and related services. Although some of this subsidization had to do with the unique political economy of Russian–Ukrainian relations during this period, some of these subsidies actually came from the Ukrainian state itself, at the expense of the population as a whole, and benefited specific economic groups related to these exports, as in the case of subsidies to coal mines and also those covering the losses incurred by politically well-connected natural gas traders. How did this interact with Russian power and influence? At first glance, actors such as Akhmetov were not keen on too-close relations with Russia, because they did not want to compromise valued exports to EU markets, and also wanted to avoid competition from Russian companies. At a deeper level, however, the kind of energy-political system they helped to set up and benefited from could not but weaken Ukrainian unity, and could be seen as partially contributing to the success of Russian-backed separatism in 2014. How Ukraine will find a role in the international division of labor under new, post-2014 conditions is a key question.

External Power: Energy Power as Russian Power?

Indeed, the way energy was used for a variety of domestic goals also affected exporters' ability to use it for purposes of international pressure, as well as consumer states' level of resilience vis-à-vis this pressure. In its impact on post-Soviet states such as Ukraine, what was the key element? Was there something specific about fossil fuels and nonrenewables that fostered these processes, or was it something about dependency on networked types of energy, as opposed to more autarchic systems? Or is it simply that fossil fuels, by being available to the USSR as a political and economic center (and, later, to Russia), led to long-term changes in the whole economic system of its peripheries, including energy-scarce constituent republics, in the direction of developing energy-intensive economies that would be highly dependent on types of energy that, centrally supplied, were plentiful and inexpensive?

One way to approach this question is by looking at the situational coalitions that could form around the types of interests and technical requirements of the fossil fuels involved. Materiality-related production and processing patterns helped create opportunities and constraints for these actors, facilitating domestic and transborder coalitions. The case of coal in Ukraine and specifically in the Donetsk area, discussed in chapter 6, presents an interesting example: coal's high-volume/low-caloric value energy ratio, requiring significant human labor, set the stage for the high social costs of coal sector reform, helping regional oligarchs such as Rinat Akhmetov and Serhii Taruta to instrumentalize miners' grievances. This situational coalition allowed coal-metallurgical oligarchs to privatize the benefits of state subsidies while socializing their cost.[16]

How did the specificities of various energy types constrain or amplify Russia's ability to use energy supplies as a means of leverage? Throughout the three chains presented in this book, we could see how constitutive power interacted with "power as influence," sometimes potentiating and sometimes constraining an energy supplier's ability to use energy as a means of leverage. For example, the decline in the role of incumbent gas suppliers in Germany (e.g., Ruhrgas) discussed in chapter 4 highlighted the importance of both the constitutive elements (e.g., companies losing the ability to act as powerful natural gas policy lobbyists after their merger into larger, broader-profile companies[17]) and influence elements of power. With the German natural gas sector becoming fragmented and in many cases taken over by electricity companies, the imbalance vis-à-vis an increasingly centralized Gazprom becomes evident.

Not surprisingly, the use of energy (systems) for the pursuit of multiple goals could often not create a coherent policy, including a coherent external policy. In the case of the EU and its policies, the contradictions inherent in the multiple uses of energy (policy) were seen in the tension between two goals the EU sought to fulfill through its energy policy: on one hand, fostering competition to reduce consumer prices, which was also related to the goal of creating a level playing field and functioning single energy market; and, on the other hand, pursuing security of supply and climate security goals, which would require a degree of public intervention above and beyond free markets.

In the Russian case, the oil export taxation system that was in place in the 2000s tried to simultaneously fulfill several goals, not only supporting exports and especially value-added ones, but also giving preferences to friendly post-Soviet states such as Belarus by providing tax incentives for Russian companies to refine oil in (and reexport it from) these states. Using tax measures (taxing gasoline at a higher level than less-processed heavy oil products), throughout the 2000s the system also sought to disincentivize the exporting of gasoline as a way of preventing politically dangerous domestic shortages. Similarly, the generous asset-swap policies pursued by Gazprom to incentivize EU-country companies to participate in the Nord Stream project despite its apparent lack of economic rationale may have made sense from the perspective of political goals such as the building of a situational coalition to amplify support for the pipeline, but not from the perspective of increasing Gazprom's asset valuation.[18]

We also saw that various nodes in the value chains could play the role of gateways and gatekeepers able to act as gate openers or closers to Russian influence under particular circumstances. We saw this, for example, in the case of the Velké Kapušany (Slovak Republic) gas entry/exit point and the impact of decisions both by the managers of the physical node and by the regulatory nodes affecting its behavior (with Brussels and the Slovak government as regulatory nodes) on Ukraine's ability to access natural gas supplies above and beyond its contractual relationship with Gazprom, and thus be able to achieve a degree of energy independence from its main supplier.

In the case of natural gas, the reduced price transparency related to its materiality characteristics helped make possible extensive price manipulations, often involving a situational coalition of corrupt actors on both sides of the Russian-Ukrainian border, as seen in the example of Dmytro Firtash's sharing of the profits of his unique arrangements with Gazprom with associates of then–president Yanukovich.[19]

This also opened the door to a specific type of Russian influence: weakening the political system through corruption. In addition, some of the profits and rents gained through special, lower-than-market-price sales of Russian gas to Firtash between 2009 and 2014 resulted in more than $3 billion in gains for Firtash, some of which was recycled into funds to support Yanukovich's bid for the presidency in 2010.[20]

In the case of the EU, the impact of these situational, transborder coalitions could be seen through the case of new gas importation and infrastructure projects, such as Nord Stream 1 and 2 and the companies brought together by the project (in addition to Gazprom, Wintershall, Ruhrgas, Gasunie, and GDF Suez for Nord Stream 1; and ENGIE, OMV, Shell, Uniper, and Wintershall for Nord Stream 2), whose lobbying power was strong enough to overcome political and environmental objections at the EU and national levels. This coalition was strong enough to make an impact on European Commission (EC)–level regulatory decisions, such as that on providing Gazprom with a temporary exemption to EU regulations governing the use of pipelines on EU territory, so that Gazprom could use the OPAL pipeline further, carrying inland Nord Stream gas, without reserving capacity for third-party access to other parties. Although we cannot necessarily speak of a single coalition encompassing the entire space from production in Russia to end-use in Germany, a chain of partial situational coalitions formed around physical, commercial, and regulatory nodes could go a long way in bringing the interests of key Russian players to the European Commission table.

LOOKING AHEAD

As we look ahead, what we have learned by following these chains may also help us keep our eyes open to important developments. These include not only events in the countries located in the path of the value chains analyzed in this book but also broader global trends.

The End of Some Supply Chains: Threat and Opportunity Revisited

Although infrastructure and its related path dependencies can have strong staying power, we should not forget that value and supply chains can decline and even disappear. We saw this most clearly in the case of Ukraine—important value and supply chains going through Ukraine lost currency in the mid-2010s, first and foremost due to Russia's redirection of transportation routes aimed at avoiding transit states and Ukraine in particular. Although the issue intensified after the opening of Nord Stream 1 in 2011, this process started well before, in the 1990s, with the building of the Yamal pipeline aimed at moving gas transit volumes away from Ukraine. These new transportation routes avoiding Ukraine were in many ways (technically, and in what they meant for Russia's role as a supplier) remarkably similar to the old ones; in fact, Russia's share in the EU's imports of natural gas and oil did not decline, but actually increased.

This process of change in oil and gas transit routes also involved end markets. Although supplies to the German market via the exemplary supply and value chains followed in this book were key for Ukrainian players (e.g., Metinvest exports and NAK Naftohaz's natural gas and oil transit earnings), this was not the case for the producers of the original energy good (LUKoil, the Urals Mining and Metallurgical Company, or even Gazprom). And though their supplies reached Germany via the exemplary chains analyzed in this book, other routes (e.g., Druzhba North via Poland for oil and, starting in 2011, Nord Stream for natural gas) were much more significant. Transit of Russian natural gas via Ukraine declined from about 20 percent of all German gas imports in the 2000s to about 10 percent by 2014.[21] (Let us not forget, however, that demand in end markets is also related to regulatory issues, which may also be seen from a political lens involving the role of interest groups. For example, the high demand for diesel in Germany—and EU markets on a whole—was predicated on tax preferences given to that fuel as compared with its close competitor gasoline, and was based on the assumption of diesel being more environmentally friendly than gasoline. After a series of scandals in 2017 unveiled automobile industry manipulation of data on the issue, that rationale came crumbling down.)

The shutting out of Ukraine from Russia's export value chain can in some ways be seen as a cataclysmic event. At issue is not only lost transit revenue (and the resulting flight of wealth away from Ukraine) but also power—in two ways: first, the loss of the counterpower involved in providing a service needed by the country's largest supplier of natural gas (the so-called bilateral monopoly between Ukraine and Russia discussed in chapter 2); and second, the loss of the power implied in multilateralizing the supply of natural gas from Russia to the EU, in a way that also made Ukraine important for the EU.

In addition, losing this transit role would also mean that Ukraine would not be able to fully use its complex transit infrastructure, thus losing not only the investments made in system modernization (sunk costs) but also the employment provided by transit and related services such as storage. Here, materiality issues become important once again: because of natural gas's gaseous state, maintaining a certain pressure is essential for the gas to flow at all; below a specific load level, a natural gas pipeline simply cannot function—dropping from a 100 percent load to a 50 percent load means much more than a 50 percent drop in functionality. This is the context in which various Russian promises (i.e., promises that some level of transit via Ukraine would continue despite increasing volumes being shipped via Nord Stream 1 and 2) need to be understood. From a security perspective, transit power for Ukraine also means that, as long as the country is a significant transit carrier of Russian gas, this role offers a degree of protection against an all-out military intervention by Russia.

Some of the reasons for the decline in Ukraine's transit role are discussed in chapters 4 and 5. A look at the governance of the natural gas sector during the focus period—which can be seen as representative of the postindependence period as a whole—also shows how infrastructure that could in theory bring both income and some counterpower vis-à-vis suppliers may see this possible role squandered if misused for other purposes such as domestic rent-seeking, which affected both Ukraine's use of infrastructure and Ukraine's reputational capital as a transit state.

The issues discussed in this book are not simply theoretical ones. The question of the possible end of some value chains and survival of others has important practical implications for the ability of various actors to balance risk and opportunity—"threat" and "temptation"—in their participation in European and global energy markets. Concretely concerning Ukraine, and leaving aside repeated tensions with Gazprom, as well as the company's assertions about its ability to unilaterally terminate its contracts, other developments may affect the gas molecule's path through the country's transit system.[22] Despite objections by Sweden and Poland, Nord Stream 2 may be completed by 2021. And despite the signing of a new contract with Gazprom in late 2019, these developments, together with the change in Ukraine's political guard signaled by the election of Volodymyr Zelensky in March 2019, have opened a new era of uncertainty about Ukraine's continued role in transit.

Much discussion of Nord Stream 1 and 2 has focused on what these projects would mean to Ukraine by reducing its role in transit. These debates also raise the question: Is there a "right" to playing a transit role? Until now, initiatives such as the Energy Charter Treaty process, and also widely used concepts of energy supply security and energy security more generally, have focused on the need to guarantee an energy good's safe passage from producer to consumer, and the ability of diverse producers to access energy transit infrastructure (e.g., through the principle of third-party access), but always with the end consumer as the focus of attention. Can we also talk of a country's right to maintaining a profitable role in an energy exports system that, in a different (Soviet) political context, that country was key to maintaining in working order, not only through transit services but also through broader networkness management services (see chapter 4), such as storage and pressure management?

Yet despite the obvious significance of its technical role in this system, the question of Ukraine's role in transit cannot be answered at a solely technical level; rather, it raises political and even moral questions calling for a deep understanding of history. Should countries and regions that were for decades subject to the dependency ("threat") effects of being made part of certain supply and infrastructure chains built under a previous political system (the Soviet Union) also be guaranteed access to the benefits ("opportunity") side of being part of these chains? Does the European Union have a moral duty to extend solidarity to Ukraine on the basis of what many see as its historical and contemporary role as bulwark vis-à-vis Russian expansionism as well as against Nazi aggression and enormous loss of life in World War II?

Ukraine and the New Gas Molecule

At the same time, the diversification of natural gas and oil supply options in the European Union—such as direct physical supplies, physical swaps, and virtual swaps (through which, for example, a country such as the Slovak Republic could purchase Russian natural gas as contractually German without this gas ever having physically been in Germany[23])—further forces a rethinking of our long-standing understanding of European energy space and value chain space, an understanding that originally took shape together with the beginning of large scale Soviet natural gas supplies to Western Europe in the early 1970s.

The important value chains tied to Russian exports on which Ukraine bet its future for a significant part of its postindependence period are in crisis—and not only because of Russian policy. Indeed, the fact of the building of Nord Stream as a project largely intended to bypass Ukraine is a problem. But other trends are likely to be as important for Ukraine in the medium term. Transitioning from a world of contractually fixed transportation paths to one based on real competition ushers in a new world where the gas (methane) molecule will be increasingly free. Thus perhaps an equally fundamental problem seems to be the fact that Ukrainian energy transit policy still seems to be tied to the concept of contractually defined, fixed transit paths closely tied to Russia's export value chain. In addition, the increased role of electricity-based systems, and competition between the combustion engine world and the electric engine world, between the gas (methane) and oil molecules and the watt—even if this watt was produced from natural gas or oil—opens new challenges. These challenges will need to be addressed directly.

Materiality and the Decarbonization Transition

This book has focused on the differences between various fossil fuels and their power implications—both in terms of "power over" and "power to." The analysis of fossil fuel diversity undertaken here could also be extended to a broader set of primary energy sources, such as various types of renewables, with different physical characteristics affecting key secondary features, such as transportability, the sizes of typical markets, distribution, and storage. Such structured comparisons also have practical policy implications related to the challenge of drastically reducing the carbon footprint of human activity, a key goal if global warming is to be kept under control. Moreover, moving toward the goal of decarbonization will entail replacing a variety of fossil fuels, not only widely talked about oil. Each of these fossil fuels involves not only technical-use specificities but also a variety of social and political relationships related to their use—including but by no means limited to the issue of the interest groups related to each of these businesses. Only by understanding this diversity will we be able to develop a realistic understanding of the manifold challenges on the way to decarbonization—and a feasible road map to get there.[24]

———————

This book is about the threat and opportunity made possible by certain value chains involving Russian fossil fuels reaching Western Europe via Ukraine—but also about their crisis and near demise, as in the case of the Ukrainian transit of Russian natural gas and oil to Western Europe, which had declined sharply by 2014. What risks and opportunities, threats and temptations, will the new energy chains of an EU set on decarbonization bring?

CHAPTER EIGHT

Disruptive Energies and the Tentative End of a System: An Epilogue

EARLY IN THIS BOOK, our focus period, October 2011 to March 2014, was described as one of "calm before the storm." Some aspects of the storm were swift, such as the April 2014 Russian military incursion in Ukrainian territory and the annexation of Crimea. Others had been years in the making but reached a critical point in 2014. All put under pressure fossil fuel value chains that had remained largely stable since 1991, value chains that had supported the maintenance of particular types of post-Soviet political systems. Already during the focus period, these value chains had started to come under pressure. By 2014, they were facing crucial changes. In this epilogue, we look at these chains' disruption, at the impact of this disruption on the countries crossed by these value chains, and across the ocean at the political crisis involving Donald Trump's presidency.

VALUE CHAINS UNDER PRESSURE

The energy value chains analyzed in this book were, first, affected by changes in global market conditions. Key factors included the entrance into the global market of new energy sources and a global low price environment for fossil fuels.

A first factor concerned the explosively increasing role of energy types that had until then not played a significant role in the world market, including new production forms of fossil fuels (unconventionals), old fossil fuels seeing a resurgence due to price dynamics (coal), and renewables. Although—with the partial exception of Poland—shale gas did not make significant inroads in Central and Eastern Europe, unconventionals played a disruptive role due to the global changes set in motion by the fall in prices unleashed by the U.S. boom.[1]

A second type of disruptive energy (and, many would argue, the only truly disruptive one) concerned renewables. Their increased role in the European Union's market resulted from targets and regulations—including increasingly stringent motor fuel requirements—that synergized with national-level measures such as guaranteed prices for renewables-generated electricity.[2] In addition, as a result of economies of scale, the cost of producing renewable energy—in particular wind-generated electricity—went down significantly. The increase in the use of renewables was much more significant in the case of countries such as Germany (where it more than doubled, from 17 percent to 40 percent of electricity generation between 2010 and 2019[3]) than in the case of other countries crossed by this book's value chains. Especially in the German case, in addition to their direct impact on displacing fossil fuels, the growing role of renewables also synergized with increased public sentiment, not only against fossil fuels but also against large (natural-gas-based) electricity generating companies.[4] Thus the Nürnberg power plant at the end of the natural gas value chain discussed in chapter 4 was not only left waiting for a cloudy and windless day, but also faced an increasingly hostile public opinion, further disincentivizing investments in such infrastructure.

Let us now take a look at changes taking place at the level of each of the value chains.

The Natural Gas Value Chain

The natural gas chain deserves special consideration—as well as a somewhat lengthier discussion—due to its being exemplary of processes also going on in the oil and coal value chains, as well as to its importance for EU policies as a whole. In the case of natural gas, three key disruptive developments involved changes in Russian transit policy, changing EU regulations, and the increased role of liquefied natural gas (LNG).

Russian transit policy. A key change affecting the course of the chains after 2014 was Russia's redirection of transportation routes aimed at moving away from reliance on transit states, and especially on Ukraine, replacing existing physical chains with new ones such as the Yamal pipeline and, later, projects through the Baltic (Nord Stream 1 and 2) or Black Sea (the never-realized South Stream, as well as the Turk-Stream project unveiled in 2014). Their impact was seen especially clearly on transit volumes through Ukraine, where changes already in motion since the 1990s gained speed in about 2011–14. By 2014, transit via Ukraine (62.2 billion cubic meters) had declined by more than 40 percent from its 2011 level;[5] despite temporary increases in the following three years, even the maximum post-2011 transit figure of 93.5 billion cubic meters (2017) was a full 20 to 30 percent lower than the volumes transported in the 1991–2006 period. In 2018, transit declined again, to 86.8 billion cubic meters. If both Nord Stream 2 and a further Gazprom project, the TurkStream pipeline to Turkey under the Black Sea, were to be completed and used at full capacity by Gazprom, this could mean a further substantial reduction in transit, and also in Ukraine's bargaining power.

The increasing role of LNG. Second, the growing role of LNG was slowly but surely affecting the natural gas value chain. Although LNG supplies did not involve the entrance of a new type of energy (LNG can come from both conventionally or unconventionally produced gas), transforming natural gas into a liquid substance made possible LNG's rise as a globally traded commodity. And though LNG had been used for decades to supply markets lacking pipeline access, its rise as a global commodity came only in the 2000s, having been made possible by price trends equalizing the higher costs required by the liquefaction process. LNG's share in global gas trade increased from less than 30 percent in 2003 to 46 percent in 2018,[6] with supply increasing by almost 10 percent in 2018 alone.[7] Even with Europe as the "market of last resort" for LNG exporters due to generally lower prices than in Asian markets with less access to alternative (pipeline) supplies, this growth helped kick-start supply chains different from the ones that had dominated European gas supplies since the early 1970s. These new chains involved increased supplies by tanker from various locations (mainly Qatar, Algeria, and Nigeria, and, slowly at first, the United States) to Northern European ports (as opposed to Southern European areas, where LNG supplies had a long tradition), regasification, and, now in gaseous form, transit along inland pipelines. This affected the constellation of actors coalescing around the chain, and it challenged the idea of natural gas markets as first and foremost regional, not global, markets.[8]

LNG reminds us of the ways in which technological change—through the way it affects midstream operations—can set into motion new technical-social chains and coalitions. Indeed, the very start of modern oil in the 1860s provides an example of how technical changes opening new transportation possibilities could set one group of actors against another. When the first rudimentary oil pipelines were developed, they upended the prevailing transportation technology, which until then consisted of oil being transported in barrels (whatever barrels could be found: "wine, whiskey, fish, nails, or salt pork barrels"), hauled by teamsters organized around the Brotherhood of Pennsylvania Oil Haulers, "a notoriously tight clique" whose members "earned five times the average wage of other union workers."[9] As the first pipelines were put into use, angry teamsters, seeing the danger of a pipeline that was making them superfluous, "vandalized one pipeline installation after another as the pipeline industry emerged."[10] Similarly, the rise of LNG in the 2010s could be seen as threatening established ways of doing business, which centered on pipeline-transported natural gas, first and foremost from Russia.

A number of factors limited the impact of LNG in Central and Eastern Europe, however. Its high (and largely fixed) liquefaction and regasification costs make LNG less competitive in a low-price than a high-price environment,[11] making it less competitive in the wake of the 2014 global slump in oil (and natural gas) prices; during the period 2010–17, average LNG prices in EU states were about 15 to 25 percent higher than prices for pipeline natural gas (see table 8.1).[12] This was especially the case for price competition from Russian pipeline gas, given Russia's lower production cost and transportation advantages;[13] the marginal cost of supply, including liquefaction costs, for U.S. LNG in Europe is about 25 percent higher than Gazprom's.[14] Although nearly half of LNG supplies to the EU were to old LNG markets lacking pipeline import infrastructure, such as Spain and Portugal, supplies to northwestern European ports gained increased momentum later in the decade.[15]

TABLE 8.1

Average Price of Germany's Pipeline Natural Gas Imports versus the EU
Price for Liquefied Natural Gas, in Dollars per Million BTUs, 2010–17

Year	Average Price of Germany's Pipeline Gas Imports	Price for EU Member States of Liquefied Natural Gas
2010	6.04	6.9
2011	7.62	9.5
2012	8.58	10.3
2013	8.08	10.6
2014	6.90	8.8
2015	5.93	6.6
2016	4.51	4.8
2017	4.99	5.5

Sources: Germany's average pipeline imports: International Energy Agency, "Natural Gas
Information 2018," table 2: selected natural gas import prices into Europe by pipeline, p.
IV.4; liquefied natural gas price for EU member states: International Energy Agency, "Natu-
ral Gas Statistics," https://www.iea.org/statistics/naturalgas/.

Although the much-hyped idea that U.S. LNG supplies would
change Europe's energy and political landscape did not materialize,
LNG's impact could be seen in more indirect ways.[16] For instance,
shortly after Lithuania's first regasification facility (a floating unit aptly
named "Freedom," which was also the first in the region) was put into
operation in 2014, even when its actual use remained limited given the
high price of LNG supplies as compared with pipeline imports from
Russia, it helped Lithuania negotiate a 23 percent price discount from
Gazprom.[17] Similarly, though Central European hopes that regasified
LNG from the Świnoujście terminal in Poland (opened in 2016) could
be easily transported throughout the region and serve as a real diversification factor were probably overstated, the very existence of this
option could bolster their bargaining power vis-à-vis Gazprom.[18] However, this will not necessarily mean more independence from Russian
gas—Russian producers, first and foremost Novatek, were investing
heavily in LNG facilities and seemed intent on conquering a significant
share of the European (as well as global) LNG market in the 2020s.
At the same time—akin to the situation in natural gas-fired electricity
generation facilities, which had been kept on standby for a "cloudy
and windless day"—LNG regasification facilities were often used at

partial capacity but were kept on standby, acting as a counterweight to Gazprom's market power. This raises a key issue: at which cost should this infrastructure be kept in operation if maintaining this capacity is considered key for national security—and who should pay for this?

Despite it not being fully competitive with pipeline gas supplies, U.S. LNG also became a disruptive factor through its discursive use, as U.S. administrations and energy companies argued that it could be crucial for breaking Russia's role as monopolist gas supplier. This was accompanied by strong lobbying efforts by well-connected U.S. suppliers, as would come to light in the course of the presidential impeachment investigations that started in 2019 (discussed below).

Changes in the EU's regulatory environment. Last but not least, changes in the EU's regulatory environment also made 2014 a key year for changes in the gas value chain. December 31, 2014, had been set by the European Council as the deadline for completing the preconditions for the EU's internal energy market integration.[19] Two sets of official EU regulations were especially important: competition-related regulations and infrastructure-related initiatives.

Related to long-term intellectual trends favoring the liberalization of network-related industries, competition-related policy regulations aimed to create a level playing field in support of more market integration.[20] Among these, the most significant were measures codified in the 2009 Gas Directive and Third Internal Energy Market Package (often referred to as the Third Package), which called for third-party access (TPA) to pipeline capacity, the breakup of national monopolies, and the unbundling of gas and electricity systems—that is, outlawing a single company from owning the production, transportation, and distribution of natural gas or electricity. Although the Third Package formally entered in force in 2009, its enforcement became more stringent starting in 2014.

Such competition-focused regulations also had a key impact on infrastructure issues. Although not mentioning Gazprom explicitly, these regulations limited the company's ability to own pipelines transiting its gas in the EU, as well as its ability to use 100 percent of a pipeline's capacity without providing TPA to other users. TPA came to the forefront of attention through issues related to the Nord Stream underwater pipeline connecting Russia and Germany while circumventing Ukraine. In particular, at issue was the question of the terms under which Gazprom would be able to use the OPAL pipeline connecting directly with Nord Stream's terminal in Lubmin (Germany) and, traveling south, reaching consumers in Germany and the Czech Republic.[21] Gazprom's holding a legal monopoly on pipeline natural gas exports from Russia made it impossible for other companies at the point of origin to supply gas to the pipeline, meaning that it was not clear how the TPA requirement could be fulfilled. (The other alternative proposed by the EC, for Gazprom to implement a so-called gas release program "by selling at least 3 bcm [billion cubic meters] of natural gas at auctions to stimulate competition in the Czech Republic's gas market," was not considered seriously by Gazprom, because selling this gas at auctions would have helped depress prices for its gas.[22]) The specifics of the story on Gazprom's access to OPAL capacity are rather complex, with numerous changes between 2015 and 2020. A key point, however, is that up to the fall of 2019, Gazprom was able to use more of the pipeline's capacity (i.e., without capacity set aside for other potential shippers). This resulted from a 2009 agreement reached with Germany's energy regulator Bundesnetzagentur and with reference to a provision of the EU Gas Directive relaxing TPA rules for "energy infrastructure projects that enhance competition and security of supply, but, given their project risks, would not happen without the exemption."[23] The "project risks" noted by the EC as grounds for an exemption were directly related to natural gas's materiality characteristics, which in turn were related to its gaseous form, in particular the limited transportation options and high investment costs complicating the possibility of bringing additional gas supplies to a starting point (Lubmin), and the technical and financial burden of operating a pipeline at less than full capacity (see chapter 4). Such decisions also brought to the fore issues related to Gazprom's lobbying power vis-à-vis the EC, which was exemplified by the role played by high-level politicians, such as former German chancellor Gerhard Schröder, who, after leaving office, became chairman of Nord Stream's Shareholders' Committee Board.[24]

In September 2019, the European Court of Justice placed OPAL back under full EU jurisdiction and limited Gazprom's use of the pipeline to 50 percent of its capacity. This called into question how Gazprom would be able to fulfill its sale contracts to inland markets served by OPAL now that its ability to use its full transit volume would be limited. In addition, in December 2019 the United States imposed sanctions on companies participating in Nord Stream 2; and in May 2020 the German regulator ruled that it would not be exempted from EU unbundling regulations banning the same-company ownership of both the pipeline and the gas being supplied. Though these developments do not prevent the pipeline from being completed, they complicate its operation; and, thus, they mean that—at least in the short term—Gazprom needs to maintain or even increase transit via Ukraine in order to be able to fulfill its contractual obligations.

This situation, together with delays in the completion of Nord Stream 2—which Gazprom had hoped would be ready before the December 31, 2019, expiration of its transit contract with Ukraine's Naftohaz—partially explains Gazprom's December signing of the contract—after a year of speculation that Gazprom would not enter into a new contract and that, as a result, Ukraine could be left with dangerously low transit volumes (see chapter 7). These zigzags around Nord Stream 2's regulation and the question of OPAL's use, however, should not turn our attention away from the reality that both the Nord Stream 2 and TurkStream pipelines are likely to be completed in the early 2020s, with the implication that Gazprom's need for transit through Ukraine is likely to decrease significantly.

The developments described above were taking place within the context of the EU's security-of-supply goals, which aimed at diversifying away from reliance on one dominant supplier. December 31, 2014, was also the deadline for putting in place measures that would guarantee that all EU states would have continued emergency supplies in the case of a disruption of external supply.[25] As became increasingly clear with Russia's 2014 intervention in Ukraine, and as the investigations of Gazprom's possible abuse of market power progressed, such issues could also have important "hard security" implications.

In addition to official regulations, no less important were what could be called quasi-regulatory developments, which mainly related to a number of EC legal proceedings against Gazprom. In 2015, the EC opened a case against Gazprom, arguing it had engaged in "abuse of dominant position" and hindering of competition in the supply of natural gas to Bulgaria, the Czech Republic, the Slovak Republic, Hungary, Estonia, Latvia, and Lithuania, for which Gazprom was the sole supplier, as well as in imposing unfair pricing and contractual conditions hindering gas supply diversification.[26] As of 2020, the case had not been fully concluded—the May 2018 EC decision suspending the antitrust case against Gazprom, but imposing a number of binding obligations on the company to change its business practices, was appealed by Poland, which imposed its own $7.6 billion fine on the company in October 2020.[27] In a separate but related development, in May 2020 the Arbitration Institute of the Stockholm Chamber of Commerce, which is commonly known as the Stockholm Arbitration Court, ruled that Gazprom owed Poland's PGNiG $1.5 billion due to having overcharged it for natural gas between 2014 and 2020.

These developments were calling into question key elements of a natural gas contractual model that had been dominant for nearly four decades. Key elements of this system were destination clauses preventing importers from reselling gas volumes outside their borders, long-term contracts (with a typical duration of twenty to twenty-five years), oil-based price indexation, take-or-pay commitments holding importers financially responsible for purchasing a certain minimal amount (typically, 75 to 85 percent of the nominal quantities) of contracted volumes, and commercial secret regulations hindering transparent pricing.[28] From the EC's perspective, such clauses created obstacles to competition and to the free movement of goods within the EU. In calling into question this contractual system, the EC was also reducing Gazprom's indirect regulatory power and its headquarters' power as not only commercial but also de facto regulatory nodes.

These events took place in a context where typical natural gas contracts were also changing as a result of market developments.[29] As discussed above, the oversupply of natural gas experienced in the European market after 2010 led to more gas-on-gas competition, higher market liquidity, and an increase in spot market transactions.[30] These market developments affected contractual issues as increased supply options gave importers more power to counter Gazprom's conditions. For example, as a reaction to high oil-indexed prices that they saw as fully out of sync with a new, low-price environment,[31] a number of Gazprom customers in Europe started to successfully pressure the company to renegotiate long-term contracts to move a portion of their contracted volumes to spot prices; by 2015, we start to see a closer alignment between the Russian gas price charged to Germany and spot prices.[32]

The Oil Value Chain

Key pressures on the oil value chain had to do with Russian transit policy and EU regulations. Already since the 2000s, Russia had been pursuing a strategy of building new infrastructure (e.g., the new oil terminals Primorsk and Ost Luga and the BPS-1 and BPS-2 pipelines) as a way to circumvent Ukraine and the Baltic states as oil export routes. Such views were also enshrined in official documents, such as Russia's Energy Strategy to 2020 (2003) and Russia's Energy Strategy to 2030 (2008); this strategy intensified after 2014. Thus, EU oil imports from Russia remained stable, but now increasingly taking place directly, without the participation of transit states. A key factor affecting our chain was changes in Russian tax rules favoring oil product exports. These changes contributed to making Russia the largest exporter of refined oil products to the EU, supplying nearly a third of its oil product imports throughout the 2010s.[33] Compounded with the problems besieging Ukrainian refining discussed in chapter 5, they meant that now more Russian exports to Ukraine would be in the form of refined products rather than crude oil, further weakening Ukraine's transit role.

Although, in the 2000s, oil as a "low-networkedness" type of energy had been less central to EU policy than natural gas, Russia's 2014 annexation of Crimea and the worsening of relations with Russia brought oil closer to the EU's attention concerning security of supply. With Russia's status as the largest source of refined oil products imports for the EU, the EC realized that the prior emphasis given to emergency reserves of crude oil would likely not be sufficient in the case of a crisis, and so it started to pay increased attention to oil product imports from Russia as well as Russian investments in EU refineries.[34] The shift in EC views on the importance of various segments of the oil value chain—that is, from a primary interest in the supply of *crude* oil to increased attention to its midstream refining component— is especially significant. This concerned not only the EU's stated need for diversification of oil import sources but also the transportation routes for oil and oil products, an area where an official Russian public relations campaign had long sought to unfairly cast Ukraine as an unreliable transit partner vis-à-vis the EU.

With regard to oil and oil products, most EU regulations came in the form of progressively more stringent environmental standards affecting automotive fuels (from EURO 1 fuel standards in 1992 to EURO 6 in 2014 and EURO 7 standards expected to be implemented in 2021[35]). These increasingly ambitious standards affected the oil value chain because, given the EU's growing demand for refined product imports, only refineries able to comply with these conditions had a chance to export to the EU market, limiting Ukraine's ability to export to these markets despite its physical proximity.

The Coal-Metallurgical Value Chain

Key changes in the coal value chain had to do with changes in the market role of coal, EU regulations, and the effects of Russian military intervention in Ukraine. A temporary but at the time very important trend was the growing role of coal in power generation in about 2014, aided by the boom in unconventionals (which drove down natural gas prices in the United States, increasing its market share and leading many U.S. coal users to substitute natural gas for it, creating a surplus of low-priced coal, much of which found a market in Europe). This lower-price surplus coal (whose import prices in Europe fell more than 50 percent between March 2008 and May 2014[36]) drove a temporary increase in coal use in the EU, at the same time as the EU's emissions trading system—seen by many as ineffectual due to the low price assigned to CO_2[37]—put few hurdles on the way for coal to gain a larger share, despite its worse CO_2 profile compared with those other fuels and a number of EU regulations affecting its use in power generation.[38]

However, the most important change to our coal-metallurgical value chain came from an unexpected direction: Russian military intervention and the military conflict in the Donbas. Despite the fact that Ukraine continued to purchase coal from Russia even after the 2014 military incursion and the fact that Metinvest's supply chains—including factories on both sides of the conflict line—continued to function until disrupted by separatists in 2017, the coal-metallurgical value chain analyzed in chapter 5 was profoundly affected by the military conflict in the Donbas and, in particular, by the establishment of entities in the area propped up by the Russians—the so-called Luhansk People's Republic (LNR) and Donetsk People's Republic (DNR). It was affected by coordination problems involving the connection between physical nodes located on both sides of the conflict line. In particular, it was affected by the changed balance of forces in the Azov and Black Sea areas after Russia's armed annexation of Crimea. Starting in 2018, Russia's intensive patrolling of the Azov Sea and forcible inspection—and intimidation—of ships coming in and out of Mariupol created a de facto naval blockade, threatening to bring to a halt Ukraine's metallurgical exports through the city, home to two of the country's most important metallurgical factories, the MMK Iron and Steel Works and Azovstal, as well as a major port. Table 8.2 provides

TABLE 8.2

Natural Gas, Oil, and Coal from Russia to Germany via Ukraine: Main Changes in About 2014

Commodity	Key Change	Analysis
Natural gas	Ukraine's official consumption and imports from Russia are drastically reduced; imports of Russian-origin gas continue, but on the basis of reverse flows from neighboring states. Ukraine's transit role is drastically reduced. Gazprom's share in EU's natural gas imports did not change significantly, but continued its gradual increase, from 27% in 2011 to 35% in 2017.*	Ukraine's fall in official consumption is due more to economic contraction and fall in GDP and the fact of not counting use in heavily industrialized DNR and LNR than to increases in efficiency. Chain is affected by significant increases in prices charged Ukraine, as Russia cancels previous discounts. EU levels of natural gas imports from Russia remain stable, but now increasingly taking place directly, without the participation of transit states.
Oil	Ukraine's transit role is drastically reduced. Russia's role in the supply of oil and oil products to the EU remains stable. As Ukraine's refining industry collapses, its dependence on imports of Russian crude oil is replaced by dependence on imports of refined oil products.	EU levels of oil imports from Russia remain stable, but now increasingly taking place directly, without the participation of transit states.
Coal	Ukraine continues to buy coal from Russia, using it for metallurgical exports. Metinvest's supply chains continued to function across the conflict line until disrupted by separatists in 2017.	Ukrainian segment of the coal-metal chain is affected by coordination problems involving feedstock and nodes located in uncontrolled territories. Ukraine's metallurgical exports decrease as a result of shipping problems in the Sea of Azov as result of Russian intimidation of Ukrainian and Ukraine-bound vessels.

Source: Author's notes and analysis based on the information presented in this book.

* From James Henderson and Jack Sharples, "Gazprom in Europe: Two 'Anni Mirabiles,' but Can It Continue?," *Oxford Energy Insight* 29 (2018): 7 (based on Gazprom data), https://www.oxfordenergy.org/wpcms/wp-content/uploads/2018/03/Gazprom-in-Europe-%E2%80%93-two-Anni-Mirabiles-but-can-it-continue-Insight-29.pdf.

a summary of how each of our main three value chains changed in about 2014.

THE IMPACT OF THESE CHANGES ON THE VARIOUS COUNTRIES IN THE CHAINS

What was the impact of these changes on the key countries involved in our value chains? As is discussed below, this impact depended on each country's role in the value chain, as well as on its regulatory and governance environment.

The Impact on the Russian Segment

At first, it seemed that Gazprom's business would be significantly affected by changes in the EU market, but in the short term this was not the case, because it started to adapt to the new contractual environment by negotiating with importers and selectively offering more competitive price and contractual conditions.[39] The May 2018 EC decision suspending the antitrust case against Gazprom but imposing a number of binding obligations on the company also points in this direction. Russia also succeeded in launching its new projects aimed at diverting natural gas transit away from Ukraine, in particular the Nord Stream 2 project, which, despite ongoing disputes, started construction in 2018. Once operational, it would double Nord Stream's capacity to 55 billion cubic meters, further moving transit volumes away from Ukraine. A future EU energy balance based on renewables, however, would deeply affect future demand for Gazprom's exports. (EU demand for natural gas, originally predicted by the International Energy Agency to start flattening in 2022, went down already in the spring of 2020 as a result of the COVID-19 pandemic and related economic slump—which also led to a drastic 46 percent decline in transit through Ukraine in April 2020 alone.[40]) Similarly, the European Court of Justice's 2019 decision restricting Gazprom's OPAL use, together with the impact of EU and U.S. sanctions on specific links of Russia's energy value chains, made the outlook start to look less positive for Russia.

The Impact on the Ukrainian Segment

The impact of these changes on Ukraine was at times contradictory—but ultimately highly worrisome. The most important changes for Ukraine were the country's ability to contractually (but not physically) diversify away from Russian gas, and the further decline in both natural gas and oil transit via its territory. In the immediate aftermath of 1991, Ukraine was in a strong bargaining position due to its important transit role, leading to widespread references to a "bilateral monopoly" with Russia as (near) monopoly supplier and Ukraine as (near) transit monopolist;[41] over time, this bargaining power was significantly reduced as Ukraine's role as transit route starts to decline (on the various reasons for this decline, see chapters 4 and 5; concerning transit declines in the 2010s, however, it is important to note that in 2018, Gazprom was found to be in breach of contract for not transiting the contracted amounts for the previous years).

In about 2014, Ukraine's gas consumption as well as its gas and crude oil imports from Russia start to decrease drastically. Although Russia's military intervention strengthened the resolve of many in Ukraine to reduce dependence on energy purchases from Russia, these decreases were not necessarily the result of higher energy efficiency, higher renewables use, or use of domestic energy sources. And though crude oil imports from Russia decreased, dependency on imports of Russian refined products increased, as in the case of diesel (which increased from about 10 percent of consumption in 2010 to 25 percent in 2017) and liquefied petroleum gas (which is commonly known as LPG, and which reached 54 percent in 2016).[42] The decrease in natural gas use had to do with the sharp contraction of the economy after 2013, tensions with Russia (immediately after the April 2014 Crimea takeover, Gazprom announced an 81 percent increase in gas prices to Ukraine; after a dispute over payments, it ceased supplies for six months), and the fact that areas not under Kyiv's control (Crimea and the so-called DNR and LNR areas) were not included in the statistics. Imports of physically Russian gas continued, but through different contractual means—reverse supplies from the Slovak Republic, Poland, and Hungary. Indeed, one key impact of EU-level regulatory changes is that, by affecting these countries' contractual environment by making clear that the EU did not support key elements of the traditional contractual system such as destination clauses, they made possible Ukraine's access to reverse gas supplies. Although, as discussed in chapter 4, this was by no means a smooth process, without the EU's challenge of the traditional natural gas contractual model, it would have been simply impossible.

Ukraine and a new conceptualization of European energy space. What was behind the contractual trends discussed above—including the challenge to destination clauses that was so crucial for Ukraine to be able to access reverse supplies—was a much broader reconceptualization of energy space. The model envisioned by the EC, in contrast to the world of long-term contracts and point-to-point deliveries, involved a vision of the gas market as a (physical or virtual) space where gas from different origins would meet, and could be bought and sold freely on the basis of spot prices; this gas would come from both regasified LNG as well as pipeline supplies, where, in a "common carrier" system, a neutral system administrator would allocate access to transportation capacities—as well as the fees for these—through a transparent process. Such space, and in particular natural gas space, was gradually being reconceptualized: from one based on *fixed contractual paths* and *fixed delivery points* (where, indeed, there was not much trading but simply delivery of already-contracted volumes) to a conceptualization based on *hubs* (where trading and gas-to-gas competition would take place) and *zones*, within which distance would be contractually inconsequential and a gas/methane molecule would be freely replaceable by another—and thus, all points in the zone could be considered equivalent.

These developments presented both new opportunities and new challenges for Ukraine. Although Ukraine supported the new gas market rules proposed by the EC, paradoxically, due to Ukraine's transit role being so intrinsically tied to Gazprom's export value chain and associated contractual path, in the transition period before a move to a fully open and liquid gas market, its transit role had much to lose with this new conceptualization of energy transit space. By moving away from a long-term contract, start- to end-point-based transportation fees and movement along a fixed contractual path as the key natural gas transportation concept, and toward treating equally all gas flows leading to a trading hub, already the EU's Second Gas Directive of 2003 "phased-out transit as a concept."[43] So while Russia was busy phasing out the reality of transit states and promoting direct supply routes such as Nord Stream, the EU was set on phasing out (traditional) transit as a concept. Although concern about the threat to Ukrainian transit represented by Nord Stream 2 is only natural, overfocusing our attention on this issue may also take attention away from an even more crucial question for Ukraine: what is its role in a new energy world, a world characterized not only by a new conceptualization of energy space but also by moving away from the fossil fuels that dominated the Soviet and post-Soviet value chains in which Ukraine was so central?

Ukrainian oligarchs and changing value chains. How did these changes affect the economic and political role of traditionally dominant Ukrainian energy actors, which in the previous system often had a vested interest in maintaining Ukraine's dependency on Russian energy?[44] If the experience of 2005's political changes (the Orange Revolution) tells us anything, it is that the power of entrenched actors has been highly resilient. The difference between the experience of 2005 and that of 2014, however, is that despite significant political changes in 2005, many of the value chains remained unchanged at that time. The 2014 political changes (the Euromaidan Revolution), in contrast, coincided in time with significant changes in the energy value chains that had created rents whose circulation in the political system had supported a certain type of politics.[45]

One change was related to the significant increase in natural gas prices and the significant decrease in direct purchases from Russia, which made largely impossible the continuation of rent-seeking through arbitrage rents related to the coexistence of multiple prices for natural gas. Similarly, some of the rent-seeking related to transit lost currency and oligarchs' role in gas transit diminished.[46] At the same time, despite the Euromaidan protesters' commitment to de-oligarchization, the power of Ukrainian energy oligarchs continued unabated. The same key players from the 2011–14 period continued to play key roles in 2020, with some changes in their portfolios.

The natural gas magnate Dmytro Firtash continued to control key sectors of the Ukrainian energy sector, with an especially important role in the chemical and titanium industries, both of which, being very energy intensive, can benefit from access to low-price natural gas such as that enjoyed by Firtash in his many years as the main intermediary for murky transactions involving Russian natural gas in Ukraine (see chapter 4). He led these businesses from Vienna, where he was arrested in 2014 on a warrant from the U.S. Federal Bureau of Investigation; freed on a $172 million bail, he is facing potential extradition to the United States on charges of bribery involving titanium supplies. (The United States' extradition request was approved by a Austrian judge in 2019, but has been blocked due to technical reasons.) In the course of the U.S. impeachment inquiry in late 2019, it emerged that President Trump's attorney, Rudy Giuliani, had sought to pressure Firtash to provide information on the son of Trump's contender, former vice president Joseph Biden, in exchange for help in avoiding that extradition.[47]

After a noisy confrontation with the state in 2015 regarding his informal control of Ukrnafta (see chapter 5), Ihor Kolomoyskyi's Privat company managed to remain one of the largest players in the automotive fuel retail sector. He also gained significant influence in the government of President Volodymyr Zelensky, the surprise winner of the 2019 presidential elections; Kolomoyskyi associates were named to key cabinet positions. He has used this influence, as well as that in the Verkhovna Rada, to push for policies aligned with his interests, as well as to gain advantages vis-à-vis rival oligarchs. In particular, his group was behind a proposed law that would impose high taxes on iron ore mining, a key part of Akhmetov's coal-metallurgical value chain, though not affecting manganese ore, a related sector controlled by Kolomoyskyi.[48] At the same time, his position came under increased scrutiny as he was seen as using his new influence to have the 2016 nationalization of Privatbank reversed, a move that created a stir in the international financial community as a large International Monetary Fund loan to Ukraine was seen as being contingent on prosecuting those responsible for money misappropriated at the bank, amounts that were bailed out by the state. In May 2020, the Parliament of Ukraine passed a law banning the return of nationalized banks to former owners, showing the limits of Kolomoyskyi's new influence. Kolomoyskyi was also targeted by Giuliani as part of his efforts to unearth negative information on Biden's son.[49]

After a period of confrontation with President Petro Poroshenko in 2014–15, Rinat Akhmetov seemed to have found a modus vivendi with the new power, and—despite significant problems with industrial assets in separatist territories—remained Ukraine's strongest energy actor, with assets in several energy branches and controlling 85 percent of coal production, 23.8 percent of electricity generation, and 30.5

percent of renewable energy.[50] Although his apparent power declined in 2019 as rival oligarch Kolomoyskyi sought to use his political connections with President Volodymyr Zelensky to undermine Akhmetov's positions, his influence never disappeared. Although the party he supported—the Opposition Bloc—did not formally win any parliamentary seats in the 2019 elections, his continued power could be seen through his influence over individual deputies as well as control of a key economic sector.

The Impact on the EU and German Segment

The impact of these changes in the EU segment of the value chains had to do first and foremost with EU regulations (discussed above). These EU regulatory developments, together with the market liberalization and opening promoted by the EU, fostered the emergence of large utility companies active in several countries and benefiting from larger market areas (e.g., Vattenfall, Engie, and Enel), leading to mergers and the dissolution of traditional, single-country-based companies.[51] All this, compounded by the growing competition from renewables in power generation, exacerbated the decline of established national gas suppliers such as E.ON Ruhrgas, which had been key as Gazprom's traditional downstream partners.

Going beyond declarations, what real changes could be seen in the European markets after 2014? Three data points are central: the degree to which the market integration and liquidity envisioned by the EC were becoming a reality, the prevalence of the contractual forms favored by the EC, and the degree of dependency on Russian fossil fuels. The liquidity of major European gas hubs, as evidenced by raising "churn rates" (i.e., the frequency with which each gas molecule is traded) continued to increase, but "in different ways and at differing speeds across the continent,"[52] with Northern Europe much closer to the ideal than the rest of the continent; a fully liquid and open market encompassing the EU as a whole had not yet been achieved. (In practical terms, the closest the EU had gotten to a hub-based system by 2019 was through the system of entry/exit zones, a gas network access model allowing "users to book capacity rights independently at entry and exit points, . . . creating gas transport through zones instead of along contractual paths" as in the point-to-point contract model;[53] as of 2019, however, a single EU entry/exit space was still on the horizon, with most single states' gas markets still organized, as in 2014, as single "entry/exit zones."[54])

Concerning contractual forms, the trend toward transparent gas-on-gas competition pricing (e.g., hub-based, spot market pricing), in contrast to oil-indexed longer-term contracts, which had increased rapidly from 2009 on, started to stabilize in 2014 at about 61 percent of total volumes, with smaller gains in the following years.[55] Although some long-term contracts continued to be signed after 2010 (e.g., those between Gazprom and Bulgaria and Hungary), these were of shorter duration (four to ten years) than those that were the norm until 2010 (between twenty and twenty-five years).[56]

Given these changes, what happened to dependency on Russia? Despite the rise in renewables, EU natural gas consumption (as well as imports from Russia), which had reached a low point in 2014, started to increase again in 2015.[57] Gazprom's share in EU natural gas imports grew significantly (from about 23 percent in 2014 to 35 percent in 2016, 2017, and 2018[58]), while the share of Russian supplies in oil, oil products, and coal imports remained largely stable. A significant decline in the demand for Russian energy would also imply a significant decline in Russia's ability to use energy for leverage; contractual changes could also reduce Gazprom's ability to use its market power.

EURASIAN VALUE CHAINS AND THE CRISIS OF THE TRUMP PRESIDENCY

That the value chains analyzed in this book would reach well beyond the EU and across the Atlantic was made clear in the fall of 2019, when revelations concerning U.S. president Donald Trump's pressure on Ukraine to gain advantage against a domestic political opponent, former vice president Joseph Biden, unleashed a tumultuous impeachment process, which would be only the third in U.S. history. As the story continued to unfold in the fall of 2019, the clearer it became that Ukraine's role as the target of such pressure had everything to do with the chains analyzed in this book, with the key element connecting these and the broader story being the issue of sanctions imposed on Russia in the wake of its 2014 military intervention in Ukraine. Ukraine is key to all the chains affected by sanctions due to the simple fact that the sanctions are largely about Russia's invasion of Ukraine. For example, Ukraine is key for the Nord Stream natural gas value chain not because it is physically on its path (it is not) but because the negative effect that the full use of Nord Stream would have on Ukraine has prompted sanctions against companies participating in the project. Similarly, Ukraine is key for the potentially booming Arctic oil value chain not because it is physically on its path (it is not) but because EU and U.S. sanctions against Russia specifically targeting Arctic oil projects are about Russian aggression toward Ukraine. So, for Russian actors to be able to unlock these value chains, a solution to the sanctions issue needs to be found, and also a solution to Ukraine's concerns about Russian aggression in Eastern Ukraine. In fact, the desire to unlock these chains is one of the two key reasons (besides the desire to maintain a lever of influence on Ukrainian politics) for Russia's support of a plan (the "Steinmeier Formula") to return the LNR and DNR territories to limited Kyiv control, but in an arrangement that would give them a distinct, self-governing status.

In what ways does the crisis of the Trump presidency—in its full arch, involving both suspicions of Russian interference in the 2016 elections and the alleged 2019 quid pro quo and parallel policy vis-à-vis Ukraine—intersect with the natural gas, oil, and coal chains analyzed in this book? To understand these connections, we need to understand that the so-called Ukraine scandal was never just about Ukraine, but also very much about Russia and about how sanctions were affecting the entire value chains extending from Siberia to the EU and beyond.

In the case of natural gas, one important element of the Ukraine story concerns the 2019 efforts of two shady businessmen associated with President Trump's private lawyer to—through what amounted to a parallel foreign policy outside regular channels—reshape the leadership of Ukraine's state energy company, NAK Naftohaz, in order to get it to purchase large amounts of U.S. LNG originating from companies related to these individuals. In order to do so, they exerted pressure on the Ukrainian government to replace the reform-minded chief executive of Naftohaz, Andriy Kobolyev, with another Naftohaz senior executive, U.S. citizen Andrew Favorov, who was seen as amenable to their proposals. According to press reports, U.S. energy secretary Rick Perry was also closely involved in these attempts. In addition, natural gas was directly related to the quid pro quo at the center of the investigation, as Burisma, the company on whose board

Joseph Biden's son had served and that president Trump wanted investigated, had competed for natural gas production licenses—an area where long-standing corruption issues had made it harder for Ukraine to increase production and thus become more self-sufficient.

The oil value chain also figures in the impeachment inquiry, but from a different perspective, going back to the key Russian interest in influencing the U.S. administration: the lifting of sanctions imposed on Russia as response to its 2014 intervention in Ukraine. Some of the most damaging sectoral sanctions imposed on Russia targeted Russia's deepwater, Arctic offshore, and fracking-related oil projects and, thus, its ability to develop some of the few areas where—given the rapid increase in increasingly unprofitable mature brownfields discussed in chapter 5—growth and profits could still be expected.

Concerning the coal-metallurgical chain, the key link with the Trump-Ukraine scandal had to do with the way sanctions had affected a key player in a subbranch of this chain, the Russian Aluminum conglomerate Rusal—which produces 7 percent of the entire world's supply of aluminum—and its owner, Oleg Deripaska. Rusal and Deripaska are the best-known targets of sanctions directed at seven Russian oligarchs, twelve companies, and seventeen senior Russian officials accused of supporting malicious Russian state activity around the globe. Imposed on April 2018, the sanctions originally intended to shut Rusal entirely from international markets—the first time the United States and the EU imposed full blocking sanctions on a top-twenty Russian firm, with ripple effects all along the global aluminum value chain.[59] Deripaska emerged as one of the key behind-the-scenes players seeking to influence the U.S. administration to lift these sanctions, which were watered down in May and lifted in late 2018 in exchange for Deripaska reducing his ownership stake in Rusal's parent company. Deripaska also seems to have been the key person behind Paul Manafort's attempt to influence both U.S. policy and the Republican Party's official position on Ukraine already at the 2016 Republican National Convention.[60] The coal value chain also figures directly in the story, as related to Paul Manafort's work on behalf of Rinat Akhmetov, the key player in the coal-metallurgical chain analyzed in chapter 6. In fact, Akhmetov used some of the money made through this chain to support then–president Yanukovich, including by helping to fund a parallel, underground budget for Yanukovich's Party of Regions, which paid for Manafort's public relations services.

INTERPRETING THESE CHANGES FROM AN
ENERGY-MATERIALITY PERSPECTIVE

The changes taking place in about 2014 can be understood within the context of our general view of energy materiality: it may create constraints to actors' choices, but it does not itself dictate these choices. For example, in the case of LNG, the high energy expenditures needed to transform a gaseous substance into a liquid one created new hurdles for its marketability; in the case of renewables and renewables-produced electricity, issues of storage were key. Materiality issues also synergized with these developments in two additional ways: first, changes such as the increased use of LNG took a familiar energy good and gave it new materiality characteristics, in the process also altering our views of the size and connectiveness of natural gas markets.[61] Second, the impact of external impulses was mediated by the materiality characteristics of the various goods. For example, new rules on the need for third-party access to pipeline capacity were both co-constituted by concerns about the network significance of natural gas *and* had a particular effect on natural gas markets exactly because of natural gas's high degree of networkness.

Earlier in this book, chapter 3 discussed some of the ways in which different value chains bring to the fore different types of risk. All energy value chains present challenges concerning issues of coordination and the sharing of risk between participants (e.g., buyers and sellers), but these challenges differ depending on the type of energy being considered, and are more acute in the case of those types of energy with relatively higher sunk cost investments involved in their typical production and delivery processes, such as natural gas. Seen from a value chain perspective, the EU's unbundling legislation sought to replace vertical integration with a market relationship as a means of managing risk; in the EC-favored contractual and pricing model, there is an attempt to move risk-sharing from contractual long-term commitment and into the ongoing costs of supplies; a perfectly liquid market would (at least in theory) ameliorate some of the typical risks associated with natural gas, such as the risks of sunk costs and stranded assets.[62]

The idea behind these EU initiatives is that these risks are assessed by players in economically rational terms, but here the EU may have been too naive. Even when there were always two sides in EU policy—acknowledgment of the need for some degree of public intervention without which policies such as the move to renewables would be impossible was always present, alongside and often in tension with the push for competitive markets[63]—the EU was not always properly equipped to deal with issues requiring clear intervention and investment above and beyond that by private actors, which, for example, may not see a business rationale for investments in import diversification infrastructure to reduce dependency on Russia. Thus, not being able to tackle geographic diversification directly, the EU ended up tackling the issue through what could be called contractual and contractual diversification means—that is, the management of the risks of dependency on a single supplier through the use of a variety of contract types and duration frames and the support of new contractual models.

This also meant that the EU was ill prepared to deal with the political challenges coming from Russia's more centralized energy system, or to recognize the full impact of situations where infrastructure may be built for primarily noneconomic reasons but, once built, changes the way the value chains work. One example may be projects such as Nord Stream, which some have seen as not economically justified. This applies in particular to the Nord Stream 2 project, which—especially after a 2019 EU decision subjecting its flows to EU regulation—saw its profitability take a sharp turn downward. Although it appears that Nord Stream 2 is not the most economically efficient way of bringing Russian natural gas to Germany, it seems to be, indeed, highly profitable for close-to-the-Kremlin construction companies and pipe suppliers.[64] In this case, the interests of a subgroup of the Russian elite seem to have coincided with a particular foreign policy vision by the Russian leadership to push for a project which, though having a debatable economic basis, can play an important political role. This brings us back to the point made at the beginning of this book: energy policy has multiple uses above and beyond producing electricity, heat, and transportation fuel; no less important are the various material and social goods produced by energy systems as processes, ranging from systems of social provisioning for the many to rents for the few.

Glossary of Key Technical Terms in the Natural Gas, Oil, and Coal-Metallurgical Chains

General Terms

benchmark prices: the most important and widely used price quotations for a particular commodity, widely used as reference points. Especially used for oil and coal. For oil, some key benchmark pricing brands are West Texas Intermediate, Dubai/Oman, and Brent, with nearly two-thirds of world contracts using Brent prices as benchmark reference. While coal qualities and prices vary much more than those of oil, the prices of Central Appalachian (United States), Newcastle (Australia), South African export, and Colombian stem coal are commonly used as benchmarks, but in a less rigid manner than in the case of oil, where some prices (e.g., the Russian Urals discussed in this book) are explicitly understood in terms of a particular discount from a benchmark price, most often Brent.

brownfields: aging oil and natural gas fields with declining and increasingly inefficient production rates, close to reaching maturity.

bulk dry cargo: cargo that is dry (i.e., cannot be transported by pipeline) and has low value per unit of volume (e.g., most types of coal).

carbon dioxide (CO_2) emissions trading (cap-and-trade) system: a system in which countries and companies are given a quota for CO_2 emissions but are allowed to exceed these limits if they purchase surplus emission rights from other countries and companies. The system (under the name EU ETS) was first established in the EU in 2005 but has seen only limited success due to the overallocation of emission allowances and the resulting low price of emission rights, which have not acted as an incentive to reduce emissions.

carbon intensity: the amount (grams) of CO_2 emitted per kilowatt-hour generated as electricity; it depends on the energy source as well as the generation technology used.

commercial nodes: locations where key commercial decisions affecting a value chain (e.g., concerning prices and contractual conditions) are made; these nodes are not always coterminous with the physical ones. For example, a key commercial node in the European natural gas value chain is located in the Gazprom headquarters in Moscow (as a conceptual, not strictly physical space), where important decisions concerning the company's strategy in Europe are made.

common carrier: a transportation infrastructure (e.g., in energy, an oil or gas pipeline) open to any third party under a standard, transparent set of terms (e.g., published prices or the auctioning of capacity), in contrast to a private infrastructure serving only the owner or selected users. Closely related to the concept of third-party access (see below).

decarbonization: the process of reducing the carbon (CO_2) footprint of energy production and human activity.

differential rents: the rent or profit related to differential natural advantages available to different natural resources producers, differences which allow them to produce a good (including minerals "produced" by extraction such as oil or natural gas) at different costs.

diffuse resources: natural resources scattered widely, and at least in theory amenable to/likely to be extracted by a large number of small operators; common examples are timber and some crops such as wheat.

downstream: processes related to the marketing, distribution, and selling of final products to consumers; these final products include, among others, natural gas and its derivatives, refined products from crude oil (such as gasoline, diesel, and chemical industry feedstock), and coal and coke. Related infrastructures include local gas distributors and gasoline stations. (Some textbooks include refining as part of the downstream process.)

energy density: the amount of useful (extractable) energy per unit, usually measured in megajoules per kilogram or in terms of volume.

energy mix: the proportions of different types of energy (e.g., oil, natural gas, nuclear, and renewables) used in a particular country, locality, or sector of the economy.

final energy and energy services: energy as consumed by end users, in such forms as fuel used by motor vehicles (gasoline, diesel), electricity, or energy services such as heating (as opposed to primary energy sources).

fungibility: mutual replaceability of units of a good, which make possible their sale as standardized units. Fungible goods are goods composed of standardized, easily replaceable units. Oil, and especially oil belonging to a single brand (e.g., Brent or Urals), is an example of a fungible good.

midstream: processes related to energy transportation between markets, and further processing into usable goods, such as refining; also includes storage and other ancillary processes. In the natural gas industry the midstream includes gas treatment, separation of natural gas liquids (NGLs), liquefied natural gas (LNG) production and regasification plants, storage, and gas pipeline systems. In the oil industry it typically includes refining, transportation, and storage. In the coal sector, the midstream segment refers mainly to cleaning, transportation, and (in the case of metallurgical coal) processing into coke.

natural monopoly: refers to a situation where, due to the characteristics of the economic sector (for example economies of scale, the economic efficiency of large-scale production by a single company) and the high cost of entry for each separate participant, it may be more economically efficient for a single company to take on a monopoly position. Many have justified Gazprom's role in the Russian gas sector (where, until 2013, it held a monopoly on all gas exports and continues to hold a monopoly on pipeline gas exports) on natural monopoly grounds.

netback pricing: a price-setting mechanism (especially used in natural gas and part of Gazprom's stated pricing philosophy since the early to middle 2000s) based on the goal of maintaining equal returns for the seller in all its export markets. In this case, the price in the main markets at the end of the pipeline (Germany) would be taken as reference, and prices to other markets derived from it by subtracting the difference in transportation costs. This is in contrast to both the principle of oil-indexed prices (based on the replacement cost of the natural gas in each individual market) and the gas-to-gas competition principle, where natural gas prices are set through supply and demand in competitive markets with multiple suppliers.

network balancing: the process of making sure a networked system is maintained in safe operational balance through measures such as managing the grid system load and wattage coming in and out (in the case of electricity), the pressure of the pipelines, and natural gas intake and out-take (in natural gas). It is especially relevant for highly networked types of energy such as electricity and natural gas.

network-related industries: industries relying heavily on a network, such as electricity or natural gas, but also other industries such as telecommunications, postal services, and the internet.

networked energy: term used to denote types of energy where users depend heavily on a network, as opposed to autarchic/autonomous supplies (from off-grid residential solar panels for example); it also refers to the degree to which the overall functioning of the system depends on the network working properly *as a network* and being physically balanced as a system, for example, keeping an appropriate load (in an electricity grid) or maintaining the appropriate level of pressure (in a natural gas pipeline) in order to prevent accidents such as the system coming to a standstill (gas not moving due to insufficient pressure in the pipeline) or even collapsing (blackouts).

oil-price indexation: the indexing of natural gas prices to correspond to fluctuations in the price of oil, with a determined lag period. (De facto, it refers to indexation to the types of energy sources most prevalent in a country or market; traditionally, the specific calculation for each market and contract has been considered a commercial secret.) Such clauses go back to the 1960s and 1970s, when large-scale natural gas imports started to arrive in Western European markets; such clauses intended to smooth the entrance of this new fuel by pricing it at a similar level than other fuels used in that local market. Since the early 2000s, it has come to be gradually replaced by prices based on supply and demand.

physical nodes: refer to critical points ("nodes") where key processing takes place. Some examples involve the preprocessing of primary energy before it can be traded, refining of crude oil into higher-value products such as gasoline, gas pipeline intake points, oil import terminals, trading hubs where natural gas is further distributed, transit from a lower-price market to higher-priced one, and points where export duties and taxes are levied onto a product.

"point" (or "pointy") resources: natural resources concentrated in small areas and at least in theory amenable to/likely to be extracted by a few producers; common examples are oil, natural gas, and plantation-type crops.

primary energy sources: raw energy before conversion or processing (as opposed to final energy and energy services consumed by end users).

regulatory nodes: locations where key regulatory decisions affecting a value chain are made (e.g., decisions on taxation, rules for access to transportation infrastructure, or environmental standards). These nodes are not always coterminous with the physical ones or commercial ones. For example, a key regulatory node in the European natural gas value chain is located in the European Commission in Brussels, whose regulations affect the entire European natural gas value chain.

stranded assets: costly assets that may become economically obsolete (i.e., no longer able to earn an economic return) before the end of their expected economic life. Assets may become obsolete or "stranded" as a result of a variety of factors—changes in technology or regulations, changing societal preferences, the discovery of new types of energy, or, in the case of oil and natural gas, the discovery of new gas and oil fields leading to unused pipelines or other infrastructure. Also related to sunk costs (see separate entry); stranded assets differ from sunk costs in that sunk costs are about assets that can possibly still yield a revenue stream; once that revenue stream ceases, they become stranded assets.

sunk costs: costs that, once made, cannot be recovered; for example, those related to capital-intensive infrastructure which may go unused if circumstances such as prices or consumption patterns change. Good examples are energy infrastructure, especially highly capital-intensive infrastructure such as natural gas pipeline systems. Also related to stranded assets (see separate entry).

third-party access (TPA): a system of access to transportation infrastructure associated with natural monopolies (e.g., gas pipelines) where the owners of this infreastructure are obliged to provide access to this infrastructure to other users besides itself or its clients on a transparent, competitive basis. Various systems have different rules as to what percentage of transit volumes should be made available to third parties, including competitors.

transfer pricing: a system whereby companies use reduced prices for sales between their own entities as a way to hide profits and minimize taxes.

trunk pipelines: large-volume, large-diameter pipelines intended to transport oil or natural gas at high pressure over long distances between states or within a state. Refers to both oil and natural gas pipelines (although the technology for both pipelines is different).

upstream: processes related to the production (i.e., extraction) of a primary energy resource. Includes the searching for potential fields, drilling of exploratory wells, and subsequently operating the wells or mines to bring the crude oil, raw natural gas, coal, or other natural resources to the surface.

value chains: the entire cycle of economic activities involved in bringing a product to the end user, from conception, planning, and exploration through various stages of physical transformation with inputs from other goods, to delivery to final consumers, to disposal and after-use. As used in this book, the concept includes both the material movements in the chain, the value addition (or subtraction) that takes place as a good moves through this chain, and the financial flows and chains associated with them. In spatial terms, value chains can be of any length, involving an intra-country, continental, or global footprint.

vertical integration: a type of arrangement where a lead or mother firm and producer of the initial good controls the entire chain. In the energy sector, it most often refers to arrangements where an oil-producing company (or its subsidiaries) also refines this oil and controls its distribution and final sale at the pump as refined products such as gasoline and diesel derived from this crude oil. Thus, companies such as LUKoil, ExxonMobil, and Shell—having assets in the upstream, midstream, and downstream segments of the value chain—are referred to as "vertically integrated." (This does not mean, however, that they refine in-house all the oil they produce.) In the global value chain research tradition, vertical integration is also referred to as one of various possible systems of governance of global value chains, alongside "market," "modular," "relational," and "captive" relationships between lead firms and suppliers as alternative patterns of organizing these chains.

Natural Gas Value Chain

associated petroleum gas ("associated gas"): natural gas produced as a by-product of the oil production process. Traditionally, this gas was deemed uneconomical to collect and sell, and was vented or flared into the atmosphere, releasing significant amounts of methane (in venting) or CO_2 (in flaring). Regulatory issues may be behind these practices, such as the fact that until recently Russian oil companies were not allowed to commercialize this gas; they are still banned from exporting it via pipelines.

In the 2000s it is being increasingly used as fuel for local power stations and/or processed into propane and natural gas liquids (NGLs) for use in chemical plants.

churn rates: the frequency with which a natural gas (methane) molecule is traded; used as a measure of the degree of liquidity in a hub-based natural gas trade system.

compressor stations: stations located along a natural gas pipeline (in most pipelines, every 200 kilometers or so) in order compress the natural gas so that it can move through the pipeline. Most often, they are powered by gas drawn from the pipelines themselves—in some cases as much as 10 percent of the total gas transited—but electric pumping units exist as well.

condensate treatment plant: the second step in natural gas processing. Processes gas condensate into natural gas liquids (NGLs) and stable gas condensate, which then go into different production chains. As part of this process, a deethanization unit (deethanizer) separates ethane from the wet NGL feed, making sure crystalline solids—which can harm a pipeline—cannot form.

desulfurization: removal of sulfur compounds (e.g., hydrogen sulfide), highly lethal contaminants found in raw natural gas. These must be removed before further processing to prevent damages to humans, pipelines, and other equipment.

dry gas: natural gas after natural gas liquids and other impurities have been removed. This is the lighter-than-air, blue-burning gas most consumers experience as end users.

entry/exit zones: a gas network access model in which users book capacity rights independently at entry and exit points, rather than along a destination point-related contractual path as in the traditional system.

fixed delivery points: a contractual clause specifying that a particular volume of natural gas would be delivered to a particular end point. Under this clause, companies would not be allowed to sell gas transported over a common pipeline in each other's home markets. Part of traditional natural gas contract provisions in Europe. Closely related to destination clauses (also known as territorial sales restrictions) banning particular importers from re-selling to other markets the natural gas imported, thus preventing gas-to-gas price competition between gas from a single supplier at a delivery point (e.g., gas supplied by Gazprom and changing ownership at the Baumgarten gas hub in Austria).

gas condensate: the hydrocarbon liquids stream that is first separated from "dry" natural gas and is further processed into specific natural gas liquids; often referred to as wet gas.

gas-metering stations (GMS): stations designed to automatically measure incoming and outgoing natural gas flows into or out of a country or system.

hub-based natural gas trade: a system where natural gas is traded in points where natural gas from various suppliers meets, often the intersection point between two or more pipelines, facilitating gas-on-gas competition. For example, the Henry Hub in Louisiana is the world's largest natural gas trading hub, and its price quotation is often used as an important reference benchmark for North American pipeline natural gas and global LNG prices.

L-gas and H-gas: two qualities of natural gas that have coexisted in northeastern Europe since the 1970s through the 2020s. L-gas, produced only in the Netherlands, has a lower methane content and caloric value than H-gas, produced in the North Sea, Algeria, and, most importantly, Russia. H-gas (whose composition parameters are defined by a EU quality standard introduced in 2015, CEN EN 16726:2015) is considered as reference gas for engine building. Being noninterchageble, L- and H-gas are supplied trough separate networks. With the gradual depletion of the Groningen fields in the Netherlands, by the 2020s, L-gas would be gradually replaced by H-gas.

methane: a colorless flammable gas which is the main component of natural gas; typically, natural gas is composed of over 90 percent methane.

natural gas liquids (NGLs): substances (also known as "condensates") that are present in raw natural gas which are gaseous when under underground pressure, but become liquid once at normal atmospheric pressure on the surface. Because they can damage pipelines, they are removed after raw gas is brought to the surface, and are fractioned into their various components. These various components (e.g., propane, butane, and methane) usually fetch higher prices than dry natural gas, as they are used as specialized feedstock for other industries. In particular, chemical industries use ethylene produced from the NGL ethane as a key component in the production of plastic, paint, glue, and other products. NGLs can also be re-added to natural gas so that it can reach a certain caloric/BTU level contractually required by that pipeline or contract.

network codes: user codes (sometimes referred to as "shipping codes") containing information on the parties supplying and receiving the gas volumes and the volume of gas transferred. This allows gas to change ownership regardless of its physical location in the system. Thus, for example, a network code would signal that gas sold to the Slovak Republic should be redirected for Ukrainian use, officially making this Slovak gas sold to Ukraine, although technically this gas would never get to the Slovak Republic. However, for such virtual operation to happen, the supplier—in this example, Gazprom—needs to agree to provide the appropriate network codes; without this, ownership would need to change at a concrete physical location.

pipeline standard (gas): Refers to the caloric and quality standards for natural gas transited in specific pipelines, where the physical impossibility of batching means the gas volumes in a pipeline will mix. Bringing natural gas to a specific "pipeline standard" means making sure it reaches the minimal caloric and other quality standards for the pipeline, for example through adding high-caloric-value natural gas liquids. Not to be confused with the technical standards pipelines must fulfill as infrastructure objects.

pressure management (natural gas): the process of ensuring that, at each stage in the production and supply chain, natural gas is at the appropriate pressure for that stage so that it can be used safely and efficiently. When natural gas comes out of the reservoir, its naturally high pressure needs to be reduced so that it can be handled safely; later, pressure needs to be increased significantly, so that it can move forward in long distance pipelines. As it reaches power plants and the smaller-diameter pipelines of city networks or residential end-users, pressure needs to be reduced again to progressively lower levels for each of these respective users so that it can be delivered safely without risk of an explosion.

raw natural gas: the product which comes out of the well, in some cases mixed with oil. At this point, it still contains natural gas liquids (condensate, natural gasoline, and liquefied petroleum gas), water, and other impurities. As a first step, water must be removed, which yields gas condensate; this gas condensate must be further processed to remove natural gas liquids.

regasification (of liquefied natural gas, LNG): a process by which natural gas, which had been liquified at ultra-low temperatures, is brought back to gaseous state for distribution and transportation via pipeline. Regasification at the port of entry is necessary because, due to the need to maintain extreme low temperatures, it would be virtually impossible and prohibitively expensive to transport LNG inland in liquified form. Similarly, the high cost of LNG regasification facilities means that they will be concentrated in port areas where there is constant, high volume use. If the utilization rate is low, the (relative) cost of keeping the temperature low enough to prevent vaporization (i.e., to keep LNG liquid) increases.

reexport ban provision: a contractual clause banning importers from reexporting the natural gas imported from a supplier. Part of traditional natural gas contract provisions in Europe.

reverse supplies (natural gas): a reverse supply/flow (also known as "backhaul") may either be physical or virtual. In a physical reverse flow, natural gas which has reached a country is resold and physically sent back to a country it has passed through in its transit journey. In a virtual reverse, thanks to the use of network codes (see separate entry), a party of gas would not need to physically reach the importing state, but the last metering station in the previous state (e.g., Ukraine) would receive a message ("network code") confirming that a certain amount of gas had changed ownership, and that it should be redirected for Ukrainian use. Virtual reverse also makes it possible to receive reverse supplies from countries supplied by the same pipeline, but not immediately adjacent to the country which is to receive the supplies. Thus, for example, a virtual reverse scheme would allow Ukraine to receive contractually German gas, without this gas having to first reach Germany.

ship-or-pay clauses: contractual clauses subjecting a user of transit services (e.g., Gazprom) to penalties should it not ship a minimum volume of the natural gas volumes it agreed to ship as part of a contract covering transit; in other words, the shipper agrees to pay for contracted transportation capacity regardless of actually transported gas.

spot prices: refer to the current market price of a good (including oil, natural gas, and coal) for immediate delivery at the specific location where the good is purchased ("on the spot"), as opposed to futures prices or fixed, non-market prices.

take-or-play clauses: contractual clauses subjecting the purchaser of a gas volume to penalties should it not import a minimum volume of the natural gas; in other words, the consumer agrees to pay for a percentage of the contracted volumes capacity regardless of actually importing it. In the traditional natural gas contractual model, such clauses were intended to help share risks between suppliers and consumers.

technical gas: natural gas used to power compressor stations in natural gas pipelines. Refers to the way this portion of a pipeline's gas used for this purpose is designated, not to a different quality of natural gas.

transit system operator (TSO): in an unbundled natural gas trading system (such as that launched by the EU's 2007 Third Energy Package) where gas producers are not allowed to also own the transportation infrastructure transiting this gas, a TSO plays the role of coordinator in a system which should be open to all on the basis of transparent procedures. A country's TSO is responsible for transmission and operation control within the natural gas transmission system. While a pipeline system cannot be owned by the same gas-producing company, a country's TSO may have a variety of ownership models, such as state-owned (as in Finland) or owned by a consortium between a state entity and a private holding (as in the Slovak Republic).

underground gas storage (UGS) facilities: large underground reservoirs where natural gas is stored for later use or further transportation. Most often are depleted natural gas fields, salt cavern formations, and depleted aquifers. Access to such facilities is crucial for the efficient and safe work of the natural gas value chain, because it allows evening out daily and seasonal demand fluctuations and delivering additional natural gas during higher-demand periods (e.g., winter). The ability to store natural gas is essential for producers, because production cannot simply be turned off at short notice; if unable to store surplus production, a producer may have little option but to flare (in the case of petroleum associated gas) or let it escape. Because of the high volumes involved, all gas storage in gaseous form takes place underground; natural gas can also be stored above ground as liquefied natural gas, but this is not an efficient storage solution because it requires permanent refrigeration along with liquefaction and regasification.

working pressure (of a pipeline): the appropriate pressure for a pipeline to move its content forward safely. Varies with the content and diameter of the pipeline, among other factors.

Oil Value Chain

batching (oil): transporting crude oil via pipeline in batches of different qualities, which are kept separated in the stream by the use of a buffer fluid (often synthetic oil or a light hydrocarbon liquid), making possible the transportation of multiple types of oil per month; batching helps strengthen the branding of different oil qualities.

crude oil tank "farm": an industrial facility composed of multiple crude oil storage tanks, intended for long-term storage or for keeping at hand various types of crude oil to be blended for further use and distribution.

crude oil, key classification parameters: crude oil grades are usually classified according to two sets of parameters: place in the light–heavy continuum and place in the sweet–sour continuum (see separate entries). Thus a crude oil may be light and sweet (e.g., West Texas Intermediate), heavy and sour (Venezuela), but also medium-heavy and medium-sweet (such as Urals), or, though less commonly, heavy and relatively sweet, as in the case of Oriente (Ecuador) oil.

dieselization: a term commonly used to refer to the process as a result of which, between about 1990 and 2010, diesel cars as a percentage of the EU's total passenger car fleet increased drastically as a result of significant tax incentives. (This process was not repeated in other areas of the world.) These tax incentives where related to diesel motors' higher efficiency (which in turn was related to diesel's materiality characteristics compared with those of gasoline), which was assumed to more than compensate for diesel's higher CO_2 emissions, making it more environmentally friendly than gasoline. In reality, however, as was revealed by the 2014–16 diesel emissions scandal, this advantage had been significantly overstated; moreover, diesel car owners typically drove more miles than they would with an equivalent gasoline-run car, largely canceling the positive effect.

light versus heavy crude oil: light oil is low-density crude oil containing a high proportion of light hydrocarbon fractions. Usually priced higher than heavy crude oil types as it is easier to refine and yields a higher proportion of higher-price refined products (such as gasoline) than heavy oil. **Heavy crude oil** is a high-viscosity crude oil containing a low proportion of light hydrocarbon fractions. Usually defined as any crude oil with an API gravity (which measures the density of an oil compared to water; the lower the API gravity, the denser the oil as compared to water) of less than 20°. Not to be confused with **heavy fuel oil** (also known as residual oil), a high-contaminant, high-pollutant by-product of the crude oil refining process mainly used in commercial marine shipping.

oil derivates (also known as "oil derivatives") are products derived from crude oil as it is processed in refineries; main among these are ethylene, propylene, and "aromatics" (such as benzene and toluene) and used as key feedstock for the chemical industry. Although some of these products may also be derived from natural gas or coal, they are most often refined from oil. Not to be confused with oil-related derivatives, a type of financial instrument including futures trading based on (derived from) crude oil price fluctuations.

oil refinery specification: refers to the way a refinery is technically specified in order to work most efficiently with particular types of oil, such as light and "sweet" oil (such as West Texas Intermediate and Brent) or heavier and "sour" oil (such as Dubai and Venezuela oil), or, most often in the countries discussed in this book, medium-sour Urals/REBCO oil. While specifying an oil refinery to work with a particular type of oil does not necessarily preclude that refinery from working with other types, doing that may lead to significant efficiency loses. Thus the more the crude oil used differs from the one the refinery's distillation units have been specified for, the higher the refining cost and the lower the production yield, depth of refining, margins, and profitability. Most refineries worldwide specialize in light sweet oil, the easiest to process; only specialized "complex" refineries can efficiently process heavy "sour" oil. While such refineries can also process lighter, sweet oil, doing so in a refinery specified to work with heavier crude oils would typically lead to efficiency losses. Most refineries in the former Soviet Bloc built during the communist period are specified to most efficiently process the medium-heavy, medium-sulfur Urals and REBCO brands of crude oil.

refined oil products: include a variety of products refined from crude oil, in two main categories: motor oils used for transportation and heating (such as gasoline, diesel, heating oil) and petrochemicals used mainly for chemical industry use (such as olefins and polyolefins including ethylene, propylene, and benzene used as chemical industry feedstock). Also includes products used as industrial lubricants, and, at the end of the spectrum, residual fuel oil from which products such as asphalt to pave roads are made.

refinery product slate: the type and quality of products produced by a given oil refinery. While a refinery will try to maximize profits and adapt to market demand, there are limits to the refinery's production slate flexibility and its management's ability to modify the slate. This is so because of the constraints created by the interface between the qualities of the crude oil feedstock it can obtain and process ("crude slates") and the characteristics and complexity of the refinery's equipment ("refinery configuration"), in particular its fractional distillation setup, the most commonly used distillation process.

refining margin: the difference in value between the products produced by a refinery and the price of the crude oil used to produce them. Closely related to "crack spread"; a more basic calculation of the difference between crude oil and petroleum product prices. **Crack spread** refers to theoretical/potential refining margins a refinery may have, whereas refining margins refers to the actual margins.

sweet versus sour crude oil: sweet crude oil is crude oil containing no more than 0.5 percent of sulfur; easier to refine due to lower levels of sulfur. Western Siberian and West Texas Intermediate are examples of such oil. **Sour crude oil** is crude oil containing more than 0.5 percent of sulfur and thus is harder to refine. Urals-Volga region oil (e.g., that produced in Tatarstan and Bashkortostan by Tatneft and Bashneft) and Dubai/Oman are examples of such oil.

technological oil (sometimes referred to as "technical oil"): oil used to keep oil pipelines in good working order even if they are not being actively used; normally cannot be sold as fuel.

Urals/REBCO oil brands: Russian oil export blend based on a blend of heavy Ural-Volga oil and lighter Western Siberian oil.

Coal and Metallurgy Value Chain

basic oxygen furnace (BOF): a steel-producing process where molten pig iron and steel scrap are converted into steel using the oxidizing action of pure oxygen blown into the mixture in a blast furnace. Requires iron, coal, and limestone as feedstock. As of 2019, about 75 percent of all steel worldwide was produced through this method. The BOF process uses coke as both a heating and reducing agent, but in smaller amounts than those required by the less-advanced open hearth furnace (OHF) process (see separate entry).

coal preparation plants (CPPs): plants where the initial washing, ash removal, and sorting of run-of-the-mine coal is carried out. Here various common contaminants such as rocks are removed so that the product achieves a degree of homogeneity.

coal washing: the initial processing of run-of-the-mine coal, involving the removal of impurities (especially ash) before transportation. "Washed coal" has a significantly higher heating value (often 25 to 30 percent higher as measured in calories) per weight unit than "unwashed coal," leading to significantly more efficient use in power generation. This process, also known as "beneficiation," is part of the broader process of initial coal processing, which also involves the sizing and sorting of the coal.

coke: specialized coal after being reduced (through an industrial process, see below) to almost pure carbon. Coke is used in metallurgical production both as fuel in the smelting process and/or as reducing agent in driving off the impurities of the product in the blast furnace.

coking coal (also known as "metallurgical coal"): refers to various types of coal used in metallurgical production, in particular steel production.

coking plant: an industrial plant where, through a complex and energy-intensive process, coking/metallurgical coal (a blend of coking coals) is turned into coke (which is almost pure carbon) by heating the coal in special airless ovens to drive out impurities. Nearly 1.5 metric tons of metallurgical coal are needed to produce one ton of coke. Because of their need for large amounts of water and energy, coking plants may have their own water access infrastructure and electricity generation facilities, which may also supply areas around the plant.

crude steel: produced from pig iron after it has been cleaned of impurities.

electric arc furnace (EAF): the most advanced steel-making process currently available, based on the smelting of scrap metal. It does not require coke, but uses largely steel scrap as feedstock. (The scrap steel used in steel production using the EAF method was originally made using coke, but as this scrap is usually decades-old disposal metal, the coke contained in this scrap is usually not counted as a direct feedstock in the process.)

intermediate steel castings: a type of semifinished steel product produced from crude steel. It includes "long products," such as blooms and billets, and "flat products," such as large-format steel slabs; continuous cast slabs are the most common and best-known intermediate steel casting. These castings require additional processing (re-rolling) to produce the shapes and qualities needed by end consumers.

metallurgical plant: industrial facility where iron ore and other feedstock is transformed into steel. May use one of three key production methods: open hearth furnace (OHF), basic oxygen furnace (BOF), and electric arc furnace (EAF) (discussed separately).

open hearth furnace (OHF): steel-producing process (also known as the Siemens–Martin process) whereby iron ore is combined with coke and very small amounts of scrap metal to produce pig iron in a blast furnace. Requires coke as both heating and reducing (i.e., driving out of steel impurities in the blast furnace) agent. The least efficient steel-making process, as of 2000 had been largely phased out, and as of 2019 accounted for less than 0.4 percent of total world steel production. Currently still used commercially only in Ukraine, which that year produced about 20 percent of its steel through this method.

open-pit mining: a coal mining technique where, in contrast to traditional underground mining, a cut is made in the ground (often in a mountaintop) and explosives blow open parts of the surface to expose the coal or other minerals.

pig iron: the immediate product of the blast furnace, later refined to produce steel or iron. It contains a high level of impurities, which need to be removed by transfering the pig iron to a furnace where oxygen is blown into the iron to remove the carbon and other impurities, resulting in crude steel.

run-of-the-mine coal: coal as it comes out of the mine, before passing through a coal-processing plant or being sorted, "washed," and impurities removed.

steam coal (also known as "electricity coal"): refers to various types of coal used in electricity generation, including bituminous coal, lignite (brown coal), and various types of hard coal.

steel alloy: steel that has been alloyed with additional elements (such as manganese, nickel, chromium, molybdenum, vanadium, silicon, and boron) to give it improved characteristics, such as added strength, corrosion resistance, and machinability (ability to be cut using a machine tool). Among the many steel alloys, stainless steel is the most widely used.

steel products, semifinished: include, in order of complexity and value-added, items going from manganese alloys (e.g., silico manganese and ferro manganese) used to increase strength in steel alloys, to ferronickel used for stainless steel production, to pig iron, to intermediate castings such as blooms and heavy steel slabs, steel segments ready to be re-rolled into final products of still higher value, such as quarto plates.

steel products, finished: include items such as pipes and rails, wires and tubes.

steel quarto plates: a specialized steel product, widely used in shipbuilding and energy infrastructure such as wind turbine towers. Takes its name from the specialized equipment used in its production, the four-high "quarto" mill, a reversible mill with two work rolls and two backing rolls, where the top and bottom rolls are driven by separate motors, making it possible for the slab to be passed back and forth through the mill.

steel re-rolling: the shaping of larger pieces of steel into thinner sheets of specific thickness by passing them through two rolls. More generally, this refers to steel re-rolling mills (see below).

steel re-rolling mills: mills specializing in the shaping of larger pieces of steel into thinner ones by passing them through two rolls, thus producing specialized, higher-value-added products such as quarto plates. Re-rolling mills may import intermediate castings such as large-format steel slabs and transform them into higher-value products using more sophisticated re-rolling machinery than is available at the original mill.

steel scrap: discarded steel products such as from automobiles, industrial structures, buildings, railroads, and ships, and recycled into new uses, in particular through making of new steel through smelting as part of the Electric Arc Furnace steel production process.

Main Actors

Note: Unless specified, the information in this appendix is valid for the focus period of this book, 2011–14.

Adviivka Coking Plant: a coking plant in Adviivka, Donetsk Region, Ukraine. Acquired by the Metinvest group in 2006.

Akhmetov, Rinat: the wealthiest person in Ukraine, owner of the System Capital Management (SCM) holding group including Metinvest and DTEK. Key player in Ukrainian politics, including through his support of the Party of Regions in the Donbas. Together with Viktor Pinchuk and Serhii Taruta was active in the early 1990s takeover of state-owned coal and metallurgical companies in the Donbas. All were original members of the ISD (Donbas Industrial Union) group, from which Akhmetov would later part ways to create his own group, System Capital Management (SCM).

Alekperov, Vagit: the longtime president of LUKoil (1993–).

Azovstal: a major metallurgical company in Mariupol, Ukraine, specializing in continuous cast steel slabs, the most common type of semifinished steel, requiring further processing before final use. Owned by the Metinvest group.

Bachatskaya-Koksovaya Coal-Processing Plant: a coal-processing plant near the village of Startobachaty in Kemerovo Oblast, Russia. Owned by Kuzbassrazrezugol.

Baltic Pipeline System (BPS) I and II: an oil pipeline system inaugurated in 2001 (BPS I) and 2012 (BPS II), intended to reduce Russian reliance on transshipment through Lithuanian and Latvian ports by making possible seaborne exports via the Primorsk and Ost-Luga ports in the Russian Baltic.

Bashneft: a Russian oil (and natural gas) company based in Bashkortostan and owner of three oil refineries in the region.

Bundesnetzagentur (German Federal Network Agency): a German state agency in charge of regulating network industries such as electricity, gas, telecommunications, postal, and railways networks. Partially responsible for decisions on the use of OPAL pipeline from the Nord Stream terminal in Lubmin, Germany; the extent of such national-level decision-making on such major pipelines originating from outside the EU was a key issue of debate in the 2010s.

Central European Gas Hub: Central Europe's most important natural gas trading hub, located in Baumgarten, Austria, where physical supplies from Norway and Russia's Brotherhood pipeline meet.

Deripaska, Oleg: a key Russian metallurgical magnate, owner of major aluminum producer Rusal. In the 2010s, under U.S. sanctions for supporting malicious Russian state activity throughout the globe and suspected of a possible connection with Russian collusion in the U.S. 2016 elections.

Druzhba pipeline: a system of multiple parallel oil pipelines starting in Western Siberia and dividing in Belarus into Northern and Southern branches, with the Northern branch going through Belarus and Poland and the Southern branch through Ukraine.

DTEK: a daughter holding of Rinat Akhmetov's SCM, specializing in energy engineering including natural gas production and electricity generation.

Duisburg Intermodal Terminal (Samskip Intermodal Rail Terminal): an intermodal rail terminal in Duisburg, Germany, integrating barge, road freight, and rail logistics and one of Europe's most important freight transportation cross-points.

Enercon: a German producer of wind turbines.

Energy Community: an organization established in 2006 with the support of the EU with the goal of extending EU internal energy market rules to nonmember states in southeastern Europe, the Black Sea region, and beyond on the basis of a legally binding framework. As of 2020, its members—in addition to the EU—included Albania, Bosnia-Herzegovina, Georgia, Kosovo, Moldova, Montenegro, North Macedonia, Serbia, and Ukraine; and, as observers, Armenia, Norway, and Turkey.

E.ON: a major German energy utility company operating thermal and nuclear power plants. One of the "big four" utilities (together with RWE,

EnBW, and Vattenfall Europe) controlling a significant part of German power plants in 2011. Became a major player in natural gas as Ruhrgas became its subsidiary when it merged into E.ON in 2003. In 2016, separated its fossil-fuel assets into a new company, Uniper.

ESPO (Eastern Siberia–Pacific Ocean) pipeline: an oil pipeline (inaugurated in 2009) linking Eastern Siberian oil fields with Russia's port of Kozmino on the Pacific, and aimed at facilitating deliveries to China, Japan, and South Korea.

European Commission: the executive arm of the European Union, in charge of drawing legislation and implementing decisions.

European Court of Justice: the European Union's highest court in matters of EU law, with the authority to adjudicate key jurisdiction issues such as whether specific pipelines coming from outside the EU, such as Nord Stream, should be under full EU, national, or joint jurisdiction.

Eustream: the Slovak Republic's natural gas Transit System Operator and main entity involved in the 2014 decision on reverse supplies to Ukraine.

Firtash, Dmytro: a Ukrainian businessman and political actor owning important assets in the natural gas and chemical industries through the DF Group. In the 2000s, closely associated with intermediary company RosUkrEnergo and other nontransparent gas trade schemes also involving Gazprom. Living in Austria and since 2017 facing a U.S. extradition order on a corruption charge.

Franken I: a natural-gas-powered power plant in Nürnberg, Germany, which during our focus period was owned by E.ON and was later taken over by E.ON's spinoff company, Uniper.

Gasunie: a state-owned Dutch natural gas infrastructure and transportation company, one of the European "incumbent gas suppliers" occupying a privileged position from the 1980s to the early 2000s.

Gaz de France: a French natural gas company. One of Mingazprom's (and, later, Gazprom's) key partners in gas imports to Europe from the 1970s on. Key "incumbent gas supplier" actor in the territorially divided gas trade business where each importing company was not allowed to sell gas transported over the same pipeline in each other's home markets. Merged with Suez in 2008.

Gazprom: Russia's largest company, involved in the production, transportation, and sale of natural gas (and oil, through its subsidiary, Gazprom Neft). Majority owned by the Russian state.

Gazprom Export: Gazprom's wholly owned export subsidiary.

Gazprom Neft: Gazprom's oil and oil-refining subsidiary; Russia's third-largest oil producer.

GDF Suez: a French energy company, and Gaz de France's successor; one of Gazprom's partners in the Nord Stream project.

Gosplan: a commonly used name for the Soviet Union's State Planning Committee, in charge of economic planning.

Gossnab: a commonly used name for the Soviet Union's Soviet State Committee for Material and Technical Supply, in charge of allocating supplies to various state enterprises.

ISD (Industrialnii Soyuz Dobassa / Donbas Industrial Union): a Donbas business group started in the early 1990s by Viktor Pinchuk, Serhii Taruta, and Rinat Akhmetov, which during that period was active in the informal takeover of state-owned mining and metallurgical companies.

Khartsyzsk Pipe Plant: a key steel pipe plant in Khartsyzsk, Ukraine, part of the Metinvest group, at a time supplying materials for Gazprom pipelines in exchange for natural gas.

Kolomoyskyi, Ihor: the head of the Privat Group, the main player in Ukraine's oil market for many years. Also owner of Privatbank, which, before its contested nationalization in December 2016 counted as its clients nearly half of the Ukrainian population and through whose electronic system most salary and pension payments were made.

Kremenchug refinery: a refinery located in central Ukraine, which as of 2014 was the only refinery in Ukraine working on a permanent basis.

Kuchma, Leonid: president of Ukraine (1994–2004).

Kudrin, Alexei: Russia's finance minister (2000–2011), associated with the 2001 Tax Code oil taxation reforms, which focused on revenue extraction efficiency and revenue-based (as opposed to profits-based) taxation.

Kurchenko, Serhii: a key associate of Ukrainian president Viktor Yanukovich; involved in natural gas, oil, and mining business.

Kuzbassrazrezugol: coal-mining company based in Kemerovo, Russia, specializing in open-pit mining; owner of the Bachatsky mine.

Litvinov refinery: a refinery in the Czech Republic, using as feedstock almost exclusively Russian crude oil; farthest direct destination of Druzhba South oil. Owned by Unipetrol and its majority shareholder, Polish PKN Orlen.

LUKoil: a Russian multinational oil and energy company, and one of the world's largest crude oil producers. Russia's second-largest company after Gazprom and the largest non-state-owned company.

Magomedov, Musa: general director of the Adviivka Coking Plant (2012–19).

Mariupol Ilyich Iron and Steel Works (Mariupolskii Metallurhinii Kombinat, MMK): Ukraine's second-largest metallurgical factory; owned by Metinvest. It was established in 1897, and is the oldest metallurgical factory in the city of Mariupol.

Mazeikiu Nafta refinery: a Lithuanian refinery through which significant refining and indirect re-exporting of Russian oil took place until Russia's oil transit monopolist Transneft, arguing technical problems, closed the Lithuanian branch of the Druzhba pipeline in 2007.

Mechel: Together with Evraz and Severstal, one of Russia's top vertically integrated mining and metallurgical companies; it controls about 25 percent of coking coal production in Russia.

Medvedev, Dmitry: Russia's president (2008–12) and prime minister (2012–20).

Metinvest: a Ukrainian daughter holding of Rinat Akhmetov's SCM, specializing in mining and metallurgy. A key player in Ukraine, with additional assets in Europe and North America.

MEGAL (Mittel-Europäische-Gasleitung) pipeline: a natural gas pipeline (inaugurated in 1980) crossing Southern Germany and transporting gas from the Czech-German border (and, through a Southern branch, the Austrian-German border) to the German-French border.

Merkel, Angela: German chancellor (2005–).

MERO ČR: a Czech state-owned company in charge of oil transportation.

Mingazprom (Soviet Ministry of Gas Industry): Gazprom's predecessor and the main Soviet entity involved in the beginning of large-scale natural gas sales to Western Europe in the 1970s; also a main partner of key "incumbent gas supplier" companies such as Ruhrgas and Gaz de France.

Mozyr refinery: a Belarusian refinery through which significant refining and indirect reexporting of Russian oil has been taking place since the 1990s.

NAK Naftohaz Ukraini (Naftohaz of Ukraine): Ukraine's national oil and gas company. It is in charge of natural gas and oil production, transportation, and refining. Since 2019, it has been undergoing a process of unbundling of its production, transportation, and supply assets.

National Commission of Electricity Regulation (NKRE): Ukraine's energy regulatory agency; during our focus period, under the strong influence of Rinat Akhmetov's group.

Nord Stream pipeline: a pipeline transporting natural gas from Ust-Luga and Vyborg in Russia to Lubmin, Germany, under the Baltic Sea, allowing for large-scale gas exports to Europe without going through the territory of traditional transit partners such as Ukraine. Its first two lines (Nord Stream 1) were completed in 2011. Its second two lines (Nord Stream 2), slated to be completed in 2021, were the center of much international controversy and sanctions by the United States.

Novatek: an independent (i.e., non-Gazprom) gas producer in Russia increasingly active in LNG production and exports during our focus period.

Novopolotsk (Naftan) refinery: a Belarusian refinery through which significant refining and indirect re-exporting of Russian oil has been taking place since the 1990s.

Odesa-Brody pipeline: an oil pipeline (inaugurated in 2004) intended to diversify Ukrainian oil imports by bringing Caspian oil imported through the Odesa oil terminal and transporting it to the northwest to Brody, where it would connect with the Druzhba pipeline flowing westward.

Odesa oil terminal: a facility in the Odesa port, making it possible for the port to receive supplies from medium-sized to large oil tankers. It is controlled by Ihor Kolomoyskyi's Privat Group.

OPAL (Ostsee-Pipeline-Anbindungsleitung) pipeline: a natural gas pipeline commissioned in 2011 to bring Nord Stream gas from its Lubmin terminal to Hora Svaté Kateřiny in the northern part of the Czech-German border (together with the connecting Gazelle pipeline, commissioned in early 2013), and also to Waidhaus in the southern part of the Czech-German border.

Ostchem: a key chemical industry and nitrogen fertilizer company in Ukraine; the world's third-largest nitrate producer. It is owned by Dmytro Firtash and the GDF Group.

Party of Regions: a Ukrainian political party established in 1997 with a strong base in the Donbas; it was widely considered the "party of power" through 2014. It was strongly associated with Viktor Yanukovich's roles as prime minister (2002–4 and 2006–7) and president (2010–14), and Rinat Akhmetov as a main supporter in the Donbas area. It won a plurality in the 2006, 2007, and 2012 elections.

Pinchuk, Viktor: the second-wealthiest person in Ukraine and owner of the metallurgical company Interpipe. He is a son-in-law and close associate of former president Leonid Kuchma. Together with Rinat Akhmetov and Serhii Taruta, he was active in the early 1990s takeover of state-owned coal and metallurgical companies in the Donbas.

PKN Orlen: a Polish oil company, and Central Europe's largest oil company; during the period 2011–14, it was Central and Eastern Europe's largest company in terms of revenue.

Privat Group: a global business group based in Ukraine. In Ukraine, it controls key assets in energy (oil production, through control of Ukrnafta), transportation (through control of Ukrtransnaftna), storage, and refining (through the Kremenchug, Nadvirna, and Drohobych refineries), as well as retail (about 30 percent of the gasoline and diesel retail market) and banking through Privatbank, Ukraine's largest commercial bank before its nationalization in 2016. It is controlled by Ihor Kolomoyskyi.

Putin, Vladimir: Russian president (2000–8 and 2012–) and prime minister (2008–12).

Prydniprovsky pipeline system: a pipeline system transporting Russian (and Kazakh) oil for export through the Odesa port in Ukraine.

RAO UES: a parastatal monopoly electricity utility in Russia controlling the majority of the country's electric grid as well as a significant part of generation capacities. It was liquidated in 2008 as part of the privatization of Russia's electricity infrastructure.

Rosneft: a state-controlled Russian oil company. It is Russia's largest oil company and the world's largest publicly traded oil company. It grew substantially in the 2010s through the acquisition of a number of Yukos assets in state-run auctions (2005–7) and the acquisition of TNK-BP (2013).

RosUkrEnergo: a key intermediary company especially active between 2004 and 2008 in the arrangement of the transportation and supply of Russian and Central Asian natural gas to Ukraine. It is owned by a Gazprom daughter company and the Centragas Group Associated with Dmytro Firtash. It is registered in Zug, Switzerland.

Ruhrgas: the first Western European company to sign a contract to import natural gas from the USSR (1970); it remained Mingazprom's (and, later, Gazprom's) traditional partner in Germany. It was a key "incumbent gas supplier" actor in the territorially divided gas trade business, whereby each importing company was not allowed to sell gas transported over this pipeline in each other's home markets. It ceased to exist in 2013 when it merged into E.ON.

Rusal: a key Russian aluminum conglomerate producing about 7 percent of the world's supply of aluminum. It is owned by Oleg Deripaska, and in the 2010s it was under U.S. sanctions for supporting malicious Russian state activity around the globe.

Russian Railways (RZhD): a Russian railway company; despite privatization and reorganization since the 1990s, its freight system remained much less transparent. It carried about 95 percent of coal transported domestically in Russia.

RWE: one of the "big four" utilities (together with E.ON, EnBW, and Vattenfall Europe) that controlled a significant part of German power plants in 2011.

Schröder, Gerhard: former German chancellor (1998–2005), chairman of Nord Stream's Shareholders' Committee (2006–), and chairman of the Board of Directors of state-controlled Rosneft, Russia's largest oil producer (2017–).

Senvion: a German producer of wind turbines.

Siemens Wind Power: a German producer of wind turbines.

Slovnaft refinery: a Slovak refinery (purchased in 2004 by Hungary's MOL), processing exclusively Russian oil.

Stockholm Chamber of Commerce, Arbitration Institute of (often referred to as the "Stockholm Arbitration Court"): an international commercial arbitration institution (one of a number of such institutions worldwide), commonly specified as an arbitral forum in Gazprom contracts. Though it is related to the general framework of international commercial law, commercial arbitration institutions are not regular courts. Parties to a contract agree to submit any potential contractual disputes to a specific arbitration institution when they would prefer binding arbitration to litigation in national courts.

System Capital Management (SCM): major holding company owned by Ukrainian businessman Rinat Akhmetov. Its major subsidiaries include Metinvest (mining and metallurgy) and DTEK (power plants and other energy engineering), among others.

Taruta, Serhii: Founder and later chairman of the Board of the ISD (Donbas Industrial Union) and key Ukrainian business actor. Together with Rinat Akhmetov and Viktor Pinchuk, was active in the early 1990s takeover of state-owned coal and metallurgical companies in the Donbas.

Tatneft: Russian oil company based in Tatarstan. Its controlling shareholder is the Republic of Tatarstan within the Russian Federation. For a period, co-owner of Ukrtatnafta (owner of the Kremenchug refinery) together with (and in a long-term feud with) Kolomoyskyi's Privat Group.

TNK-BP: a major Russian vertically integrated and third-largest oil company; acquired by Rosneft in 2013.

Trametal: a secondary steel producer specializing in the re-rolling of large-format steel slabs into higher-value-added quarto plates. Located in San Giorgio di Nogaro (Italy); since 2008, owned by Metinvest.

Transneft: Russia's oil pipeline transportation monopolist.

Transpetrol: Slovak state-owned company in charge of oil transportation.

Tuleyev, Aman: Kemerovo's (region of the Russian Federation) long-standing governor (1997–2018).

Tymoshenko, Yulia: Ukrainian opposition politician and prime minister (2005 and 2007–10), main actor behind the 2009 contract between NAK Naftohaz and Gazprom, which put an end to the January 2009 stoppage by Gazprom of gas supplies to Ukraine and points West but significantly increased gas prices.

Ukrnafta: Ukraine's largest oil and gas producer; during our focus period informally controlled by Kolomoyskyi's Privat Group.

Ukrtransnafta: Ukraine's state (NAK Naftohaz Ukraini subsidiary) oil transportation monopoly, during our focus period informally controlled by Ihor Kolomoyskyi's Privat Group.

Urals Mining and Metallurgical Company (UGMK): Russian mining company, bringing together over fifty enterprises from the raw materials and metallurgical sector; Kuzbassrazrezugol's managing company.

Vattenfall Europe: one of the "big four" utilities (together with RWE, EnBW, and E.ON) controlling a significant part of German power plants in 2011.

Wingas: a German gas distribution company. Originally established in 1993 by BASF subsidiary Wintershall and Gazprom. In 2016 became solely owned by Gazprom after Wintershall sold its shares to Gazprom in a politically controversial swap.

Wintershall: a German oil and gas production company and wholly owned BASF subsidiary.

Yanukovich, Viktor: Ukrainian prime minister (2002–4 and 2006–7) and president (2010–14); left the country as a result of the popular movement known as the Euromaidan Revolution / Revolution of Dignity in 2013–14.

Yatseniuk, Arseniy: Ukrainian prime minister (2014–16) at the time of the 2014 discussion on possible reverse-based natural gas supplies.

Yukos: a highly successful vertically integrated private Russian oil company headed by Mikhail Khodorkovsky. After Khodorkovsky's arrest in 2003, most of the company's assets were seized to pay for tax claims and transferred to state-owned companies such as Rosneft.

Yuschenko, Viktor: Ukrainian prime minister (1999–2001) and president (2005–2010); a central player in 2004's Orange Revolution.

Chronologies of Main Natural Gas, Oil, and Coal Market Events for Russia, Ukraine, and the European Union

NATURAL GAS: MAIN EVENTS IN RUSSIA, UKRAINE, AND THE EUROPEAN UNION, 1990–2020

Winter 1993–94	Disruption in supplies of Russian gas and oil lead to an energy crisis and freezing home temperatures in Ukraine
May 1997	Black Sea Fleet agreements give Russia control of most of the fleet in exchange for forgiveness of Ukraine's gas-related debt
January 2006	Russia suspends gas supplies to Ukraine for three days
January 4, 2006	Gas supply agreement gives control of gas supply to Ukraine to intermediary company RosUkrEnergo
2007	Agreement on a Belarusian-Russian natural gas transit joint venture on the basis of Beltransgas signed
December 2008	Gas supply confrontation between Ukraine and Russia

January 2009	14-day suspension of gas supplies by Russia to Ukraine stops all Russian supplies to Bulgaria, Romania, Macedonia, Serbia, Bosnia-Herzegovina, and Croatia
January 19, 2009	Supplies to Ukraine are restored as a ten-year contract sharply rising prices and eliminating RosUkrEnergo's role is signed with Gazprom
2009	European Commission adopts Third Energy Package, including the requirement of unbundling between production, transportation, and supply
January 2010	Gazprom reaches 50 percent ownership in Beltransgas
2010	Building of Nord Stream gas pipeline connecting Russia and Germany directly under the Baltic Sea started
2013	Liberalization of Russia's LNG exports
May 2014	Gazprom signs 30-year, $400-billion contract to supply gas to China
June 2014	Gazprom lodges multi-billion-dollar claim against Naftohaz at Arbitration Institute of Stockholm Chamber of Commerce (hereafter, Stockholm Arbitration Court; see glossary) for nonpayment of received gas
June 2014	Naftohaz lodges multi-billion-dollar claims against Gazprom at the Stockholm Arbitration Court for not fulfilling agreed transit volumes
September 2014	Sanctions on Russian gas sector imposed as a result of Russian intervention in Ukraine
December 2014	Floating LNG regasification terminal inagurated in Lithuania, the first in the former USSR
February 2017	Gazprom forced to limit amount of gas supplied via OPAL pipeline after Polish objection to its full loading of pipeline on TPA grounds
February 2018	Stockholm Arbitration Court rules that Gazprom must pay Naftohaz $4.63 billion for Gazprom's failure to use the agreed gas transit volumes
February 2018	Stockholm Arbitration Court rules that Naftohaz must pay Gazprom $2.5 billion for unpaid gas arrears
February 2019	EC approves tighter rules on Nord Stream 2, making pipelines coming to the EU from third countries

	subject to EU regulations but leaving actual responsibility for regulation to the country where the pipeline enters the EU (Germany)
December 2019	After a year of uncertainty, Ukraine's Naftohaz and Gazprom agree on a new five-year transit contract offering Ukraine guaranteed transit volumes (albeit much lower than those in the previous contract), assuaging fears of a collapse of transit after the completion of Nord Stream 2
April 2020	Transit via Ukraine declines 46 percent as a result of COVID-19-related declines in EU demand for Russian gas
May 2020	Stockholm Arbitration Court rules that Gazprom overcharged Poland for gas deliveries between 2014 and 2020 and must pay $1.5 billion in compensation

OIL: MAIN EVENTS IN RUSSIA, UKRAINE, AND THE EUROPEAN UNION, 1990–2020

April–July 1990	Oil blockade from Moscow after Lithuania declares independence
Winter 1993–94	Disruption in supplies of Russian gas and oil lead to an energy crisis and freezing home temperatures in Ukraine
1995	As a result of Russia's Loans for Shares program, oil companies Sidanko, Yukos, and Sibneft became the property of private banks
1996	Restructuring of Russia's oil sector completed, with the former oil monopolist divided among eleven vertically integrated, partially privatized companies
1999	Construction of Butinge Oil Terminal in Lithuania is completed, allowing for non-Russian oil supplies
2003	In the largest foreign investment deal since 1991, the merger of TNK, Sideanko, and Onako with BP's Russian assets creates TNK-BP
2004	Yukos is disbanded
July 2006	Russia stops pipeline oil shipments via Druzhba North to Lithuania

January 2007	Transneft suspends oil shipments to or through Belarus, briefly
2013	Rosneft's takeover of TNK-BP completed, making Rosneft the world's largest-output oil producer
2014	Sanctions on Russian oil sector imposed as a result of Russian intervention in Ukraine
2017	Former German chancellor Gerhart Schröder becomes chairman of Rosneft's Board of Directors
April–May 2019	Severe contamination of Druzhba pipeline's Russian oil with organochlorine, a chemical that can damage refining equipment and create poisonous gas; in the most serious crisis in the history of the Druzhba pipeline, refineries in Belarus, Germany, the Slovak Republic, the Czech Republic, and Hungary stop accepting its oil; all transmission is stopped for two weeks
March 2020	There is a Russian-Saudi oil price war, as Russia refuses to reduce oil production and Saudi Arabia responds by increasing production and dumping low-price oil in the world markets to punish Russia, which has higher production costs
April 2020	Oil futures prices reach record lows (briefly reaching negative prices) as the COVID-19 pandemic leads to demand declines, unclaimed oil, and storage deficits

COAL-METALLURGY: MAIN EVENTS IN RUSSIA, UKRAINE, AND THE EUROPEAN UNION, 1990–2020

1993	Subsidization of Ukraine's mining sector reaches 4 percent of the country's GDP
1993	Miners' strikes and a march to Kyiv to protest living conditions lead to first Donetsk representative named as (acting) prime minister
2000	System Capital Management (SCM) is established
2001	Russian state eliminates support to loss-making mines
2002	Akhmetov leaves ISD, taking with him the best active operations, including Azovstal

2004	Pavlohradvukhillia, Ukraine's largest coal-mining enterprise, privatized to Akhmetov's SCM
2004	Orange Revolution in Ukraine
2005	Avdiivka Coking Plant acquisition by SCM completed
2005	DTEK established
2006	Metinvest established
2007	Metinvest's acquisition of Trametal (Italy) completed
2008	Sharp fall in steel prices
2011	Pinchuk's Interpipe shifts to coking coal-free, 100 percent Electric Arc Furnace steel production based on remelting of scrap metal
2011	Akhmetov's Azovstal closes its open-hearth furnace production, but continues to use a coking-coal-based technology
2014	Revolution of Dignity brings an end to Yanukovich regime
September 2014	Ukrainian government decides to stop subsidizing mines in Donetsk (DNR) and Luhask (LNR) areas under rebel control
2014	Value of Ukrainian metal products exports falls 38.2 percent from previous year
2016	Ukraine adopts "Rotterdam plus" price formula, significantly increasing the price at which domestically produced coal is purchased
January 2017	Veterans of Ukraine's volunteer battalions blockade coal trade with separatist-held territories DNR and LNR
March 2017	DNR nationalizes property of Ukrainian-registered companies, including DTEK and Metinvest property
2018	Start of Russian naval intimidation on Azov Sea, disrupting export of metallurgical products from Mariupol
2020	Global coal demand falls by about 8 percent in the first quarter, the largest decline of any fossil fuel

Notes

1. DEPENDENCY ON RUSSIAN ENERGY: THREAT OR OPPORTUNITY?

1. Margarita M. Balmaceda, *Energy Dependency, Politics, and Corruption in the Former Soviet Union: Russia's Power, Oligarch's Profits and Ukraine's Missing Energy Policy, 1995–2006* (London: Routledge, 2008); Margarita M. Balmaceda, *The Politics of Energy Dependency: Ukraine, Belarus, and Lithuania Between Domestic Oligarchs and Russian Pressure* (Toronto: University of Toronto Press, 2013); Margarita M. Balmaceda, *Living the High Life in Minsk: Russian Energy Rents, Domestic Populism, and Belarus' Impending Crisis* (Budapest: Central European University Press, 2014).

2. On risk as the obverse of opportunity, see Susan Strange, "Structures, Values and Risk in the Study of the International Political Economy," in *Perspectives on Political Economy*, ed. R. J. B. Jones (London: Francis Pinter, 1983).

3. On the availability of energy rents even in a situation of energy dependency, see Balmaceda, *Energy Dependency*, chap. 1; and Balmaceda, *Politics*, chap. 1.

4. See Balmaceda, *Energy Dependency*.

5. See Balmaceda, *Politics*.

6. See Balmaceda, *Living the High Life*.

7. This book uses the term "fossil fuels" to refer collectively to oil, natural gas, and coal, which are energy sources formed from decayed organic materials through millions of years, are nonrenewable, and are in finite supply.

8. International Energy Agency (IEA), *World Energy Outlook 2017* (Paris: IEA, 2016), 79 (table 2.2).

9. See Balmaceda, *Politics*.

10. Energy corruption also created threats to broader democratic governance in non–former Soviet Union Eastern European states, e.g., Bulgaria;

see Tihomir Mitev, Ivo Hristov, and Ivan Chalakov, *Chernite Dupki na bal-garskata energetika* (Sofia: Iztok-Zapad, 2011), in Bulgarian; published in English as *The Black Holes of Bulgarian Power Industry: The Transformation of Electric Power Sector after 1989* (Sofia: East-West Publishing House, 2013). For translated chapters from this book, see http://ivantchalakov.weebly .com/publications.html.

11. Michael Barnett and Raymond Duvall, "Power in International Politics," *International Organization* 59, no. 1 (2005): 39–75, at 46; Michel Foucault, *Discipline and Punish: The Birth of the Prison* (New York: Pantheon Books, 1977).

12. See Gary Gereffi, J. Humphrey, R. Kaplinsky, and T. J. Sturgeon, "Introduction: Globalisation, Value Chains and Development," *IDS Bulletin* 32, no. 3 (2001): 1–8, http://www.ids.ac.uk/files/dmfile/gereffietal323.pdf; and Immanuel Wallerstein, *World Systems Analysis: An Introduction* (Durham, NC: Duke University Press, 2004).

13. See Jean Braudillard, *The Revenge of the Crystal: A Baudrillard Reader* (London: Pluto Press, 1999); Arjun Appadurai, *The Social Life of Things: Commodities in Cultural Perspective* (Cambridge: Cambridge University Press, 1986); and Bruno Latour, "When Things Strike Back: A Possible Contribution of 'Science Studies' to the Social Sciences," *British Journal of Sociology* 51, no. 1 (2000): 107–23; Timothy Mitchell, *Carbon Democracy: Political Power in the Age of Oil* (London: Verso Books, 2011); Andrew Barry, *Material Politics: Disputes Along the Pipeline* (Oxford: Wiley-Blackwell, 2013); Douglas Rogers, *The Depths of Russia: Oil, Power, and Culture after Socialism* (Ithaca, NY: Cornell University Press, 2015); Douglas Rogers, "The Materiality of the Corporation: Oil, Gas, and Corporate Social Technologies in the Remaking of a Russian Region," *American Ethnologist* 39, no. 2 (2012): 284–96; and Stephen Collier, *Post-Soviet Social: Neoliberalism, Social Modernity, Biopolitics* (Princeton, NJ: Princeton University Press, 2011). For a discussion of other geography publications dealing with the materiality of things, see Karen Bakker and Gavin Bridge, "Material Worlds? Resource Geographies and the Matter of Nature," *Progress in Human Geography* 30, no. 1 (2006): 5–27.

14. See Chris A. Gregory, *Gifts and Commodities* (London: Academic Press, 1982); Michael Burawoy, *Manufacturing Consent* (Chicago: University of Chicago Press, 1979); and James G. Carrier, *Gifts and Commodities: Exchange and Western Capitalism Since 1700* (London: Routledge, 1995).

15. See Gabrielle Hecht, *The Radiance of France: Nuclear Power and National Identity after World War II* (Cambridge, MA: MIT Press, 2009); Gabrielle Hecht, *Being Nuclear: Africans and the Global Uranium Trade* (Cambridge, MA: MIT Press, 2012); and Timothy Mitchell, *Rule of*

Experts: Egypt, Techno-Politics, Modernity (Berkeley: University of California Press, 2002).

16. Although, in general, EU states are less dependent on Russian energy than former USSR states such as Ukraine and Belarus, serious fears of Russia using energy exports as a means to affect these states' policies have been voiced.

17. Calculated from BP, *Statistical Review of World Energy 2019* (London: BP, 2019), 38; BP, "Primary Energy," no date, http://www.bp.com/en/global /corporate/energy-economics/statistical-review-of-world-energy/primary -energy.html; and Daniel Workman, "Coal Exports by Country," March 29, 2020, http://www.worldstopexports.com/coal-exports-country/3265. In addition, the exporting of nuclear power technology has been an important element of Russia's energy-related exports.

18. See Anita Orban, *Power, Energy, and the New Russian Imperialism* (Westport, CT: Praeger, 2008); Marshall Goldman, *Petrostate: Putin, Power, and the New Russia* (Oxford: Oxford University Press, 2009); Edward Lucas, *The New Cold War* (New York: St. Martin's Press, 2014); Keith C. Smith, *Russian Energy Politics in the Baltics, Poland, and Ukraine: A New Stealth Imperialism?* (Washington, DC: Center for Strategic and International Studies, 2004); and Agnia Grigas, *The New Geopolitics of Natural Gas* (Cambridge, MA: Harvard University Press, 2017).

19. The embargo took place in the context of the Arab-Israeli war and imposed as retaliation by the Arab oil producers (loosely organized as the Organization of Arab Petroleum Exporting Countries, or OAPEC, within OPEC) against those states perceived as supporting Israel in the conflict (initially the United States but later also the Netherlands, Portugal, and South Africa). See Roy Licklider, "The Power of Oil: The Arab Oil Weapon and the Netherlands, the United Kingdom, Canada, Japan, and the United States," *International Studies Quarterly* 32, no. 2 (June 1988): 205–26, at 206. Similarly, the U.S. embargo of oil and gasoline sales to Japan in 1941 can be seen as one of the most direct uses of energy supplies as a weapon. See Timothy C. Lehmann, "Keeping Friends Close and Enemies Closer: Classical Realist Statecraft and Economic Exchange in U.S. Interwar Strategy," *Security Studies* 18, no. 1 (2009): 115–47.

20. It was in the immediate aftermath of this crisis that well-known international relations theorists such as Stephen Krasner brought the issue to the pages of key journals on the area. See Stephen D. Krasner, "Oil Is the Exception," *Foreign Policy* 14 (1974): 68–84. This is not to say that the issue had not been discussed earlier—sensitivity and vulnerability in a state's reaction to an (energy) dependency, for example, are one of the main themes explored by Albert O. Hirschman, *State Power and the Structure of Foreign Trade* (Berkeley: University of California Press, 1980; orig. pub. 1945).

21. Robert Dahl, "The Concept of Power," *Behavioral Science* 2, no. 3 (1957): 201–15.

22. See, among others, Ken Waltz, *Theory of International Politics* (New York: Addison-Wesley, 1979).

23. Tom Casier, "Russia's Energy Leverage over the EU: Myth or Reality?," *Perspectives on European Politics and Society* 12, no. 4 (2011): 493–508, at 493.

24. See IEA, *Energy Policies Beyond IEA Countries: Ukraine 2012* (Paris: IEA, 2012), 107 (table 7.3).

25. See Balmaceda, *Energy Dependency*, and Balmaceda, *Politics*.

26. On the challenge presented by Russian state firm managers' behavior to our expectations of principal–agent relationships, see Joel S. Hellman, "Winners Take All: The Politics of Partial Reform in Postcommunist Transitions," *World Politics* 50, no. 2 (1998): 203–34. Though Hellman was writing at a time when the main discussion was one of state capture by private actors and the Putin era has been mainly thought of in terms of state actors capturing private businesses, behind these state actors are often individuals acting primarily in terms of their private interests, making Hellman's discussion still relevant. On state/corporate/personal interests within Russian state-owned corporations, see Balmaceda, *Politics*, chap. 3.

27. See Karen Dawisha, *Putin's Kleptocracy: Who Owns Russia?* (New York: Simon & Schuster, 2014).

28. For an overview of energy articles published in U.S. political science journals between 1972 and 2012, see Llewelyn Hughes and Phillip Y. Lipscy, "The Politics of Energy," *Annual Review of Political Science* 16 (2013). One important exception is Mitchell, *Carbon Democracy*.

29. In particular, research on natural gas markets by economists such as Christian von Hirschhausen from the DIW in Berlin and the extensive publications series by the Oxford Institute of Energy Studies inspired by its long-term director, Jonathan P. Stern. For one among many representative publications, see Simon Pirani, ed., *Russian and CIS Gas Markets and Their Impact on Europe* (Oxford: Oxford Institute of Energy Studies, 2009).

30. The original focus of the "oil curse" and "rentier state" bodies of literature was on examples from the oil-rich Middle East. See, e.g., Hossein Mahdavy, "The Pattern and Problems of Economic Development in Rentier States: The Case of Iran," in *Studies in the Economic History of the Middle East* (Oxford: Oxford University Press, 1970); Richard M. Auty and Alan H. Gelb, "Political Economy of Resource-Abundant States," in *Resource Abundance and Economic Development*, ed. R. M. Auty (Oxford: Oxford University Press, 2001); and H. Beblawi and G. Luciani, *The Rentier State* (London: Croom Helm, 1987). Extensions of this literature to deal with cases beyond the Middle East have also focused on oil and on oil-rich countries such as

Nigeria and Venezuela. See Peter Lewis, *Growing Apart: Oil, Politics and Economic Change in Indonesia and Nigeria* (Ann Arbor: University of Michigan Press, 2007); Omolade Adunbi, *Oil Wealth and Insurgency in Nigeria* (Bloomington: Indiana University Press, 2015); John L. Hammond, "The Resource Curse and Oil Revenues in Angola and Venezuela," *Science & Society* 75, no. 3 (2001): 348–78; Jonathan DiJohn, *From Windfall to Curse? Oil and Industrialization in Venezuela, 1920 to the Present* (University Park: Pennsylvania State University Press, 2009); and Stefan Peters, "Beyond Curse and Blessing: Rentier Society in Venezuela," in *Contested Extractivism, Society and the State: Struggles over Mining and Land*, ed. B. Engels and K. Dietz (London: Palgrave Macmillan, 2017), 45–68.

31. IEA, *Key World Energy Statistics 2017* (Paris: IEA, 2017), 6, 30. All data are for 2015.

32. Total world coal consumption reached its highest level in 2014. See IEA, *Coal Information 2017* (Paris: IEA, 2017), 16 (table 7: world coal consumption, part II).

33. See Margarita M. Balmaceda, "Value-Added Links, Energy Relations, and Integration in the Former Soviet Area," paper presented at American Political Science Assocation Annual Meeting, Washington, DC, August 29–September 1, 2014. A good illustration of the possibilities opened by the processing of oil away from origin is provided by the case of Belarus in the period 1996–2007, when the refining in Belarus of oil imported from Russia was able to save Russian oil-exporting companies from paying Russian duties on their exports—which, in turn, helped create a de facto alliance between these refiners and Russian oil producers. See Balmaceda, *Living the High Life*.

34. Some recent voices (in particular from Russia) are calling for more attention to "security of demand" in our understanding of energy security. See, e.g., Nikolay Kaveshnikov, "The Issue of Energy Security in Relations between Russia and the European Union," *European Security* 19, no. 4 (December 2010): 585–605; and Jeronim Perovic, Robert W. Orttung, and Andreas Wenger, eds., *Russian Energy Power and Foreign Relations* (London: Routledge, 2009).

35. On privately provided public goods as applied to energy and the environment, see Matthew J. Kotchen, "Green Markets and Private Provision of Public Goods," *Journal of Political Economy* 114, no. 4 (2006): 816–34. See also Andreas Goldthau and Nick Sitter, "Soft Power with a Hard Edge: EU Policy Tools and Energy Security," *Review of International Political Economy* 22, no. 5 (2015): 941–65.

36. See, e.g., Meghan O'Sullivan, *Windfall: How the New Energy Abundance Upends Global Politics and Strengthens America's Power* (New York: Simon & Schuster, 2017); and Grigas, *New Geopolitics*.

37. I thank Peter Rutland for this insight. On the role of oil supplies in World War II, see W. G. Jensen, "The Importance of Energy in the First and Second World Wars," *Historical Journal* 11 (1968): 538–54, at 547–54.

38. Barnett and Duvall, "Power," 46. Connected with the constitutive "power to," the concept of "power with," focusing on cooperation and consensus, is also relevant. On "power with," see Mary Parker Follett, "Power," in *Dynamic Administration: The Collected Papers of Mary Parker Follett*, ed. Henry C. Metcalf and L. Urwick (New York: Harper Brothers, 1942), 95–116; and Amy Allen, "Rethinking Power," *Hypatia* 13, no. 1 (1998): 21–30, at 35–37.

39. See Pietra Rivoli, *The Travels of a T-Shirt in the Global Economy: An Economist Examines the Markets, Power and Politics of World Trade* (Hoboken, NJ: John Wiley & Sons, 2005); Eric Schlosser, *Fast Food Nation: The Dark Side of the All-American Meal* (New York: HarperCollins, 2002); Tom Miller, *The Panama Hat Trail: A Journey from South America* (New York; Morrow, 1986); and Lisa Margonelli, *Oil on the Brain: Adventures from the Pump to the Pipeline* (New York: Nan A. Talese / Doubleday, 2007). Other examples of single-commodity studies of global resource flows include those by Ian MacLachlan, *Kill and Chill: Restructuring Canada's Beef Commodity Chain* (Toronto: University of Toronto Press, 2001); Marlène Elias and Judith Carney, "The Female Commodity Chain of Shea Butter: Burkinabe Producers, Western Green Consumers and Fair Trade," *Cahiers de Geographie du Quebec* 48, no. 133 (2004): 71–88; and Gavin Bridge and Philippe Le Billon, *Oil* (Cambridge: Polity Press, 2013).

2. IS ENERGY A WEAPON OR A CONSTITUENT PART OF DISAGGREGATED POWER RELATIONS?

1. For a list of instances of their attempted use, see Robert W. Orttung and Indra Overland, "A Limited Toolbox: Explaining the Constraints on Russia's Foreign Energy Policy," *Journal of Eurasian Studies* 2, no. 1 (2011): 74–85.

2. See John Gillingham, *Coal, Steel, and the Rebirth of Europe, 1945–1955* (Cambridge: Cambridge University Press, 1991).

3. Some definitions subsume the midstream stage into the downstream.

4. See Stephen Fortescue, *Russia's Oil Barons and Metal Magnates: Oligarchs and the State in Transition* (Basingstoke, U.K.: Palgrave Macmillan, 2007); Stephen Fortescue, "The Russian Steel Industry, 1990–2009," *Eurasian Geography and Economics* 50, no. 3 (2009): 252–74; and Arkadiusz Sarna, "Ukrainian Metallurgy: The Economic Link in the Oligarchic Power System," *CES Studies* (2002): 70–84.

5. See Fortescue, *Russia's Oil Barons*, and Margarita M. Balmaceda, *The Politics of Energy Dependency: Ukraine, Belarus, and Lithuania between Domestic Oligarchs and Russian Pressure* (Toronto: University of Toronto Press, 2013).

6. The term "supply chains" refers to "the steps it takes to get a good or service from the supplier to the customer." In contrast, value chains refer to broader processes of transformation and value adding. In this book, I use the term "value chains" because it most accurately reflects the reality we are studying.

7. A value chain does not need to be legal or formal to exist—illegal activities, such as drug trafficking and trading in legal goods involving corruption, also have their own value chains.

8. Gary Gereffi, J. Humphrey, R. Kaplinsky, and T. J. Sturgeon, "Introduction: Globalisation, Value Chains and Development," *IDS Bulletin* 32, no. 3 (2001): 1–8, at 4, http://www.ids.ac.uk/files/dmfile/gereffietal323 .pdf. Some definitions also include "final disposal after use" as the last part of the value chain. Such an expanded definition has the advantage of also incorporating the element of after-use, which is key for discussions of ecological sustainability issues and nuclear power, where issues of disposal of used materials are key. Though in recent years there has been a proliferation of research on issues related to value chains, and various strands of the literature give different names to the chain studied ("global value chain," "global supply chain," "commodity chain"), these differences are not significant for working purposes of this book.

9. A move to a less contractual-path-based set of supply relationships, associated with the liberalization of the natural gas market proposed by the European Commission, for example (see chapters 7 and 8), does not invalidate a value chain approach as an analytical instrument, as it is applicable regardless of whether the good in question moves through a fixed contractual path or not.

10. On the GVC approach and the relocation of production to the Global South, see Neilson, Pritchard, and Wai-chung Yeung, "Global Value Chains," 4. For a first attempt at applying the related concept of global production networks to the extractive industries, see Gavin Bridge, "Global Production Networks and the Extractive Sector: Governing Resource-Based Development," *Journal of Economic Geography* 8 (2008): 389–419.

11. The volatility of energy prices means that the risk of value destruction is an everyday occurrence for industries such as refining. The Soviet and post-Soviet context provides numerous examples of value destruction, e.g., through refineries in Russia in the 1990s losing income from the sale of refined oil products, or coal mines in Ukraine in the 2000s, where the monetary and caloric cost of producing coal was often higher than either the revenue or heating/caloric value that could be derived from them. On

other differences between the global value chains of extractive as compared with those of manufacturing industries, see Bridge, "Global Production Networks," 398.

12. These data are for the May 2020 prices of futures contracts for WTI oil, which went from $20 to a negative price of –$37.62 on April 20, 2020. The source for these data is "Oil Futures Crash: Crude Oil WTI Futures, Dollars per Barrel," https://theindustryspread.com/wp-content/uploads/2020/04/FactSet-CNBC-WTI-Crude-Oil-Futures-Chart-21-April-2020.png.

13. From the perspective of Gereffi et al., "Introduction," 5, lead firms exercise this power through their "control over key resources needed in the chain, decisions about entry to and exit from the chain and monitoring of suppliers." This refers to the mainstream GVC literature, which has significantly moved away from its Wallersteinian origins emphasizing world-systems as a critical concept. See P. Gibbon, J. Bair, and S. Ponte, "Governing Global Value Chains: An Introduction," *Economy and Society* 37, no. 3 (2008): 315–38. For a critique of this turn, see Jeffrey Neilson, Bill Pritchard, and Henry Wai-chung Yeung, "Global Value Chains and Global Production Networks in the Changing International Political Economy: An Introduction," *Review of International Political Economy* 21, no. 1 (2014): 1–8; and for a discussion of enduring tensions between the original Wallersteinian and newer incarnations of this literature, see Jeffrey Neilson, "Value Chains, Neoliberalism and Development Practice: The Indonesian Experience," *Review of International Political Economy* 21, no. 1 (2014): 38–69.

14. Gereffi et al., "Introduction."

15. Much of this work conceptualizing transit relationships has been done from the perspective of formal modeling of monopoly supply, transit monopoly vs. supply monopoly (i.e., bilateral monopoly), and bargaining between the supplier and transit provider states. See, e.g., Yuri Yegorov and Franz Wirl, "Ukrainian Gas Transit Game," *ZfE Zeitschrift für Energiewirschaft*, no. 2 (2009): 147–55; and Ekpen J. Omonbude, "The Transit Oil and Gas Pipeline and the Role of Bargaining: A Nontechnical Discussion," *Energy Policy* 35, no. 12 (December 2007): 6188–94. Recently, scholars have started to pay attention to the oil market as composed of a series of discrete but interrelated linked segments, including refining as one of these. See Llewelyn Hughes and A. Long, "Is There an Oil Weapon? Security Implications of Changes in the Structure of the International Oil Market," *International Security* 39, no. 3 (2015): 152–89.

16. See Phillipe LeBillon, "The Political Ecology of War: Natural Resources and Armed Conflicts," *Political Geography* 20, no. 5 (2001): 561–84; Michael L. Ross, "Oil, Drugs and Diamonds: The Varying Roles of Natural Resources in Civil War," in *The Political Economy of Armed Conflict: Beyond Greed and Grievance*, ed. Karen Ballentine and Jake Sherman (Boulder, CO: Lynne

Rienner, 2003), 47–72; and Karen Ballentine and Jake Sherman, eds., *The Oil Curse: How Petroleum Wealth Shapes the Development of Nations* (Princeton, NJ: Princeton University Press, 2012), 170–78.

17. See Chris A. Gregory, *Gifts and Commodities* (London: Academic Press, 1982); and James G. Carrier, *Gifts and Commodities: Exchange and Western Capitalism Since 1700* (London: Routledge, 1995). On the use of energy rents—and opportunities for access to rent-seeking possibilities—as currency for "balancing" various oligarchic interest groups ("clans") in Ukraine, see Margarita M. Balmaceda, *Energy Dependency, Politics, and Corruption in the Former Soviet Union: Russia's Power, Oligarchs' Profits, and Ukraine's Missing Energy Policy, 1995–2006* (London: Routledge, 2008).

18. On other constraints to Russia's use of its energy power, see also Orttung and Overland, "Limited Toolbox."

19. See Arjun Appadurai, *The Social Life of Things: Commodities in Cultural Perspective* (Cambridge: Cambridge University Press, 1986); and Bruno Latour, "When Things Strike Back: A Possible Contribution of 'Science Studies' to the Social Sciences," *British Journal of Sociology* 51, no. 1 (2000): 107–23.

20. Stephen Collier, *Post-Soviet Social: Neoliberalism, Social Modernity, Biopolitics* (Princeton, NJ: Princeton University Press, 2011), 213–14.

21. Karen Bakker, *An Uncooperative Commodity: Privatizing Water in England and Wales* (Oxford: Oxford University Press, 2004). See also Robert A. Young and John B. Loomis, *Determining the Economic Value of Water: Concepts and Methods* (London: Routledge, 2014), 4–6.

22. See Rafael Kandiyoti, *Pipelines: Flowing Oil and Crude Politics* (London: I. B. Tauris, 2012); and Andrew Barry, *Material Politics: Disputes Along the Pipeline* (Oxford: Wiley-Blackwell, 2013).

23. On the role of lootable/nonlootable resources as sources of revenue in civil conflict situations, see LeBillon, "Political Ecology"; and Ross, "Oil, Drugs and Diamonds." For a different perspective on the issue, see Ostrom's broader discussion of obstructability and excludability: Elinor Ostrom, "How Types of Goods and Property Rights Jointly Affect Collective Action," *Journal of Theoretical Politics* 15, no. 3 (2003): 239–70; and James Acheson, "Ostrom for Anthropologists," *International Journal of the Commons* 5, no. 2 (2011): 319–39.

24. See H. Beblawi and G. Luciani, *The Rentier State* (London: Croom Helm, 1987).

25. See Beblawi and Luciani, *Rentier State*. See also Kiren Aziz Chaudhry, *The Price of Wealth: Economies and Institutions in the Middle East* (Ithaca, NY: Cornell University Press, 1997); and Dirk J. Vandewalle and Dirk Vandewalle, *Libya since Independence: Oil and State Building* (London: I. B. Tauris, 1998).

26. See, e.g., Balmaceda, *Politics*, 33 (table 1.5).

27. See Balmaceda, *Energy Dependency.*

28. See Balmaceda, *Living the High Life in Minsk*, chaps. 3 and 5.

29. For classic discussions of the role of domestic sectors and groups in international interactions, see Helen V. Milner, *Interests, Institutions, and Information: Domestic Politics and International Relations* (Princeton, NJ: Princeton University Press, 1997); and Andrew Moravcsik, *Why the European Community Strengthens the State: International Cooperation and Domestic Politics*, Working Paper 52 (Cambridge, MA: Center for European Studies at Harvard University, 1994), http://aei.pitt.edu/9151/; and Robert Baldwin, "The Political Economy of Trade Policy: Integrating the Perspective of Economists and Political Scientists," in *The Political Economy of Trade Policy*, ed. R. C. Feenstra, G. M. Grossman, and D. A. Irwin (Cambridge, MA: MIT Press, 1996). On domestic veto players and international trade agreements, see E. D. Mansfield and H. V. Milner, *Votes, Vetoes, and the Political Economy of International Trade Agreements* (Princeton, NJ: Princeton University Pres, 2012).

30. For additional information on the choosing of the reference period, see Margarita M. Balmaceda, "Methodology: Choosing the Reference Period," unpublished paper for workshop on "The Political Economy of Post-Soviet Energy," Delmenhorst, Germany, May 31–June 2, 2017.

31. Although virtual swaps where only ownership rights change hands are a well-established part of natural gas and oil trade, they do not invalidate the usefulness of analyzing underlying physical flows.

32. The importance of governance systems as a key framing condition for energy transit (and by implication for comparing value chains passing through the same countries) is well established in the literature. See, e.g., Caroline Kuzemko, Andrei Belyi, Andreas Goldthau, and Michael F. Keating, eds., *Dynamics of Energy Governance in Europe and Russia* (Houndmills, U.K.: Palgrave Macmillan, 2012).

33. I thank Andrian Prokyp for this insight and the related discussion.

34. The image of "three molecules" is actually a placeholder for a technically more complex situation: it is not technically accurate to speak of a "crude oil molecule," because crude oil is actually a mixture of hydrocarbons, each composed of a variety of molecules. It is also not possible to talk of a "coal molecule"—coal is a combustible rock containing varying proportions of carbon (from about 50 to 90 percent, depending on the type of coal) as well as other materials, including hydrogen, oxygen, nitrogen, ash, and sulfur. In the case of natural gas, it would be tempting to designate the unit to be followed as a "methane molecule," because methane composes over 90 percent of natural gas; methane (composed of 1 carbon atom and 4 hydrogen atoms) is the simplest hydrocarbon. However, limiting our natural gas story to methane would deprive us of one of the things that makes natural gas interesting— natural gas liquids (NGLs) and their profitable commercialization.

35. See Timothy Mitchell, *Carbon Democracy: Political Power in the Age of Oil* (London: Verso Books, 2011).

36. I thank Simon Blakey for this phrasing.

37. Compare with Mitchell's discussion of "points of vulnerability" (e.g., oil wells, pipelines, refineries, railways, docks, and shipping lanes across), where "movements could organize and apply pressure" and "sites at which a series of claims for political freedoms and more egalitarian forms of life would be fought." Mitchell, *Carbon Democracy*, 103. On how not all energy "governing" is done by state institutions, see "Introduction," in *Dynamics*, ed. Kuzemko et al., 5–6.

38. The use of individuals' administrative power to set regulations giving them access to rent-seeking opportunities has a long history in post-Soviet states. From the case of Ukraine in the 1990s, we know how much power barter and IOUs (*zaliki/zacheti*) operations gave to those state officials in the position to set barter equivalencies or the crucial value of the discount component in specific bills of exchange operations. See V. Khmurych and T. Tkachenko, "Opportunities for Corruption in the Ukrainian Gas Market," Eurasia Foundation, 1999, www.eurasia.org/programs/eerc/Kyiv/papers/khtk.htm; and Balmaceda, *Politics*, 110.

39. In his history of the Mediterranean region, Fernand Braudel discusses not only the physical nodes through which pepper and grain moved to continental Europe but also the smaller number of commercial centers or nodes where prices for these were determined, e.g., Venice. See Fernand Braudel, *The Mediterranean and the Mediterranean World in the Age of Phillip II* (London: Harper Collins, 1992), 462–541.

40. For examples of such intentional lack of transparency by key players, see Katrin Ganswindt, Sebastian Rötters, and Heffa Schücking, *Bitter Coal* (Cologne: Urgewald and Food First Information and Action Network, 2013), 8ff. On the broader empirical challenges of following globalized value chains given existing statistics, see Timothy J. Sturgeon, "Global Value Chains and Economic Globalization," in *Towards a New Measurement Framework: Report to Eurostat*, ed. Eurostat (Brussels: European Commission, 2013), http://ec.europa.eu/eurostat/documents/54610/4463793/Sturgeon-report-Eurostat. The multiplicity of national statistical classification systems further complicates the endeavor; this is especially the case with coal, where the boundaries between types are more flexible than in the case of other goods. See Katarzyna Stala-Szlugaj, "Polish Imports of Steam Coal from the East (CIS) in the Years 1990–2011," 15–16, www.min-pan.krakow.pl/se/ksiazki/12_10ks_sir179_z.pdf.

41. In 1991, the Russian Federation signed the Energy Charter declaration, and then applied it in a provisional manner from its coming into force in 1998 to 2009; but it failed to ratify or implement its key Transit Protocol.

42. See, e.g., the discussion of natural gas as compared with oil regulation by Jeff D. Malkholm, *The Political Economy of Pipelines: A Century of Comparative Institutional Development* (Chicago: University of Chicago Press, 2012).

43. On the case of Singapore, see Rex J. Zedalis, *Singapore, the Energy Economy: From the First Refinery to the End of Cheap Oil, 1960—2010* (London: Routledge, 2012).

3. ENERGY: MATERIALITY AND POWER

1. Portions of this chapter first appeared as "Differentiation, Materiality, and Power: Towards a Political Economy of Fossil Fuels," *Energy Research and Social Sciences* 39 (2018): 130–40, and are reprinted with permission.

2. In addition, the exporting of nuclear power technology has been an important element of Russia's energy-related exports.

3. See Arjun Appadurai, *The Social Life of Things: Commodities in Cultural Perspective* (Cambridge: Cambridge University Press, 1986); and Bruno Latour, "When Things Strike Back: A Possible Contribution of 'Science Studies' to the Social Sciences," *British Journal of Sociology* 51, no. 1 (2000): 107–23.

4. See, e.g., Margarita M. Balmaceda, *The Politics of Energy Dependency: Ukraine, Belarus, and Lithuania between Domestic Oligarchs and Russian Pressure* (Toronto: University of Toronto Press, 2013), 33.

5. Focusing on physical characteristics of different energy sources is not the only way to understand materiality in energy; rather, the term has been understood in myriad ways, ranging from the physical to the discursive. For an overview of the ways in which materiality has been understood within the context of energy issues, see Margarita M. Balmaceda, Per Högselius, Corey Johnson, Heiko Pleines, Douglas Rogers, and Veli-Pekka Tynkkynen, "Energy Materiality: A Conceptual Review of Multi-Disciplinary Approaches," *Energy Research & Social Science* 56 (2019), https://www.sciencedirect.com/science/article/pii/S2214629618309198?via%3Dihub101220.

6. I thank Douglas Rogers for this insight.

7. On this issue, see the literature on political ecology, e.g., Timothy Forsyth, *Critical Political Ecology: The Politics of Environmental Science* (London: Routledge, 2004). See also Karen Bakker and Gavin Bridge, "Material Worlds? Resource Geographies and the 'Matter of Nature,'" *Progress in Human Geography* 30, no. 1 (2006): 5–27.

8. See Ian Hodder, *Entangled: An Archeology of the Relationships between Humans and Things* (Malden, MA: Wiley-Blackwell, 2012); and Christopher Tilley, *The Materiality of Stone: Explorations in Landscape Phenomenology* (Oxford: Berg, 2004).

9. See Thomas R. De Gregori, "Resources Are Not; They Become: An Institutional Theory," *Journal of Economic Issues* 21, no. 3 (1987): 1241–63, at 1243ff. For an early discussion, see also Erich Zimmermann, *World Resources and Industries: A Functional Appraisal of the Availability of Agricultural and Industrial Resources* (New York: Harper Brothers, 1933).

10. Similarly, it is worth noting the chipping away at the materiality-based division of oil and natural gas companies, with an increasing number of international oil companies also starting to work on natural gas in the last decades.

11. The U.S. Geological Survey refers to "proved reserve estimates" as estimating not what reserves exist but what is proven to be "economically producible" using current technology. James G. Speight, *An Introduction to Petroleum Technology, Economics, and Politics* (New York: John Wiley & Sons, 2011), 219.

12. Judith Rees, *Natural Resources: Allocation, Economics and Policy* (London: Routledge, 1990), 18–21. Similarly, a recent publication on coal notes that coal proved reserves change according to the price of coal; if the price of coal will decrease to the point of affecting what reserves are considered to be recovered economically, the size of "proven reserves" will go down. Herminé Nalbandian and Nigel Dong, "Coal and Gas Competition in Global Markets," 2013, 9, https://usea.org/sites/default/files/072013_Coal%20and%20gas%20 competition%20in%20power%20generation%20in%20global%20markets _ccc220.pdf, citing World Coal Association, *Coal Facts 2012: Where Is Coal Found?*, 5 (London: World Coal Association, 2012), available at www .worldcoal.org.

13. Chris Park and Michael Allaby, "Recoverable Resource," in *A Dictionary of Environment and Conservation* (New York: Oxford University Press, 2013), http://www.oxfordreference.com/view/10.1093/acref/9780199641666 .001.0001/acref-9780199641666-e-6718.

14. On energy and populism, see Parvin Alizadeh, "The Political Economy of Petro Populism and Reform, 1997–2011," in *Iran and the Global Economy: Petro Populism, Islam and Economic Sanctions*, ed. P. Alizadeh and H. Hakimian (New York: Routledge, 2013), 76–102; Sebastián L. Mazzuca, "The Rise of Rentier Populism," *Journal of Democracy* 2 (2013): 108–22; and Egil Matsen, Gisle J. Natvik, and Ragnar Torvik, "Petro Populism," *Journal of Development Economics* 118 (2016): 1–12.

15. See, e.g., the discussion of "socialist oil," and how it functioned according to very different rules than those in capitalist states, by Douglas Rogers, *The Depths of Russia: Oil, Power, and Culture after Socialism* (Ithaca, NY: Cornell University Press, 2015).

16. E.g., one of the main critiques to Gazprom's Nord Stream 1 and 2 projects has been that they do not make sense from an economic perspective. But in this, as in other cases, other types of logic may be at play: a political logic

to limit political risk, or "punish" a no-longer-friendly neighbor, or the logic of (possibly corrupt) actors involved in the pipeline-building process, who are more interested in their own profit, even if this implies economically irrational (from the perspective of the producing firm as a whole) overinvestments.

17. An excellent example of the intersection of what is physically doable and economically sensible given different priorities comes from the case of oil. One difference between oil and natural gas is that oil, in contrast to natural gas, can be transported by rail car. But the actual way in which this transportation takes place depends not only on materiality issues but also on profit calculations. Rail transportation of unprocessed oil rich in the volatile gases it contains when it first comes out of the ground increases the risk of a fire in the tanks (e.g., the high-profile one in Lac-Mégantic in Quebec in 2013 that killed forty-seven people). The reason why oil trains continue to ship this explosive mixture has less to do with technical requirements than with profit motivations *directly related to oil's distinct value-added chain*: "Oil companies have a financial stake in keeping the volatile gases in the oil. When the gas-laden oil arrives at refineries, the gases can be separated, processed, and sold for added profit. The gases can even be sold overseas, something that can't be done with oil as [U.S.] crude oil can't be exported. . . . If producers are forced to remove these lucrative gases at the well, that significant additional revenue would be lost." Marcus Stein, "How to Prevent an Oil Train Disaster" (op-ed), *New York Times*, May 19, 2015. At the same time, a simple regulatory change—allowing exports—could change the dynamics of the value chain.

18. See Per Högselius, Anna Åberg, and Arne Kaijser, "Natural Gas in Cold War Europe: The Making of a Critical Infrastructure," in *The Making of Europe's Critical Infrastructure*, ed. Per Högselius, Anna Åberg, Arne Kaijser, and Erik van der Vleuten (New York: Palgrave, 2013), 30.

19. See Stephen J. Collier, *Post-Soviet Social: Neoliberalism, Social Modernity, Biopolitics* (Princeton, NJ: Princeton University Press, 2011).

20. Some paragraphs of the second and third sections of this chapter have been modified from "Differentiation, Materiality, and Power: Towards a Political Economy of Fossil Fuels," by Margarita M. Balmaceda, *Energy Research and Social Sciences* 39 (2018): 130–40.

21. All fossil fuels are nonrenewable, but not all nonrenewables are fossil fuels; e.g., uranium used for nuclear power generation is nonrenewable but is not a fossil fuel.

22. See Rogers, *Depths of Russia*.

23. The reference temperature usually used in both oil and natural gas calculations is 15 degrees Celsius, the ISO Standard Reference Conditions standard.

24. On the standardization of oil as a key process making possible its trade as an international commodity and the very creation of an international

3. Energy: Materiality and Power   299

economy of oil, see Gavin Bridge and Philippe Le Billon, *Oil* (Cambridge: Polity Press, 2013), 71–74.

25. The source for these data is Yasar Demirel, *Energy: Production, Conversion, Storage, Conservation, and Coupling* (London: Springer, 2012), 40 (table 2.9).

26. "API Gravity," http://www.petroleum.co.uk/api.

27. See Investopedia, "Benchmark Oils: Brent Crude, WTI and Dubai," figure 1, http://www.investopedia.com/articles/investing/102314/understanding-benchmark-oils-brent-blend-wti-and-dubai.asp.

28. Investopedia.

29. Low-caloric value Dutch and German "L-gas" is an exception.

30. On "virtual" exports of Czechoslovak natural gas to Austria in the 1960s, see Per Högselius, *Red Gas* (Basingstoke, U.K.: Palgrave, 2013), 50.

31. In addition, contractual conditions (e.g., long-term contracts as opposed to spot pricing) kept such hubs from wide use in continental Europe until recently.

32. Watts (as in kilowatts, kW), calories, and other measures such as BTUs all refer to energy content. For conversion tables, see U.S. Energy Information Administration, *Energy Conversion Calculators*, https://www.eia.gov/energyexplained/index.cfm?page=about_energy_conversion_calculator.

33. In the U.S. Liquid Measure System, oil is measured in barrels (42 U.S. gallons); 7.14 barrels make a metric ton weight equivalent.

34. See Demirel, *Energy*, 40 (table 2.9).

35. The values here are from C. Ronneau, *Energie, pollution de l'air et developpement durable* (Louvain-la-Neuve: Presses Universitaires de Louvain, 2004). The data for brown coal are from "Some Energy Units, Definitions and Conversions," http://ramblingsdc.net/EnUnits.html.

36. These data are from World Nuclear Association, "Heating Values of Various Fuels," September 2016.

37. On energy density, see Vaclav Smil, *Power Density* (Cambridge, MA: MIT Press, 2015).

38. For comparative data on carbon intensity in electricity generation, see Sylvie Cornot-Gandolphe, "The European Coal Market: Will Coal Survive the EC's Energy and Climate Policy?," *Note de l'ifri*, 2012, 39 (figure 16). See also the concept of energy return on investment, measuring the ratio of usable energy obtained from a resource relative to the energy used to obtain that energy; this can be calculated in various ways, depending on whether the energy expenditures throughout the entire value chain are included, or only the direct production process. See Kenneth Mulder and Nathan John Hagens, "Energy Return on Investment: Toward a Consistent Framework," *AMBIO: A Journal of the Human Environment* 37, no. 2 (2008): 74–79.

39. By "differential rents" is meant the rent or profit related to differential natural advantages available to different producers, allowing them to produce a good (including minerals "produced" by extraction, e.g., oil or natural gas) at different costs. See David Ricardo, *On the Principles of Political Economy and Taxation* (London: J. Murray, 1817).

40. Gavin Bridge, "Global Production Networks and the Extractive Sector: Governing Resource-Based Development," *Journal of Economic Geography* 8 (2008): 389–419, at 403–4.

41. See, among others, Robert E. Baldwin, "Patterns of Development in Newly Settled Regions," *Manchester School* 24, no. 2 (1956): 161–79; Philippe Le Billon, "The Political Ecology of War: Natural Resources and Armed Conflicts," *Political Geography* 20, no. 5 (2001): 561–84; Richard M. Auty, ed., *Resource Abundance and Economic Development* (Oxford: Oxford University Press, 2001); and Richard M. Auty, "The Political Economy of Resource-Driven Growth," *European Economic Review* 45, nos. 4–6 (2001): 839–46. For a discussion of the literature from the perspective of the danger of ascribing to the resource itself characteristics related not to the resource itself but to human decisions concerning its development, see Mehrdad Vahabi, "The Resource Curse Literature as Seen Through the Appropriability Lens: A Critical Survey," *Public Choice* 175, nos. 3–4 (2018): 393–428.

42. See International Energy Agency (IEA), *Energy Policies of IEA Countries: European Union—2014 Review* (Paris: IEA, 2014), 205.

43. IEA, *Energy Policies: EU 2014*, 182–83.

44. Perhaps a better example of natural gas acquiring similar characteristics to those of oil would be the still-rare transformation of natural gas into liquid synthetic fuel.

45. A seldom-used exception are coal slurry pipelines carrying a mixture of pulverized coal and water.

46. See Timothy Mitchell, *Carbon Democracy: Political Power in the Age of Oil* (London: Verso Books, 2011), 37.

47. See Mitchell, 36–37, 151–55, on how the more cumbersome (and requiring of direct human intervention) transportation of coal as compared with oil gave workers in the industry a stronger sense of agency, as well as made it possible for them to forge an alliance with workers in other areas of the economy, such as "miners, railwaymen and dockworkers, allowing them unprecedented power"; Mitchell, 52. On coal miners and the rise of European social democracy, see Gregory M. Luebbert, *Liberalism, Fascism, or Social Democracy: Social Classes and the Political Origins of Regimes in Interwar Europe* (Oxford: University Press, 1991); and Alan Campbell, Nina Fishman, and David Howell, eds., *Miners, Unions and Politics, 1910–1947* (Aldershot, U.K.: Ashgate, 1996).

48. See Vitalija Markova and Viktor Čurašev, "Put' uglja," *Ekspert Sibir'*, no. 22 (377), June 3, 2013, http://expert.ru/siberia/2013/22/put-uglya/; and IEA, *Energy Policies Beyond IEA Countries: Russia 2014* (Paris: IEA, 2014), 167.

49. Although LNG technology is contributing to the creation of a global gas market independent of pipeline networks, its impact has thus far been limited by its high relative cost, especially with lower gas prices. However, this is expected to change as gas prices rise and the relative cost of LNG technology decreases.

50. In mid-2014, average natural gas prices in Asian markets were more than twice higher than those in the United States, while prices for oil tracked closely in both markets, with the largest difference in price never exceeding 15 percent. See, for natural gas, IEA, *Energy Policies: EU 2014*, 196 (figure 7.16); and Organization for Economic Cooperation and Development, "Oil Import Prices, Historical Chart for Crude Oil Import Prices 2000–2016," https:// data.oecd.org/energy/crude-oil-import-prices.htm.

51. See Morris Albert Adelman, "International Oil Agreements," *Energy Journal* 5, no. 3 (1984): 1–9; and for adjustment costs, see Albert O. Hirschman, *National Power and the Structure of Foreign Trade* (Berkeley: University of California Press, 1945), 13–39.

52. A. H. Younger and P. Eng, "Natural Gas Processing Principles and Technology, Part I," Gas Processors Association, Tulsa, 2004, 21.

53. Crude (i.e., still unrefined) oil is also less expensive to transport because, usually, larger tanker vessels are used than those used for shipping refined oil products, reducing per-unit costs. See also note 17 above on the risks of transporting oil by rail.

54. Thus, e.g., whether a refinery uses light or heavy oil as main feedstock will affect the proportion of each key product (gasoline, diesel, kerosene heating oil, aviation fuel, and asphalt) it can produce from each barrel of crude oil.

55. At issue were not only the technical characteristics of Belarusian refineries but also the political and governance context—the fact that refining specifically in Belarus provided Russian oil-exporting companies the opportunity to avoid paying Russian duties on their exports, which, in turn, helped create a de facto alliance between these refiners and Russian oil producers. See Margarita M. Balmaceda, *Living the High Life in Minsk: Russian Energy Rents, Domestic Populism, and Belarus' Impending Crisis* (Budapest: Central European University Press, 2014).

56. For examples from Western Europe and the United States, see Jeff D. Makholm, *The Political Economy of Pipelines* (Chicago: University of Chicago Press, 2012).

57. On asset specificity, see James E. Alt, Fredrik Carlsen, Per Heum, and Kåre Johansen, "Asset Specificity and the Political Behavior of Firms: Lobbying for Subsidies in Norway," *International Organization* 53, no. 1 (1999): 99–116. On asset specificity, see also Makholm, *Political Economy*.

58. On the issue of which goods are more viable as objects for cartel building, see Debora L. Spar, *The Cooperative Edge: The Internal Politics of International Cartels* (Ithaca, NY: Cornell University Press, 1994).

59. Despite multiple discussions in the 2000s about the possible creation of a "natural gas cartel" led by Russia, no such cartel took shape. Although Russia is not a member of the Organization of the Petroleum Exporting Countries, on a number of occasions (most recently, in April 2020), it reached an agreement with several other large oil producers to cut production in an attempt to limit a decline in prices.

60. See Apostolos Serletis, Govinda R. Timilsina, and Olexandr Vasetsky, "International Evidence on Sectoral Interfuel Substitution," *Energy Journal* 4, no. 4 (2010): 1–29, at 27.

61. Natural gas liquids (NGLs), which are often also referred to as "condensates," exist "in a gaseous state at underground pressures" but become liquid at normal atmospheric pressure due to condensation and, after removal, are "fractioned" into their various components, which usually fetch higher prices than natural gas in general. See EIA, Office of Oil and Gas, "Natural Gas Processing: The Crucial Link Between Natural Gas Production and Its Transportation to Market," January 2006, 2, https://www.eia.gov/pub/oil_gas/natural_gas/feature_articles/2006/ngprocess/ngprocess.pdf. NGLs such as propane, butane, and methane provide important feedstock for other production processes, in particular chemical companies, especially through ethylene produced from NGL ethane, which is a key component of plastic, paint, glue, and other products. NGLs can also be re-added to natural gas so that it can reach the BTU level contractually required by a specific pipeline or contract.

62. See Högselius, *Red Gas*, chaps. 4 and 5.

63. Some of these derivates can also be produced from natural gas or coal.

64. For some uses, coking coal can be replaced by petcoke, which is produced from oil.

65. An illustration: Russian natural gas plays two roles in the production of fertilizers in Belarus (the country's second source of export revenue, after the refining and reexporting of Russian crude oil). For the production of potash-based fertilizers, natural gas plays a key role as a supplier of energy in its very energy-intensive production process. In the production of nitrogen fertilizers, natural gas plays a key role not only as a source of energy but also as a raw material (because natural gas constitutes 80 percent of the material needed for its production); Balmaceda, *Living the High Life*, 70.

66. Andrej Pustišek and Michael Karasz, *Natural Gas: A Commercial Perspective* (Berlin: Springer, 2017), 53.

67. This also affects the electricity system, which is closely related to that of natural gas due to the important role of natural gas in electricity generation.

68. See U.S. National Transportation Safety Board, "Safety Recommendation Report Natural Gas Distribution System Project Development and Review (Urgent)," December 6, 2018, https://www.ntsb.gov/investigations/AccidentReports/Reports/PSR1802.pdf.

69. M. Barnett and R. Duvall, "Power in International Politics," *International Organization* 59, no. 1 (2005): 39–75.

70. Gary Gereffi, J. Humphrey, R. Kaplinsky, and T. J. Sturgeon, "Introduction: Globalisation, Value Chains and Development," *IDS Bulletin* 32, no. 3 (2001): 1–8, at 5–6.

71. Gereffi et al., 2.

72. Gary Gereffi, John Humphrey, and Timothy Sturgeon, "The Governance of Global Value Chains," *Review of International Political Economy* 12, no. 1 (2005): 78–104, at 83–84.

73. On the impact of vertical integration vs. vertical segmentation of oil markets, especially on the issue of oil processing, see Llewelyn Hughes, *Globalizing Oil: Firms and Oil Market Governance in France, Japan, and the United States* (Cambridge: Cambridge University Press, 2014); and Llewelyn Hughes and Austin Long, "Is There an Oil Weapon? Security Implications of Changes in the Structure of the International Oil Market," *International Security* 39, no. 3 (2015): 152–89.

74. From the perspective of Gereffi et al., lead firms exercise this power through their "control over key resources needed in the chain, decisions about entry to and exit from the chain and monitoring of suppliers." Gereffi et al., "Introduction," 5.

75. See also Gereffi, Humphrey, and Sturgeon, "Governance"; and P. Dicken, P. F. Kelly, K. Olds, and H. Yeung, "Chains and Networks, Territories and Scales: Towards a Relational Framework for Analyzing the Global Economy," *Global Networks* 1, no. 2 (2001): 89–112.

76. Peter Gibbon, Jennifer Bair, and Stefano Ponte, "Governing Global Value Chains: An Introduction," *Economy and Society* 37, no. 3 (August 2008): 315–38, at 316, https://doi.org/10.1080/03085140802172656.

77. See also Malkholm's discussion of natural monopolies in U.S. natural gas and oil pipeline regulation; Malkholm, *Political Economy*, 39–42. Also see Wengle's discussion of Russian electricity utility RAO AES on how the materiality associated with a good can be important not only or necessarily because of materiality itself but also because of the discourses—and their related policy preferences—that materiality characteristics may make possible. Susanne Alice Wengle, "Power Politics: The Political Economy of Russia's Electricity Sector Liberalization" (PhD diss., University of California, Berkeley, 2010), 137ff.

78. See Mitchell, *Carbon Democracy*.

79. See Collier, *Post-Soviet Social*.

80. See Margarita M. Balmaceda, *Energy Dependency, Politics, and Corruption in the Former Soviet Union: Russia's Power, Oligarchs' Profits, and Ukraine's Missing Energy Policy, 1995–2006* (London: Routledge, 2008).

81. Thus, the very concept of and need for "governance" of value chains discussed by the global value chain literature; see Gereffi et al., "Introduction."

82. The International Energy Agency defines stranded assets as those investments that are made but which, at some time before the end of their economic life (as assumed at the investment decision point), are no longer able to earn an economic return; see IEA, *World Energy Outlook 2013* (Paris: IEA, 2013), 436. Assets may become obsolete or "stranded" as a result of a variety of factors—changes in technology or regulations, changing societal preferences, the discovery of new types of energy, or, in the case of oil and natural gas, the discovery of new gas oil fields leading to unused pipelines or other infrastructure. For examples, see Malkholm, *Political Economy*. Stranded assets differ from sunk costs in that sunk costs are assets that can possibly still yield a revenue stream; once that revenue stream ceases they become stranded assets. There is a significant body of literature on both stranded assets and sunk costs in the case of natural gas (see the contributions by von Hirschhausen, Stern, and Omonbude, among others), but not nearly as much theorization of these questions in the case of oil, coal, and other energy value chains.

83. Economists have discussed a number of alternative ways of dealing with these challenges—e.g., vertical integration, contractual forms intended to share the risk between buyers and sellers, and short-term trading in anonymous spot markets—each of which also imply different types of relationships between actors in the chain. See Makholm, *Political Economy*, 4; and A. S. Neumann, S. Ruester, and C. V. Hirschhausen, "Long-Term Contracts in the Natural Gas Industry: Literature Survey and Data of 426 Contracts (1965–2014)," DIW Berlin, 2015, 6.

84. This was, e.g., the case in Ukraine's (NAK Naftohaz') January 2009 contract with Gazprom (going up to 2019), requiring it to pay for 80 percent of the "yearly contractual volume," regardless of whether it actually consumed that amount of gas. For other examples from Western Europe and the United States, see Makholm, *Political Economy*.

85. See European Union, "Third Gas Directive (Directive 2009/73/EC)," 2009, https://eur-lex.europa.eu/LexUriServ/LexUriServ.do?uri=OJ:L:2009:211:0094:0136:en:PDF.

4. NATURAL GAS: MANAGING PRESSURE FROM WESTERN SIBERIA TO THE NÜRNBERG POWER PLANT

1. International Energy Agency (IEA), *Energy Policies of IEA Countries: European Union* (Paris: IEA, 2014), 175; hereafter, *Energy Policies: EU 2014*.

2. Paul May and Simon Cotton, *Molecules That Amaze Us* (Boca Raton, FL: CRS Press, 2015), 322; see also Patrick A. Narbel, Jan Petter Hansen, and Jan R. Lien, *Energy Technologies and Economics* (Berlin: Springer, 2014),

89. Natural gas also contains some amounts of ethane, propane, and heavier hydrocarbons, as well as trace amounts of nitrogen, carbon dioxide, hydrogen sulfide, and water. Of these other substances, the most damaging to health, machinery, and the environment is hydrogen sulfide—a sulfur-bearing compound—which must be removed at the well and is only allowed in the pipeline in trace concentrations usually not exceeding 4 parts per million. See Andrej Pustišek and Michael Karasz, *Natural Gas: A Commercial Perspective* (Berlin: Springer, 2017), 28 (figure 4.2).

3. Typical end uses for natural gas include electricity generation, district heating, residential use, and as feedstock for the chemical industry.

4. Low-caloric value Dutch "L-gas" is an exception (discussed below).

5. In a physical swap operation, natural gas is delivered by the buyer at one location and redelivered by the seller of the swap at another location with which there is no physical connection. See Andrej Pustišek and Michael Karasz, *Natural Gas: A Commercial Perspective* (Berlin: Springer, 2017), 85–87, 86 (figure 5.10).

6. Some high-pressure petroleum liquids pipelines exist, but in that case 70 bar is the upper limit rather than the operating standard. See Natural Resources Canada, "Frequently Asked Questions (FAQs) Concerning Federally Regulated Petroleum Pipelines in Canada," January 18, 2019, https://www.nrcan.gc.ca/energy/infrastructure/5893#h-1-1.

7. European Parliament, *Gas and Oil Pipelines in Europe*, IP/A/ITRE/NT/2009-13, November 2009, 15, http://www.europarl.europa.eu/RegData/etudes/note/join/2009/416239/IPOL-ITRE_NT(2009)416239_EN.pdf.

8. There is no full uniformity in the way the entire pipeline is designated, with the terms Brotherhood (Bratsvo), Urengoy-Pomary-Uzhhorod, and Transgas often used interchangeably. This is partially due to the fact that different sections of the pipeline connected with and overlapped with portions of previously built pipeline systems (e.g., the Northern Lights system built in the 1950s and 1960s to bring Siberian gas to Moscow and Leningrad), as well as to changes in usage in Gazprom's official materials. By 2013, Gazprom Export was referring to the entire system, from Urengoy to the Slovak Republic, as Brotherhood (Bratsvo) (see http://www.gazpromexport.ru/en/projects/transportation/). In the interest of simplicity, when referring to the pipeline system as a whole, I refer to it as the Brotherhood pipeline.

9. The choice of the focus period is explained in chapter 2.

10. In 2012, EU natural gas consumption was 477 billion cubic meters. IEA, *World Energy Outlook 2014*, 173.

11. IEA, *Energy Policies: EU 2014*, 173 (figure 7.1), 175.

12. IEA, *Energy Policies: EU 2014*, 16.

13. In 2012, LNG imports made up 15 percent of the EU's total natural gas imports; and LNG regasification terminals located in the EU were being utilized to only 23.5 percent of their capacity. IEA, *Energy Policies: EU 2014*, 175, 180.

14. IEA, *Energy Policies: EU 2014*, 15.

15. IEA, *Energy Policies: EU 2014*, 180. For an exhaustive discussion of EU energy legislation, see Tim Kalus, *EU Energy Law and Policy: A Critical Account* (Oxford: Oxford University Press, 2013).

16. See Andrei Vavilov, "Introduction," in *Gazprom: An Energy Giant and Its Challenges in Europe*, ed. Andrey Vavilov (New York: Palgrave Macmillan, 2014), 7.

17. For a cinematic rendering of common people's lives along this journey, see Vitaly Mansky, director, *Pipeline* (film), Russia / Czech Republic / Germany, 2013, 121 minutes.

18. See, among others, Per Högselius, *Red Gas* (Basingstoke, U.K.: Palgrave Macmillan, 2013); and Jeronim Perovic, ed., *Cold War Energy: A Transnational History of Soviet Oil and Gas* (New York: Palgrave Macmillan: 2017). Two fictionalized Soviet films cover the tensions around the building of the pipeline: *Otvetnaya Mera* (Ukraine/USSR, 1974) and *Kontrakt Veka* (Russia/USSR, 1985).

19. There is no official English translation for the enterprise; Gazprom's materials in English refer to it as Gazprom Dobycha Urengoy.

20. Although Novo-Urengoy only became related to gas exploration and the Brotherhood pipeline in the 1970s, it was from long before that tied to ambitious transportation projects—through Stalin's idea of a transpolar railroad, which, although never fully completed, brought the first infrastructure investments to the region.

21. In 2012, monthly salaries in Novo-Urengoy averaged 67,500 rubles compared with 26,500 rubles for Ekaterimburg. No author given, "Tak vot on kakoj, severnyj ritejl," *Èkspert Ural* 33 (566), August 18, 2013, http://expert.ru/ural/2013/33/tak-vot-on-kakoj-severnyij-ritejl/.

22. See, e.g., Tatjana Asabina, "Sil'nye, Smelye, Uspešnye," *Gaz Urengoja* 12 (2392), March 28, 2015, 5, on youth sports. Gazprom also sought to emphasize its connection with native populations and traditions. The same issue of the newspaper provides a sense of Gazprom's attempts to emphasize its connection with native populations and traditions by the blending of local elements into official celebrations of Gazprom Dobycha Urengoy anniversaries in the region by means of a new tradition of reindeer races, for example. See Elena Kalinina, "Po zasnežennoj trasse," *Gaz Urengoja* 12 (2392), March 28, 2015, 5.

23. See, e.g., Ivan Nazarov, "Overview of the Russian Natural Gas Industry," in *Gazprom: An Energy Giant and Its Challenges in Europe*, ed. Andrey Vavilov (New York: Palgrave Macmillan, 2014), 21.

24. Nazarov, 24.

25. Nazarov, 24.

26. Nina Poussenkova, "Rossiskii 'Gazprom' v gazpromovskoy Rossii," *Istoria Novoy Rossii* 2010 (online magazine), www.ru-90.ru/node/1320, cited by Nazarov, "Overview," 23.

27. Nazarov, "Overview," 24–25.

28. Nazarov, 18.

29. I. A. Golubeva, "Gazopererabatyvajuščie predprijatija gruppy 'GAZ-PROM,'" *Neftepererabotka i Nefteximija* 1 (2015): 18–26, at 24.

30. The discussion here is perforce a simplified outline of natural gas processing. For a comprehensive analysis of the multiple steps involved in natural gas processing as well as of how it interfaces with the further value chains of various subproducts, see Energy Information Administration, "Natural Gas Processing: The Crucial Link Between Natural Gas Production and Its Transportation to Market," January 2006, 9, https://www.eia.gov/pub/oil_gas/natural _gas/feature_articles/2006/ngprocess/ngprocess.pdf.

31. Though in gaseous form underground, once brought to "normal atmospheric pressure," these substances will condensate (thus the concepts of "wet gas" and natural gas liquids) and may create crystalline structures ("plugs") that may damage the pipe.

32. This tells us that the constraints imposed by materiality are not absolute, but are mediated by both the state of technology and what is considered to be economically efficient or "profitable"—a topic to which I return in chapter 7 of this book.

33. Russian H-gas typically has a 96.96 percent methane content, in comparison with Dutch and German L-gas, at 83.64 and 86.46 percent methane content, respectively. INGAS, "Report on Gas Composition Range in Europe DB0.1," 2011, 10, 11 (table 2, "Average Values of Natural Gases in Germany, 2007"), http://www.ingas-eu.org/docs/DB0.1.pdf.

34. In addition to being marketed to oil refineries and petrochemical plants, NGLs are sometimes reinjected into a hydrocarbon reservoir to help mobilize hydrocarbons and increase production.

35. The name of the plant in Russian is Novourengojskij zavod po podgotovke kondensata k transportu (ZPKT); I. A. Golubeva and E. V. Rodina, "Gazopererabatyvajuščie predprijatija Rossii Stat'ja 6, Novourengojskij zavod po podgotovke kondensata k transportu (Ooo 'Gazprom Pererabotka')," *Neftepererabotka i Nefteximija* 5 (2015): 19–25, at 23.

36. A. H. Younger and P. Eng, "Natural Gas Processing Principles and Technology-Part I," Gas Processors Association, Tulsa, 2004, 18.

37. On ZPKT's establishment in the context of Soviet energy industry strategy, see Matthew J. Sagers, *Natural Gas Liquids and the Soviet Gas Processing Industry* (Washington, DC: Center for International Research, 1986), vol. 3, 24, 31.

38. This was named in honor of the late Russian prime minister and long-time head of Gazprom's board, Viktor Chernomyrdin, who is credited with establishing the company by creating the State Gas Concern, Gazprom in 1989, while he was minister for the gas industry.

39. Golubeva and Rodina, "Gazopererabatyvajuščie," 22–23.

40. Golubeva and Rodina, 25.

41. Domestic and export prices were set according to different principles. In 2013, the retail gas prices set by the Federal Tariff Service averaged 3,268 rubles per 1,000 cubic meters ($99.38), while export prices to the "near abroad" averaged 8,523 rubles ($259.19) and to the "far abroad" 12,046 rubles per 1,000 cubic meters ($366.33); electricity prices for industry were at about $12 per MWh. Interfax-CAN, *A Comprehensive Insight into Russia's Gas Industry*, 2014, 39 (graph 10), by subscription, http://www.interfax.com/txt.asp?rbr=7&id=275. For industrial prices, see also IEA, *Energy Policies Beyond IEA Countries: Russia 2014* (Paris: IEA, 2014), 108 (figure 5.8). Calculated on the basis of exchange rate valid on December 31, 2013 (x-rates.com). On different systems of price formation for domestic and foreign buyers during this period, see Interfax-CAN, *Comprehensive Insight*, 38–43; and IEA, *Russia 2014*, 106–8.

42. Although in general NGLs need to be removed in order for natural gas to make it to pipeline standard, there is a degree of leeway concerning what amount will be set aside for further processing, what portion reinjected into fields, and what part eventually used to enrich pipeline gas in situations where a particular caloric level needs to be reached. See Energy Information Administration, "Natural Gas Processing."

43. A total of 49.1 percent of electricity generation (2012) was based on natural gas, a significant increase since 2002. IEA, *Russia 2014*, 183, 185. On gas consumption, see IEA, *Russia 2014*, 99 (figures 5.5 and 5.6).

44. See IEA, *Russia 2014*, 211 (figure 8.16).

45. Susanne Alice Wengle, "Power Politics: The Political Economy of Russia's Electricity Sector Liberalization" (PhD diss., University of California, Berkeley, 2010), 60. In the early 2000s, pricing policies kept domestic gas prices not only significantly below international ones but also artificially low compared with other fuels, prompting consumers and power plants to move to lower-price gas (especially from coal), leading to an increase in the already-high share of gas in the country's energy mix, and affecting the amount of natural gas available for export.

46. See Susanne Alice Wengle, *Post-Soviet Power: State-Led Development and Russia's Marketization* (New York: Cambridge University Press, 2015), 166 (table 4.2, on European Russia); and IEA, *Russia 2014*, 196 (figure 8.9, on Russia as a whole).

47. Sergey Seliverstov, "The Electricity Sector Reforms in Russia: European Legal Concepts and Russian Reality," cited by Anatole Boute, *Russian Electricity and Energy Investment Law* (Leiden: Brill, 2015), 112.

48. See Margarita M. Balmaceda, *The Politics of Energy Dependency: Ukraine, Belarus, and Lithuania between Domestic Oligarchs and Russian Pressure* (Toronto: University of Toronto Press, 2013), 73–74.

49. See Wengle, *Post-Soviet Power*, 99–133.

50. Calculated from IEA, *Russia 2014*, 81–82.

51. This calculation is based on the assumption that about 70 percent of Gazprom's profits come from exports to Europe, and that about 80 percent of those exports transited through Ukraine. The 70 percent figure is from Jonathan Stern, declarations to "Commons Defence Select Committee Evidence Session on U.K. Relations with Russia," March 17, 2009, http://www.epolitix.com/latestnews/article-detail/newsarticle/committee-briefing-uk-relations-with-russia/.

52. James Henderson, "Commercial and Political Logic for Altai Gas Pipeline," OIES Energy Comment, December 2014, 3.

53. Exports to northwestern China via a proposed Altai Pipeline (also known as "Power of Siberia 2"), in discussion since 2002 as part of Gazprom's Eastern Gas Program, would have originated in Urengoy but faced repeated delays and was postponed indefinitely in 2015. On the Altai Pipeline project during our focus period, see Henderson, "Commercial and Political Logic." A much different route, which would deliver gas to eastern China, started to be discussed in 2020.

54. This monopoly, inherited from Gazprom's Soviet predecessor Mingazprom, was enshrined into law in 2006's Law on Gas Exports. Article 3 of the law confers this monopoly on the owner of the UGSS transit network, i.e., Gazprom and Gazprom Export. Jonathan Stern, "The Russian Gas Balance to 2015: Difficult Years Ahead," in *Russian and CIS Gas Markets and Their Impact on Europe*, ed. Simon Pirani (Oxford: Oxford University Press, 2009), 91n80.

55. Nazarov, "Overview," 27.

56. These two other levels, where Gazprom had no monopoly rights, where subject to different levels of regulation. Intraregional gas networks could be owned by private companies, but "still subject to regulation by the federal government and regional authorities." Local distribution grids supplying gas "through small-diameter, low pressure pipelines directly to end-users," were independent of the other two levels (UGSS and the intraregional network) and controlled by local municipal authorities. Nazarov, "Overview," 28.

57. See Jonathan Stern, *The Future of Russian Gas and Gazprom* (Oxford: Oxford University Press, 2005), quoted by Katja Yafimava, "Evolution of Gas Pipeline Regulation in Russia: Third-Party Access, Capacity Allocation and Transportation Tariffs," OIES NG95, March 2015, 3.

58. See Yafimava, "Evolution," 13–17.

59. See Tatiana Mitrova, *Shifting Political Economy of Russian Oil and Gas* (Washington, DC: Center for Strategic and International Studies, 2106), 22–23.

60. Concerning Gazprom's only limited ability to set its own export prices for sales to member countries of the Commonwealth of Independent States, such as Ukraine until the early 2000s, one strategy that was ascribed to the company was the use of intermediary companies such as Itera to sell this gas at higher, uncontrolled prices. See Balmaceda, *Politics*, 74–75.

61. Interfax-CAN, *Comprehensive Insight*, 44 ("Graph 11: Share of Gazprom in Russia's Production of Natural Gas in 2008: Jan.–May 2014"). See also IEA, *Russia 2014*, 83 ("Figure 5.1: Gas Production by Leading Russian Gas Companies, 2007–13"). On discount levels, see Mitrova, *Shifting Political Economy*, 22–23.

62. See Mitrova, *Shifting Political Economy*, 22–23.

63. If, in 2011, 35.6 percent of Russia's UGSS system was thirty years old or older, by 2013 this had grown to 42.2 percent. Interfax-CAN, *Comprehensive Insight*, 28 ("Table 14: Unified Gas Supply System Years in Use in 2011–2013"). On underinvestment in the 1990s, see IEA, *Optimizing Russian Natural Gas* (Paris: IEA, 2006), 19–20.

64. Thus, e.g., in some cases these compressor stations only use a small percentage of gas, and in others as much as 10 percent of the gas transited, as was the case of Russia due to lack of investments. Nazarov, "Overview," 33.

65. Nazarov, 29.

66. See Simon Pirani, "Ukraine: A Gas-Dependent State," in *Russian and CIS Gas Markets and Their Impact on Europe*, ed. Simon Pirani (Oxford: Oxford University Press for Oxford Institute for Energy Studies, 2009), 113, table 3.6. Before 2004, Ukraine received all transit payments from Gazprom mainly in kind; starting with the 2006 gas contracts, in cash; Pirani.

67. IEA, *Energy Policies Beyond IEA Countries: Ukraine 2012* (Paris: IEA, 2012), 106. Data on Gazprom were calculated by the author from IEA, *Russia 2014*, 111 (figure 5.9).

68. For a detailed analysis of the agreements, see Jonathan Stern, Simon Pirani, and Katja Yafimova, *The Russo-Ukrainian Gas Dispute of January 2009: A Comprehensive Assessment*, Paper NG 27 (Oxford: Oxford Institute of Energy Studies, 2009), 26–30, https://www.oxfordenergy.org. The agreements were leaked to *Ukrainsksa Pravda* and published there on January 22, 2009, http://www.pravda.com.ua/articles/4b1aa351db178/ and http://www.pravda.com.ua/articles/4b1aa355cac8c/.

69. In the period between 1994 and 2009, intermediary companies such as Itera, EuralTransgas, and RosUkrEnergo were able to make very large profits by using political connections to force themselves as (unneeded) intermediaries in gas supplies, in the process pocketing a large part of the supplies (often between 37.5 and 41 percent of these) for their "services." Margarita M. Balmaceda, *Energy Dependency, Politics, and Corruption in the Former Soviet Union: Russia's Power, Oligarchs' Profits, and Ukraine's Missing Energy*

Policy, 1995–2006 (London: Routledge, 2008), 92. On the role of intermediary companies such as Itera, EuralTransgas, and RosUkrEnergo in Ukraine's gas imports, rent-seeking, and corruption, see Balmaceda, *Energy Dependency*, 112–13; and Balmaceda, *Politics*, 114–20.

70. In previous contractual arrangements (and in particular in those in force in 1994–2005), transit, storage fees, and prices paid for Russian gas imports were "negotiated as a package"—IEA, *Ukraine Energy Policy Review 2006* (Paris: IEA, 2006), 219—and transit and storage fees charged Russia, extremely low by international comparison, were partially compensated for by low gas import prices, during most of the 1994–2005 period, nominally set at $50 per 1,000 cubic meters. During this period, Ukraine also imported gas from Turkmenistan; these imports, regulated by separate contracts, were mostly on a merchandise barter basis and through intermediary companies. For details see Balmaceda, *Energy Dependency*.

71. Netback pricing refers to prices based on the replacement value of gas (based on the price of competing fuels, in particular fuel oil) at the delivery point. In the case of Gazprom contracts with states of the former Soviet Union, it usually referred to the replacement cost of gas in Germany (Gazprom's largest Western European export market) minus transportation costs between Germany and the specific country; see Energy Charter Secretariat, *Putting a Price on Energy: International Pricing Mechanisms for Oil and Gas* (Brussels: Energy Charter Secretariat, 2007). Although this was far from the hub-based pricing based on transparent competition between gas from various suppliers that some European companies started to demand of Gazprom as early as 2012, it was a major improvement over previous contracts. However, as noted by Pirani, though the contract "appeared to reflect the European netback principle," by 2013 it "was doing so very inaccurately, because (i) the base price was about 10 percent higher than the level of European netback to Ukraine in January 2009" and (ii) the changes on the European market resulted by 2013 in Gazprom granting price reductions to European customers that closed the differential between Gazprom's contract prices and hub prices (via price reductions, sale of volumes above take-or-pay at hub-related prices, and rebates). Ukraine's import prices had been reduced, but on the basis of a political, rather than commercial, arrangement (the 2010 agreement on the Black Sea naval base)"; Simon Pirani, "Ukraine's Imports of Russian Gas: How a Deal Might Be Reached," Oxford Energy Comments, Oxford Institute for Energy Studies, July 2014, https://www.oxfordenergy.org/wpcms/wp-content/uploads/2014/07/Ukraines-imports-of-Russian-gas-how-a-deal-might-be-reached.pdf.

72. See Pirani, "Ukraine's Imports."

73. The Kharkiv agreements of April 2010 extended Russia's lease on military bases in Crimea from 2017 (when they were supposed to end) to 2042,

in exchange for a gas price discount. The discount, nominally 30 percent, was only applicable under certain conditions, and did little to stop the rapid increase in import prices.

74. If companies such as Austria's OMV, Germany's E.ON, and Poland's PGNiG had been able to negotiate lower prices and new contract modalities as early as mid-2012, in part because of pressure of new gas volumes from the United States' shale gas revolution, Ukraine was not able to do so.

75. See Igor Lyubashenko, "Ukraine's First Year in the Energy Community: Restart Needed," PISM Policy Paper 28, April 2012, 12. (A November 2009 addendum waived take-or-pay clauses for 2009 and reduced gas supply volumes for 2010 from 52 to 33.75 billion cubic meters in recognition of Ukraine's weaker gas demand as a result of the world economic crisis.)

76. This was through a Gazprom daughter company. On the connection between the danger of bankruptcy and Gazprom's taking away of clients from NAK Naftohaz, commented Volodymyr Saprykyn: "We got an European, market contract for the supply of gas to Ukraine. But inside the country we really do not have a market." Volodymyr Saprykyn, cited by Tetyana Yarmoshuk, "Naftohaz mozhe vlizti u borghi pered 'Gazpromom'," Radio Svoboda (Ukrainian program), February 19, 2009, available at www.radiosvoboda.org.

77. Ukrtranshaz charged $1.60 per 1,000 cubic meters per 100 kilometers for transit; only Belarus's Beltransgas charged Gazprom lower fees. Ukrainian transit fees were subsequently increased.

78. See Balmaceda, *Politics*, 134–35.

79. IEA, *Eastern Europe, Caucasus and Central Asia* (Paris: IEA, 2015), 343–44. The official name of the law is the Law on Introducing Amendments into the Law of Ukraine on Pipeline Transport Concerning the Reforming of the Oil and Gas Complex, April 12, 2012, no. 4658-VI.

80. See Dixi Group, *Analìtìčna zapiska šodo stanu realìzacìï Zakonu "Pro zasadi funkcìonuvanná rinku prirodnogo gazu"* (Kyiv: Dixi Group, 2012).

81. It has been argued that the company was created in 1998 specifically with rent-seeking purposes. On the rationale for the establishment of NAK Naftohaz in 1998 from the perspective of then-president Leonid Kuchma and rent-seeking, see Balmaceda, *Energy Dependency*, 40; and Balmaceda, *Politics*, 113.

82. The joining of the Energy Community, as well as steps toward closer relations with the EU, such as negotiations for the establishment of a deep and comprehensive free trade agreement (although that was ultimately jettisoned in October 2013), could also be seen as part of Yanukovich's own bargaining for better trade conditions from Russia, including a possible renegotiation of the 2009 gas contract.

83. IEA, *Eastern Europe and the Caucasus 2015* (Paris: IEA, 2015), 358; and Pirani, "Ukraine," 110, based on materials from NAK Naftohaz and Ukrtranshaz. By 2011, Ukraine was crisscrossed by 13,800 kilometers

of large-diameter pipelines including, in addition to Brotherhood's multiple parallel lines, the Soiuz pipeline from the Orenburg gas field in the Urals, as well as pipelines bringing Russian gas through Belarus and then joining the main pipeline, a corridor crossing Ukraine from northeast to south, and a corridor from Central Russia to Eastern Ukraine. Pirani, "Ukraine," 110–11. On compressor stations, see Pirani, "Ukraine," 110.

84. See Högselius, *Red Gas*, 144–45, on the crisis of missing supplies to the Brotherhood pipeline at the time of its launching in the early 1970s and on how the need to assure Central Asian gas could reach the pipeline led to the development of an additional intra-Ukrainian, East-West gas transportation infrastructure.

85. In addition, two GMSs for incoming gas were located in Belarusian territory and one on the Polish side of the border. GMS cost information (for a four-line station) is from "Ukraïnì potrìbno bude buduvati novì gazovimìrÛval'nì stancìï pìslâ ob'êdnannâ GTS z ÊvropoÛ," *Dzerkalo Tyzhnia*, October 17, 2014, http://dt.ua/ECONOMICS/ukrayini-potribno -bude-buduvati-novi-gazovimiryuvalni-stanciyi-pislya-ob-yednannya-gts-z -yevropoyu-154092_.html.

86. This is also why, at the height of the 2009 gas crisis, the EU made a point of sending representatives to the Sudzha station.

87. IEA, *Ukraine 2012*, 104 (on "accountability and transparency"). For related examples—concerning gas reexports, stealing of gas from the pipelines, and misuse of barter transactions—from the 1994–2004 period, see Balmaceda, *Energy Dependency*, 99–105.

88. At least in theory, such a change could help guarantee continued transit through Ukraine as a change in the delivery point means transferring the title (and, with it, the associated risks) to the purchaser at a different location.

89. On the "obsolescent bargain," see note 104.

90. As a result of a modernization drive started in about 2008, by late 2011 about 35 percent of Ukraine's compressor stations had electric pumping units. IEA, *Ukraine 2012*, 104. Using updated technology, the Nord Stream pipeline inaugurated in 2011 was able to significantly reduce the number of compressor stations used.

91. The significance of these investments is made clear by the Soviet reliance on Western credits to finance the building of compressor stations along the Brotherhood pipeline in the early 1970s. See Högselius, *Red Gas*, 142.

92. Andrei V. Belyi, *Transnational Gas Markets and Euro-Russian Energy Relations* (Basingstoke, U.K.: Palgrave Macmillan, 2015), 42. At the time of the January 2009 crisis, Russian accusations of Ukraine's stealing 63.5 million cubic meters from Gazprom's transit gas surfaced, but were not confirmed by international observers especially deployed to monitor possible siphoning of gas from the export pipeline.

93. Pirani, "Ukraine," 123.

94. For the specific amounts involved, see Pirani, "Ukraine," 117 (table 3.7).

95. As of 2014, Ukraine had thirteen underground gas storage facilities with a total working capacity of 30.9 billion cubic meters a year. IEA, *Eastern Europe, Caucasus and Central Asia* (Paris: IEA, 2015), 360.

96. For a detailed discussion of the development of Ukraine's UGS facilities, see O. T. Černova, "Analìz rozvitku merežì pìdzemnih shovîŝ gazu Ukraïni," *Rozrovka rodovishh* 8 (2014): 261–76. On Western Ukrainian fields as the source of the USSR's first natural gas exports, see Högselius, *Red Gas*, 14, 216.

97. Nazarov, "Overview," 29.

98. See GLE LNG, "Gas LNG Europe" Map, http://www.gie.eu/download /maps/2013/GLE_LNG_JULY2013.pdf. In particular, the Bìlche-Volicko-Ugerske gas storage merits mentioning: with an active capacity of 1.7 billion cubic meters, one of Europe's largest underground gas deposits, planned in the mid-1980s to fit the needs of increased Soviet gas exports to Western Europe, and completed after is demise, in 1992. See Černova, "Analìz rozvitku merežì pìdzemnih shovîŝ gazu Ukraïni," 261–76, at 267.

99. IEA, *Eastern Europe, Caucasus and Central Asia*, 362.

100. IEA, *Ukraine 2012*, 112.

101. IEA, *Eastern Europe, Caucasus and Central Asia*, 362.

102. See Mykhailo Gonchar, Alexander Duleba, and Oleksandr Malynovskyi, *Ukraine and Slovakia in a Post-Crisis Architecture of European Energy Security* (Bratislava: RC SFPA, 2011), 18–19.

103. In January of 2009, the government of PM Tymoshenko ordered 11 billion cubic meters of RosUkrEnergo gas (which Firtash co-owned, at 45 percent, together with Gazprom, at 50 percent, and businessmen Ivan Fursin, at 5 percent) seized from storage facilities. This was part of a complex operation in which the company had placed this gas as collateral for a loan from Gazprom, and Gazprom had decided to "seize the gas" from RosUkrEnergo against this debt "and sell it to Naftohaz"; Pavel Korduban, "Ukraine Shows No Hurry to Return Gas to RosUkrEnergo," *Eurasia Daily Monitor*, July 2, 2010, https://jamestown.org/program/ukraine-shows-no-hurry-to-return-gas-to-rosukrenergo/. However, Firtash disagreed, arguing that the gas had been bound for consumers in the European Union, and sued NAK Naftohaz at the Stockholm Arbitration Institute (commonly referred to as the Stockholm Arbitration Court), accusing it of illegally appropriating this gas. After a suit in which many argued the Yanukovich government had not defended NAK Naftohaz's interests proactively, RosUkrEnergo won the process in June 2010. The Stockholm Arbitration Court ordered NAK Naftohaz to return 11 billion cubic meters of natural gas to RosUkrEnergo, in addition

to 1.1 billion cubic meters in lieu of penalties; the transfer was completed in April 2011, which added to the higher prices to weaken NAK Naftohaz's situation. See Balmaceda, *Politics*, 334n157, 131–43. The Arbitration Institute of the Stockholm Chamber of Commerce is a unique regulatory node; though not a court in the commonly used sense of the word, it is an international commercial arbitration institution to which parties to a contract may agree to appeal in case of a contractual dispute when they want binding arbitration of potential disputes.

104. On the obsolescing bargain between transit states and energy suppliers and how the relative bargaining power between both evolves, see Raymond Vernon, *Sovereignty at Bay: The Multinational Spread of U.S. Enterprises* (New York: Basic Books, 1971); and Ekpen J. Omonbude, "The Transit Oil and Gas Pipeline and the Role of Bargaining: A Nontechnical Discussion," *Energy Policy* 35, no. 12 (December 2007): 6188–94.

105. Balmaceda, *Politics*, 3.

106. As of 2017, among the ten enterprises officially stated as having direct feed from the trunk pipeline were Europe's largest producer of iron ore concentrate, the North Mining and Concenrate Plant, in Kryvyi Ryh; the large steel producer, Mariupol Illich Iron Works; Euroammonia, operator of the Ukrainian segment of the Toliatti-Odesa ammonia pipeline; and also seven more companies. Ukrtranshaz, "Ìnstrukcìâ prisvoênnâ EÌS-kodìv dlâ točok vhodu/vihodu gazorozpodìl'nih merež," 3–4, utg.ua/img/.../instruction-to-create-eic-for-grm-04-04-2017.docx.

107. See John E. Sawyer, "Natural Gas Prices Impact Nitrogen Fertilizer Costs," http://lib.dr.iastate.edu/cgi/viewcontent.cgi?article=2672&context=cropnews.

108. For other examples, see Balmaceda, *Energy Dependency*.

109. Ukraine accounted for 3 percent of total world production of nitrogen fertilizers. L. V. Klimenko, "Tendencìï rozvitku vìtčiznânogo ta svìtovogo rinku mìneral'nih dobriv," *Agrosvìt* 1 (January 2011): 37–40, at 40.

110. Although Ostchem purchased this gas from Gazprom (through Gazprom Schweiz, a Gazprom subsidiary) and it transited through its pipelines, it is believed that the contract was for Central Asian gas, which (not being Russian gas) would not be subject to 30 percent export taxes, thus allowing for an equivalent discount. See Simon Pirani, "Consumers as Actors in the Russian Gas Sector," Oxford Energy Comment, January 2013, 8.

111. Some have referred to this process as one of "Ukraine's evolution from an oligarchy to a cronyist state." Taras Kuzio, "Ukraine Sliding from Oligarchy to Cronyism," *Eurasia Daily Monitor*, January 16, 2013.

112. Stephen Grey, Tom Bergin, Sevgil Musaieva, and Jack Stubbs, "Special Report: How a 29-Year-Old Ukrainian Made a Killing on Russian Gas,"

December 11, 2014, http://www.reuters.com/article/us-russia-capitalism-kurchenko-specialre-idUSKBN0JP1KO20141212. According to the Reuters investigation, Firtash sold the gas to Kurchenko's Lidergas for $397 per 1,000 cubic meters, which it resold for $430 per 1,000 cubic meters to the NAK Naftohaz subsidiary, with the deal being a way for Firtash to "reward" Yanukovich for "political favors that had benefited Firtash's business empire."

113. Stephen Grey, Tom Bergin, Sevgil Musaieva, and Roman Anin, "Special Report-Putin's Allies Channelled Billions to Ukraine Oligarch," Reuters, http://uk.reuters.com/article/russia-capitalism-gas-special-report-pix-idUKL3N0TF4QD20141126. On the comparative "recycling" of profits related to energy dependency on Russia in Ukraine in the 1994–2011 period, see Balmaceda, *Politics*, 265–66.

114. Russia as a destination for Ukrainian exports went down from 29 to 18.3 percent between 2011 and 2014; Ukraine as a destination for Russian exports went down from 3.5 to 2.5 percent in the same period. Ricardo Giucci, Robert Kirchner, Woldemar Walter, and Vitaliy Kravchuk, "Economic Links between Russia and Ukraine. A Fact-Based Analysis," Policy Briefing PB/07/2015, German Advisory Group in Ukraine, Berlin/Kyiv, June 2015, 4–7, http://www.beratergruppe-ukraine.de/wordpress/wp-content/uploads/2014/06/PB_07_2015_en.pdf.

115. In June 2014, Gazprom announced that it would cease transit through Ukraine at the end of 2019, when the 2009–2019 transit contract expires. The position was subsequently softened.

116. Calculated on the basis of Federal Ministry for Economic Affairs and Energy, Zahlen Und Fakten Energiedaten, table 17, http://www.bmwi.de/Redaktion/DE/Artikel/Energie/energiedaten-gesamtausgabe.html.

117. There was a short-lived exception: after the 2009 agreements, Gazprom used high-priced exports to Ukraine to compensate for lower demand from the EU.

118. The 2012 imports from Gazprom amounted to 32.9 billion cubic meters, and 28 billion cubic meters in 2013. Data for 2011 from IEA, *Eastern Europe, Caucasus and Central Asia*, 337; data for 2012–14 are from NAK Naftohaz Ukraini, as presented by Georg Zachmann and Dmytro Naumenko, "Ukraine Energy Update 2015/16," German Advisory Group / Institute for Economic Research and Policy Consulting, Technical Note TN/01/2016, March 2016, 7, http://www.beratergruppe-ukraine.de/wordpress/wp-content/uploads/2016/05/TN_01_2016_en.pdf. Gas demand also declined significantly, from 59.3 billion cubic meters in 2011 to about 50 billion cubic meters in 2013 to 41.5 in 2014. Data for 2011 are from IEA, *Ukraine 2012*, 101; data for other years were calculated by the author from figure 1 in "Ukraine Energy Update," by Zachmann and Naumenko, 5. Please note that the figures for gas demand and the imports number for 2014 do not include

supplies to the areas not under Kyiv's control ("LNR," "DNR," and Crimea) after mid-2014; it is estimated that 45 percent of the fall in gas demand is due to this. See Zachmann and Naumenko, "Ukraine Energy Update," 6 ("Figure 3: Drivers of Gas Demand Reduction"). See Zachmann and Naumenko, "Ukraine Energy Update," 6 ("Figure 3: Drivers of Gas Demand Reduction").

119. See Zachmann and Naumenko.

120. IEA, *Ukraine 2012*, 140.

121. In April 2014, Gazprom cancelled the discounts associated with the April 2010 Kharkiv agreements along with the discounts granted in December 2013 as part of an action plan intended to support President Yanukovich. As a result, prices charged Ukraine went from $268 per 1,000 cubic meters in March to $485 per 1,000 cubic meters in April 2014.

122. Although, as discussed above, Ukraine had received gas via reverse supplies from Poland already in 2012, the size of shipments (0.06 billion cubic meters of gas) was negligible compared with 2014 and later supplies.

123. This meant Gazprom had to arrange and pay for all the transit up to that point, including negotiating transit fees with the countries en route (Ukraine), while the importer did the same for transit via the countries West of the transfer point, i.e., Slovakia and the Czech Republic. As noted elsewhere in this chapter, there have been repeated debates about whether this contractual delivery point should be moved east to the Russian-Ukrainian border. On the evolution of delivery points for Gazprom contracts since the Cold War, see Kalus, *EU Energy Law*, 240–41.

124. Kalus, 240.

125. See IEA, *Energy Policies: EU 2014*, 192. An entry/exit system is "a gas network access model which allows network users to book capacity rights independently at entry and exit points, . . . creating gas transport through zones instead of along contractual paths" as in the point-to-point contract model. DNV Kema, "Study on Entry-Exit Regimes in Gas: Part A—Implementation of Entry/Exit Systems," July 2013, 4.

126. Tomasz Dąborowski, "Breaking the Boundaries: The Transformation of Central European Gas Markets," *OSW Point of View*, December 2014, 25.

127. See Andreas Goldthau, *A Liberal Actor in a Realist World: The European Union Regulatory State and the Global Political Economy of Energy* (New York: Oxford University Press, 2015).

128. This was the case with the EU states Lithuania, Latvia, and Estonia. Although a first connection—an electricity grid connector between Estonia and Finland—was inaugurated in 2006, its significance was limited due to its small size. It was only in 2014 that the Baltic states gained access to non-Russian natural gas with the set up of the Freedom LNG terminal in Lithuania.

129. Thus the EU did not include oil in its trans-European energy infrastructure priority development plan until 2013, and as of 2016 had not included other types of energy such as coal. See Regulation (EU) 347/2013 of the European Parliament and of the Council, April 17, 2013, on guidelines for trans-European energy infrastructure, http://eur-lex.europa.eu/legal-content/EN/TXT/?qid=1489667585678&uri=CELEX:32013R0347.

130. On the very different implications of synchronous as compared with asynchronous international energy collaborations and a comparison between both, see Vincent Lagendijk and Erik van der Vleuten, "Inventing Electrical Europe: Interdependencies, Borders, Vulnerabilities," in *The Making of Europe's Critical Energy Infrastructure*, ed. Erik van der Vleuten, Arne Kaijser, Anique Hommels, and Per Högselius (London: Palgrave 2013), 62–104. A very visible example of the impact of synchronous systems came to light in late February 2018, when, due to tensions between Kosovo and Serbia regarding electricity transmission, the electricity that was provided to the system was less than that contracted, leading electricity-regulated clocks all over Europe to slow down. See Valerie Hopkins and Richard Pérez-Peña, "Clocks Slow in Europe? Blame Kosovo-Serbia Row," *New York Times*, March 7, 2018.

131. Using the case of natural gas as an example, it is possible to trace how unbundling and deregulation policies moved from the United States (Natural Gas Policy Act of 1978) to the United Kingdom and, later, the EU (first Natural Gas Directive of 1998). See Jeff D. Makholm, *The Political Economy of Pipelines: A Century of Comparative Institutional Development* (Chicago: University of Chicago Press, 2012); and Anne Neumann, Sophia Rüster, and Christian von Hirschhausen, "Long-Term Contracts in the Natural Gas Industry: Literature Survey and Data on 426 Contracts (1965–2014)," *Data Documentation* (DIW Berlin), no. 77 (2015): 9. See also Thane Gustafson, *The Bridge: Natural Gas in a Redivided Europe* (Cambridge, MA: Harvard University Press, 2020), chap. 6. Such ideas moved not only across the Atlantic, from the Chicago School to the United Kingdom to Brussels, but also from more typical "networked industries," such as telecommunications, to "networked" types of energy, such as electricity and natural gas. In this movement, as discussed in chapter 3, the material characteristics of natural gas as a good requiring a networked system were discursively recruited for this purpose.

132. See chapter 3 for other examples of how material characteristics may be discursively recruited to support specific policy initiatives.

133. These data are from IEA, *Energy Supply Security 2014* (Paris: IEA, 2014), 388.

134. Though the contracts were not public, Slovakia's TSO Eustream made reference to this clause during reversal negotiations.

135. These were the Uzhhorod, Drozdovychi, Beregovo, and Tekovo GMSs.

136. These data are for 2012; they were calculated by the author on the basis of data from the Office of the Prime Minister of Ukraine, "Report for 2015 Following the Results of Monitoring Security of Natural Gas Supplies," September 2015, submitted to the Secretariat of the Energy Community, 12, https://www.energy-community.org/portal/page/portal/ENC_HOME/DOCS/3842350/2198FDD2CC031492E053C92FA8C0BE17.PDF; and IEA, *Russia 2014*, 111.

137. The Uzhhorod GMS did not exist as a full-fledged GMS until 1997, when it was built by UkrGazprom. Ûrij Ponomarev and Nikolaj Bolhovitin, "Kak izmerâetsâ kačestvo i količestvo gaza na vhode i vyhode GTS 'Ukrtransgaza'," *Dzerkalo Tyzhnia*, October 17, 2015, http://zn.ua/columnists/kak-izmeryaetsya-kachestvo-i-kolichestvo-gaza-na-vhode-i-vyhode-gts-ukrtransgaza-156266_.html. On the area as a possible gas hub, see also Dixi Group, "Ukrainian Gas Hub: A Chance for Europe," Policy Paper, 2016.

138. Patrick Heather, *The Evolution of European Traded Gas Hubs*, OIES Paper NG 104, December 2015, 5–7. Not all "hubs" are equal, however—some may be virtual and some physical; some may include largely natural gas from one geographical origin (as in the case of the Baumgartnen hub near Vienna, where about 70 percent of the gas traded is of Russian origin), and some a broader mix of gas from different origins.

139. Matúš Mišík, personal communication, May 4, 2017.

140. On network codes, see DNV Kema, "Study," 36–38.

141. "Czech Company Wins Landmark Case Against Gazprom," Euractiv, October 26, 2012, http://www.euractiv.com/section/energy/news/czech-company-wins-landmark-case-against-gazprom/; Teraz.sk, Obchodníci nemusia mať o reverzný tok plynu na Ukrajinu záujem, 2013, http://www.teraz.sk/ekonomika/rusko-ukrajina-plyn-preprava-kapacity/54773-clanok.html.

142. Matúš Mišík, "Shale Oil/Gas in Slovakia," unpublished report, 2017.

143. See Jan Osička, Filip Černoch, Tomáš Dráb, Tomáš Martanovic, and Jiří Vlcek, *Natural Gas Reverse Flows in the Danube Strategy Region: Current State and Outlook* (Prague: Center for Energy Studies, 2014), 43.

144. Barbara Lewis, "Ukraine Appeals to EU over 'Illegal' Gazprom-Slovak Pipeline Contract," Reuters, June 23, 2015, http://uk.reuters.com/article/uk-ukraine-gas-slovakia-idUKKBN0P31W620150623; Teraz.sk, "Eustream má záujem o riešenie reverzného toku plynu na Ukrajinu," 2015, http://www.teraz.sk/ekonomika/eustream-ma-zaujem-o-riesenie-reverzneho/142370-clanok.html.

145. The final report of this investigation—which held Gazprom responsible for abuse of market power vis-à-vis Poland, Hungary, Bulgaria, Estonia,

Latvia, and Lithuania—was released in April 2015. See European Commission, "Antitrust: European Commission Sends Statement of Objections to Gazprom—Factsheet," Memo/15/4829, April 22, 2015, http://europa.eu /rapid/press-release_MEMO-15-4829_en.htm.

146. Ukrtranshaz, "Modernisation and Reconstruction of Urengoy-Pomary -Uzhhorod Gas Pipeline," presentation, Energy Community, https://www .energy-community.org/portal/page/portal/ENC_HOME/DOCS/3398175 /0633975ADD357B9CE053C92FA8C06338.PDF.

147. See Wikborg Rein, "Facilitating Reverse Flow Capacity from West to East," Memo to Naftohaz, June 2, 2015, http://www.naftogaz.com/files /Information/2015-06-02%20-%20Facilitating%20Reverse%20Flow%20 Capacity%20from%20West%20to%20East.pdf; and Barbara Lewis, "Ukraine Appeals to EU Over 'Illegal' Gazprom-Slovak Pipeline Contract," Reuters, June 23, 2015, http://uk.reuters.com/article/uk-ukraine-gas-slovakia-idUKKBN 0P31W620150623.

148. Slovakia's TSO Eustream was owned by the Slovak state (51 percent, without managerial control) and the EHP (Energetický a průmyslový holding, 49 percent). EHP had bought its shares from E.ON Ruhrgas and Gas De France (new name Engie) in 2013 (Eustream, 2017), which had bought 49 percent of shares during the privatization in 2002. (Originally, Gazprom was also supposed to be a part of this consortium, but it changed its mind at the very last minute and Ruhrgas and GdF became owners of the shares in 2002.) Mišík, "Shale Oil/Gas."

149. This paragraph is derived from Osicka et al., *Natural Gas Reverse Flows*, 46.

150. SITA, "Fico: SR je pripravená organizovať spätný chod plynu na Ukrajinu," 2014, http://www.sita.sk/sk/blog/2014/04/fico-sr-je-pripravena-organizovat -spatny-chod-plynu-na-ukrajinu/.

151. Filip Černoch et al., *The Future of Natural Gas Security in the V4 Countries: A Scenario Analysis and the EU Dimension* (Brno: Muni Press, 2012), 70.

152. SITA, "Fico."

153. Pravda, "Fico: Slovensko je pripravené spustiť reverzný tok plynu," 2014, http://spravy.pravda.sk/ekonomika/clanok/314611-fico-slovensko-je -pripravene-spustit-reverzny-tok-plynu/.

154. SITA, "Fico." These attitudes also go back to the 2009 crisis, where the Slovak Republic was the only EU country that openly blamed Ukraine for the crisis. Alexander Duleba, "Poučenie z plynovej krízy v januári 2009: Analýza príčin vzniku, pravdepodobnosti opakovania a návrhy opatrení na zvýšenie energetickej bezpečnosti SR v oblasti dodávok zemného plynu," Výskumné centrum slovenskej spoločnosti pre zahraničnú politiku, Bratislava, http://www.sfpa .sk/dokumenty/publikacie/281 (translation by Matúš Mišík).

155. "The Vojany power plant was originally designed as a coal-fired power plant, however, with an option to also use heavy oil and natural gas; for this purpose, a special pipeline was built from Uzhhorod that was not directly connected to the Brotherhood pipeline." Mišík, "Shale Oil/Gas."

156. The cost of upgrading the pipeline to increase its capacity from 6.5 (2014) to 14.6 billion cubic meters a year (2015) and be able to use a compressor station was $27 million; after much negotiation, both sides agreed to finance the upgrades themselves (i.e., without the EU funding). See NRSR, "Hodina otázok: Otázka od—Marián Kéry," 2014, https://www.nrsr.sk /web/Default.aspx?sid=schodze/ho_detail&MasterID=14129; and Eustream, "Numerical Capacities," 2017, https://tis.eustream.sk/TisWeb/#/? nav=bd .cap.

157. On contractual as compared with geographic diversification, see Balmaceda, *Politics*, 31–32.

158. Although Baumgarten underwent transformation into a trading hub where gas from different sources is traded, during the years 2012–14 most of the natural gas passing through the Baumgarten hub was still subject to long-term, "legacy" contracts.

159. Calculated by the author from IEA, *Czech Republic 2016* (Paris: IEA, 2016), 122 (figure 9.1).

160. Gas transited through Ukraine also entered Germany through Olbernhau; additional Russian supplies (about 20 percent of the total) transited via the Yamal pipeline through Belarus and Poland.

161. On system builders, see Högselius, *Red Gas*, 5–6, 229–34.

162. See Högselius, *Red Gas*, chap. 7.

163. Though not illegal at the time, the companies continued to enforce the agreement even after it became illegal in 2000 with the application of the EU's Gas Directive (Directive 98/30/EC) on the opening of domestic gas markets to competition. The EU Commission found Ruhrgas's successor, E.ON Ruhrgas, and Gaz de France's successor, GDF Suez, to have infringed on EU rules on the abuse of a dominant market position, imposing fines of over $1.5 billion, the first large fine imposed by the EU concerning energy markets. See Kalus, *EU Energy Law*, 121ff, 132, 291; and IEA, *Energy Policies EU 2014*, 39. On the Ruhrgas–Gas de France pipeline-building coalition, see Alain Beltran and Jean-Pierre Wiellot, "Gaz de France and Soviet Natural Gas: Balancing Technological Constraints with Political Considerations, 1950s to 1980s," in *Cold War Energy: A Transnational History of Soviet Oil and Gas*, ed. Jeronim Perović (New York: Palgrave Macmillan, 2017), 231–52, at 239.

164. See Andrey Vavilov and Georgy Trofimov, "A Phamtom Energy Empire: The Failure of Gazprom's Downstream Integration," in *Gazprom: An Energy Giant and Its Challenges in Europe*, ed. A. Vavilov (New York: Palgrave Macmillan, 2014), 76–77, 85; and Marian Radetzki, "European

Natural Gas: Market Forces Will Bring About Competition in Any Case," *Energy Policy* 27 (1999): 17–24, at 20–21.

165. As this new infrastructure was built, it also had to adapt to the materiality characteristics of Soviet gas, in particular its high caloric value. The differences in quality between Russian and Dutch natural gas imports also meant that in Germany a system of at times parallel pipelines ensued, whereupon L-gas from Dutch fields (with an upper caloric value of 44.44 million joules per kilogram) was delivered through separate pipelines than Russian H-gas, whose upper caloric value was significantly higher at 54.30 million joules per kilogram. See INGAS, "Report on Gas Composition Range in Europe DB0.1," 2011, 10, 11 (table 2, "Average Values of Natural Gases in Germany, 2007"), http://www.ingas-eu.org/docs/DB0.1.pdf. Data are from "Annex 7: Average Compositions of Natural Gases in Germany Transported by E.ON Ruhrgas," INGAS, "Report," 76. The much higher methane value of Russian gas also affected end-user infrastructures, as if H-gas were to be used in appliances specified for L-gas, "carbon monoxide would be emitted"; see https://energytransition.org/2017/03/germany-runs-out-of-dutch-gas/. By the mid-1970s, however, H-gas had become the standard in Germany as well as in most of Western Europe. Per Högselius, Anna Åberg, and Arne Kaijser, "Natural Gas in Cold War Europe," in *Making of Europe's Critical Infrastructure*, ed. Högselius et al., 48. On the implications of the end of L-gas due to the depletion of Dutch fields, see Margarita M. Balmaceda, Per Högselius, Corey Johnson, Heiko Pleines, Douglas Rogers, and Veli-Pekka Tynkkynen, "Energy Materiality: A Conceptual Review of Multi-Disciplinary Approaches," *Energy Research & Social Science* 56 (2019): 101–220.

166. See Kirsten Westphal, "Institutional Change in European Natural Gas Markets and Implications for Energy Security: Lessons from the German Case," *Energy Policy* 74 (2015): 35–43, at 40.

167. IEA, *Germany 2013*, 74–75; Westphal, "Institutional Change," 37.

168. Westphal, "Institutional Change," 37.

169. I thank Thane Gustafson for the related discussion.

170. Westphal, "Institutional Change," 37. Thus, e.g., Ruhrgas, which had been one of Germany's largest natural gas traders, became a 100 percent daughter company of E.ON (under the name E.ON Ruhrgas) in 2003 and merged with E.ON Global Commodities in 2013.

171. See Westphal, "Institutional Change." See also Jonathan Stern and Howard V. Rogers, *The Dynamics of a Liberalised European Gas Market: Key Determinants of Hub Prices, and Roles and Risks of Major Players*, Paper NG 94 (Oxford: Oxford Institute of Energy Studies, 2014), https://ora.ox.ac.uk/objects/uuid:66b7bc5e-209f-433e-92fc-33efd1b6117c.

172. See IEA, *Energy Supply Security 2014*, 138.

173. See also Kalus, *EU Energy Law*, 183–84, on the Third Internal Energy Market Package's Third Country Clause (often referred to as "Gazprom clause"), requiring non-EU companies to satisfy unbundling requirements before being allowed to own or operate transmission networks in the EU and giving individual states additional power within their territory to refuse permission to non-EU companies deemed to have a negative impact on their security of supply.

174. Nord Stream AG's shareholders as of 2011 were Gazprom, 51 percent; Wintershall, 15.5 percent; Ruhrgas, 15.5 percent; Gasunie, 9 percent; and GDF Suez, 9 percent.

175. Franken I was able to also use some types of light oil in case of need.

176. Data on gas use for electricity generation are from IEA, *Energy Policies of IEA Countries: Germany 2013 Review* (Paris: IEA, 2013), 133.

177. This was calculated from Federal Ministry for Economic Affairs and Energy, "Zahlen Und Fakten Energiedaten," table 17, http://www.bmwi.de /Redaktion/DE/Artikel/Energie/energiedaten-gesamtausgabe.html. See also IEA, *Energy Policies of IEA Countries: Germany 2013*, 70.

178. For daily information on electricity generation in Germany by power plant, see the interactive tool at https://www.energy-charts.de.

179. For natural price differences between U.S. and European markets in the years 2011–14, see IEA, *Energy Policies of IEA Countries: European Union 2014 Review* (Paris: IEA, 2014), 194 (figure 7.16). In addition, the failure of the EU's CO_2 Emission Trading System to devise a strong-enough system of incentives to move away from coal also played a role. See IEA, *Energy Policies EU 2014*, 173. See also Westphal, "Institutional Change," 39, on the role of renewables on making only coal-fired power plants commercially viable. In 2014, coal accounted for 44 percent of Germany's power generation. Although the coal lobby was not able to demand that a specific percentage of coal-fueled generation be guaranteed, it was able to derail a proposal for a carbon emissions tax on coal power plants, the so-called climate levy (*Klimaabgabe* in German).

180. The Renewable Energy Sources Act (Erneuerbare-Energien-Gesetz) of 2000, and subsequent amendments, limited sunk-cost risks for renewables-based power plants by guaranteeing stable payment ("feed-in tariffs") for twenty years.

181. In May 2011, after the Fukushima nuclear accident, the decision was made to immediately close eight nuclear power plants plus the remaining nine by 2022.

182. In its decision, the Bundenetzagentur refered in particular to the situation in February 2012 where, as a result of an extreme cold wave, supplies of Russian gas went down even as demand increased, creating electricity supply problems in particular in Southern Germany, home of the Franken

I power plant. On the February 2012 crisis as related to system-relevance and networkness, see Bundesnetzagentur, *Jahresbericht 2012*, 58–59.

183. By 2011, Germany was generating 20.2 percent of its electricity from renewables; by 2014, this had increased to 27.2 percent. These data are from Bundesministerium fur Wirschaft und Energie, "Zeitreihen zur Entwicklung der erneuerbaren Energien in Deutschland 1990–2016," 37, 40, http://www.erneuerbare-energien.de/EE/Redaktion/DE/Downloads/zeitreihen-zur-entwicklung-der-erneuerbaren-energien-in-deutschland-1990-2016.pdf.

184. In 2016, Wintershall sold its shares in a politically controversial swap, and Gazprom became Wingas's sole owner.

5. OIL: MANAGING VALUE SWINGS FROM SIBERIAN FIELDS TO GASOLINE STATIONS IN GERMANY

1. As discussed in chapter 3, while dozens of geographically designated brands of oil exist, most oil is traded as one of three benchmark brands: Brent, West Texas Intermediate, and Dubai. See Gavin Bridge and Philippe Le Billon, *Oil* (Cambridge: Polity Press, 2013), chap. 3.

2. See Daniel Kurt, "Benchmark Oils: Brent Blend, WTI and Dubai," Investopedia, June 25, 2018, http://www.investopedia.com/articles/investing/102314/understanding-benchmark-oils-brent-blend-wti-and-dubai.asp.

3. For representative data using the Brent dated quotation, see BP, *Annual Report and Form 20-F 2014* (London: BP, 2014), 20, https://www.bp.com/content/dam/bp-country/fr_ch/PDF/BP_Annual_Report_and_Form_20F_2014.pdf.

4. International Energy Agency (IEA), *World Energy Outlook 2014* (Paris: IEA, 2014), 96.

5. See IEA, *Energy Policies of IEA Countries: European Union* (Paris: IEA, 2014), 162.

6. IEA, *Energy Policies: EU 2014*, 153.

7. IEA, *Energy Policies: EU 2014*, 167, 169.

8. See BP, *BP Statistical Review of World Energy 2016* (London: BP, 2016), 15 (table: Regional Refining Margins), http://oilproduction.net/files/especial-BP/bp-statistical-review-of-world-energy-2016-full-report.pdf.

9. Calculated by the author on the basis of information given by IEA, *Energy Policies: EU 2014*, 156, 162.

10. The reason has to do with the structure of the molecules found in crude oil, and with the physics of fractional distillation: in a distillation tower, oil that is heated to about 400°C vaporizes and rises in the fractioning tower;

as this vapor cools, its components condense into several distinct liquids, from lighter ones like kerosene, to gasoline, to progressively heavier ones like diesel, lubricants, fuel oil, and, finally, bitumen used for paving roads. (Though it is possible to further refine some of these goods by cracking, there are limits to the amount of each oil product that a refinery may produce.) See Patrick A. Narbel, Jan Petter Hansen, and Jan R. Lien, *Energy Technologies and Economics* (Berlin: Springer, 2014), 90.

11. Organizationally, Vateganskoe was part of the territorial production enterprise Kogalymneftegaz; after its reorganization in January 2013, of the TPP Povneftegaz, both with headquarters in Kogalym; see http://zs.LUKoil .ru/ru/About/Structure/Povkhneftegaz.

12. "OOO 'LUKOJL-Zapadnaja Sibir,' " on the website for LUKoil-WS, http://zs.LUKoil.ru/ru.

13. On the "oil generals," see Thane Gustafson, *Wheel of Fortune: The Battle for Oil and Power in Russia* (Cambridge, MA: Belknap Press of Harvard University Press, 2012); and Nina Poussenkova, "From Rigs to Riches: Oilmen vs. Financiers in the Russian Oil Sector," in *The Energy Dimension in Russian Global Strategy* (Houston: James A. Baker III Institute for Public Policy of Rice University, 2004), https://scholarship.rice.edu/bitstream /handle/1911/91474/from-rigs-to-riches-oilmen-vs-financiers-in-the-russian -oil-sector.pdf.

14. See Biblioteka pro literaturu avtorov i biblioteki, http://koglib.ru/index .php/83-kogalym/112-gorod-kogalym. Oil production at Kogalym had started in 1978.

15. One example is the glossy photograph book published by LUKoil in honor of the city, featuring several photographs highlighting the city's Muslim houses of worship alongside Orthodox ones. See *Kogalym: Žemčužina Zapadnoj Sibiri*, 93–94, http://zs.LUKoil.ru/ru/About/Geography?wid =widS7oOTRom5E-jiKBBLBeTng. On LUKoil's engagement with multiethnic heritages in the Perm and adjacent area, see Douglas Rogers, *The Depths of Russia: Oil, Power, and Culture after Socialism* (Ithaca, NY: Cornell University Press, 2015).

16. See Gustafson, *Wheel*, 36–37.

17. On issues of lack of diversification in the Hantsy-Mantsy region, see Irina Perečneva, "Samostojatel'naja rabota," *Èkspert Ural*, nos. 28–31 (519), 2012, http://expert.ru/ural/2012/31/samostoyatelnaya-rabota.

18. See LUKoil, "Osnovnye fakty 2007," 24, http://www.LUKoil.ru /Handlers/DownloadPartialPdfHandler.ashx?fid=4048&fc=9&pages=23,34.

19. According to LUKoil's statements, as of 2006 all the associated gas produced in area fields (i.e., fields belonging to the Langepasneftegaz, Kogalymneftegaz, Povkhneftegaz, and Pokachevneftegaz territorial production units) was being utilized and processed; http://zs.LUKoil.ru/ru/Responsibility/Ecology.

20. For a characterization of Vateganskoe as compared with other major Russian oil fields, see "Mestoroždenija nefti i gaza," at Neftjaniki: Neft' i gaz, http://www.nftn.ru/oilfields/russian_oilfields/khanty_mansijskij_ao/vateganskoe/6-1-0-566.

21. On the transition to a high-cost resource environment, see IEA, *Energy Policies Beyond IEA Countries: Russia 2014* (Paris, IEA, 2014), 125–26. Production recovered starting in 2000 as a response to technological improvements, such as horizontal drilling and the reorganization of private producers such as LUKoil. IEA, *Russia 2014*, 127.

22. See LUKoil, *Analyst Databook 2013* (Moscow: LUKoil, 2013), 4, 46.

23. In 2013, LUKoil (Russian-produced oil only) refined 53.16 percent of the oil it produced in Russia; of the crude oil exported by LUKoil, about 40 percent was later refined at LUKoil-owned refineries abroad. Calculated by the author from LUKoil, *Analyst Databook 2013*, 60. On the significance of the degree of oil refined in its own refineries for issues of market segmentation, see Llewelyn Hughes and Austin Long, "Is There an Oil Weapon? Security Implications of Changes in the Structure of the International Oil Market," *International Security* 39, no. 3 (2015): 152–89, esp. 159–61. It was only after the Russian incursion into Ukraine in 2014 that the European Union started to express official concern over growing Russian investments in the EU refinery sector. See IEA, *Energy Policies: EU 2014*, 169. See also European Commission, *European Energy Security Strategy* (Brussels: European Commission, 2014), 166.

24. IEA, *Russia 2014* (Paris: IEA, 2014), 150.

25. See LUKoil, *Analyst Databook 2015* (Moscow: LUKoil, 2015), 41.

26. IEA, *Russia 2014*, 150.

27. Data for Russia were calculated from IEA, *Russia 2014*, 141–42. Data for the EU are from IEA, *Oil Information 2016* (Paris: IEA, 2016), III 45, III 212.

28. The issue can also be approached from the perspective of transaction costs incurred in both types of operations; see note 132 below.

29. IEA, *Russia 2014*, 139.

30. IEA, 156. LUKoil's exports record was lower, at less than 30 percent of production. (Data cover non–Commonwealth of Independent States, CIS, exports via the Transneft system.) See "Figure 92: 2008–2012 Non-CIS Crude Oil and Condensate Exports through Transneft by Company, Percent of Output," in *Oil and Gas Yearbook 2013*, by Otkritie Capital, 94, based on data from InfoTEK, Interfax, and RPI's *FSU Oil and Gas Statistics Yearbook*, and company data. Accessed through the by-subscription-only Emerging Markets Information System portal, available at www.securities.com and www.emis.com; hereafter, EMIS (subscription).

31. Data for 2014 are from EY, "Oil and Gas Tax Alert: Tax Maneuver: Parameters and Impact Assessment," December 2014, http://www

.ey.com/Publication/vwLUAssets/EY-oil-and-gas-tax-alert-december-2014-eng/$FILE/EY-oil-and-gas-tax-alert-december-2014-eng.pdf. For an overview of hydrocarbon taxes in place in 2014, see IEA, *Russia 2014*, 144–48.

32. See Gustafson, *Wheel*, 258–59.

33. See Tatiana Mitrova, *Shifting Political Economy of Russian Oil and Gas* (Washington, DC: Center for Strategic and International Studies, 2016), 26. Revenue-based taxation, in turn, was a response to a more complex (and more loophope-prone) system of taxes in the 1990s, which in the 2000s the state sought to simplify by reducing the number of taxes and shifting the "tax burden to 'easy to monitor' gross income taxes." Daniel Fjaertoft and Lars Petter Lunden, "Russian Petroleum Tax Policy: Continuous Maneuvering in Rocky Waters," *Energy Policy* 87 (2015): 553–61, at 554. See also Michael Alexeev and Robert Conrad, "The Russian Oil Tax Regime: A Comparative Perspective," *Eurasian Geography and Economics* 50, no. 1 (2009): 93–114.

34. Gustafson, *Wheel*, 371.

35. Thus Gustafson refers to this goal as "a policy objective essentially based on ideological grounds"; Gustafson, *Wheel*, 372.

36. See, e.g., James H. Gary, Glenn E. Handwerk, and Mark J. Kaiser, *Petroleum Refining: Technology and Economics* (Boca Ration, FL: CRC Press, 2007), 22ff.

37. Gustafson, *Wheel*, 372.

38. This also meant that for much of this period, Russian refineries could boast a high refining margin, but without engaging in modernization. For data on refining margins in Russia during this period, see LUKoil, *Yearly Report 2009* (Moscow: LUKoil, 2009), 51, http://www.LUKoil.be/fr/pdf/AR_ENG_2009.pdf.

39. For details on the changes in Russian oil export duties between 1999 and 2011, see Bassam Fattouh and James Henderson, "The Impact of Russia's Refinery Upgrade Plans on Global Fuel Oil Markets," Oxford Institute for Energy Studies, July 12, 2012, 3–5, doi:10.26889/9781907555541.

40. By 2011, the average Nelson Complexity Index for Russian refineries was 5, while it was 6.5 for European ones and 9.6 for U.S. ones. Fattouh and Henderson. "Impact," on the basis of data from *Oil & Gas Journal*, company data, and Bank of America Merrill Lynch Research.

41. Gustafson, *Wheel*, 478.

42. The taxation of Russian oil (and gas) exports to former Soviet states has been subject to a variety of complex and changing regulations involving country-of-origin or country-of-destination application of value-added, export, and excise taxes. For background on the issue and its impact on Ukraine, see Clinton R. Shiells, "Optimal Taxation of Energy Trade: The Case of Russia and Ukraine," Joint Vienna Institute, August 2005, 2–6, http://

www.etsg.org/ETSG2005/papers/shiells.pdf; and Clinton R. Shiells, "VAT Design and Energy Trade: The Case of Russia and Ukraine," *IMF Staff Papers* 52, no. 1 (2005): 103–19. Though it is impossible to fully trace the changing regulations here, it is worth noting that the very complexity of these regulations facilitated their manipulation for both tax-evasion and political purposes. See also Shinichiro Tabata, "Russian Revenues from Oil and Gas Exports: Flow and Taxation," *Eurasian Geography and Economics* 43, no. 8 (2002): 610–27, at 625–26, DOI: 10.2747/1538-7216.43.8.610.

43. See Margarita M. Balmaceda, *The Politics of Energy Dependency: Ukraine, Belarus, and Lithuania between Domestic Oligarchs and Russian Pressure* (Toronto: University of Toronto Press, 2013), 87–88, 316n84.

44. This was called the "60-66-90-100" system, in reference to the duties to be applied to light oil products, heavy oil products, and petrol (i.e., gasoline) in proportion to the export duties on crude oil. With small modifications (further lowering the rate on light products and increasing that of heavy products), it remained in place throughout our focus period.

45. See LUKoil, *Analyst Databook 2015*, 67. Excise tax levels did not differentiate only between gasoline and diesel (as well as other oil products), but, within each type of gasoline and diesel, between products fulfilling various EU quality and environmental standards—EURO-3, EURO-4, EURO-5, etc.—with higher excises per ton on lower EURO-standard products.

46. See Interfax-CAN, *Russia's Oil Sector in 2011* (Moscow: Interfax-CNA, 2012), 59.

47. Mitrova, *Shifting Political Economy*, 26–27. The tax revenue data are from Ministry of Energy of the Russian Federation, as cited by Szymon Kardaś, "The Twilight of the Oil Eldorado: How the Activity of Russian Oil Companies on the EU Market Has Evolved," *OSW Studies* 55 (2016): 8.

48. IEA, *Russia 2014*, 143.

49. See Rogers, *Depths*. On regionally patterned pacts, see Susanne Alice Wengle, *Post-Soviet Power: State-Led Development and Russia's Marketization* (New York: Cambridge University Press, 2014), 99–133.

50. See "Sxemy magistral'nyx truboprovodov PAO 'Transneft,'" http://transneft.ru/pipelines/; and "Karta: Sxema truboprovodov," for the Siberian division of Transneft, www.siberia.transneft.ru/about/map/. For a map of Transneft's oil pipelines in about 2012, see IEA, *Russia 2014*, 153.

51. IEA, *Russia 2014*, 151.

52. LUKoil, *Analyst Databook 2013*, 62.

53. Andrei V. Belyi, "Institutional Trends in Russia's Oil and Gas Sectors," *Journal of World Energy Law & Business* 6, no. 3 (2013): 163–78, at 170. See also the discussion of Russia's Unified Gas System and exceptions to rules prohibiting private gas pipelines in chapter 4 of this book.

54. By the beginning of our focus period—2011—the access to the trunk oil pipelines had been formally modified by regulations on nondiscriminatory access. See Resolution No. 218 of the Russian Government of March 29, 2011 ("Resolution No. 218"), approving the Rules of Securing Non-Discriminatory Access to Services of State Natural Monopolies in Transportation of Crude Oil (Petroleum Products) via Trunk Pipelines.

55. IEA, *Russia 2014*, 163. E.g., the export tax (duty) component of Urals oil exports to the Czech Republic (on a CIF—cost, insurance, and freight—basis) for the high-price period December 2011–June 2013 ranged from 50 to 60 percent of the CIF price. The source for these data is "Figure 143: Typical Export Route Costs for Russian Crude, $/bbl," in *Oil and Gas Yearbook 2013*, by Otkritie Capital, 158, available via EMIS (subscription).

56. E.g., when LUKoil gained access to the ESPO Pipeline and the Baltic ports by swapping with Rosneft its export quotas for supplies via Druzhba to the Czech Republic in 2013. Kardaś, "Twilight," 19. On Rosneft obtaining additional allocations in exchange for permission to allocate export quotas to LUKoil, see "Rosneft, LUKoil Exchange Export Quotas," *Nefte Compass*, July 25, 2013, http://www.energyintel.com/pages/searchresult.aspx (subscription required).

57. For a discussion of the heyday of special exporters ("spetsy") in the mid-1990s, when they "handled 93 percent of Russia's total exports of crude oil," see Gustafson, *Wheel*, 90–92. Even after a change in policy in 1994, oil companies continued to receive additional export quotas throughout the 1990s and mid-2000s for a variety of reasons, including a company receiving "additional quotas due to the need to rebuild after damage sustained in an earthquake, another because it supplied oil to hardship-stricken Kamchatka, another because it operated in Dagestan, in the border with war-ridden Chechnya. These examples show that the system of additional export quotas was often used not only or not so much to regulate exports, but as a way to deal with a variety of domestic concerns." Balmaceda, *Politics*, 314–15. On the late 1990s, see also Yakov Pappe, *Oligarkhi* (Moscow: Vyschaya Shkola Ekonomiki, 2000).

58. Mikhail Glazunov, *Corporate Strategy in Post-Communist Russia* (New York: Routledge, 2016), 94–95.

59. Russia's pipeline oil export capacity increased significantly with the commissioning of the BPS-1 and BPS-2 in 2001 and 2012, respectively, and the ESPO pipeline linking Eastern Siberia to Asian markets in 2009.

60. In 2010, a major scandal emerged concerning Transneft's executives' alleged misappropriation of $4 billion during the building of the ESPO pipeline. On state, corporate, and personal interests as coexisting within the management of formally state companies, see Balmaceda, *Politics*, 73–74.

61. IEA, *Russia 2014*, 151. E.g., the "tariff from West Siberia" component of Urals oil exports price to the Czech Republic (CIF) for the high-price period December 2011–June 2013 ranged from 5.46 to 6.2 percent of the CIF price; the source is "Figure 143: Typical Export Route Costs."

62. Depending on its viscosity, the nature of the terrain, the diameters of pipelines, and the state of pumping stations, oil in pipelines is estimated to move at between 4 and 8 kilometers per hour.

63. In oil pipelines linking major hubs, shipment often takes place in batches separated by a buffer fluid (often synthetic oil or a light hydrocarbon liquid), making possible the transporting of multiple types of oil per month. Setting a batching operation requires significant investments, because it requires building dedicated storage tanks for each type of oil at both ends of the pipeline.

64. Tamara J. U. Safonova, "Vlijanie de-èskalatorov po kačestvu na cenu rossijskoj nefti," *Neft', Gaz i Biznes*, no. 4 (2013): 29–32, at 29. The REBCO denomination, "close to Urals in terms of the composition but meant exclusively for open trade" was introduced as a separate brand in 2006 as part of the Russian government's attempts to secure a separate quotation for it (i.e., not simply a quotation based on a set discount from Brent prices) in an attempt to increase prices and reduce the gap between the price of the Urals brand vis-à-vis the Brent oil quotation, but with limited success due to limited demand. Anna Annenkova, "Russian Benchmarks of Black Gold," *Oil of Russia*, no. 4 (2012): 44–46, at 45. See also Nikolaj N. Nikolajuk, "Ulučšenie Kačestva Èksportiruemoj Nefti Kak Faktor Povyšenija Konkurentosposobnosti Rossijskogo TÈK Na Ènergetičeskom Rynke ES," *Neft', Gaz i Biznes*, no. 1 (2013): 20–22, at 20; and Vadim Zajcev, "Kak pojavilis' sorta Brent, WTI i Urals (Deržat' marku)," *Kommersant Vlast'*, no. 13, April 8, 2013, 43. Some of the materials related to Druzhba supplies in the period 2011–14 refer to this oil as REBCO and some as Urals. Because the pipeline did not have the technical capacity to ship different qualities of oil sequentially ("batching"), it can be assumed that during this period both designations were used interchangeably.

65. An intermediate option is not to use batching per se, but a "quality bank," in the sense that, even when different oil sorts become mixed in the pipeline and what each company takes at the destination point is not its original grade of oil but a composite mixture, it receives compensation for oil quality losses (price differentials between low-sulfur [e.g., Western Siberian or West Texas Intermediate] and high-sulfur oil [e.g., Dubai Crude or Volga-Urals], which can amount to several U.S. dollars per barrel), paid by producers that experience oil quality increases in the mixing. However, the Bashneft leadership is reported to have also refused that option. See "'Tatneft" i 'Bašneft'" prosjat V. Putina ne vvodit' položenie o 'banke kačestva

nefti' v zakon o truboprovodnom transporte," March 13, 2002, at Higher Schoool of Economics, Research, and Educational Portal IQ, https://iq.hse .ru/news/177807247.html; and Galina Starinskaja, "Štraf neft'ju: 'Transneft'' predlagaet sozdat' bank kačestva nefti, osnovannyj na ob"eme," *RBK*, April 4, 2013, https://www.rbc.ru/newspaper/2013/04/04/56c1afca9a7 947406ea09dc8.

66. "Sweet," low-sulfur oil is easier to refine than "sour," high-sulfur oil because it does not contain as many impurities, which would need to be removed before processing.

67. Between 2011 and 2014, the share of Russian crude oil exports to the EU fluctuated from 65.8 to 63.9 percent of total crude oil exports. These data are from Russia's Federal Customs Service and the Observatory of Economic Activity, as cited by Kardaś, "Twilight," 10.

68. Russian Federation, *Energetičeskaja strategia Rossii na period do 2020 goda: Utverždena rasporjaženiem Pravitel'stva Rossijskoj Federacii 28 avgusta 2003 g.* (Energy Strategy of Russia until 2020: Approved by the directive of the Government of Russian Federation on August 28, 2003), no. 1234; Russian Federation, *Energetičeskaja strategia Rossii na period do 2030 goda: Utverždena rasporjaženiem Pravitel'stva Rossijskoj Federacii 27 avrusta 2008* (Energy Strategy of Russia until 2030: Approved by the directive of the Government of Russian Federation on August 27, 2008).

69. Thus, Ukraine's role in the seaborne transit of Russian oil (i.e., through Ukrainian ports such as Odesa and Feodosia) fell dramatically, from an average of 190,000 barrels per day over the period 2009–12, to 30,000 barrels per day in 2013. IEA, *Energy Policies: EU 2014*, 168.

70. See Balmaceda, *Politics*, 207–24.

71. M. Gonchar, A. Duleba, and O. Malynovskyi, *Ukraine and Slovakia in a Post-Crisis Architecture of European Energy Security* (Kyiv: Research Center of the Slovak Foreign Policy Association, 2011), 138.

72. IEA, *Russia 2014*, 165.

73. Calculated by the author from "Figure 6.12: Flows by Major Export Direction, January 2009 to January 2014," in *Russia 2014*, by IEA, 159. In volume terms, the decrease was from 60.18 million tons in 2011 to 48.23 million tons in 2014. Data from Argus FSU, as reported by Kardaś, "Twilight," 16.

74. Data for 2011 from Otkritie Capital, *Oil and Gas Yearbook 2013*, 94 (figure 93; based on data from Transneft, Neftyanaya Torgovlya, and Otkritie Capital estimates); data for 2013 from "Graph 22: Breakdown of Russia's Oil Exports Routes in 2012–2013," in *Russia's Oil Sector in 2013*, by Interfax-CAN (Moscow: Interfax-CAN, 2014), 52, based on data from Transneft.

75. "Table 28: Breakdown of Oil Exports by Russian Companies to Outside the CIS by Main Routes in 2011–2015," in *Russia's Oil Sector in 2015*,

by Interfax-CAN (Moscow: Interfax-CAN, 2016), 47, based on data from the Fuel and Energy Central Dispatch Center of the Russian Federation.

76. A further subbranch of the Druzhba South pipeline separates near Bratislava and supplies Hungary and points south.

77. Otkritie Capital, *Oil and Gas Yearbook 2013*, 94 (figure 93).

78. For a detailed discussion, see Margarita M. Balmaceda, *Living the High Life in Minsk: Russian Energy Rents, Domestic Populism, and Belarus' Impending Crisis* (Budapest: Central European University Press, 2014).

79. IEA, *Energy Policies of the Russian Federation 2002* (Paris: IEA, 2002), 94.

80. The sources for these data are, for 2011, https://www.ukrinform .net/rubric-economics/1349681-Ukrtransnafta_fails_to_implement_plans _for_processing_belarusian_black_oil_at_Kremenchug_refinery_281891.html; and for 2014, "Statements of Ukrtransnafta PJSC," as reported by EY (Ernst & Young), *Extractive Industries Transparency Initiative National Report of Ukraine 2014–2015* (Kyiv: Ernst & Young, 2015), 77 (figures 5.7 and 5.8), and Naftohaz Ukraini, *Annual Report for 2015*, 113, http://naftogaz.com/files /Zvity/Naftogaz_Annual_Report_2015_engl.pdf.

81. IEA, *Energy Policies Beyond IEA Countries: Eastern Europe, Caucasus, and Central Asia 2015* (Paris: IEA, 2015), 337.

82. Crude oil imports from Russia fell from 1.6 to 0.8 million tons between 2012 and 2013. IEA, *Energy Policies Beyond IEA Countries: Eastern Europe*, 337.

83. On economic actors' interests and the stalling of Ukrainian energy supply diversification, see Margarita M. Balmaceda, *Energy Dependency, Politics, and Corruption in the Former Soviet Union: Russia's Power, Oligarchs' Profits, and Ukraine's Missing Energy Policy, 1995–2006* (London: Routledge, 2008); and Balmaceda, *Politics*, chap. 4.

84. Ukrtransnafta transferred operational control to the offshore company Collide.

85. The Odesa oil terminal operator Collide was accused of overcharging for services provided, preventing potential Caspian suppliers from shipping their oil via the Odesa-Brody pipeline to Europe. Vitalii Kniazhans'kyi, "Comrade Reverse," *The Day* (Kyiv), March 16, 2004; orig. pub. in Ukrainian in *Den'*, March 12, 2004.

86. Such corrupt deals, it has been argued, were conducted in collaboration with Transneft executives also benefiting from them. See Balmaceda, *Energy Dependency*, 113.

87. See Balmaceda, *Energy Dependency*, 94.

88. Even such reverse use of Odesa-Brody as Brody-Odesa was ended in 2007.

89. From the very start of the project, the Odesa-Brody pipeline became the subject of significant speculation and confrontation between affected interest groups within Ukraine. See Balmaceda, *Energy Dependency*, 93–95.

90. See Wojciech Kononczuk, *The Never-Ending Collapse: The State of the Ukrainian Oil Sector* (Warsaw: OSW, 2017).

91. See also Leonid Nester (head of the International Cooperation Division at Ukrtransnafta), "Krušenie xrustal'noj mečty, ili neskol'ko slov o mifax i realijax kaspijskoj nefti" *Zerkalo nedeli*, no. 42/517, October 16, 2004, 8. See also Balmaceda, *Energy Dependency*, 93. On the reversal, see also Ivan Gonta, "S čem vošla 'Ukrtransnafta' v 2005 god," *Zerkalo nedeli*, no. 3, January 28, 2005, http://gazeta.zn.ua/ECONOMICS/s_chem_voshla_Ukrtransnafta_v_2005_god.html.

92. In 2011, Ukraine's refineries had the design capacity to process 51.4 million tons of oil, while the country consumed only 14.4 million tons. IEA, *Energy Policies Beyond IEA Countries: Ukraine 2012* (Paris: IEA, 2012), 135, 142.

93. By 2000, TNK had acquired control of the Lysychansk refinery. In 2013, the Odesa refinery was purchased by a close Yanukovich associate, Serhii Kurchenko, and, after his fleeing Ukraine in 2014, taken over by the Russian bank VBN as security against unpaid debts. On Kurchenko and the Odesa refinery, see Kononczuk, *Never-Ending Collapse*, 18.

94. See "Chart 3: Oil Processing at Ukrainian Refineries (Million Tonnes)," in *Never-Ending Collapse*, by Kononczuk, 11; and IEA, *Ukraine Energy Policy Review 2006* (Paris: IEA 2006), 233.

95. Balmaceda, *Energy Dependency*, 107, 183n58. This is closely related to transfer pricing tax evasion, by which "the oil companies 'optimized' their taxes by paying a very low internal price to their producing divisions, thus lowering all local taxes based on that price." Gustafson, *Wheel*, 262.

96. See Balmaceda, *Energy Dependency*, 106–8.

97. Sergei Kujun (director, Konsaltingovoj gruppy A-95), cited at http://oilnews.com.ua/a/columns/Patsient_skoree_mertv_u_ukrainskih_NPZ_perspektiv_net/221279, 2015. See also author's interview, oil sector analyst, Kyiv, September 30, 2016. On Lysychansk modernization, see IEA, *Energy Policies Beyond IEA Countries: Ukraine 2012*, 144.

98. Kujun, cited at http://oilnews.com.ua/a/columns/Patsient_skoree_mertv_u_ukrainskih_NPZ_perspektiv_net/221279. By 2005, most oil products refined in Ukraine did not fulfill 1992 EURO-1 standards, let alone the more stringent EURO-2, EURO-3, and EURO-4 standards that were implemented between 1992 and 2005. IEA, Ukraine 2008, 192.

99. T. I Salašenko and G. M. Fedenko, "Energetična bezpeka Ukraïni u sferì naftopererobki," *Problemi ekonomìki*, no. 4 (2014): 141–52, at 147 (diagram 4), http://www.problecon.com/pdf/2014/4_0/141_152.pdf.

100. See Kononczuk, *Never-Ending Collapse*, 26.

101. IEA, *Russia 2014*, 156.

102. For a discussion of the impact of Eurasian Customs Union regulations on Ukraine's oil products market, see IEA, *Energy Policies Beyond IEA Countries: Ukraine 2012*, 144.

103. See Energy Charter Secretariat, *Bringing Oil to the Market: Transport Tariffs and Underlying Methodologies for Cross-Border Crude Oil and Products Pipelines* (Paris: Energy Charter Secretariat, 2012), 62.

104. Although the term "Privat Group" is used to refer collectively to the group of businesses under Kolomoyskyi's control, it was not a formally constituted business conglomerate.

105. On Privat's retail market, see Kononczuk, *Never-Ending Collapse*, 38.

106. See "Kak Kolomojskij neft' otkačival," *Komsomol'kie Vesti*, June 26, 2014, https://prozoro.info/2014/06/26/kak-kolomojskij-neft-otkachival/.

107. See Kononczuk, *Never-Ending Collapse*; and Sergei Kujun, "Neulovimyj akciz," *Zerkalo Nedeli*, April 24, 2015, http://gazeta.zn.ua/energy_market/neulovimyy-akciz-_.html.

108. Ukrainian Institute for the Future, "The Future of Ukrainian Oligarchs," Kyiv, 2018, 25.

109. See also DiXi Group, "Behind Ukraine's Energy Transition: Overcoming Key Challenges," Policy Brief, 2016, 23–24.

110. Kononczuk explains this survival by highlighting how Kolomoyskyi was able to "bribe" (and, one could argue, by implication also blackmail) members of successive governments by being able to support them through his media holdings, in particular the popular TV channel 1+1. See Kononczuk, *Never-Ending Collapse*, 23.

111. See RFE Ukrainian Service, *Rankova Svoboda* radio program, December 19, 2016, recording at www.Radiosboboda.ua, https://ain.ua/2016/12/21/privatbank-chto-my-poteryali-i-alternativa; and Oleksandr Moiseenko, "Majže deržavnij: Šo bude z Privatbankom," *Ekonomichna Pravda*, December 16, 2016, https://www.epravda.com.ua/publications/2016/12/16/614619/. On the origins of Privatbank as a special instrument available to Kolomoyskyi but not to other "oligarchs," see Volodimir Golovko, "Formuvannâ pervinnogo kapìtalu v umovah krizi upravlìnnâ ukraïns'koÛ promislovìstÛ (1991–1998 rr.)," *Problemi ìstorìï Ukraïni: Fakti, sudženná pošuki*, no. 21 (2012): 5–17, at 10. In December 2016, the Ukrainian government initiated Privatbank's nationalization, arguing that its risky lending policies had led to a serious capital shortfall and liquidity problems threatening the banking system as a whole.

112. In addition to Druzhba, Ukraine also transited Russian and Kazakh oil via the Samara-Lysychansk and the Nizhnevartovsk-Lysychansk-Kremenchug-Odesa pipelines. IEA, *Energy Policies Beyond IEA Countries: Ukraine 2012*, 139.

113. See Oleg Gavriš and Natal'ja Neprjaxina, "Kontrabanda xlynula potokom: V Ukraine rastet nezakonnyj import benzina," *Kommersant'—Ukraina*, November 15, 2011; and IEA, *Energy Policies Beyond IEA Countries: Ukraine 2012*, 133.

114. This episode is part of a larger story concerning these groups' encroachment on the business of established "oligarchs" during the Yanukovich period. On this issue, see also chapter 6 of this book.

115. IEA, *Energy Policies Beyond IEA Countries: Ukraine 2012*, 142.

116. For a summary of changes in Ukrainian oil products' import duties, see IEA, *Energy Policies Beyond IEA Countries: Ukraine 2012*, 146. On the negative impact of politically well-connected, tax-exempt importers on Ukraine's refining sector during the first two decades of Ukrainian independence, see Balmaceda, *Politics*, 112–13; and Balmaceda, *Energy Dependency*, 107–8, 183–84nn59 and 60.

117. See Ekaterina Sakova, "V Ukraine snižaetsja dobyča nefti i ee pererabotka," October 31, 2014, http://www.capital.ua/ru/publication/33318-v-ukraine-snizhaetsya-dobycha-nefti-i-ee-pererabotka. In August 2014, the Permanent Court of Arbitration in The Hague ruled in favor of Tatneft and asked Ukraine to pay $112 million in compensation to the company.

118. See IEA, *Energy Policies Beyond IEA Countries: Ukraine 2012*, 143. See also Kononczuk, *Never-Ending Collapse*, 11.

119. Interview with Rada deputy Ihor Eremeev, April 14, 2014, http://www.pravda.com.ua/articles/2014/04/14/7022421/.

120. Ihor Eremeev and others have noted that soon after the re-reversal of the pipeline, Kremenchug stopped importing Azerbaijan oil due to its high price, moving to domestic (Ukrnafta) supplies. Eremeev argues that the idea of diversification through supplies from Azerbaijan was a "fiction" used instrumentally by Kolomoyskyi as a means, not for real oil supply diversification, but for justifying the re-reversal of the pipeline and, through it, the closing of production at the Odesa refinery. Interview with Eremeev, April 14, 2014.

121. For video footage of the March 19, 2015, confrontation, see http://www.radiosvoboda.org/a/26910861.html. Lazorko was subsequently dismissed, and Kolomoyskyi was forced to resign as governor of the Dnipropetrovsk region, yet his influence continued in the background. See "Kolomojs'kij plativ Vanheke za te, šob UkrnaftoÛ keruvali Pustovarov ì Kuŝ," *Ukrainska Pravda*, September 17, 2015, https://www.pravda.com.ua/news/2015/09/17/7081608/.

122. See IEA, *Energy Policies Beyond IEA Countries: Ukraine 2012*, 136.

123. For details of multiple examples of such overcharging, see the audit of Ukrtransnafta conducted by Deloitte and Touche, "Oglâd konsolìdovanoï finansovoï zvìtnostì PAT "Ukrtansnafta" stanom na 31 grudnâ 2014 ta za rìk, âkij zakìnčivsâ cìèÛ datoÛ," March 2016, https://www.ukrtransnafta.com/wp-content/uploads/2017/08/konsolidovana-fin-zvitnust-2014.pdf.

124. See DiXi Group, "Behind Ukraine's Energy Transition," 23–24; and Mikola Yakovenko, "Ukraine Oil Transit," unpublished paper, September 2016, 3.

125. See Daniil Nesterov and Sergej Ljamec, "Pozvolit li Kabmin opustošit' truboprovody," *Ekonomichna Pravda*, June 25, 2014, https://www.epravda .com.ua/rus/publications/2014/06/25/470618/; and Yakovenko, "Ukraine Oil Transit," 2.

126. See Nesterov and Ljamec, "Pozvolit li Kabmin opustošit' truboprovody"; "Ukrtransnafta načinaet vikačivat texnologičeskuju neft iz nefteprovodov," http://www.oilnews.com.ua/a/news/Ukrtransnafta_nachinaet_vikachivat _tehnologicheskuyu_neft_iz_nefteprovodov/212297; Sergei Kujun, "Dìvoča pam'ât' mìl'ârdera," *Dzerkalo Tyzhnia*, December 11, 2015, http://gazeta.dt.ua /energy_market/divocha-pam-yat-milyardera-_.html; and Yakovenko, "Ukraine Oil Transit," 2. See also Deloitte and Touche's audit of Ukrtransnafta, in "Oglâd konsolìdovanoï fìnansovoï zvìtnostì PAT "Ukrtansnafta" stanom na 31 grudnâ 2014 ta za rìk, âkij zakìnčivsâ cìêÛ datoÛ," by Deloitte and Touche, March 2016, https://www.ukrtransnafta.com/wp-content/uploads/2017/08 /konsolidovana-fin-zvitnust-2014.pdf.

127. See "Kak Kolomojskij neft' otkačival," *Komsomol'skie Vesti*, June 26, 2014, https://prozoro.info/2014/06/26/kak-kolomojskij-neft-otkachival/.

128. See Kujun, "Dìvoča pam'ât' mìl'ârdera"; and Yakovenko, "Ukraine Oil Transit," 2. See also Kononczuk, *Never-Ending Collapse*, 24.

129. IEA, *Energy Policies Beyond IEA Countries: Ukraine 2012*, 137.

130. IEA, *Ukraine 2012*, 137.

131. See Balmaceda, *Living the High Life in Minsk*. On the comparison of Ukraine's and Belarus refinery modernization investments policy, see Volodymyr Omelchenko, cited in *Ekonomicheskie novosti*, April 21, 2011, reprinted in http://old.razumkov.org.ua/ukr/expert.php?news_id=2744.

132. In seeking to understand why some transactions are internalized through vertical integration, while others are given to other actors through contracts and outsourcing, Williamson argues that the decision will be based on the relative costs of doing the transaction within the firm (the costs of coordination within the firm, and internalization of risks given volatile markets) and across markets (transaction costs). See Oliver E. Williamson, "The Vertical Integration of Production: Market Failure Considerations," *American Economic Review* 61, no. 2 (1971): 112–23; and Oliver E. Williamson, *Contract, Governance and Transaction Cost Economics*, ed. Gengxuan Chen (Singapore: World Scientific, 2017), https://doi.org/10.1142/10316.

133. See Johann Graf Lambsdorff, *The Institutional Economics of Corruption and Reform: Theory, Evidence and Policy* (Cambridge: Cambridge University Press, 2007), 212–13.

134. See Tomás Vlček, *Alternative Oil Supply Infrastructure for the Czech Republic and Slovak Republic* (Brno: IIPS and Muni Press, 2015), 19–20.

135. Given the variety of alternative transportation options open for oil transportation and distribution in addition to pipelines, the assumption in the

European Union has traditionally been that oil constitutes an "open market" and that, as such, no specific measures concerning third-party access to pipelines are needed, which may explain why oil infrastructure was not included in EU-supported Trans-European Networks until 2013. See European Union, "Regulation (EU) No. 347/2013 of the European Parliament and of the Council," April 17, 2013, http://eur-lex.europa.eu/legal-content/EN/TXT/?qid=1489667585678&uri=CELEX:32013R0347.

136. See, e.g., European Union.

137. Although, in contrast to natural gas, oil was not included in the Energy Community's field of responsibility and thus member states were not required to apply oil-related EU legislation besides that related to competition and environmental standards, other EU rules would also affect exporters to the EU through what authors such as Damro and Goldthau and Sitter have referred to as the EU's "regulatory and market power," including items such as the requirements needed to access the EU as a market. See Andreas Goldthau and Nick Sitter, "A Liberal Actor in a Realist World? The Commission and the External Dimension of the Single Market for Energy," *Journal of European Public Policy* 21, no. 10 (2014): 1452–72; and Chad Damro, "Market Power Europe," *Journal of European Public Policy* 19, no. 5 (2012): 682–99.

138. In 2001, Yukos (specifically, Yukos Finance) had acquired 49 percent of Transpetrol's shares, as well as effective control over it; after Yukos's liquidation in 2004, a complex battle ensued concerning the fate of these shares. After protracted negotiations involving Russia as well as European and local Slovak courts, in 2009 the Slovak state repurchased Yukos's 49 percent stake in Transneft. See Viera Pochybova, "Yukos' Stake in Slovak Transpetrol," *Journal of East-West Business* 11, nos. 3–4 (2006): 97–107; and Anita Orban, *Power, Energy and the New Russian Imperialism* (Westport, CT: Praeger, 2008).

139. Thus, e.g., in 2013, the main Russian oil companies exporting to Slovakia were LUKoil, Russneft, Tatneft, and Bashneft, which—with the exception of LUKoil, which supplied both countries—did not coincide with the companies exporting to the Czech Republic that year. Nefte Compass, "Russian Crude Oil Exports to NonCIS Markets, 2013," January 23, 2013, http://www.energyintel.com/pages/about_ncm.aspx (subscription).

140. IEA, *Energy Supply Security 2014* (Paris: IEA, 2014), 393–94; IEA, *Energy Policies of IEA Countries: Slovak Republic—2012 Review* (Paris, IEA, 2012), 87.

141. Alexander Duleba, "The Slovak-Ukrainian-Russian Security Triangle," in *On the Edge: The Ukrainian–Central European–Russian Security Triangle*, ed. Margarita M. Balmaceda (Budapest: Central European University Press, 2000), 88.

142. Although the Slovak Republic produced some oil domestically, much of it was further exported to Austria. See IEA, *Energy Policies of IEA Countries: Slovak Republic*, 94.

143. IEA, 88.

144. Calculated by the author on the basis of data on oil transportation revenues from *Alternative Oil Supply Infrastructures*, by Vlček, 99 (table 4.5).

145. Between 2011 and 2014, this ranged from 66.27 to 70.43 percent. Calculated by the author on the basis of Slovnaft's yearly reports for 2011, 2013, and 2014.

146. Calculated by the author on the basis of Comtrade data for 2012, for products in HS group 2710 and HS 334.

147. IEA, *Energy Policies of IEA Countries: Slovak Republic*, 94.

148. The Slovak section of the Druzhba pipeline is connected to the Adria pipeline indirectly, via a reduced-capacity pipeline linking Šahy with the Százhalombatta refinery in Hungary, which in turn is connected to Adria. This connection, however, was not used for normal operations; moreover, in order for the Adria pipeline to be able to supply Slovakia in addition to Hungary, it would have needed to have its throughput capacity significantly expanded. IEA, *Energy Supply Security 2014: Emergency Response of IEA Countries* (Paris, IEA, 2014), 395. For a detailed discussion, see Vlček, *Alternative Oil Supply Infrastructures*, 125–36.

149. The rationale for such an extension would be that, if set up to reach the Leuna refinery in Germany, a more technologically advanced refinery than Litvinov and with "the potential to make very good returns," this could increase Druzhba South's utilization rate. PKN Orlen, "PNK Orlen Facts, Figures, Comments 2014," 26, http://integratedreport.PKN Orlen.pl/sites/PKN Orlen14ar/files/pkn_PKN Orlen_facts_figures_comments_2014.pdf. (Others have suggested a reverse-flow pipeline, making it possible for the Litvinov refinery to also receive supplies from Druzhba North; this would further reduce Druzhba South's load.) See also Vlček, *Alternative Oil Supply Infrastructures*, 161–69.

150. For assumptions on oil flow speed, see note 62 above.

151. IEA, *Energy Supply Security 2014*, 133. In 1996, the Czech Republic gained access to the IKL pipeline bringing in oil from the Trieste port. Though most of the oil imported via IKL came from Caspian exporters, it also included Russian oil arriving by tanker.

152. Figures for the Czech Republic and Slovakia were calculated by the author from export/import data given by IEA, *Oil Information 2014*; and IEA, *Oil Information 2016* (Paris: IEA, various years).

153. Calculated by the author from "Twilight," by Kardaś, 16 ("Figure 3: Crude Oil Supplies via the Druzhba Pipeline to Recipient Countries in the Period 2011–14, Million Tonnes").

154. See Tomáš Vlček, "The Petroleum Sector of the Czech Republic and the Involvement of the Russian Federation," unpublished paper, December 2016, 2. See also Vlček, *Alternative Oil Supply Infrastructures*, 67–68, 98–99; and Tomáš Vlček and Filip Černoch, *The Energy Sector and Energy Policy of the Czech Republic* (Brno: International Institute of Political Science of Masaryk University, 2013), 91–92. Slovakia's Transpetrol oil transit company also played a role, because it affected the transit fees that the Czech Republic's Unipetrol had to pay to get Druzhba-borne oil to arrive to its borders and, later, to the Litvinov refinery.

155. Filip Černoch et al., *The Future of the Druzhba Pipeline as a Strategic Challenge for the Czech Republic and Poland* (Brno: International Institute of Political Science of Masaryk University, 2012), 32. According to the EU's 2009 Oil Stocks Directive (implemented in 2012), EU member states are required to keep emergency stocks of oil and/or petroleum products "equivalent to 90 days of net imports or 61 days of inland consumption, whichever is higher." IEA, *Energy Policies of IEA Member Countries: European Union*, 161.

156. Despite assumptions to the contrary—on which, see James Marriott and Mika Minio-Paluello, *The Oil Road: Journeys from the Caspian Sea to the City of London* (New York: Verso Books, 2013), 324—the first evidence of the refinery using any non-Russian oil at all comes from 2012, when Unipetrol reported Litvinov's use of small amounts of oil from Kazakhstan for purposes of achieving a better yield; Unipetrol, *Annual Report 2012* (Prague: Unipetrol, 2012), 28.

157. On Litvinov as a "geopolitical pawn" since the late 1930s, see Marriott and Minio-Paliello, *Oil Road*, 329.

158. On the history of the Druzhba pipeline see Falk Flade, "Creating a Common Energy Space: The Building of the Druzhba Oil Pipeline," in *Cold War Energy: A Transnational History of Soviet Oil and Gas*, ed. Jeronim Perovic (New York: Palgrave Macmillan, 2017), 321–44. See also Vlček, *Alternative Oil Supply Infrastructures*, 54ff. Urals and REBCO are technically different blends, but are often referred to as interchangeable as they are close in composition.

159. In other words, the Litvinov refinery would not be able to use more than 0.5 million ton per year of light (Caspian) oil in its crude oil intake of nearly 5 million tons per year; calculated by the author from table 19 in *Future*, by Černoch et al. In theory, Iranian oil could be used as a substitute for REBCO oil, as it is also heavy and high-sulfur. Interview with Tomáš Vlček, assistant professor in the Energy Security Studies Program, Department of International Relations and European Studies, Faculty of Social Studies, Masaryk University, Brno, Czech Republic, November 29, 2016. See also Vlček, "The Petroleum Sector of the Czech Republic and the Involvement of

the Russian Federation" (unpublished paper, December 2016), 6. On refinery specification to various types of crude, see Robert Clews, *Project Finance for the International Petroleum Industry* (London: Elsevier / Academic Press, 2016), 121–23.

160. There have been discussions about a possible reversal of the IKL pipeline to transit Russian oil from Druzhba to refineries in Southeastern Germany. See Černoch et al., *Future*, 29.

161. Although in July 2008 an instance of a 50 percent cut in oil supplies via Druzhba South was compensated for with IKL supplies, this was an exception; and in practice, most or all crude oil sent to the Litvinov refinery was supplied via Druzhba South. See Vlček, "Petroleum Sector," 4.

162. See Balmaceda, *Politics*, 32.

163. Stratfor, "Russia's New Export Routes Leave Czechs Short of Oil," April 14, 2012, https://www.stratfor.com/analysis/russias-new-export-routes-leave-czechs-short-oil.

164. Vlček, "Petroleum Sector," 3.

165. Černoch et al., *Future*, 35.

166. Kardaś, "Twilight," 18–19; Georgy Bovt, "Rosneft's Chinese Oil Card," *Moscow News*, June 24, 2013, https://themoscowtimes.com/articles/rosnefts-chinese-oil-card-25224.

167. Gustafson, *Wheel*, 319.

168. Unipetrol, *Annual Report 2013*, 6, http://www.unipetrol.cz/cs/VztahySInvestory/vyrocni-zpravy/Documents/2013%20ANNUAL%20REPORT/Unipetrol_Annual_Report_2013.pdf.

169. The corridor covering "60 percent to 100 percent" of Unipetrol's REBCO demand was intended to provide the company with flexibility to react to changing conditions in the crude oil market. Unipetrol, 9.

170. For more details on oil supply contracts signed by PKN Orlen to the benefit of Unipetrol refineries Litvinov and Kralupy valid during our reference period, see PKN Orlen, "Consolidated Management Board Report 2014," 28, 61, http://integratedreport.PKN Orlen.pl/en/financial-results/consolidated-menagerial-board-report.

171. This change also coincided with a time period of sharp reduction in the role of trading companies—such as Normeson, Gunvor, and Mercuria—in the supply of oil to Druzhba destinations. See Kardaś, "Twilight," 24–29. It is not clear, however, what role such companies played in supplies sent specifically to Druzhba South destinations.

172. In addition, two smaller refineries in Pardubice and Kolín (operated by a Unipetrol subsidiary) produced lubricants, bitumen, and other products using as feedstock mainly Russian oil, as well as semiproducts from the Litvinov and Kralupy refineries. Černoch et al., *Future*, 20–21.

173. Unipetrol, *Annual Report 2013*, 34.

174. Jonas Grätz, *Russland als globaler Wirtschaftsakteur: Handlungsressourcen Und Strategien Der Öl-Und Gaskonzerne* (Munich: Oldenbourg Verlag, 2013), 37. Intertwined with this goal was, according to some authors, another goal that was more political than economic: keeping the Czech Republic dependent on Russian oil (Grätz, 338–39), as well as the symbolic gains related to the branding of LUKoil as a global company (Grätz, 347).

175. Although LUKoil could have imported such products from its refineries in Russia, Bulgaria, Romania, Ukraine, Italy, and the Netherlands, given transportation constraints and costs for refined products, to do this would have made little sense; during the 2011–14 period, the Czech Republic imported only small amounts of oil products from these countries. See Grätz, *Russland*, 345 and table 7.22.

176. Grätz, *Russland*, 347, citing LUKoil, *Analyst Databook 2011*.

177. E.g., in April 2012, Gazprombank purchased a controlling interest in Czech oil services firm Eriell. See Stratfor, "Russia's New Export Routes Leave Czechs Short of Oil," April 14, 2012, https://www.stratfor.com/analysis/russias-new-export-routes-leave-czechs-short-oil. For other examples, see chapter 4 above; and Grätz, *Russland*, 349–51. For a discussion of domestic debates on Russian investments in the Czech energy sector, see Hana Biolková, *Postoje k ruským investicím přicházejících do České republiky* (MA thesis, Masaryk University, Brno, 2014), 77ff.

178. See also Grätz, *Russland*, 343. This makes sense especially if one considers that in the previous five years, Česká Rafinérská's refining margins for Urals/REBCO oil have been, on the average, $0.50 lower per barrel than those of refineries in Northern Europe, including the Netherlands. See Grätz, *Russland*, 366 (table 7.23, based on data from IEA, *Oil Market Report*, various issues; and Unipetrol, *Annual Report*, various years). Česká Rafinérská's margins were influenced by the much lower complexity of the Paramo refinery, whose crude oil refining unit was in service until mid-2012, bringing down the refining margin numbers for Unipetrol as a whole.

179. During our focus period, Litvinov was operated by Česká Rafinérská, in turn a joint venture where Unipetrol was the majority shareholder (51.22 percent, in addition to ENI and Shell Overseas Investments; in 2014, Unipetrol increased its share to 67.55 percent, which secured it a qualified majority of votes). Unipetrol, *Annual Report 2013*, 6. (Later, in April 2015, Unipetrol increased its shares to 100 percent.) In turn, since 2004, Unipetrol shares have been controlled by Poland's PKN Orlen (62.99 percent), in addition to 37.01 percent of publicly traded shares. Černoch et al., *Future*, 19.

180. During the period 2011–14, PKN Orlen was the largest company in Central and Eastern Europe in revenue. See Deloitte, "CE Top 500 Ranking," 42, https://www2.deloitte.com/content/dam/Deloitte/global/Documents/About-Deloitte/ce-top500-2013.pdf; Deloitte, "CE Top 500 Ranking," 44,

https://www2.deloitte.com/rs/en/pages/about-deloitte/articles/central
-europe-top500-2014.html#; and Deloitte, "CE Top 500 Ranking," 50,
https://www2.deloitte.com/global/en/pages/about-deloitte/articles/central
-europe-top500.html.

181. Calculated by the author from PKN Orlen, "Consolidated Management Board Report 2014," 42, http://integratedreport.PKN Orlen.pl/en
/financial-results/consolidated-menagerial-board-report.

182. PKN Orlen, "PNK Orlen Facts, Figures, Comments 2014," 26,
http://integratedreport.PKNOrlen.pl/sites/PKNOrlen14ar/files/pkn
_PKN Orlen_facts_figures_comments_2014.pdf.

183. During our focus period, Unipetrol losses amounted to $159 million
(2011), $160 million (2012), $71 million (2013), and $27 million (2014).
Calculated by the author from Vlček, "Petroleum Sector," 12; and "Unipetrol loni prodělal 1,4 miliardy, tržby klesly o sedm procent (January 24,
2014)," *iDNES.cz*, http://ekonomika.idnes.cz/hospodareni-unipetrolu-v
-roce-2013-d4o-/ekoakcie.aspx?c=A140124_074254_ekoakcie_vez. Unipetrol's refining margin went down from $3.50 to $1 per barrel between 2012
and 2013. See Unipetrol, *Annual Report 2013*.

184. Unipetrol, *Annual Report 2013*, 60.

185. Černoch et al., *Future*, 35–36. The refinery was supplied with crude
oil by its shareholders in proportion of their shareholding stake—e.g., PKN
Orlen's 62.99 percent; Černoch et al., 19–20.

186. Although PKN Orlen (and Płock as commercial node) made decisions
about crude oil supplies sent to, and product mixes by, the Litvinov refinery,
EU-level regulations (and Brussels as regulatory node) were key in terms of
environmental standards for the motor fuels produced, and state-level legislation was key in other areas. Thus, e.g., measures against unfair competition
specifically related to "gray" imports involving tax evasion (a situation repeatedly noted by Unipetrol as an important contributing factor to difficulties in
the domestic market; see Unipetrol, *Annual Report 2013*, 35) remained a state-level prerogative, coexisting with broader EU-level mandates (overseen by the
DG Competition) on mergers, antitrust measures, and state aid. On the division
and partial overlap of member state and EU energy-related competencies in the
competition area, see IEA, *Energy Policies of IEA Member Countries: European
Union*, 30–32; Christopher W. Jones, *EU Energy Law* (Deventer, Netherlands:
Claeys & Casteels, 2016), 469–526; and Kim Talus, *EU Energy Law and Policy:
A Critical Account* (Oxford: Oxford University Press, 2013), 110–74.

187. On "minimal impact," see Vlček, "Petroleum Sector." On security considerations during the 2007–10 period, see Ondřej Nowak and Jiří
Hnilica, "Rafinérský průmysl v České republice a energetická bezpečnost v
oblasti dodávek ropy," *Ekonomika a Management* 2010 (3), cited by Vlček,
"Petroleum Sector," 3–5.

188. PKN Orlen, "5.4.2 Risks and Threats of Conducted Operations of PKN Orlen Group," 99–103, http://integratedreport.PKNOrlen.pl/sites/PKN Orlen14ar/files/pkn_PKN Orlen_2014_consolidated_managerial_board_report.pdf. See also Vlček, "Petroleum Sector," 5.

189. For Unipetrol diesel production figures, see Unipetrol, *Annual Report 2013*, 33.

190. A study by the European sustainable transportation nongovernmental organization Transport & Environment notes the role of refineries in the push for diesel as follows: as the market for middle distillates (e.g., heating oil) started to decline in the 1970s as a result of the growing role of nuclear power (in countries such as France) and natural gas (in Western Europe as a whole), the increasing number of diesel vehicles in use helped compensate for this decline, as the growing use of diesel, also a middle distillate, could help compensate for the decline in demand for other middle distillates. See Transport & Environment, "Diesel: The True (Dirty) Story: Why Europe's Obsession with Diesel Cars Is Bad for Its Economy, Its Drivers & the Environment," September 2017, 11, www.transportenvironment.org/sites/te/files/2017_09_Diesel_report_final.pdf.

191. As it became clear in the "diesel scandal" of 2016–18, however, the hope that diesel vehicles would significantly help reduce emissions was misplaced. Not only was the actual difference in CO_2 emissions per kilometer smaller (5.5 percent) than expected, but the results were often manipulated, and any gains in efficiency were compensated for by the fact that diesel vehicles were, on average, driven more kilometers per year than gasoline ones, presumably because of diesel's lower price at the pump.

192. See Transport & Environment, "Diesel," "Figure 1: Diesel Share in the Main OECD Markets."

193. International Council on Clean Transportation, "European Vehicle Market Statistics 2013," 6, https://www.theicct.org/sites/default/files/publications/EU_vehiclemarket_pocketbook_2013_Web.pdf.

194. In fact, the Czech Republic was a net importer of oil products, covering only about 80 percent of gasoline and diesel demand with domestic production. IEA, *Energy Policies of IEA Countries: Czech Republic 2016 Review* (Paris: IEA, 2016).

195. No separate data are available on sales to Germany, specifically from Litvinov, but they can be inferred based on indirect evidence.

196. Unipetrol, *Annual Report 2013*, 36.

197. These are the amounts for Czech diesel exports to Germany for specific years: 2011, 133,000 tons; 2012, 146,000 tons; 2013, 160,000 tons; and 2014, 252,000 tons. *IEA Oil Information 2014*, III 167; *IEA Oil Information 2016*, III 155. Germany's diesel consumption is from *IEA Oil Information*, various years.

198. "The Directive on the taxation of energy products and electricity (Energy Taxation Directive 2003/96/EC, ETD) sets minimum tax levels for electricity and for energy products used for heating or motor fuel. Member states are free to decide on the taxation above these minimum levels." IEA, *Energy Policies of IEA Member Countries: European Union*, 158. For price information see IEA, 159–61.

199. The channeling of oil's heterogeneity into a smaller number of benchmark brands (in European markets, first and foremost Brent) also affected our value chain by making it necessary for both Russian (Urals/REBCO) oil producers and the owners of refineries using this oil to adapt to changes in the Urals/Brent price differential.

200. Balmaceda, *Energy Dependency*, 115.

201. On Aruba, Curaçao, and Singapore as refining centers, see Davis Bond, "Oil in the Caribbean: Refineries, Mangroves, and the Negative Ecologies of Crude Oil," *Comparative Studies in Society and History* 59, no. 3 (2017): 600–628; and Rex J. Zedalis, *Singapore, the Energy Economy: from the First Refinery to the End of Cheap Oil, 1960–2010* (London: Routledge, 2012).

202. Lydia Woellwarth, "Transneft Reduces Oil Transit through Ukraine Amid Crude Oil Quality Complaints," *World Pipelines*, May 15, 2018, https://www.worldpipelines.com/business-news/15052018/transneft-reduces-oil-transit-through-ukraine-amid-crude-oil-quality-complaints/. Despite the 1.6 percent sulfur content threshold for Urals oil, early 2018 shipments were closer to the 1.75 percent marker as a result of low-sulfur oil from Siberia being rerouted to China and thus not able to lower average sulfur levels in oil exported through Druzhba.

203. IEA, *Energy Policies of Ukraine 1996* (Paris: EIA, 1996), 132.

6. COAL: MANAGING SUBSIDIES FROM KUZBASS TO UKRAINE'S METALLURGICAL COMPLEX IN THE DONBAS TO GERMANY

1. The name "quarto plates" comes from the specific machinery used for their production—the four-high "quarto" mill, a reversible mill with two work rolls and two backing rolls, where the top and bottom rolls are driven by separate motors, making it possible for the slab to be passed back and forth through the mill (http://www.planete-tp.com/en/manufacture-of-thick-sheet-in-four-high-quarto-a978.html). This makes it possible for steel slabs to be individually rolled along both axes (https://www.noviostaal.nl/en/assortiment/heavy-quarto-plates/).

2. Coking coal is not *transformed* into steel but is a key component of the raw materials mix going into its production.

3. IEA, *Energy Policies Beyond IEA Countries: Russia 2014* (Paris: IEA, 2014), 172.

4. SCM had consolidated revenues of $11.385 billion in 2016, making it the largest such group in Ukraine.

5. While "DTEK" comes from the initials of the company's name in Russian, Donbasskaja toplivno-ènergetičeskaja kompanija, the full name has not been used in any corporate materials since at least 2012, possibly because of the politically complicated hint at the primacy of the Russian language. The initials in Ukrainian would be "DPEK," from Donbas'ka palivno-energetična kompanìà.

6. Metinvest's value chain, however, is not the only one connecting Siberian coking coal and end consumers in Germany. An alternative chain (to date not verified) may run through the supply chains of Metinvest's rival ISD involving the re-rolling in Poland or Hungary of steel plates produced in Ukraine. Other value chains end in other EU states, not Germany.

7. The technical process outlined in this chapter is that centered on the basic oxygen furnace (BOF) technology, which was the most commonly used in the former USSR during our focus period. Steel is currently also produced using the open hearth furnace (OHF) and electric arc furnace (EAF) processes (discussed below in the text).

8. "Basics of Iron and Steel Making," *Steel Times International*, www.steel-timesint.com/contentimages/features/Basics_of_Iron_and_Steel_Making .doc. If not refined into steel, pig iron can be used to make cast iron.

9. In integrated steel plants, pig iron is transferred directly to the steel plant as liquid steel.

10. Thus, technically speaking, coking coal does not "become" steel but is used for its production.

11. IEA, *Energy Policies of IEA Countries: European Union—2014 Review* (Paris: IEA, 2014), 223; 224 (figure 8.5).

12. IEA, *Russia 2014*, 176.

13. International Energy Agency (IEA), *Coal Information 2015* (Paris: IEA, 2015), 56 (table 4.7, "Coking Coal Prices for Industry," part III).

14. See European Commission, Directorate-General for Enterprise & Industry, "Study on the Competitiveness of the European Steel Sector," 2008, 28 (table 2.9), https://ec.europa.eu/growth/content/study-compet -itiveness-european-steel-sector-0_en; and World Steel Association, *Steel Statistical Yearbook 2007* (Brussels: World Steel Association, 2007), https://www .worldsteel.org/en/dam/jcr:5a3cd3bc-79f9-44e5-ac54-ed231832cb21/Steel %2520statistical%2520yearbook%25202007.pdf.

15. See various issues of *European Steel in Figures* (http://www.eurofer. org/News%26Events/Publications.itpl) and *World Steel in Figures* (https:// www.worldsteel.org/steel-by-topic/statistics/steel-statistical-yearbook /World-Steel-in-Figures.html).

16. Novosibirsk, Tomsk, and Krasnoyarsk are, respectively, 366, 431, and 747 kilometers away from the regional administrative center Novokuznetsk.

17. See the information on Kuzbassrazrezugol's official website, http://www.kru.ru/ru/about/about/bachatsk/.

18. These data are for 2012. IEA, *Russia 2014*, 170.

19. See Kuzbassrazrezugol's website, http://www.kru.ru/ru/about/.

20. Aleksandr Sazonov, "Vo glave uglja," *Forbes.ru*, August 3, 2005, http://www.forbes.ru/forbes/issue/2005-08/21792-vo-glave-uglya.

21. Katrin Ganswindt, Sebastian Rötters, and Heffa Schücking, *Bitter Coal* (Cologne: Urgewald/FIAN, 2013), 17.

22. Ganswindt, Rötters, and Schücking, 17.

23. IEA, *Russia Energy Survey 2002* (Paris: IEA, 2002), 155–56.

24. IEA, *Russia Energy Survey*, 158.

25. IEA, *Russia 2014*, 170, 180.

26. IEA, *Russia 2014*, 170.

27. Gennadij S. Beljanin, "Obogatitel'naja fabrika 'Koksovaja'—garantija kačestvauglja dlja filiala 'Bačatskij ugol'nyj razrez' OAO U.K. 'Kuzbassrazrezugol'," *Ugol*, June 2010, 58–61, at 59.

28. In another tragedy attributed to neglect, a March 2018 fire in a Kemerovo shopping center took the lives of over forty children, which finally put an end to Tuleyev's political career. He resigned a week later.

29. On corruption accusations against Tuleyev, see materials from the racketeering case opened in a U.S. court involving Sibirsky Aluminum, Russia's largest aluminum company, with operations in Kemerovo. *Base Metal Trading v. Russian Aluminum*, official lawsuit documents, http://www.allcourtdata.com/law/case/base-metal-trading-sa-v-russian-aluminum/cw6zaieK and https://www.thefreelibrary.com/Russia's+Largest+Aluminum+Company+Named+in+US$2.7+Billion+RICO+Suit.-a068267137. A new federal investigation was opened in November 2016.

30. For a detailed discussion of the 1989 strikes, see Stephen Crowley, *Hot Coal, Cool Steel: Russian and Ukrainian Workers from the End of the Soviet Union to the Post-Communist Transformations* (Ann Arbor: University of Michigan Press, 1997), chap. 2.

31. This decline in domestic coal consumption was related to consumers' migration from coal to lower-cost natural gas, as well as to the relatively low (and declining since 1998) role of coal in Russia's electricity generation (15.7 percent in 2012) and total primary energy supply (17 percent in 2012). IEA, *Russia 2014*, 167; for 1998 figures, see IEA, *Russia 2002*, 194.

32. In Russia, CPPs are known as "*obogatitelnie fabriki*" (enriching factories), and their product is called coal concentrate. For an example from a Western-planned CCP in Russia, see Beljanin, "Obogatitel'naja fabrika 'Koksovaja,'" 58–61.

33. Mixail Kičanov, "Ugol'nyj peregruz," *Ekspert Sibir'* 4, no. 360 (2013), http://expert.ru/siberia/2013/04/ugolnyij-peregruz/.

34. Beljanin, "Obogatitel'naja fabrika 'Koksovaja,'" 58–61, at 59–60.

35. Mixail Kičanov, "Ugol'nyj peregruz."

36. For details of this processing, see Beljanin, "Obogatitel'naja fabrika 'Koksovaja,'" 58–61.

37. IEA, *Russia Energy Survey*, 165.

38. V. I. Jakunin, "Desjat' šagov k èffektivnosti," *Ekspert*, no. 33 (August 31, 2009), 36–42, cited by F. I. Xusainov, *Reforma železnodorožnoj otrasli: Problemy nezaveršennoj liberalizacii* (Moscow: Higher School of Economics, 2014), 16.

39. For data on transportation costs for coal, oil, and metallurgical products, see Vitalija Markova and Viktor Čurašev, "Put 'uglja," *Ekspert Sibir'*, no. 22 (377), June 3, 2014, http://expert.ru/siberia/2013/22/put-uglya/; IEA, *Energy Policies Beyond IEA Countries: Russia 2014* (Paris: IEA, 2014), 167. Xusainov puts transportation costs for coal at about 30–50 percent of its price. See Xusainov, *Reforma železnodorožnoj otrasli*, 12.

40. That transportation issues had a serious impact on both exports and domestic supply possibilities was also made clear by official Russian policy documents. The long-term program for the development of the Russian coal industry for the period 2012–30, for instance, makes the intended additional coal production dependent on "the development of railroad tariffs and transportation costs." IEA, *Energy Policies Beyond IEA Countries: Russia*, 167.

41. No author stated, "Èksport uglja čerez morskie porty Rossii," *Morskie porty*, no. 3 (2013), http://www.morvesti.ru/tems/detail.php?ID=23803.

42. IEA, *Russia 2014*, 175.

43. See Kateryna Grushevska and Theo Notteboom, "Dry Bulk Cargo in Ukrainian Ports," *Port Technology*, no. 61, (February 2014): 64–69.

44. Peter Rutland, "Russian Railways: An Emerging Force," Oxford Analytica, 2012.

45. In addition to his interests in the railway industry, Yakukin played a role in energy business through involvement in, among others, natural gas intermediary companies active in Lithuania. See Margarita M. Balmaceda, *The Politics of Energy Dependency: Ukraine, Belarus, and Lithuania between Domestic Oligarchs and Russian Pressure* (Toronto: University of Toronto Press, 2013), 238–39.

46. Freight tariffs for transportation by the RZhD were set by the Federal Tariff Service and included separate charges for infrastructure use as well as services and wagon use. They involved several components, including consideration of distance, type of good, and ownership. IEA, *Russia 2014*, 167. See also Rutland, "Russian Railways."

47. Rutland, "Russian Railways."

48. IEA, *Russia 2104*, 175; Xusainov, *Reforma železnodorožnoj otrasli*, 14, based on materials from Rosstat.

49. See IEA, *Russia 2014*, 175.

50. IEA, *Russia 2014*, 187.

51. On coal purchases by the Avdiivka Coking Plant from Bachatsky and Kuzbassrazrevugol, see "Yearly Report of the Avdiivka Coking Plant 2014."

52. See World Bank, *Ukraine: Coal Industry Restructuring Sector Report* (Washington, DC: World Bank, 1996), 2, http://documents.worldbank.org/curated/en/1996/03/696696/ukraine-coal-industry-restructuring-sector-report.

53. Quotation taken from an interview given by Serhii Ermilov, energy minister during Viktor Yuschenko's presidency. Alla Dubrovyk and Vitalij Knjažanskij, "Sergej Ermilov: Kak tol'ko NAK Naftogaz isčeznet kak sub"ekt, to, pover'te, s gazom u nas vse budet v porjadke," *Den'*, December 24, 2014, http://m.day.kyiv.ua/ru/article/ekonomika/s-chego-nachinat-reformy.

54. On the mythologization of the Donbas, see also Yuri Andrukhovich, *Diâvol hovaêt'sá v sirì* (*The Devil's Hiding in the Cheese*) (Kyiv: Krytyka, 2006); and Serhii Zhadan, *Voroshylovhrad* (Kharkiv: Folio, 2010), translated into English as *Voroshilovgrad* (Dallas: Deep Vellum, 2016).

55. Richard M. Levine and Andrew R. Bond, "Prospects for Ukrainian Ferrous Metals in the Post-Soviet Period," *Post-Soviet Geography and Economics* 39, no. 3 (1998): 151–63, at 155, citing Craig ZumBrunnen and Jeffrey Osleeb, *The Soviet Iron and Steel Industry* (Totowa, NJ: Rowman & Allenheld, 1986).

56. Mikhail G. Sklyar, "Ukrainian Coals: Resources, Output, Utilization," *Fuel* 73, no. 10 (1994): 1672–78, at 1672.

57. In a metallurgical context, reduction refers to the process of driving of steel impurities in the blast furnace.

58. In some cases, this specific grade of coking coal can be replaced by semicoking coal of compatible characteristics as part of a master-blended mixture.

59. See Allan Rodgers, "Coking Coal Supply: Its Role in the Expansion of the Soviet Steel Industry," *Economic Geography* 40, no. 2 (April 1964): 113–50, at 122. On the quality of Ukrainian coking coal, see IEA, *Energy Policies Beyond IEA Countries: Ukraine 2012* (Paris: IEA, 2012), 156, 157.

60. World Bank, *Ukraine*, 13. See also IEA, *Ukraine Energy Policy Review 2006* (Paris: IEA, 2006), 141.

61. See Rodgers, "Coking Coal Supply," 123; and Ilona V. Kochura, "Coal Market of Ukraine: Analysis and Development Background," *GeoScience Engineering* 58, no. 1 (2012): 17–23, at 18.

62. World Bank, *Ukraine*, 2.

63. World Bank, 41–42.

64. Leslie Dienes, "Energy, Minerals, and Economic Policy," in *The Ukrainian Economy*, ed. I. S. Koropeckyi (Cambridge, MA: Harvard Ukrainian Research Institute, 1992), 129.

65. On industrial development and pressures for regional autarchy during the Soviet period, see Stephen Fortescue, "Die russische Stahlindustrie und die Ukraine," *Ukraine-Analysen*, no. 86 (February 2, 2011): 2–5, at 5. Similar processes could also be observed in other key industrial sectors outside Ukraine.

66. On demonetarization and liquidity problems in the early post-Soviet period, see D. M. Woodruff, *Money Unmade: Barter and the Fate of Russian Capitalism* (Ithaca, NY: Cornell University Press, 1999).

67. World Bank, *Ukraine*, 26.

68. IEA, *Energy Policies of Ukraine: 1996 Survey* (Paris: IEA, 1996), 159. See also Sklyar, "Ukrainian Coals," 1674, figure 2.

69. For a critical perspective on this engagement, see Adam Swain, "Soft Capitalism and a Hard Industry: Virtualism, the 'Transition Industry' and the Restructuring of the Ukrainian Coal Industry," *Transactions of the Institute of British Geographers* 31, no. 2 (2006): 208–23.

70. Of course, neither the fear of social instability nor the subsidization of the coal mining sector were phenomena unique to Ukraine—multiple examples of such phenomena can be found, from Victorian England to the contemporary United States.

71. On the political implications of this in an early twentieth-century context, see Timothy Mitchell, *Carbon Democracy: Political Power in the Age of Oil* (London: Verso Books, 2013).

72. World Bank, *Ukraine*, 11. For the official Ukrainian policy covering this period, see "National Program for the Development of the Ukrainian Coal Industry and Its Social Aspects to the Year 2005," the focus of which was the reconstruction of existing mines and construction of twenty-one new ones; cited by Sklyar, "Ukrainian Coals," 1674.

73. World Bank, *Ukraine*, 41–42.

74. See World Bank, 2–3. See also IEA, *Energy Policies of Ukraine*, 157–58.

75. On supply chain problems during the Soviet system, see the section "Soviet Energy Value Chains: Myth and Reality" in "Energy Materiality and the Governance of Post-Soviet Supply Chains," by Margarita M. Balmaceda, unpublished paper prepared for the Exploring Energy Regionalisms Workshop, GIGA-Hamburg, September 22–23, 2016.

76. Although it is technically possible to produce steel without immediate access to coke through the melting of scrap steel, such technology was not available in Ukraine until 2011.

77. Some have alluded to Akhmetov's background in the Donetsk under-world at the time; see, among others, Taras Kuzio, "Crime, Politics and Business in 1990s Ukraine," *Communist and Post-Communist Studies* 47 (2014): 195–210, at 197; and Hans von Zon, "The Rise of Conglomerates in Ukraine: The Donetsk Case," in *Big Business and Economic Development: Conglomerates and Economic Groups in Developing Countries and Transition Economies under Globalization*, ed. A. E. F. Jilberto and B. Hogenboom (London: Routledge, 2007), 378–97, at 386.

78. V. Golovko, *Oligarxi iz goroda roz: Stanovlenie i razvitie krupnogo kapitala Donbassa (1991–2014 gg.)* (Kyiv: Institut istorii Ukrainy, 2014), 11.

79. The supply coordination activities engaged in by Pinchuk, Taruta, and their like started even before Ukrainian independence, and were made possible by the combination of new economic prerogatives gained by enterprises (Law on Enterprises, 1987) and the supply problems already evident during the perestroika period. Such activities were widely spread throughout the entire USSR, as was the Russian term *tolkach*. Thus, I use that here rather than the Ukrainian *štovhač* (more often transliterated as *shtovkhach*).

80. On the regional factor as determinant in the emergence of Ukrainian Business-Administrative Groups, see Balmaceda, *Energy Dependency*, chap. 2; and B. Pinto, V. Drebentsov, and A. Morozov, "Give Macroeconomic Stability and Growth in Russia a Chance: Harden Budgets by Eliminating Non-Payments," *Economics of Transition* 8, no. 2 (2000): 297–324, at 304.

81. World Bank, *Ukraine*, 11.

82. Serhii Taruta, quoted by S. Lešenko and M. Naem, "Sergìj Taruta: Koli vbili Šerbanâ, u nas ne bulo problem z ÊESU," *Ukrainskaya pravda*, February 8, 2013, https://www.pravda.com.ua/articles/2013/02/8/6983135/. Gosplan is the State Planning Committee, in charge of economic planning; Gossnab means State Supplies of the USSR, which was in charge of allocating supplies to various state enterprises.

83. On this issue as related to privatization processes, see A. Saržan, "Privatizacìâ vugìl'nih pìdprièmstv Ukraïni: Dosvìd, problemi," *Novì storìnki ìstorìï Donbasu*, no. 22 (2013): 76–86, at 78ff.

84. In seeking to understand why some transactions are internalized through vertical integration, while others are given to other actors through contracts and outsourcing, Williams argues that the decision will be based on the relative costs of doing the transaction within the firm (the costs of coordination within the firm, and internalization of risks given volatile markets) and across markets (transaction costs). See Oliver E. Williamson, "The Vertical Integration of Production: Market Failure Considerations," *American Economic Review* 61, no. 2 (1971): 112–23; and Oliver E. Williamson, *Contract, Governance and Transaction Cost Economics* (Singapore: World Scientific, 2017).

85. G. Gereffi, J. Humphrey, and T. Sturgeon, "The Governance of Global Value Chains," *Review of International Political Economy* 12, no. 1 (2005): 78–104. The five types of governance of global value chains noted in this article are market, modular, relational, captive, and vertically integrated relationships.

86. By 2000, ISD controlled 70 percent of Ukraine's mining machinery market. "Kak zakaljalas' stal'," *Delovoj žurnal*, January 14, 2015, http:// ukrrudprom.ua/digest/ndzh140105.html. Referring to the situation during our focus period, Virkhov and Butchenko note that, as per an unwritten agreement, coal mines were not allowed to purchase imported machinery, but only from Ukrainian oligarchs, in particular Rinat Akhmetov, whose machine-building interests included the Corum Group, part of SCM. Maksim Vixrov and Maksim Butčenko, "Fenomen 'narodnyx respublik' Donbassa," Carnegie Moscow Center, April 12, 2016, no p. no., https://carnegie .ru/2016/04/12/ru-pub-63295. Akhmetov also had important interests in the machine-building sector.

87. O. Bogatov, "Recent Developments in the Donbass Coal Industry," *Mining Technology* 111, no. 3 (2002): 159–66, at 161.

88. Hans Van Zon, "Is The Donetsk Model Sustainable?," *Geographia Polonica* 78, no. 2 (Fall 2005): 77–90, at 81.

89. Laszlo Lovei, *Coal Industry Restructuring in Ukraine: The Politics of Coal Mining and Budget Crises* (Washington, DC: World Bank, 1998), 2, http:// documents.worldbank.org/curated/en/1998/12/441539/coal-industry -restructuring-ukraine-politics-coal-mining-budget-crises.

90. World Bank, *Mining Communities of Ukraine: Advancing Restructuring for the Benefit of All* (Washington, DC: 2003), 6.

91. These numbers were calculated by the author from the table "Coal Production: Hurt by Below-Cost Prices," in *Energy Policies of Ukraine* by IEA, 162.

92. As seen from their confrontation with the first Tymoshenko government in the early 2000s, coal and steel actors interested in maintaining non-transparent pricing practices (e.g., Akhmetov and others) were not shy to use any available means to maintain this system. In particular, reforms pursued by Timoshenko (and Prime Minister Yuschenko) to sell coal by means of auctions would have deprived the steel industry, which until then was able to "get coke [i.e., coking coal] for half of the world price," of such underpriced inputs. Van Zon, "Is The Donetsk Model Sustainable?," 83. See also Balmaceda, *Energy Dependency*, 55, 69.

93. In 2004, the State Property Fund sold to the Avdiivka Coking Plant (controlled by SCM) 60 percent of Krasnodonvukhillia's shares, and in 2005 a further 39.91 percent. On this transition, see also Hans van Zon, "The

Reform of Ukraine's Energy Complex and Its Consequences for Donetsk," in *Re-Constructing the Post-Soviet Industrial Region: The Donbas in Transition*, ed. Adam Swain (New York: Routledge, 2007), 47–61; and Adam Swain and Vlad Mykhnenko, "The Ukrainian Donbas in 'Transition,'" in *Re-Constructing the Post-Soviet Industrial Region*, ed. Swain, 7–46, at 37.

94. See Joel S. Hellman, "Winners Take All: The Politics of Partial Reform in Postcommunist Transitions," *World Politics* 50, no. 2 (1998): 203–34.

95. Sevgil' Musaeva-Borovik and Dmitrij Denkov, "Glavnyj oligarx èpoxi Janukoviča: God spustja," *Ukrainskaya Pravda*, April 29, 2015, https://www.pravda.com.ua/cdn/cd1/2015year/akhmetov/index.html.

96. IEA, *Energy Policies Beyond IEA Countries: Ukraine*, 155.

97. V. Mazur and M. Timošenko, "Aktual'nye Èkonomičeskie Voprosy v Metallurgičeskoj Otrasli Ukrainy," *Upravlenie Èkonomikoj: Teorija i Praktika*, no. 6 (2012): 13–23, at 14.

98. World Bank, *Mining Communities*, 5.

99. Ukrpromvnešèkspertiza, *Rynok koksujuščego uglja i koksa v Ukraine i mire: Tekuščee sostojanie i prognoz na 2010 god* (Kyiv: GP Ukrpromvnešèkspertiza, 2010), 32. Data for 2011 are from *Energy Policies Beyond IEA Countries: Ukraine*, by IEA, 154.

100. In 2013, 79.06 percent of Vorkutaugol's coking coal exports went to Ukraine. This finding is from a company profile for Vorkuyaugol AOA, at https://www-emis-com.ezp-prod1.hul.harvard.edu/php/companies/index?pc =RU&cmpy=1516177, via ISI/EMIS, by subscription service.

101. V. L. Mazur, M. V. Timošenko, and C. V. Mazur, "Èkologičeskie, texnologičeskie i èkonomičeskie aspekty razvitija metallurgii Ukrainy," *Èkologija i promyšlennost'*, no. 4 (2014): 32–36, at 35.

102. IEA, "Russian Federation: Coking Coal Exports by Destination," p. V.52, in *Coal Information 2015* (Paris: IEA, 2015). Occasional differences between numbers reported in the Ukrainian and Russian tables (IEA, p. V.62) are related to occasional divergences in the way specific coal subtypes may be classified as coking coal or steam coal. See IEA, *Coal Information 2015*, pp. V.52n1, V.62.

103. IEA, "Russian Federation: Coking Coal Exports by Destination," p. V.52. See note 102 regarding occasional differences between numbers reported in the Ukrainian and Russian tables (IEA, p. V.62).

104. Avdiivka's yearly report for 2012 notes purchases from, among a variety of suppliers, the trading company Gunvor Singapore Pte Ltd. "Publične akcionerne tovaristvo 'Avdiïvs'kij koksohimičnij zavod,' Rìčna ìnformacìâ emìtenta cìnnih paperìv za 2012 rìk," http://akhz.metinvestholding .com/upload/akhz/shareholders/pao_akhz_-annual-report-_2012.pdf. Gunvor, registered in Cyprus and with main offices in Switzerland, was cofounded by close Putin associate Gennadyi Tymchenko.

105. Harold Schobert and N. Schobert, "Comparative Carbon Footprints of Metallurgical Coke and Anthracite for Blast Furnace and Electric Arc Furnace Use," 2015, 10, http://www.blaschakcoal.com/wp-content/uploads/Carbon-Footprint-Archival-Report-v-4-September-2015.pdf.

106. In about 2012, Metinvest accounted for 47.27 percent of Ukraine's overall coke production. Elena Leonidovna Černelevskaja, "Stadija èkonomičeskoj koncetracii, kak predvestnik poteri konkurentosposobnosti èkonomikoj Ukrainy," *Economics: Yesterday, Today and Tomorrow*. nos. 7–8 (2013): 42–58, at 48.

107. Some sources, such as the plant's "Yearly Report for 2012," refer to it as the largest coking plant in Europe. Avdiivka CP Yearly Report 2012, http://akhz.metinvestholding.com/upload/akhz/shareholders/pao_akhz_-annual-report-_2012.pdf.

108. M. S. Magomedov, "Nam–50," *Ugleximičeskij žurnal*, no. 5 (2013): 1–6, at 1, referring to Decree 2894 of the USSR Council of Ministers of April 11, 1955.

109. Magomedov, 1–6.

110. Magomedov, 3. He notes Avdiivka as being the first coking plant "in our country" with covered storage—this could be interpreted as meaning the USSR or Ukraine.

111. The quotation in the heading just above is from Tatiana Shokot, an Adviikva resident and a retired worker from the Adviivka Coking Plant, on the radio program *Donbass realii*, November 8, 2016, http://www.radiosvoboda.org/a/28104142.html.

112. Although non-Soviet company towns shared some of these features, the role of enterprises as purveyors of basic consumer goods was heightened in the Soviet case by the difficult accessibility of consumer goods in the free market. On the Soviet enterprise as a central point of life orientation, see, e.g., Crowley, *Hot Coal, Cool Steel*, 50.

113. See Stephen Kotkin, *Magnetic Mountain: Stalinism as Civilization* (Berkeley: University of California Press, 1995), esp. 14–16, 29.

114. See M. Burawoy, *Manufacturing Consent* (Chicago: University of Chicago Press, 1979).

115. For an example of analysis of shop-floor work and identity in a post-Soviet metallurgical factory located in a separatist borderland (the Moldavian Steel Works, known as MMZ, in Rybnitsa in separatist Transnistria), see Rebecca A. Chamberlain-Creanga, "Cementing Modernisation: Transnational Markets, Language and Labour Tension in a Post-Soviet Factory in Moldova" (PhD diss., London School of Economics and Political Science, 2011). For other micro-level analyses of Soviet and Post-Soviet metallurgical companies, see Lisa A. Baglione and Carol L. Clark, "A Tale of Two Metallurgical Enterprises: Marketization and the Social Contract in Russian

Industry," *Communist and Post-Communist Studies* 30, no. 2 (1997): 153–80, on the Staleprokatnyi Zavod (steel-rolling factory) in Saint Petersburg and the Tulachermet kontsern (Tula ferrous metallurgy concern) in Tula; Stephen Kotkin, *Steeltown USSR: Soviet Society in the Gorbachev Era* (Berkeley: University of California Press, 1991); and Kotkin, *Magnetic Mountain*, on the Magnitogorsk Works. For an overview, see Boris Z. Rumer, *Soviet Steel: The Challenge of Industrial Modernization in the USSR* (Ithaca, NY: Cornell University Press, 1986).

116. The tenacity of these ties was demonstrated, almost to the absurd, by a scene playing out in an Adviivla café from which Radio Svoboda was broadcasting a special program in November 2016—the only radio program that could be heard in the café was from the far-away city of Barnaul in Siberia. This was reported on the Radio Svoboda program *Donbass realii*, November 8, 2016.

117. In 2016, the factory director Musa Magomedov justified this by arguing that the newspaper was only about corporate and factory news. Musa Magomedov, on the radio program *Donbass realii*, November 8, 2016.

118. On coke supplies to Azovstal from Avdiivka, see "Avdiivka CP Annual Report, 2012," http://akhz.metinvestholding.com/upload/akhz/shareholders/pao_akhz_-annual-report-2012.pdf; and Ukrpromvnešèkspertiza, *Rynok koksujušćego uglja i koksa v Ukraine: Faktičeskie dannye za prošedšij mesjac i prognoz na 2 mesjaca № 7 ot 15 ijulja 2011 goda* (Kyiv: GP Ukrpromvnešèkspertiza, 2011), 3, 8. Azovstal also used coke produced in its own coke batteries. In addition to Azovstal, the Adviivka Coking Plant also supplied MMK in Mariupol, and Yenakiieve Steel in Yenakiieve, both of which were part of Metinvest's vertically integrated production chain.

119. This is the amount needed when using the BOF process; the amount required is even larger when using the less advanced OHF process—an example of how different technical processes create different levels of dependence on a supply chain.

120. On Metinvest's Ukrainian iron ore assets, see Mark Brininstool, "Ukraine," in *Minerals Yearbook 2011*, ed. U.S. Department of the Interior and U.S. Geological Survey (Washington, DC: U.S. Government Publishing Office, 2011), Area Reports, Europe and Central Eurasia, vol. III, section 47.2.

121. See C. Kul'čic'kij, *Radáns'ka industrializaciá na Donbasì//Studiï z regìonal'noï istoriï: Stepova Ukraïna* (Kyiv: Institutut Istorii Ukraini, 2015), 29, http://history.org.ua/LiberUA/978-966-02-7571-3/978-966-02-7571-3.pdf. Azovstal can be compared with the Magnitogorsk Works, established in the same period. See Kotkin, *Magnetic Mountain*. On the coal and metallurgical industry in the Donbas as prestige object of Soviet propaganda, see Tanja Penter, *Kohle für Stalin und Hitler: Arbeiten und Leben im Donbass 1929 bis 1953* (Essen: Klartext, 2010).

122. David Marples, "Crisis in Soviet Industry? An Examination of the Soviet Steel Industry in the 1980s," *Canadian Slavonic Papers* 28, no. 4 (1986): 369–84, at 369.

123. See Metinvest, "Products," https://azovstal.metinvestholding.com /en/activity/products. See also Azovstal, "Yearly Report for 2011" (Rìčna ìnformacìâ VAT "Metalurgìjnij kombìnat Azovstal," 2011), https://azovstal .metinvestholding.com/upload/azovstal/shareholders/pao_azst_godovoj _otchet.pdf; and Azovstal, "Yearly Report for 2012" (Rìčna ìnformacìâ VAT "Metalurgìjnij kombìnat Azovstal," 2012), https://azovstal.metinvestholding .com/upload/azovstal/shareholders/new_pao_azst_godovoj_otchet_2012 .pdf.

124. Of course, the scrap metal used in steel production using the EAF method was originally made using coke, but because this scrap is usually decades-old disposal metal, the coke contained in this scrap is usually not counted as a direct feedstock in the process.

125. Azovstal's technologically outdated OHF-technology furnace ceased operations in May 2011, by the beginning of our focus period. See Volody- myr Shatokha, "The Sustainability of the Iron and Steel Industries in Ukraine: Challenges and Opportunities," *Journal of Sustainable Metallurgy* 2, no. 2 (2016): 106–15; and Azovstal, "Yearly Report," various years (Rìčna ìnfor- macìâ VAT "Metalurgìjnij kombìnat Azovstal").

126. These numbers are for 2013 and were calculated by the author from Wirschaftsvereinigung Stahl, *Statististisches Jahrbuch der Stahlindustrie 2016/2017* (Düsseldorf: Verlag Stahleisen, 2016), 371, citing Worldsteel; https://www.worldsteel.org/en/dam/jcr:41f65ea2-7447-4489-8ba7 -9c87e3975aab/Steel+solutions+in+the+green+economy%253A+Wind+turbines .pdf.

127. Most of Ukraine's OHF-based steel production originated from the Donetsk Oblast. International Iron and Steel Institute, *World Steel in Figures*, 2002, cited by Van Zon, "Is the Donetsk Model Sustainable?," 82; and by Vlad Mykhnenko, *Rusting Away? The Ukrainian Iron and Steel Industry in Transition*, CEU International Policy Fellowship Programme Research Paper (Budapest: Central European University, 2004), 40 (table 5).

128. On the broader social impact of barter systems, see Douglas Rogers, "Petrobarter: Oil, Inequality, and the Political Imagination in and after the Cold War," *Current Anthropology* 55, no. 2 (2014): 131–53.

129. The late 1990s and early 2000s saw an unprecedented wave of vio- lence in the Donbas, with Azovstal directors repeatedly targeted.

130. This process included a 2000 sale of 20 percent of shares to Azovstal's management, by now controlled by ISD, and the 2003 indirect sale of 25 per- cent of shares to a company affiliated with Taruta, Akhmetov, and Deputy Prime Minister Vitaly Hayduk. Neil Andrew Abrams, "Political Thugs: Criminal

Corporate Raiding and Property Rights in Early-Capitalist Eastern Europe" (PhD diss., University of California, Berkeley, 2014), 149, http://digitalassets.lib.berkeley.edu/etd/ucb/text/Abrams_berkeley_0028E_14690.pdf.

131. No author stated, "Kommunisty xotjat otobrat' zavod u Axmetova," *Fokus*, August 17, 2007, https://focus.ua/country/8157/. Years later, Serhii Taruta, in an interview with *Ukrainska Pravda*, stressed that Akhmetov insisted on taking Azovstal's stocks, due to its supply chain importance as steel slabs supplier to the key pipe exporter Khartsyzsk Pipe Plant. Mustafa Najêm and Sergìj Lešenko, "Sergìj Taruta: Lazarenko perekonav Kučmu, šo potrìbno postaviti Ânukoviča," *Ukraiskaya Pravda*, February 11, 2013, http://www.pravda.com.ua/articles/2013/02/11/6983216/.

132. Although these features characterize the Donbas region as a whole—which includes most of Luhansk and Donetsk oblasts—here we focus specifically on the Donetsk Oblast, as the spatial overlap between administrative unit (oblast) and the political and administrative resources to be controlled was crucial.

133. Swain and Mykhnenko, "Ukrainian Donbas," 8.

134. Swain and Mykhnenko.

135. The numbers here are from Ûliâ Samaêva, "Subsidiï: Nova suspìl'na zmova," *Dzerkalo Tyzhnia*, January 15, 2016, https://dt.ua/macrolevel/subsidiyi-nova-suspilna-zmova.html.

136. One case in point was the role of the Akhmetov associate Serhii Titenko in the National Commission of Electricity Regulation (NKRE), which he headed on three occasions: between 2004 and 2005, for ten months in 2007, and between 2010 and 2014. Soon after regaining control of the NKRE in 2010, the 25 percent limit on a single company's control of the electricity generation market was raised to 33 percent. See Musaeva-Borovik and Denkov, "Glavnyj oligarx èpoxi Janukoviča."

137. See also Serhiy Kudelia, "The Donbas Rift," *Russian Politics & Law* 54 (2016): 1, 5–27, at 12.

138. Kuzio, "Crime, Politics and Business," 199. Though Akhmetov would become the central member of the "Donetsk group" (also known as "Donetsk clan"), the group went well beyond him, also including a changing array of other important local actors, including the businessmen Yevhen Shcherban (who was assassinated in 1996), Serhii Taruta, Vitaliy Hayduk, and later President Viktor Yanukovych.

139. As noted by Heiko Pleines, however, it is important to keep in mind that the new rent-seekers installed by Yanukovich were not oligarchs in the sense of building their power through patronage and the exchange of favors, but had their positions based on sheer nepotism. Heiko Pleines, "Oligarchs and Politics in Ukraine," *Demokratizatsiya* 24, no. 1 (Winter 2016): 105–27, at 118.

140. These exports were related to the uniqueness of the Khartsyzsk Pipe Plant's production technology and did not imply Ukraine's metallurgical industry as a whole had a competitive advantage over Russia's. That Khartsyzsk's high competitive edge was an exception rather than the rule is substantiated by Ukraine's import of high-grade steel from Russia, by the fact that Ukraine and Russia remained competitors in most metallurgical markets, and by Russia's more advantageous metallurgical raw materials availability.

141. These foreign trade statistics are from National Bank of Ukraine, "Dinamìka tovarnoï strukturi eksportu," https://bank.gov.ua/doccatalog /document?id=19257909. Metallurgical exports are defined in the official statistics as "ferrous and non-ferrous metals and their products," and correspond roughly with commodity group 72, "iron and steel," in the Harmonized Commodity Description and Coding System.

142. Mykhnenko, *Rusting Away?*, 36. The numbers here are the author's calculations on the basis of Ukrainian State Statistics Committee, *Statystychnyi shchorichnyk Ukrainy za 2002 rik* (Kyiv: Technical, 2003); and International Iron and Steel Institute, *World Steel in Figures: 2003 Edition* (Brussels: International Iron and Steel Institute, 2003).

143. This role was especially clear in the segments for "long" (including pipes and tubes) and "flat" products (including, among others, blooms, billets, and slabs; see note 154 below for a definition). Ukraine accounted for 16 percent of the EU's long product imports (after Turkey, at 18 percent) and 13 percent of flat product imports (fourth, after China [22 percent] and Russia [17 percent]). European Steel Association (Eurofer), "European Steel in Figures 2015 Edition, Covering 2010–14," 14, http://www.steelonthenet .com/kb/files/Eurofer_Steel_in_Figures_2010-2014.pdf.

144. These numbers are from data on exports in Azovstal's "Yearly Report 2011," 76; and "Yearly Report 2012," 27.

145. National Bank of Ukraine, "Dinamìka tovarnoï strukturi eksportu."

146. See Bogatov, "Recent Developments," 165. For a general, former-USSR-wide argument about the role of subsidies in keeping alive industries involved in value subtraction rather than value adding, see C. G. Gaddy and B. W. Ickes, "Underneath the Formal Economy: Why Are Russian Enterprises Not Restructuring?," *Transition* 9, no. 4 (1998): 1–5; and G. Gaddy and B. W. Ickes, *Russia's Virtual Economy* (Washington, DC: Brookings Institution Press, 2002).

147. More generally, it has been argued that throughout the middle to late 1990s, it was impossible to accurately calculate unit costs for steel production due to subsidized prices. See Richard M. Levine and Andrew R. Bond, "Prospects for Ukrainian Ferrous Metals in the Post-Soviet Period," *Post-Soviet Geography and Economics* 39, no. 3 (1998): 151–63, at 155. The authors note that Ukrainian officials acknowledged "higher than the world average" unit production costs for steel production.

148. In the case of Ukraine, manganese alloys meant mainly silico manganese and ferro manganese, related to Ukraine's large manganese ore reserves.

149. As reported by Azovstal, much smaller shipments occasionally took place through Sevastopol, Odesa, Mykolaiv, and Zaporizhia. Lisa Barrington, "European Heavy Plate Import Prices Hold Steady," *Metal Bulletin Daily*, March 21, 2013, 14. Musaeva-Borovik and Denkov argue that during the Yanukovich period, each main port was controlled by a specific oligarch, with the Mariupol port under de facto Akhmetov control. Musaeva-Borovik and Denkov, "Glavnyj oligarx èpoxi Janukoviča."

150. For additional evidence of Metivest shipments to Monfalcone port, see "Supply Chain Intelligence about: Metinvest Trametal SpA," no date, https://panjiva.com/Metinvest-Trametal-SpA/5738982.

151. See *Notiziario Marketpress*, April 14, 2008, www.marketpress.info/notiziario_det.php?art=62386; and Rossano Cattivello, "Alternativa alla Strada," *Friuli.it*, July 3, 2013, http://www.ilfriuli.it/articolo/Economia/Alternative_alla_strada/4/123404.

152. What later became Trametal was originally established in 1992 as Metallurgica San Giorgio, which two years later was taken over by the Malacalza Group from Genoa. Francesca Artico, "La Metinvest scommette sul Friuli," *Messagero Veneto*, http://messaggeroveneto.gelocal.it/udine/cronaca/2016/03/06/news/la-metinvest-scommette-sul-friuli-1.13081617?refresh_ce. In 2004, Metinvest acquired a large package of shares in the company and completed the purchase by 2007.

153. In addition, Akhmetov engaged in and/or lobbied for other measures improving access to export markets in the European Union, such as Ukraine's joining of the World Trade Organization (2008) and the European Coal Association, the liberalization of exports to the EU, and having pipes built by the Khartsyzk Pipe Plant certified for export to the EU. See Evghenia Sleptsova and Elena Gnedina, "From Multi-Vector to Vectorless: Ukraine's Policy towards Russia and the European Union," in *Russia's Changing Economic and Political Regimes*, ed. Andrey Makarychev and Andre Mommen (New York: Routledge, 2013), 189–212.

154. Slabs are flat products in the same family of products ("intermediate castings," which are produced in foundries) that also include ingots, blooms, and billets. These differ in shape and size (with ingots generally larger than blooms, which are in turn larger than billets, which are in turn larger than slabs). They also differ in terms of stage in the production process and technology used: ingots are produced by pouring molten steel in ingot castings; the first rolling after this produces blooms, which are further rolled into billets or slabs. They are all related to thick steel plates, which are defined as plates with a thickness of 5 millimeters or larger.

155. See also Rimma Men, "Steel Groups Extend Grip into Europe," *Kyiv Post*, March 1, 2006, https://www.kyivpost.com/article/content/business /steel-groups-extend-grip-into-europe-23965.html.

156. Wirschaftsvereinigung Stahl, *Statististisches Jahrbuch*, 143–46.

157. See, e.g., SteelOrbis, "Evraz Group Acquires Italy's Palini & Bertoli," August 15, 2005, https://www.steelorbis.com/steel-news/latest-news/evraz -group-acquires-italy8217s-palini—bertoli-152748.htm.

158. In an official Canadian investigation, Azovstal was found to be dumping the export price by 19.1 percent; see Canada Border Services Agency, Trade Programs Directorate, Anti-Dumping and Countervailing Program, "Statement of Reasons," January 15, 2010, 9, http://www.cbsa-asfc.gc.ca/sima-lmsi /i-e/ad1384/ad1384-i09-fd-eng.pdf.

159. See Lucy Davis, "Ten Years of Anti-Dumping in the EU: Economic and Political Targeting," *Global Trade & Customs Journal* 4 (2009): 213–32 (table 1, "Annex 1: All Investigations Launched from 1998–2008, Ranked by Country and Sector"). For a summary of EU antidumping investigations involving Ukrainian products, see European Commission, "Investigations," http://trade.ec.europa.eu/tdi/completed.cfm.

160. Antonio Marcegaglia, chief executive of Marcegaglia, "Perspectives for Italian Steel Producers, Re-Rollers and Processors," slide show, April 4, 2013, http://www.people.marcegaglia.com/made_in_steel_2013/pdf/slides/4 /MM_Marcegaglia.pdf. For data on Italy's BOF and EAF steel production, see European Commission, Directorate-General for Enterprise & Industry, "Study."

161. Marcegaglia, "Perspectives."

162. Although focused on a steel factory in another area of Italy, Tuscany's coast, Silvia Avallone's novel, *Acciaio*—(Milan: Rizzoli, 2010); translated into English by Antony Shugaar as *Swimming to Elba* (New York: Penguin Books, 2012)—provides a picture of the deep intersections between steel materiality, family-owned factories, and the eco-social environment. The steel plant on which the novel is based, the Lucchini plant in Piombino, also found itself, as Trametal, in the aim of non-EU investors. In 2014, Lucchini workers staged a strike in protest "against the potential sale of the factory to an Indian investment group." Enrico Cesaretti, "'A Life of Metal': An Ecocritical Reading of Silvia Avallone's *Acciaio*," *Ecozone European Journal of Literature Culture and Environment*, October 1, 2014, 109.

163. Marcegaglia, "Perspectives."

164. Marcegaglia.

165. During our focus period, Germany was the largest importer of Italian-produced quarto plates; nearly 25 percent of these exports went to Germany. Wirschaftsvereinigung Stahl, *Statististisches Jahrbuch*, 149. On the destination of Trametal's exports, see Artico, "Metinvest."

166. A second Metinvest Trading office was located in Munich.

167. World Steel Association, as cited by S&P Global Platts, "Steel for Windpower: A Burgeoning Market," *Metals Insight*, December 7, 2017, 1–7.

168. "In 2015–16 alone, Metinvest supplied over 86,500 metric tons of steel to build wind towers in Germany, Italy, Spain and Portugal." *Metinvest Annual Report and Accounts 2016*, 48. Quarto plates are used in the towers, access platforms, and foundations of wind turbines. On the fundamentals of steel use in wind turbines, see World Steel Association, *Steel Solutions in the Green Economy: Wind Turbines* (Brussels: World Steel Association, 2012), http://www.scm.com.ua/m/documents/MET_27160_AR2016_AW_web.pdf.

169. See Wirschaftsvereinigung Stahl, *Statististisches Jahrbuch*, 54–55. A number of wind turbine builders buy the needed steel plates from a variety of suppliers depending on price. S&P Global Platts, "Steel for Windpower."

170. See, e.g., Miseror, *Rohstoffe für die Energiewende* (Aachen: Miseror, 2018), 18, https://www.misereor.de/fileadmin/publikationen/studie-rohstoffe-fuer-die-energiewende.pdf.

171. World Coal Association, "How Is Steel Produced?," http://www.worldcoal.org/coal/uses-coal/how-steel-produced. Viktor Pinchuk's Interpipe facility is especially telling concerning the issue of actors' interest differentiation, and its effects on policies vis-à-vis steel production feedstock. The case of Pinchuk's state-of-the-art EAF technology steel-making facility, Interpipe (inaugurated in 2012), is especially telling. Interpipe does not need to purchase coal or coke as feedstock, because its main raw material is scrap metal, as opposed to steel produced through the BOF method, the most widely used in Ukraine during our reference period; scrap metal needs a steady supply of iron ore and coke immediately at the time of production, while EAF methods not only used negligible amounts of coke but also less electricity and coal in general (about 150 kilograms per ton of steel, compared with 770 kilograms for BOF steel).

172. Rimma Men, "Steel Groups Extend Grip into Europe," *Kyiv Post*, March 1, 2006, https://www.kyivpost.com/article/content/business/steel-groups-extend-grip-into-europe-23965.html.

7. AND THE CHAINS MEET AGAIN

1. Steel pipes produced at the Khartsyzsk Pipe Factory (owned by the industrial group ISD) were used, in part, for building the Yamal pipeline; however, this is not part of the exemplary chain analyzed in chapter 6 because the exemplary chain that is followed is in the direction of Germany, not Russia.

2. Although, in general, this was true of prices for Russian natural gas imports in the 1991–2011 period, this was not necessarily true after 2011, with Gazprom charging "captive" markets such as Lithuania and Ukraine higher prices than those charged Germany, despite a shorter transit path and lower transportation expenses.

3. Despite often been referred to as similar to oil in terms of having a global market, liquefied natural gas (LNG) prices in Asia and Europe maintained a significant differential until at least 2017. For Japan's LNG prices, see World Bank, "Commodity Markets," http://www.worldbank.org/en/research /commodity-markets; and for the EU's LNG prices, see International Energy Agency, "Natural Gas Statistics," https://www.iea.org/statistics/naturalgas/.

4. Although the examples provided here come mainly from the Ukrainian segment of the spatial chain, as noted in the case study chapters, corruption and rent-seeking took place throughout the chain, not only in this specific segment.

5. Susanne Alice Wengle, *Post-Soviet Power: State-Led Development and Russia's Marketization* (Cambridge: Cambridge University Press, 2015), 101. See also Jeff D. Makholm, *The Political Economy of Pipelines* (Chicago: University of Chicago Press, 2012).

6. For economic considerations affecting other aspects of natural gas processing—e.g., when and how to commercialize various NGLs—see the section "Natural Gas Processing Cost Recovery," in "Natural Gas Processing: The Crucial Link Between Natural Gas Production and Its Transportation to Market," Energy Information Administration, January 2006, 9, https://www.eia.gov/pub/oil_gas/natural_gas/feature_articles/2006/ngprocess /ngprocess.pdf.

7. On the obsolescing bargain between transit states and energy suppliers and how the relative bargaining power between both evolves, see Raymond Vernon, *Sovereignty at Bay: The Multinational Spread of U.S. Enterprises* (New York: Basic Books, 1971); and Ekpen J. Omonbude, "The Transit Oil and Gas Pipeline and the Role of Bargaining: A Nontechnical Discussion," *Energy Policy* 35, no. 12 (December 2007): 6188–94.

8. Margarita M. Balmaceda, *The Politics of Energy Dependency: Ukraine, Belarus, and Lithuania between Domestic Oligarchs and Russian Pressure* (Toronto: University of Toronto Press, 2013), 3.

9. This book has followed three exemplary value chains, chosen from a universe of hundreds if not thousands of natural gas, oil, and coal chains starting from Russia and extending to the EU, some of which were vertically integrated. Some of these were the following: for natural gas, the Nord Stream gas pipeline; for oil, oil products refined in Belarus exported to the Netherlands and then to Germany (Russia–Belarus–Lithuania–the Netherlands–other EU states), or gasoline refined at the Leuna (Germany) refinery

from crude oil produced by LUKoil in Russia and transited via Belarus and Poland (Druzhba North); for coal, Russian steam coal supplies to other EU states—delivered by sea (to the United Kingdom) or train (to Poland). However, none of the chains originating in Russia, crossing through Ukraine, and reaching Germany were vertically integrated.

10. Thus, e.g., Manfred Hafner's statement that "any Ukrainian politician is very well aware that the day he sells Ukrainian GTS to Gazprom will be the last day of his (or her) political career." Manfred Hafner, *Russian Strategy on Infrastructure and Gas Flows to Europe*, Polinares Working Paper 73 (Brussels: European Commission, 2012), 14.

11. This is along with sales to industrial users in Ukraine through Gazprom subsidiary Gazprom Sbyt, 2009–14,

12. Michael Barnett and Raymond Duvall, "Power in International Politics," *International Organization* 59, no. 1 (2005): 39–75, at 46.

13. In a complementary perspective, Tynkkynen focuses on hydrocarbon culture as key for understanding the connection between fossil energy and political power in Russia. See Veli-Pekka Tynkkynen, *The Energy of Russia: Hydrocarbon Culture and Climate Change* (Cheltenham, U.K.: Edward Elgar, 2019).

14. On such uses of energy in the 1991–2006 period, see Margarita M. Balmaceda, *Energy Dependency, Politics, and Corruption in the Former Soviet Union: Russia's Power, Oligarch's Profits and Ukraine's Missing Energy Policy, 1995–2006* (London: Routledge, 2008).

15. Russia was also an important market for Germany's industrial production, but, overall, only 2 percent of German exports went to Russia; in contrast, over 7 percent of Russian exports went to Germany. See Bundesministerium für Wirtschaft und Energie (BMWi), *Fakten zum Deutschen Aussenhandel* (Berlin: BMWi, 2018).

16. One may ask: if the materiality of coal was the same, why did coal reforms succeed in Russia, but not in Ukraine? Perhaps a clue to the answer is to be found in the impact of the Soviet dissolution on both cases. With Ukraine as a periphery receiving more of a hit from this dissolution than the Russian Federation, actors (as discussed in chapter 6, e.g., Rinal Akhmetov and Serhii Taruta) that could help put back into functioning value chains that had been disrupted gained a larger impact—and power—in Ukraine than in Russia.

17. Ruhrgas became a 100 percent daughter company of E.ON (under the name E.ON Ruhrgas) in 2003, and merged with E.ON Global Commodities in 2013. As part of this process, the experienced voices of individual employees with decades of experience in dealing with natural gas trade were also lost.

18. See Andrey Vavilov and Georgy Trofimov, "A Phantom Energy Empire: The Failure of Gazprom's Downstream Integration," in *Gazprom: An Energy Giant and Its Challenges in Europe*, ed. Andrey Vavilov (New York: Palgrave Macmillan, 2015), 72–104.

19. For other examples of such de facto transborder coalitions, see Balmaceda, *Energy Dependency*, and Balmaceda, *Politics*.

20. See Reuters, "Special Report: Putin's Allies Channeled Billions to Ukraine Oligarch," 2019, in the Comrade Capitalism series, https://www.reuters .com/article/russia-capitalism-gas-special-report-pix/special-report-putins-allies -channelled-billions-to-ukraine-oligarch-idUSL3N0TF4QD20141126. In addition, favorable-condition credit lines of more than $10 billion were offered to Firtash, which allowed him to establish himself as a major player in the country's chemical and fertilizers business, as discussed in chapters 2 and 4, linked to natural gas through horizontal ties.

21. Calculated by the author on the basis of Federal Ministry for Economic Affairs and Energy, "Zahlen Und Fakten Energiedaten," table 17, http://www .bmwi.de/Redaktion/DE/Artikel/Energie/energiedaten-gesamtausgabe.html.

22. This statement was made in response to the imposition in early 2018 by the Arbitration Institute of the Stockholm Chamber of Commerce—commonly known as the Stockholm Arbitration Court—of a judgment on the company for failing to live up to its transit commitments via Ukraine.

23. Such virtual swaps require no actual movement of the methane molecules, in contrast to the physical swaps used by Ukraine since 2012 for the "reverse" importation of Russian-origin natural gas from Poland, the Slovak Republic, and Hungary, as discussed in chapter 4.

24. This paragraph was adapted from "Differentiation, Materiality, and Power: Towards a Political Economy of Fossil Fuels," by Margarita M. Balmaceda, *Energy Research and Social Sciences* 39 (2018): 130–40.

8. DISRUPTIVE ENERGIES AND THE TENTATIVE END OF A SYSTEM: AN EPILOGUE

1. Fracking was banned in some EU states, while in others it was not outlawed, but did not take root; even in the case of Poland, the only country where it made some inroads, the low-price environment limited growth in the sector. In the case of Ukraine, despite a $10 billion shale gas contract with Shell to develop these resources (2013), actual progress was limited.

2. Although such guaranteed pricing systems differed from country to country, in many cases these were discontinued after a few years, once economies of scale made renewables-produced electricity more competitive.

3. AG Energiebilanzen, "Stromerzeugung nach Energieträgern 1990–2019 (Stand Februar 2020)," https://www.ag-energiebilanzen.de/.

4. However, the success of the Energiewende in Germany has been called into question, as the replacement of nuclear generation capacity by fossil fuels has meant that CO_2 emissions had not been reduced.

5. These numbers were calculated by the author on the basis of data from Office of the Prime Minister of Ukraine, submitted to the Secretariat of the Energy Community, "Report for 2015 Following the Results of Monitoring Security of Natural Gas Supplies," September 2015, 12, https://www.energy-community.org/portal/page/portal/ENC_HOME/DOCS/384235 0/2198FDD2CC031492E053C92FA8C0BE17.PDF.

6. Economist Intelligence Unit, "LNG in Europe: Energy, Disrupted," October 3, 2019, http://www.eiu.com/industry/article/968515280/lng-in-europe-energy-disrupted/2019-10-03.

7. BP, *BP Statistical Review of World Energy 2019* (London: BP, 2019), 3, 6, https://www.bp.com/content/dam/bp/business-sites/en/global/corporate/pdfs/energy-economics/statistical-review/bp-stats-review-2019-full-report.pdf; Economist Intelligence Unit, "LNG."

8. Because LNG still depends on transportation via pipelines once it reaches a port and is regasified, this can also create its own regulatory challenges: for newly contracted LNG to be able to use an existing pipeline, the pipeline needs to be covered by a third-party access regulatory framework; in this sense, LNG represents a governance challenge to the existing system.

9. Thomas O. Miesener and William L. Leffler, *Oil and Gas Pipelines in Nontechnical Language* (Tulsa: PennWell, 2006), 12, 18.

10. Miesener and Leffler, 12.

11. Under current (2020) technologies, LNG use is not highly efficient, using about 10 percent of the gas for the liquefaction process itself.

12. The trend was temporarily reversed in 2015–17 as a result of global LNG oversupply, which depressed LNG prices.

13. See, e.g., James Henderson and Jack Sharples, "Gazprom in Europe: Two '*Anni Mirabilies*,' but Can It Continue?," *Oxford Energy Insight* 29 (2018): 16.

14. In the late 2010s, Gazprom's marginal cost of pipeline gas supply to Europe, at about $5 per million BTUs, is significantly lower than that for U.S. LNG, which, including liquefaction costs, is about $6 to $7 per million BTUs.

15. International Energy Agency (IEA), *Energy Policies of IEA Countries: European Union. 2014 Review* (Paris: IEA, 2014), 182; Henderson and Sharples, "Gazprom," 11, using data from Gazprom.

16. For such a view, see, e.g., Meghan L. O'Sullivan, *Windfall: How the New Energy Abundance Upends Global Politics and Strengthens America's Power* (New York: Simon & Schuster, 2017).

17. Georgi Kantchev, "With U.S. Gas, Europe Seeks Escape from Russia's Energy Grip," *Wall Street Journal*, February 25, 2016, https://www.wsj.com /articles/europes-escape-from-russian-energy-grip-u-s-gas-1456456892. A few other EU importers were able to negotiate discounts as well.

18. In particular, hopes were placed on a planned (but widely considered to be economically unviable) North-South pipeline interconnector between Polish (Świnoujście) and Croatian LNG terminals that would link Poland, the Czech Republic, the Slovak Republic, and Hungary. See Matúš Mišík, "Crisis as Remedy? The 2009 Gas Crisis and Its Influence on the Increase of Energy Security within Visegrad Group Countries," *International Issues & Slovak Foreign Policy Affairs* 21, nos. 1–2 (2012): 56–73, at 58. Also see official energy policy documents from the Slovak government, e.g., Ministry of Economy of the Slovak Republic, "Report on the Results of Natural Gas Supplies Security Monitoring, 2015," http://www.economy.gov.sk/sprava-o -vysledkoch-monitorovania-bezpecnosti-dodavok-plynu—2015-/145946s.

19. Although (even considering extensions given to individual states) member states were supposed to transpose the Third Package directives into national legislation by 2011, this had been significantly delayed; by the end of 2014, fourteen member states had still not done so completely. IEA, *Energy Policies: EU 2014*, 36.

20. Although measures intended to create a working single EU market have been central to the EU process since its inception, initiatives such as those related to third-party access to energy transit infrastructure were also rooted in broader institutional developments in the United States, the United Kingdom, and the Energy Charter Treaty process and became part of the EU's policy goals in the 2000s. For a detailed review of EU energy legislation, see Tim Kalus, *EU Energy Law and Policy: A Critical Account* (Oxford: Oxford University Press, 2013); and Christopher Jones, *EU Energy Law* (Deventer, Netherlands: Claeys & Casteels, 2016).

21. Related issues also concerned the NEL pipeline from Lubmin to northwestern German locations.

22. Dixi Group, "DiXi Group Experts: Gazprom's Special Status Revoked: What Consequences the Court Ruling on OPAL Will Have," September 12, 2019, https://ua-energy.org/en/posts/dixi-group-experts-gazproms-special -status-revoked-what-consequences-the-court-ruling-on-opal-will-have.

23. Article 36 of the 2009 Gas the Directive (Directive 2009/73/EC); IEA, *Energy Policies: EU 2014*, 188.

24. In September 2017, Schröder was additionally appointed as chairman of the Board of Directors of state-controlled Rosneft.

25. In technical terms, fulfilling the requirement that "in case of a disruption of the single largest gas infrastructure, the capacity of the remaining infrastructure be able to satisfy the total exceptionally high gas demand in a

member state." EU Regulation 994/2010; IEA, *Energy Policies: EU 2014*, 200.

26. See IEA, *Energy Policies: EU 2014*, 40. Although the Gazprom case was the most prominent, abuse of dominant market position cases were also initiated against other companies, including RWE, EDF, and E.ON in 2008–10. See IEA, *Energy Policies: EU 2014*, 38–39.

27. See Natalia Drozdiak and Emre Peker, "EU to Settle Antitrust Case against Gazprom Soon," *Wall Street Journal*, May 7, 2018, https://www.wsj.com/articles/eu-set-to-settle-antitrust-case-against-gazprom-soon-1525686870. For details of the EU allegations and concerned countries, see Jonathan Stern and Katja Yafimova, *The EU Competition Investigation of Gazprom's Sales in Central and Eastern Europe: A Detailed Analysis of the Commitments and the Way Forward*, Paper NG 121 (Oxford: Oxford Institute of Energy Studies, 2017), available at https://www.oxfordenergy.org.

28. See Kirsten Westphal, "Institutional Change in European Natural Gas Markets and Implications for Energy Security: Lessons from the German Case," *Energy Policy* 74 (2015): 35–43, at 40.

29. Some of these changes had already taken place in U.S. and U.K. natural gas markets, which were traditionally much more liquid than those in Europe. See Jeff D. Malkholm, *The Political Economy of Pipelines: A Century of Comparative Institutional Development* (Chicago: University of Chicago Press, 2012).

30. IEA, *Energy Policies: EU 2014*, 211.

31. Why would oil-indexed prices for natural gas remain high in an environment of low oil prices? Although the price formula used for each natural gas supply contract is considered a commercial secret, they typically involve a base price to which an indexable portion is added, and such indexation is usually based on the price index for a basket of market-specific fuels (where oil usually plays a prominent role) with a lag of six to nine months.

32. See "Russian Gas Price versus European Gas Price," in "Gazprom," 4, figure 3, using data from Argus Media. The price at the title transfer facility in the Netherlands was used as a benchmark for European spot prices. For a discussion of some of the main effects of these renegotiations on contractual clauses and specific contracts, see European Commission, Directorate-General for Energy, *Quo Vadis EU Gas Market Regulatory Framework: Study on a Gas Market Design for Europe*, EUR 2017.3462 EN (Brussels: European Commission, 2018), 70–74, 270–73; and Tatiana Mitrova, "Changing Gas Price Mechanisms in Europe and Russia's Gas Pricing Policy," presentation at International Association for Energy Economics 38th international conference, Antalya, May 2015.

33. See IEA, *Energy Policies: EU 2014*, 166.

34. See IEA, 169. See also European Union, "European Energy Security Strategy," May 2014, 166.

35. Standards for gasoline (EN 228) and, of particular interest to the value chain followed in this book, diesel fuel (EN 590) change in tandem with the EU emissions standards to assure that these can be met.

36. IEA, *Energy Policies: EU 2014*, 223, 224 (figure 8.5).

37. IEA, 212.

38. Key among regulations affecting power generation was the 2001 Large Combustion Plants Directive (LCPD) (in force from 2008 to 2015), which aimed at limiting the emissions of nitrogen oxides (NO_X), sulfur dioxide (SO_X), and particulates from large combustion plants. Although not applying exclusively to coal-fired plants, LCPD had a special impact on coal plants due to their emissions profile. After the expiration of LCDP, a more stringent Industrial Emissions Directive (IED) valid for 2016–23, further tightened the regulation of nitrogen oxides and sulfur. See IEA, *Energy Policies: EU 2014*, 222.

39. Henderson and Sharples, "Gazprom."

40. IEA, *Gas 2017* (Paris: IEA, 2017), 3; Reuters, "Update 2: Russia's Gazprom Expects Gas Exports to Drop by 16 percent in 2020," April 29, 2020, https://af.reuters.com/article/commoditiesNews/idAFL5N2CH2SR; Natural Gas World, "Russian Gas Transit Via Ukraine Down 46 percent in April," May 5, 2020, https://www.naturalgasworld.com/ukraine-78726 (subscription).

41. See, e.g., Yuri Yegorov and Franz Wirl, "Ukrainian Gas Transit Game," *ZfE Zeitschrift für Energiewirschaft*, no. 2 (2009): 147–55; and Christian von Hirschausen et al., "Transporting Russian Gas to Western Europe: A Simulation Analysis," *Energy Journal* 26, no. 2 (2005): 49–68.

42. These data are from Wojciech Konończuk, "A Dangerous Energy Policy: Ukraine, Despite War, Is Making Itself Dependent on Russian Oil," *Energy Post*, September 8, 2017, http://energypost.eu/15647-2/.

43. IEA, *Energy Policies: EU 2014*, 183n3.

44. See Margarita M. Balmaceda, *Energy Dependency, Politics, and Corruption in the Former Soviet Union: Russia's Power, Oligarchs' Profits, and Ukraine's Missing Energy Policy, 1995–2006* (London: Routledge, 2008).

45. See Margarita M. Balmaceda, *The Politics of Energy Dependency: Ukraine, Belarus, and Lithuania between Domestic Oligarchs and Russian Pressure* (Toronto: University of Toronto Press, 2013), esp. chaps. 1 and 4.

46. Ukrainian Institute for the Future, *The Future of Ukrainian Oligarchs* (Kyiv: Ukrainian Institute for the Future, 2018), 24.

47. See Joe Becker, Walt Bogdanich, Maggie Haberman, and Ben Protess, "Why Giuliani Singled Out 2 Ukrainian Oligarchs to Help Look for Dirt," *New York Times*, November 25, 2019.

48. See Konstantin Skorkin, "Ukraine's President Can't Avoid Showdown with His Oligarch Backer," Carnegie Moscow Center, October 2, 2019, https://carnegie.ru/commentary/79972.

49. See Becker et al., "Why Giuliani Singled Out 2 Ukrainian Oligarchs."

50. Ukrainian Institute for the Future, *Future*, 22.

51. See IEA, *Energy Policies: EU 2014*, 37.

52. See Oxford Institute for Energy Studies, "European Traded Gas Hubs: An Updated Analysis on Liquidity, Maturity and Barriers to Market Integration," 2017, 28, https://www.oxfordenergy.org/wpcms/wp-content/uploads/2017/05/European-traded-gas-hubs-an-updated-analysis-on-liquidity-maturity-and-barriers-to-market-integration-OIES-Energy-Insight.pdf.

53. DNV Kema, "Study on Entry-Exit Regimes in Gas, Part A: Implementation of Entry-Exit Systems," July 2013, 4.

54. Tomasz Dąborowski. "Breaking the Boundaries: The Transformation of Central European Gas Markets," *OSW Point of View*, no. 46, December 2014, 25.

55. The share of gas sold on the basis of the Gas-on-Gas (GOG) pricing mechanism, which includes any pricing linked to gas-on-gas competition (including spot prices), rose from 15 percent in 2005 to 37 percent in 2010, 44 percent in 2012, 50 percent in 2013, 61 percent in 2014, 64 percent in 2015, and 66 percent in 2016—all these percentages being approximate. These data are from International Gas Union, "Wholesale Gas Price Survey"—2015, 2016, and 2017 editions—available at www.igu.org, and were estimated from figure 3.4, "Regional Price Formation 2015: Pipeline Imports," p. 15 in the 2016 edition. This is consistent with data putting the share of oil-indexed Gazprom contracts at a third of the total in 2017. See Henderson and Sharples, "Gazprom," 26. For a definition of GOG and other gas-pricing mechanisms, see International Gas Union, "Wholesale Gas Price Survey, 2017," 13.

56. European Commission, Directorate-General for Energy, *Quo Vadis*, 76.

57. After a downward trend from 2010 (498 billion cubic meters) and reaching a low point of 383 billion cubic meters in 2014, EU natural gas consumption (as well as imports from Russia), which had reached a low point in 2014, started to increase again in 2015 and reached a high in 2016. These data are from Statista, "Natural Gas Consumption in the European Union from 1998 to 2018," https://www.statista.com/statistics/265406/natural-gas-consumption-in-the-eu-in-cubic-meters/. See also Eurostat, "Gross Inland Consumption of Natural Gas in EU-28, in Thousand Terajoules (Gross Calorific Value)," 2017, http://ec.europa.eu/eurostat/statistics-explained/index.php?title=File:Gross_inland_consumption_of_natural_gas_in_EU-28,_in_thousand_terajoules_(Gross_Calorific_Value)_figure_1.png. Imports from Russia reached 150 billion cubic meters in 2015, and over 167 billion

cubic meters in 2017. See the methodological note on calculating natural gas import volumes given by Henderson and Sharples, "Gazprom," 6.

58. Data from Gazprom; Reuters, "Gazprom Grabs Record Share of Europe Gas Market Despite Challenges," February 25, 2019, https://www .reuters.com/article/us-russia-gazprom-europe/gazprom-grabs-record -share-of-europe-gas-market-despite-challenges-idUSKCN1QF067.

59. U.S. Congressional Research Service, "U.S. Sanctions on Russia," 29, updated periodically, https://fas.org/sgp/crs/row/R45415.pdf.

60. This is in addition to Manafort frantically seeking to access funds to pay back Deripaska $18.9 owed owned him from a failed joint business, and for the recovery of which Deripaska had sued Manafort.

61. While LNG technology was patented nearly a century before 2014 (1915), here we make reference to the impact of its exponentially broader use.

62. Such a system does not, however, automatically solve the issue of how to share large infrastructure investment costs.

63. As noted by Henderson and Sharples, "It is difficult to impose restrictions on a competitive source of energy [i.e., Gazprom natural gas] when the European Commission and national governments have spent 20 years creating a liberalized market to encourage lower prices for consumers." Henderson and Sharples, "Gazprom," 16.

64. See Friedrch Schmidt, "Sind so teure Röhren," *Franlkfurt Allgemaine Zeitung*, February 14, 2019; and Mikhail Kriutikhin, comments in the radio program *Dorogi Svobodi*, January 26, 2019, https://www.svoboda.org /a/29729068.html.

Selected Bibliography

Abrams, Neil Andrew. "Political Thugs: Criminal Corporate Raiding and Property Rights in Early-Capitalist Eastern Europe." PhD diss., University of California, Berkeley, 2014. http://digitalassets.lib.berkeley.edu/etd/ucb/text/Abrams_berkeley_0028E_14690.pdf.

Acheson, James. "Ostrom for Anthropologists." *International Journal of the Commons* 5, no. 2 (September 2011): 319–39. https://doi.org/10.18352/ijc.245.

Adelman, Morris Albert. "International Oil Agreements." *Energy Journal* 5, no. 3 (1984): 1–9.

Adunbi, Omolade. *Oil Wealth and Insurgency in Nigeria*. Bloomington: Indiana University Press, 2015.

AG Energiebilanzen. "Stromerzeugung nach Energieträgern 1990–2017." https://ag-energiebilanzen.de/4-1-Home.html.

Alexeev, Michael, and Robert Conrad. "The Russian Oil Tax Regime: A Comparative Perspective." *Eurasian Geography and Economics* 50, no. 1 (2009): 93–114.

Alizadeh, Parvin. "The Political Economy of Petro Populism and Reform, 1997–2011." In *Iran and the Global Economy: Petro Populism, Islam and*

Economic Sanctions, edited by Parvin Alizadeh and Hassan Hakimian. New York: Routledge, 2014.

Allen, Amy. "Rethinking Power." *Hypatia* 13, no. 1 (1998): 21–30.

Alt, James E., Fredrik Carlsen, Per Heum, and Kåre Johansen. "Asset Specificity and the Political Behavior of Firms: Lobbying for Subsidies in Norway." *International Organization* 53, no. 1 (1999): 99–116. https://doi.org/10.1162/002081899550823.

Andrukhovich, Yuri. *Diàvol hovaêt'sâ v sirì (The Devil's Hiding in the Cheese)*. Kyiv: Krytyka, 2006.

Annenkova, Anna. "Russian Benchmarks of Black Gold." *Oil of Russia* 4 (2012): 44–46.

"API Gravity." Petroleum.co.uk. http://www.petroleum.co.uk/api.

Appadurai, Arjun. *The Social Life of Things: Commodities in Cultural Perspective*. Cambridge: Cambridge University Press, 1986.

Artico, Francesca. "La Metinvest scommette sul Friuli." *Messagero Veneto*, March 7, 2016. http://messaggeroveneto.gelocal.it/udine/cronaca/2016/03/06/news/la-metinvest-scommette-sul-friuli-1.13081617?refresh_ce.

Auty, Richard M. "The Political Economy of Resource-Driven Growth." *European Economic Review* 45, nos. 4–6 (2001): 839–46. https://doi.org/10.1016/S0014-2921(01)00126-X.

Auty, Richard M., and Alan H. Gelb. "Political Economy of Resource-Abundant States." In *Resource Abundance and Economic Development*, edited by Richard. M. Auty. Oxford: Oxford University Press, 2001.

Avallone, Silvia. *Swimming to Elba*. Trans. Antony Shugaar. New York: Penguin Books, 2012.

Avdiivka Coking Plant from Bachatsky and Kuzbassrazrevugol. *Yearly Report of the Avdiivka Coking Plant 2014*.

Azovstal. "Yearly Report for 2011" (Rìčna ìnformacìâ VAT "Metalurgìjnij kombìnat Azovstal," 2011). https://azovstal.metinvestholding.com/upload/azovstal/shareholders/pao_azst_godovoj_otchet.pdf.

——. "Yearly Report for 2012" (Rìčna ìnformacìâ VAT "Metalurgìjnij kombìnat Azovstal," 2012). https://azovstal.metinvestholding.com/upload/azovstal/shareholders/new_pao_azst_godovoj_otchet_2012.pdf.

——. Various years. "Yearly Reports" (Rìčna ìnformacìâ VAT "Metalurgìjnij kombìnat Azovstal").

Baglione, Lisa A., and Carol L. Clark. "A Tale of Two Metallurgical Enterprises: Marketization and the Social Contract in Russian Industry." *Communist and Post-Communist Studies* 30, no. 2 (1997): 153–80.

Bakker, Karen J. *An Uncooperative Commodity: Privatizing Water in England and Wales*. Oxford: Oxford University Press, 2004.

Bakker, Karen, and Gavin Bridge. "Material Worlds? Resource Geographies and the Matter of Nature." *Progress in Human Geography* 30, no. 1 (2006): 5–27. https://doi.org/10.1191/0309132506ph588oa.

Baldwin, Robert E. "Patterns of Development in Newly Settled Regions." *Manchester School* 24, no. 2 (1956): 161–79. https://doi.org/10.1111/j.1467-9957.1956.tb00981.x.

——. "The Political Economy of Trade Policy: Integrating the Perspective of Economists and Political Scientists." In *The Political Economy of Trade Policy*, edited by Robert Feenstra, Gene Grossman, and Douglas Irwin. Cambridge, MA: MIT Press, 1996.

Balmaceda, Margarita M. "Differentiation, Materiality, and Power: Towards a Political Economy of Fossil Fuels." *Energy Research and Social Sciences* 39 (2018). 130–40.

——. *Energy Dependency, Politics, and Corruption in the Former Soviet Union: Russia's Power, Oligarch's Profits, and Ukraine's Missing Energy Policy, 1995–2006.* London: Routledge, 2008.

——. "Energy Materiality and the Governance of Post-Soviet Supply Chains." Unpublished paper prepared for Exploring Energy Regionalisms Workshop, GIGA-Hamburg, September 22–23, 2016.

——. *Living the High Life in Minsk: Russian Energy Rents, Domestic Populism, and Belarus' Impending Crisis.* Budapest: Central European University Press, 2014.

——. "Methodology: Choosing the Reference Period." Unpublished paper for workshop on "The Political Economy of Post-Soviet Energy," Delmenhorst, Germany, May 31–June 2, 2017.

——. *The Politics of Energy Dependency: Ukraine, Belarus, and Lithuania between Domestic Oligarchs and Russian Pressure.* Toronto: University of Toronto Press, 2013.

——. "Value-Added Links, Energy Relations, and Integration in the Former Soviet Area." Paper presented at American Political Science Association Annual Meeting, Washington, DC, August 29–September 1, 2014.

Barnett, Michael, and Raymond Duvall. "Power in International Politics." *International Organization* 59, no. 1 (2005): 39–75. https://doi.org/10.1017/S0020818305050010.

Barrington, Lisa. "European Heavy Plate Import Prices Hold Steady." *Metal Bulletin Daily*, March 21, 2013.

Barry, Andrew. *Material Politics: Disputes along the Pipeline.* Oxford: Wiley-Blackwell, 2013.

Beblawi, Hazem, and G. Luciani. *The Rentier State in the Arab World.* London: Croom Helm, 1987.

Becker, Joe, Walt Bogdanich, Maggie Haberman, and Ben Protess. "Why Giuliani Singled Out 2 Ukrainian Oligarchs to Help Look for Dirt." *New York Times*, November 25, 2019.

Beljanin, Gennadij S. "Obogatitel'naja fabrika 'Koksovaja'—garantija kačestvauglja dlja filiala 'Bačatskij ugol'nyj razrez' OAO U.K. 'Kuzbassrazrezugol.'" *Ugol*, June 2010.

Belyi, Andrei V. "Institutional Trends in Russia's Oil and Gas Sectors." *Journal of World Energy Law & Business* 6, no. 3 (2013): 163–78.

——. *Transnational Gas Markets and Euro-Russian Energy Relations*. London: Palgrave Macmillan, 2015.

Belyi, Andrei V., Caroline Kuzemko, Andreas Goldthau, and Michael F. Keating. "Dynamics of Energy Governance in Europe and Russia." *International Political Economy Series*. London: Palgrave Macmillan, 2012. https://doi.org/10.1057/9780230370944.

Beltran, Alain, and Jean-Pierre Williot. "Gaz de France and Soviet Natural Gas: Balancing Technological Constraints with Political Considerations, 1950s to 1980s." In *Cold War Energy: A Transnational History of Soviet on Gas*, edited by Jeromin Perovic. New York: Palgrave Macmillan, 2017.

Biblioteka pro literaturu avtorov i biblioteki. http://koglib.ru/index.php/83-kogalym/112-gorod-kogalym.

Biolková, Hana. "Postoje k ruským investicím přicházejících do České republiky." MA thesis, Masaryk University, Brno, 2014.

Bjørnmose, Jens, Ferran Roca, and Tatsiana Turgot. *An Assessment of the Gas and Oil Pipelines in Europe*. IP/A/ITRE/NT/2009-13. Brussels: European Parliament, 2009. http://www.europarl.europa.eu/RegData/etudes/note/join/2009/416239/IPOL-ITRE_NT(2009)416239_EN.pdf.

Bogatov, O. "Recent Developments in the Donbass Coal Industry." *Mining Technology* 111, no. 3 (2002): 159–66.

Bond, Davis. "Oil in the Caribbean: Refineries, Mangroves, and the Negative Ecologies of Crude Oil." *Comparative Studies in Society and History* 59, no. 3 (2017): 600–628.

Bovt, Georgy. "Rosneft's Chinese Oil Card." *Moscow News*, June 24, 2013. https://themoscowtimes.com/articles/rosnefts-chinese-oil-card-25224.

BP. *BP Statistical Review of World Energy 2017*. London: BP, 2017. https://www.bp.com/content/dam/bp-country/de_ch/PDF/bp-statistical-review-of-world-energy-2017-full-report.pdf.

——. *BP Statistical Review of World Energy 2019*. London: BP, 2019. https://www.bp.com/content/dam/bp/business-sites/en/global/corporate/pdfs/energy-economics/statistical-review/bp-stats-review-2019-full-report.pdf.

Braudel, Fernand. *The Mediterranean and the Mediterranean World in the Age of Philip II*. New York: HarperCollins, 1972.

Braudillard, Jean. *The Revenge of the Crystal: A Baudrillard Reader.* London: Pluto Press, 1999.

Bridge, Gavin. "Global Production Networks and the Extractive Sector: Governing Resource-Based Development." *Journal of Economic Geography* 8, no. 3 (May 2008): 389–419. https://doi.org/10.1093/jeg/lbn009.

Bridge, Gavin, and Philippe Le Billon. *Oil.* Cambridge: Polity Press, 2013.

Brininstool, Mark. "Ukraine." In *Minerals Yearbook 2011*, edited by U.S. Department of the Interior and U.S. Geological Survey. Washington, DC: U.S. Government Publishing Office, 2011.

Bundesministerium für Wirtschaft und Energie. "Energiedaten: Gesamtausgabe." Federal Ministry of Economy and Energy, October 2019. https://www.bmwi.de/Redaktion/DE/Artikel/Energie/energiedaten-gesam-tausgabe.html.

——. *Fakten zum Deutschen Aussenhandel.* Berlin: Bundesministerium für Wirtschaft und Energie, 2018.

Burawoy, Michael. *Manufacturing Consent: Changes in the Labor Process under Monopoly Capitalism.* Chicago: University of Chicago Press, 1979.

Campbell, Alan, and Nina Fishman. *Miners, Unions and Politics, 1910–1947.* Aldershot, U.K.: Scolar Press, 1996.

Canada Border Services Agency, Trade Programs Directorate, Antidumping and Countervailing Program. "Statement of Reasons." January 15, 2010. http://www.cbsa-asfc.gc.ca/sima-lmsi/i-e/ad1384/ad1384-i09-fd-eng.pdf.

Cardoso, Ricardo, Yizhou Ren, and Carolina Luna Gordo. "Antitrust: Commission Sends Statement of Objections to Gazprom." European Commission, April 22, 2015. https://ec.europa.eu/commission/presscorner/detail/en/IP_15_4828.

Carrier, James G. *Gifts and Commodities: Exchange and Western Capitalism Since 1700.* London: Routledge, 1995.

Casier, Tom. "Russia's Energy Leverage over the EU: Myth or Reality?" *Perspectives on European Politics and Society* 12, no. 4 (2011): 493–508.

Cattivello, Rossano. "Alternativa alla Strada." *Friuli.it*, July 3, 2013. http://www.ilfriuli.it/articolo/Economia/Alternative_alla_strada/4/123404.

Černelevskaja, Elena Leonidovna. "Stadija èkonomičeskoj koncetracii, kak predvestnik poteri konkurentosposobnosti èkonomikoj Ukrainy." *Economics: Yesterday, Today and Tomorrow* 7–8 (2013): 42–58.

Černoch, Filip, Břetislav Dančák, Hedvika Koďousková, Anna Leshchenko, Petr Ocelík, Jan Osička, Václav Šebek, Tomáš Vlček, and Veronika Zapletalová. *The Future of the Druzhba Pipeline as a Strategic Challenge for the Czech Republic and Poland.* Brno: Muni Press, 2012. https://munispace.muni.cz/library/catalog/download/70/136/102-1.

Černoch, Filip, Břetislav Dančák, Jana Kovačovská, Petr Ocelík, Jan Osička, Tomáš Vlček, and Veronika Zapletalová. *The Future of Natural Gas Security in the V4 Countries: A Scenario Analysis and the EU Dimension.* Brno: Muni Press, 2012.

Cesaretti, Enrico. " 'A Life of Metal': An Ecocritical Reading of Silvia Avallone's *Acciaio.*" *Ecozone European Journal of Literature Culture and Environment,* October 1, 2014. http://ecozona.eu/article/download/616/661/.

Chamberlain-Creanga, Rebecca A. "Cementing Modernisation: Transnational Markets, Language and Labour Tension in a Post-Soviet Factory in Moldova." PhD diss., London School of Economics and Political Science, 2011.

Chaudhry, Kiren Aziz. *The Price of Wealth: Economies and Institutions in the Middle East.* Ithaca, NY: Cornell University Press, 1997.

Clews, Robert. *Project Finance for the International Petroleum Industry.* London: Elsevier / Academic Press, 2016.

Collier, Stephen J. *Post-Soviet Social: Neoliberalism, Social Modernity, Biopolitics.* Princeton, NJ: Princeton University Press, 2011.

Cornot-Gandolphe, Sylvie. "The European Coal Market: Will Coal Survive the EC's Energy and Climate Policy?" Notes de l'ifri, Institut français des relations internationales, October 2012. https://www.ifri.org/en/publications/enotes/notes-de-lifri/european-coal-market-will-coal-survive-ecs-energy-and-climate.

Crowley, Stephen. *Hot Coal, Cool Steel: Russian and Ukrainian Workers from the End of the Soviet Union to the Post-Communist Transformations.* Ann Arbor: University of Michigan Press, 1997.

Dąborowski. Tomasz. "Breaking the Boundaries: The Transformation of Central European Gas Markets." *OSW Point of View* 46, December 2014. http://aei.pitt.edu/58855/.

Dahl, Robert. "The Concept of Power." *Behavioral Science* 2, no. 3 (1957): 201–15.

Damro, Chad. "Market Power Europe." *Journal of European Public Policy* 19, no. 5 (2012): 682–99.

Davis, Lucy. "Ten Years of Anti-Dumping in the EU: Economic and Political Targeting." *Global Trade & Customs Journal* 4 (2009): 213–32.

Dawisha, Karen. *Putin's Kleptocracy: Who Owns Russia?* New York: Simon & Schuster, 2014.

De Gregori, Thomas R. "Resources Are Not; They Become: An Institutional Theory." *Journal of Economic Issues* 21, no. 3 (1987): 1241–63.

Deloitte. "CE Top 500 Ranking." 2013. https://www2.deloitte.com/content/dam/Deloitte/global/Documents/About-Deloitte/ce-top500-2013.pdf.

——. "CE Top 500 Ranking." 2014. https://www2.deloitte.com/rs/en/pages/about-deloitte/articles/central-europe-top500-2014.html#.

——. "CE Top 500 Ranking." 2016. https://www2.deloitte.com/global/en/pages/about-deloitte/articles/central-europe-top500.html.

——. "Oglâd konsolìdovanoï fìnansovoï zvìtnostì PAT 'Ukrtansnafta' stanom na 31 grudnâ 2014 ta za rìk, âkij zakìnčivsâ cìêÛ datoÛ." March 2016. https://www.ukrtransnafta.com/wp-content/uploads/2017/08/konsolidovana-fin-zvitnust-2014.pdf.

Demirel, Yaşar. *Energy: Production, Conversion, Storage, Conservation, and Coupling.* London: Springer, 2012.

Dicken, Peter, Philip F. Kelly, Kris Olds, and Henry Wai-Chung Yeung. "Chains and Networks, Territories and Scales: Towards a Relational Framework for Analysing the Global Economy." *Global Networks* 1, no. 2 (2001): 89–112. https://doi.org/10.1111/1471-0374.00007.

Dienes, Leslie. "Energy, Minerals, and Economic Policy." In *The Ukrainian Economy*, edited by I. S. Koropeckyi. Cambridge, MA: Harvard Ukrainian Research Institute, 1992.

DiJohn, Jonathan. *From Windfall to Curse? Oil and Industrialization in Venezuela, 1920 to the Present.* University Park: Pennsylvania State University Press, 2009.

DiXi Group. "Behind Ukraine's Energy Transition: Overcoming Key Challenges." Policy Brief, 2016.

——. "DiXi Group Experts: Gazprom's Special Status Revoked: What Consequences the Court Ruling on OPAL Will Have." September 12, 2019. https://ua-energy.org/en/posts/dixi-group-experts-gazproms-special-status-revoked-what-consequences-the-court-ruling-on-opal-will-have.

——. "Ukrainian Gas Hub: A Chance for Europe." December 19, 2016. http://dixigroup.org/eng/publications/ukrainian-gas-hub—a-chance-for-europe/.

Drozdiak, Natalia, and Emre Peker. "EU to Settle Antitrust Case against Gazprom Soon." *Wall Street Journal*, May 7, 2018. https://www.wsj.com/articles/eu-set-to-settle-antitrust-case-against-gazprom-soon-1525686870.

Dubrovyk, Alla, and Vitalij Knjažanskij. "Sergej Ermilov: 'Kak tol'ko NAK Naftogaz' isčeznet kak sub"ekt, to, pover'te, s gazom u nas vse budet v porjadke." *Den'*, December 24, 2014. http://m.day.kyiv.ua/ru/article/ekonomika/s-chego-nachinat-reformy.

Duleba, Alexander. "The Slovak-Ukrainian-Russian Security Triangle." In *On the Edge: The Ukrainian-Central European-Russian Security Triangle*, edited by Margarita M. Balmaceda. Budapest: Central European University Press, 2000.

East European Gas Analysis. "Gas Export Pipelines of Uzhgorod Area, Western Ukraine." December 7, 2014. https://eegas.com/uzhgorod.htm.

Economist Intelligence Unit. "LNG in Europe: Energy, Disrupted." October 3, 2019. http://www.eiu.com/industry/article/968515280/lng-in-europe-energy-disrupted/2019-10-03.

Elias, Marlène, and Judith Carney. "The Female Commodity Chain of Shea Butter: Burkinabe Producers, Western Green Consumers and Fair Trade." *Cahiers de Geographie du Quebec* 48, no. 133 (2004): 71–88.

Energy Charter Secretariat. *Bringing Oil to the Market: Transport Tariffs and Underlying Methodologies for Cross-Border Crude Oil and Products Pipelines.* Paris: Energy Charter Secretariat, 2012.

——. *Putting a Price on Energy-International Pricing Mechanisms for Oil and Gas.* Brussels: Energy Charter Secretariat, 2007.

Eremeev, Ihor. Interview, April 14, 2014. http://www.pravda.com.ua/articles /2014/04/14/7022421/.

Ernst & Young. *Extractive Industries Transparency Initiative National Report of Ukraine 2014–2015.* Kyiv: Ernst & Young, 2015.

——. "Oil and Gas Tax Alert: Tax Maneuver: Parameters and Impact Assessment." December 2014. http://www.ey.com/Publication/vwLUAssets/EY-oil-and -gas-tax-alert-december-2014-eng/$FILE/EY-oil-and-gas-tax-alert -december-2014-eng.pdf.

Euractiv. "Czech Company Wins Landmark Case Against Gazprom." October 26, 2012. https://www.euractiv.com/section/energy/news/czech-company -wins-landmark-case-against-gazprom/.

European Commission. "Council Regulation (EC) 139/2004." http://eur-lex .europa.eu/legal-content/EN/TXT/?uri=CELEX%3A32013M6801.

——. *European Energy Security Strategy.* Brussels: European Commission, 2014. https://www.eesc.europa.eu/resources/docs/european-energy-security -strategy.pdf.

European Commission, Directorate-General for Energy. *Quo Vadis EU Gas Market Regulatory Framework: Study on a Gas Market Design for Europe.* EUR 2017.3462 EN. Brussels: European Commission, 2018.

European Commission, Directorate-General for Enterprise & Industry. "Study on the Competitiveness of the European Steel Sector (2008)." https://ec.europa.eu/growth/content/study-competitiveness-european -steel-sector-0_en.

European Parliament and Council of the European Union. "Directive 2009/73/EC of the European Parliament and of the Council of 13 July 2009 Concerning Common Rules for the Internal Market in Natural Gas and Repealing Directive 2003/55/EC." *Official Journal of the European Union,* July 13, 2009. https://eur-lex.europa.eu/LexUriServ/LexUriServ .do?uri=OJ:L:2009:211:0094:0136:en:PDF.

——. "Regulation (EU) 347/2013 of the European Parliament and of the Council of 17 April 2013 on Guidelines for Trans-European Energy

Infrastructure and Repealing Decision No. 1364/2006/EC and Amending Regulations (EC) No. 713/2009, (EC) No. 714/2009 and (EC) No. 715/2009—Text with EEA Relevance, Pub. L. No. 32013R0347, 115 OJ L (2013)." http://data.europa.eu/eli/reg/2013/347/oj/eng.

European Steel Association (Eurofer). "European Steel in Figures 2015 Edition, Covering 2010–2014." http://www.steelonthenet.com/kb/files/Eurofer _Steel_in_Figures_2010-2014.pdf.

Fattouh, Bassam, and James Henderson. "The Impact of Russia's Refinery Upgrade Plans on Global Fuel Oil Markets." Oxford Institute for Energy Studies, July 12, 2012. doi:10.26889/9781907555541.

Federal Ministry for Economic Affairs and Energy, Zahlen Und Fakten Energiedaten. "Energiedaten: Gesamtausgabe." No date. http://www.bmwi.de /Redaktion/DE/Artikel/Energie/energiedaten-gesamtausgabe.html.

Fjaertoft, Daniel, and Lars Petter Lunden. "Russian Petroleum Tax Policy: Continuous Maneuvering in Rocky Waters." *Energy Policy* 87 (2015): 553–61.

Flade, Falk. "Creating a Common Energy Space: The Building of the Druzhba Oil Pipeline." In *Cold War Energy: A Transnational History of Soviet Oil and Gas*, edited by Jeronim Perovic. New York: Palgrave Macmillan, 2017.

Forsyth, Timothy. *Critical Political Ecology: The Politics of Environmental Science.* London: Routledge, 2004.

Fortescue, Stephen. "Die russische Stahlindustrie und die Ukraine." *Ukraine-Analysen* 86 (February 2, 2011): 2–5.

——. "The Russian Steel Industry, 1990–2009." *Eurasian Geography and Economics* 50, no. 3 (2009): 252–74. https://doi.org/10.2747/1539-7216 .50.3.252.

——. *Russia's Oil Barons and Metal Magnates: Oligarchs and the State in Transition.* Basingstoke, U.K.: Palgrave Macmillan, 2014.

Foucault, Michel. *Discipline and Punish: The Birth of the Prison.* New York: Pantheon Books, 1977.

Fraunhofer Institute for Solar Energy Systems ISE. "Energy Charts." No date. https://www.energy-charts.de/.

Gaddy, Clifford G., and Barry W. Ickes. *Russia's Virtual Economy.* Washington, DC: Brookings Institution Press, 2002.

——. "Underneath the Formal Economy: Why Are Russian Enterprises Not Restructuring?" *Transition* 9, no. 4 (1998): 1–5.

Ganswindt, Katrin, Sebastian Rötters, and Heffa Schücking. *Bitter Coal.* Cologne: Urgewald and Food First Information and Action Network, 2013.

Gary, James H., Glenn E. Handwerk, and Mark J. Kaiser. *Petroleum Refining: Technology and Economics*, 5th ed. Boca Raton, FL: CRC Press, 2007.

Gavriš, Oleg, and Natal'ja Neprjaxina. "Kontrabanda xlynula potokom: V Ukraine rastet nezakonnyj import benzina." *Kommersant–Ukraina*, November 15, 2011.

Gazprom Export. "Overseas Transportation of Russian Gas." http://www .gazpromexport.ru/en/projects/transportation/.

Gereffi, Gary, John Humphrey, Raphael Kaplinsky, and Timothy J. Sturgeon. "Introduction: Globalisation, Value Chains and Development." *IDS Bulletin* 32, no. 3 (July 2001): 1–8. https://doi.org/10.1111/j.1759-5436.2001. mp32003001.x.

Gereffi, Gary, John Humphrey, and Timothy Sturgeon. "The Governance of Global Value Chains." *Review of International Political Economy* 12, no. 1 (2005): 78–104. https://doi.org/10.1080/09692290500049805.

Gibbon, Peter, Jennifer Bair, and Stefano Ponte. "Governing Global Value Chains: An Introduction." *Economy and Society* 37, no. 3 (August 2008): 315–38. https://doi.org/10.1080/03085140802172656.

Gillingham, John. *Coal, Steel and the Rebirth of Europe, 1945–1955: The Germans and French from Ruhr Conflict to Economic Community.* New York: Cambridge University Press, 1991.

Giucci, Ricardo, Robert Kirchner, Woldemar Walter, and Vitaliy Kravchuk. "Economic Links between Russia and Ukraine. A Fact-Based Analysis." Policy Briefing PB/07/2015, German Advisory Group in Ukraine, Berlin/Kyiv, June 2015. http://www.beratergruppe-ukraine.de/wordpress /wp-content/uploads/2014/06/PB_07_2015_en.pdf.

Glazunov, Mikhail. *Corporate Strategy in Post-Communist Russia.* New York: Routledge, 2016.

Goldman, Marshall. *Petrostate: Putin, Power, and the New Russia.* Oxford: Oxford University Press, 2009.

Goldthau, Andreas, and Nick Sitter. "A Liberal Actor in a Realist World? The Commission and the External Dimension of the Single Market for Energy." *Journal of European Public Policy* 21, no. 10 (2014): 1452–72.

——. *A Liberal Actor in a Realist World: The European Union Regulatory State and the Global Political Economy of Energy.* Oxford: Oxford University Press, 2015.

——. "Soft Power with a Hard Edge: EU Policy Tools and Energy Security." *Review of International Political Economy* 22, no. 5 (2015): 941–65.

Golovko, Volodimir. "Formuvannâ pervinnogo kapìtalu v umovah krizi upravlìnnâ ukraïns'koÛ promislovìstÛ (1991–1998 rr.)." *Problemi ìstorìï Ukraïni: Fakti, sudžennâ pošuki* 21 (2012): 5–17.

——. *Oligarxi iz goroda roz: Stanovlenie i razvitie krupnogo kapitala Donbassa (1991–2014 gg.).* Kyiv: Institut istorii Ukrainy, 2014.

Gonchar, M., A. Duleba, and O. Malynovskyi. *Ukraine and Slovakia in a Post-Crisis Architecture of European Energy Security.* Kyiv: Research Center of the Slovak Foreign Policy Association, 2011.

Gonta, Ivan. "S čem vošla 'Ukrtransnafta' v 2005 god." *Zerkalo nedeli* 3, January 28, 2005. http://gazeta.zn.ua/ECONOMICS/s_chem_voshla _Ukrtransnafta_v_2005_god.html.

Graf Lambsdorff, Johann. *The Institutional Economics of Corruption and Reform: Theory, Evidence and Policy.* Cambridge: Cambridge University Press, 2007.

Grätz, Jonas. *Russland als globaler Wirtschaftsakteur: Handlungsressourcen und Strategien der Öl-und Gaskonzerne.* Munich: Oldenbourg Verlag, 2013.

Gregory, Chris A. *Gifts and Commodities.* Cambridge: Academic Press, 1982.

Grey, Stephen, Tom Bergin, Sevgil Musaieva, and Roman Anin. "Special Report: Putin's Allies Channelled Billions to Ukraine Oligarch." Reuters, November 26, 2014. https://uk.reuters.com/article/russia-capitalism-gas -special-report-pix-idUKL3N0TF4QD20141126.

Grey, Stephen, Tom Bergin, Sevgil Musaieva, and Jack Stubbs. "Special Report: How a 29-Year-Old Ukrainian Made a Killing on Russian Gas." Reuters, December 12, 2014. https://www.reuters.com/article/us-russia -capitalism-kurchenko-specialre-idUSKBN0JP1KO20141212.

Grigas, Agnia. *The New Geopolitics of Natural Gas.* Cambridge, MA: Harvard University Press, 2017.

Grushevska, Kateryna, and Theo Notteboom. "Dry Bulk Cargo in Ukrainian Ports." *Port Technology* 61 (February 2014): 66–69.

——. *The Bridge: Natural Gas in a Redivided Europe.* Cambridge, MA: Harvard University Press, 2020.

Gustafson, Thane. *Wheel of Fortune: The Battle for Oil and Power in Russia.* Cambridge, MA: Belknap Press of Harvard University Press, 2012.

Hafner, Manfred. *Russian Strategy on Infrastructure and Gas Flows to Europe.* Polinares Working Paper 73. Brussels: European Commission, 2012.

Hammond, John L. "The Resource Curse and Oil Revenues in Angola and Venezuela." *Science & Society* 75, no. 3 (2001): 348–78.

Heather, Patrick. "The Evolution of European Traded Gas Hubs." Oxford Institute for Energy Studies, 2015. https://ora.ox.ac.uk/objects/uuid:3f7dfc77 -85d0-400b-8d66-60c67ac39af3.

Hecht, Gabrielle. *Being Nuclear: Africans and the Global Uranium Trade.* Cambridge, MA: MIT Press, 2012.

——. *The Radiance of France: Nuclear Power and National Identity after World War II.* Cambridge, MA: MIT Press, 2009.

Hellman, Joel S. "Winners Take All: The Politics of Partial Reform in Post-Communist Transitions." *World Politics* 50, no. 2 (1998): 203–34.

Henderson, James. "The Commercial and Political Logic for the Altai Pipeline." Oxford Institute for Energy Studies, Oxford Energy Comment, 2014.

Henderson, James, and Jack Sharples. "Gazprom in Europe: Two '*Anni Mirabilies*,' but Can It Continue?" *Oxford Energy Insight* 29 (2018). https://www.oxfordenergy.org/wpcms/wp-content/uploads/2018/03/Gazprom-in-Europe-%E2%80%93-two-Anni-Mirabiles-but-can-it-continue-Insight-29.pdf.

Hirschausen, Christian von, Berit Meinhart, and Ferdinand Pavel. "Transporting Russian Gas to Western Europe: A Simulation Analysis." *Energy Journal* 26, no. 2 (2005): 49–68.

Hirschman, Albert O. *National Power and the Structure of Foreign Trade.* Berkeley: University of California Press, 1980; orig. pub. 1945.

Hodder, Ian. *Entangled: An Archaeology of the Relationships between Humans and Things.* Malden, MA: Wiley-Blackwell, 2012.

Högselius, Per, Anna Åberg, and Arne Kaijser. "Natural Gas in Cold War Europe: The Making of a Critical Infrastructure." In *the Making of Europe's Critical Infrastructure,* edited by Per Högselius, Anna Åberg, Arne Kaijser, and Erik van der Vleuten. London: Palgrave Macmillan, 2013.

Hopkins, Valerie, and Richard Pérez-Peña. "Clocks Slow in Europe? Blame Kosovo-Serbia Row." *New York Times,* March 8, 2018. https://www.nytimes.com/2018/03/08/world/europe/kosovo-serbia-clocks-europe.html.

Hughes, Llewelyn. *Globalizing Oil: Firms and Oil Market Governance in France, Japan, and the United States.* Cambridge: Cambridge University Press, 2014. https://doi.org/10.1017/CBO9781107323643.

Hughes, Llewelyn, and Austin Long. "Is There an Oil Weapon? Security Implications of Changes in the Structure of the International Oil Market." *International Security* 39, no. 3 (2014–15): 152–89.

Hughes, Llewelyn, and Phillip Y. Lipscy. "The Politics of Energy." *Annual Review of Political Science* 16 (2013): 449–69.

IEA (International Energy Agency). *Coal Information 2015.* Paris: IEA, 2015.

——. *Coal Information 2017.* Paris: IEA, 2017.

——. *Eastern Europe, Caucasus and Central Asia.* Paris: IEA, 2015.

——. *Energy Policies Beyond IEA Countries: Eastern Europe, Caucasus and Central Asia 2015.* Paris: IEA/OECD, 2015.

——. *Energy Policies Beyond IEA Countries: Russia 2014.* Paris: IEA, 2014.

——. *Energy Policies Beyond IEA Countries: Ukraine 2012.* Paris: IEA, 2012.

——. *Energy Policies of IEA Countries: Czech Republic 2016 Review.* Paris: IEA, 2016.

——. *Energy Policies of IEA Countries: European Union—2014 Review.* Paris: IEA, 2014.

——. *Energy Policies of IEA Countries: Germany 2013 Review.* Paris: IEA, 2013.

——. *Energy Policies of IEA Countries: Slovak Republic. 2012 Review*. Paris: IEA, 2012.

——. *Energy Policies of the Russian Federation 2002*. Paris: IEA, 2002.

——. *Energy Policies of Ukraine 1996*. Paris: IEA, 1996.

——. *Energy Supply Security 2014: Emergency Response of IEA Countries*. Paris: IEA, 2014.

——. "Natural Gas Statistics." https://www.iea.org/statistics/naturalgas/.

——. *Oil Information 2014*. Paris: IEA, various years.

——. *Oil Information 2016*. Paris: IEA, various years.

——. *Optimizing Russian Natural Gas*. Paris: IEA, 2006.

——. *Russia Energy Survey 2002*. Paris: IEA, 2002.

——. *Ukraine Energy Policy Review 2006*. Paris: IEA, 2006. https://webstore.iea.org/energy-policy-review-2006-ukraine-ukrainian.

——. *World Energy Outlook 2013*. Paris: IEA 2013.

——. *World Energy Outlook 2014*. Paris: IEA, 2014.

——. *World Energy Outlook 2017*. Paris: IEA, 2016.

Interfax-CAN. "A Comprehensive Insight in Russia's Gas Industry (2014)." http://www.interfax.com/txt.asp?rbr=7&id=275.

——. *Russia's Oil Sector in 2011*. Moscow: Interfax-CNA, 2012. http://www.interfax.com/txt.asp?rbr=7&id=158.

——. *Russia's Oil Sector in 2013*. Moscow: Interfax-CNA, 2014. http://www.interfax.com/txt.asp?rbr=7&id=264.

——. *Russia's Oil Sector in 2015*. Moscow: Interfax-CNA, 2016. http://www.interfax.com/txt.asp?rbr=7&id=337.

International Council on Clean Transportation. "European Vehicle Market Statistics 2013." https://www.theicct.org/sites/default/files/publications/EU_vehiclemarket_pocketbook_2013_Web.pdf.

International Gas Union. "Wholesale Gas Price Survey, 2015." Available at www.igu.org.

——. "Wholesale Gas Price Survey, 2016." Available at www.igu.org.

——. "Wholesale Gas Price Survey, 2017." Available at www.igu.org.

International Iron and Steel Institute. *World Steel in Figures: 2003 Edition*. Brussels: International Iron and Steel Institute, 2003.

Jakunin, V. I. "Desjat' šagov k èffektivnosti." *Ekspert* 33 (August 31, 2009): 36–42.

Jensen, W. G. "The Importance of Energy in the First and Second World Wars." *Historical Journal* 11 (1968): 538–54.

Jones, Christopher W. *EU Energy Law*. Deventer, Netherlands: Claeys & Casteels, 2016.

"Kak Kolomojskij neft' otkačival." *Komsomol'skie Vesti*, June 26, 2014. https://prozoro.info/2014/06/26/kak-kolomojskij-neft-otkachival//.

"Kak zakaljalas' stal.'" *Delovoj žurnal*, January 14, 2015. http://ukrrudprom.ua /digest/ndzh140105.html.

Kalus, Tim. *EU Energy Law and Policy: A Critical Account*. Oxford: Oxford University Press, 2013.

Kandiyoti, Rafael. *Pipelines: Flowing Oil and Crude Politics*. London: I. B. Tauris, 2008.

Kantchev, Georgi. "With U.S. Gas, Europe Seeks Escape from Russia's Energy Grip." *Wall Street Journal*, February 25, 2016. https://www.wsj.com /articles/europes-escape-from-russian-energy-grip-u-s-gas-1456456892.

Kardaś, Szymon. "The Twilight of the Oil Eldorado: How the Activity of Russian Oil Companies on the EU Market Has Evolved." *OSW Studies* 55 (2016). https://www.osw.waw.pl/en/publikacje/osw-studies/2016-03 -17/twilight-oil-eldorado-how-activity-russian-oil-companies-eu.

"Karta: Sxema truboprovodov." No date. www.siberia.transneft.ru/about /map/.

Kaveshnikov, Nikolay. "The Issue of Energy Security in Relations between Russia and the European Union." *European Security* 19, no. 4 (December 2010): 585–605.

Khmurych, V., and T. Tkachenko. "Opportunities for Corruption in the Ukrainian Gas Market." Eurasia Foundation, 1999. http://www. eurasia.org /programs/eerc/Kyiv/papers/khtk.htm.

Kičanov, Mixail. "Ugol'nyj peregruz." *Ekspert Sibir'* 4, no. 360 (2013). http://expert.ru/siberia/2013/04/ugolnyij-peregruz/.

Kiewiet, Bert, David Balmert, Petra Szaloky, Anna Butenko, and Maurice Vos. "Entry Exit Regimes in Gas, Part A: Implementation of Entry-Exit Systems." DNV Kema, July 2013.

Kniazhans'kyi, Vitalii. "Comrade Reverse." *The Day* (Kyiv), March 16, 2004.

Kochura, Ilona V. "Coal Market of Ukraine: Analysis and Development Background." *GeoScience Engineering*, 58, no. 1 (2012): 17–23.

"Kogalym: Žemčužina Zapadnoj Sibiri." http://zs.LUKoil.ru/ru/About /Geography?wid=widS7oOTRom5E-jiKBBLBeTng.

"Kolomojs'kij plativ Vanheke za te, ŝob UkrnaftoÛ keruvali Pustovarov ì Kuŝ." *Ukrainska Pravda*, September 17, 2015. https://www.pravda.com.ua/news /2015/09/17/7081608/.

"Kommunisty xotjat otobrat' zavod u Axmetova." *Fokus*, August 17, 2007. https://focus.ua/country/8157/.

Konończuk, Wojciech. "A Dangerous Energy Policy: Ukraine, Despite War, Is Making Itself Dependent on Russian Oil." *Energy Post*, September 8, 2017. http://energypost.eu/15647-2/.

——. "The Never-Ending Collapse, the State of the Ukrainian Oil Sector." *OSW*, April 4, 2017. https://www.osw.waw.pl/en/publikacje/osw-report /2017-05-04/never-ending-collapse-state-ukrainian-oil-sector.

Korduban, Pavel. "Ukraine Shows No Hurry to Return Gas to RosUkrEnergo." Jamestown Foundation, *Eurasia Daily Monitor* 7, no. 127 (July 1, 2010). https://jamestown.org/program/ukraine-shows-no-hurry-to-return-gas-to-rosukrenergo/.

Kostromenko, Vadim. *Otvetnaya mera*. Film. Goskino, 1975. http://www.imdb.com/title/tt0478220/.

Kotchen, Matthew J. "Green Markets and Private Provision of Public Goods." *Journal of Political Economy* 114, no. 4 (2006): 816–34.

Kotkin, Stephen. *Magnetic Mountain: Stalinism as Civilization*. Berkeley: University of California Press, 1995.

——. *Steeltown USSR: Soviet Society in the Gorbachev Era*. Berkeley: University of California Press, 1991.

Krasner, Stephen D. "Oil Is the Exception." *Foreign Policy* 14 (1974): 68–84.

Kriutikhin, Mikhail. Comments in TV program *Dorogi Svobodi*, January 26, 2019. https://www.svoboda.org/a/29729068.html.

Kudelia, Serhiy. "The Donbas Rift." *Russian Politics & Law* 54, no. 1 (2016): 5–27.

Kujun, Sergei. "Dìvoča pam'ât' mìl'ârdera." *Dzerkalo Tizhnia*, December 11, 2015. http://gazeta.dt.ua/energy_market/divocha-pam-yat-milyarderi-_.html.

——. "Neulovimyj akciz." *Zerkalo Nedeli*, April 24, 2015. http://gazeta.zn.ua/energy_market/neulovimyy-akciz-_.html.

Kul'čic'kij, C. *Radáns'ka industrìalìzacìâ na Donbasì//Studìï z regìonal'noï ìstorìï: Stepova Ukraïna*. Kyiv: Instititut Istorii Ukraini, 2015. http://history.org.ua/LiberUA/978-966-02-7571-3/978-966-02-7571-3.pdf.

Kurt, Daniel. "Benchmark Oils: Brent Blend, WTI and Dubai." Investopedia, June 25, 2019. https://www.investopedia.com/articles/investing/102314/understanding-benchmark-oils-brent-blend-wti-and-dubai.asp.

"Kuzbassrazrezugol." No date. http://www.kru.ru/ru/about/about/bachatsk/.

Kuzio, Taras. "Crime, Politics and Business in 1990s Ukraine." *Communist and Post-Communist Studies* 47 (2014): 195–210.

——. "Ukraine Sliding from Oligarchy to Cronyism." Jamestown Foundation, *Eurasia Daily Monitor*, 10, no. 8 (January 16, 2013). http://www.reuters.com/article/us-russia-capitalism-kurchenko-specialre-idUSKBN0JP1KO20141212.

Lagendijk, Vincent, and Erik van der Vleuten. "Inventing Electrical Europe: Interdependencies, Borders, Vulnerabilities." In *The Making of Europe's Critical Infrastructure*, edited by Erik van der Vleuten, Arne Kaijser, Anique Hommels, and Per Högselius. London: Palgrave Macmillan, 2013.

Latour, Bruno. "When Things Strike Back: A Possible Contribution of 'Science Studies' to the Social Sciences." *British Journal of Sociology* 51, no. 1 (2000): 107–23.

Le Billon, Philippe. "The Political Ecology of War: Natural Resources and Armed Conflicts." *Political Geography* 20, no. 5 (June 2001): 561–84. https://doi.org/10.1016/S0962-6298(01)00015-4.

Lehmann, Timothy C. "Keeping Friends Close and Enemies Closer: Classical Realist Statecraft and Economic Exchange in U.S. Interwar Strategy." *Security Studies* 18, no. 1 (2009): 115–47.

Lešenko, S., and M. Naem. "Sergìj Taruta: Koli vbili Šerbanâ, u nas ne bulo problem z ÊESU." *Ukrainskaya pravda*, February 8, 2013. https://www.pravda.com.ua/articles/2013/02/8/6983135/.

Levine, Richard M., and Andrew R. Bond. "Prospects for Ukrainian Ferrous Metals in the Post-Soviet Period." *Post-Soviet Geography and Economics* 39, no. 3 (1998): 151–63.

Lewis, Barbara. "Ukraine Appeals to EU over 'Illegal' Gazprom-Slovak Pipeline Contract." Reuters, June 23, 2015. https://uk.reuters.com/article/uk-ukraine-gas-slovakia-idUKKBN0P31W620150623.

Lewis, Peter. *Growing Apart: Oil, Politics and Economic Change in Indonesia and Nigeria.* Ann Arbor: University of Michigan Press, 2007.

Licklider, Roy. "The Power of Oil: The Arab Oil Weapon and the Netherlands, the United Kingdom, Canada, Japan, and the United States." *International Studies Quarterly* 32, no. 2 (June 1988): 205–26.

Lovei, Laszlo. *Coal Industry Restructuring in Ukraine: The Politics of Coal Mining and Budget Crises.* Washington, DC: World Bank, 1998. http://documents.worldbank.org/curated/en/1998/12/441539/coal-industry-restructuring-ukraine-politics-coal-mining-budget-crises.

Lucas, Edward. *The New Cold War: Putin's Russia and the Threat to the West.* New York: St. Martin's Press, 2014.

Luebbert, Gregory M. *Liberalism, Fascism, or Social Democracy: Social Classes and the Political Origins of Regimes in Interwar Europe.* Oxford: Oxford University Press, 1991.

LUKoil. *Analyst Databook 2013.* Moscow: LUKoil, 2013. https://www.lukoil.be/pdf/Lukoil_DB_2013_eng.pdf.

——. *Analyst Databook 2015.* Moscow: LUKoil, 2015.

——. "Osnovnye fakty 2007." http://www.LUKoil.ru/Handlers/DownloadPartialPdfHandler.ashx?fid=4048&fc=9&pages=23,34.

——. *Yearly Report 2009.* Moscow: LUKoil, 2009. http://www.LUKoil.be/fr/pdf/AR_ENG_2009.pdf.

Lyubashenko, Igor. "Ukraine's First Year in the Energy Community: Restart Needed." Polski Instytut Spraw Międzynarodowyc, PISM Policy Paper 28. April 2012.

MacLachlan, Ian. *Kill and Chill: Restructuring Canada's Beef Commodity Chain.* Toronto: University of Toronto Press, 2001.

Magomedov, Musa. "Nam–50." *Ugleximičeskij žurnal* 5 (2013): 1–6.

——. On radio program *Donbass realii*, November 8, 2016. http://www
.radiosvoboda.org/a/28104142.html.

Mahdavy, Hossein. "The Pattern and Problems of Economic Development in
Rentier States: The Case of Iran." In *Studies in the Economic History of the
Middle East*, edited by M. A. Cook. London: Oxford University Press, 1970.

Makholm, Jeff D. *The Political Economy of Pipelines: A Century of Comparative
Institutional Development*. Chicago: University of Chicago Press, 2012.

Mansfield, Edward D., and Helen V. Milner. *Votes, Vetoes, and the Political Economy
of International Trade Agreements*. Princeton, NJ: Princeton University Press,
2012. https://press.princeton.edu/books/paperback/9780691135304
/votes-vetoes-and-the-political-economy-of-international-trade.

Mansky, Vitaly. *Pipeline*. Film. Deckert Distribution GmbH, 2013. https://
www.idfa.nl/en/film/07a1168c-d267-413d-86b1-cb90bb7b6a52
/pipeline.

Marcegaglia, Antonio. "Perspectives for Italian Steel Producers, Re-Rollers and
Processors." Slide show, April 4, 2013. http://www.people.marcegaglia
.com/made_in_steel_2013/pdf/slides/4/MM_Marcegaglia.pdf.

Margonelli, Lisa. *Oil on the Brain: Adventures from the Pump to the Pipeline*.
New York: Nan A. Talese, 2007.

Markova, Vitalija, and Viktor Čurašev. "Put' uglja." *Ekspert Sibir'* 22, no. 377
(June 3, 2014). http://expert.ru/siberia/2013/22/put-uglya/.

Marples, David. "Crisis in Soviet Industry? An Examination of the Soviet
Steel Industry in the 1980s." *Canadian Slavonic Papers* 28, no. 4 (1986):
369–84.

Marriott, James, and Mika Minio-Paluello. *The Oil Road: Journeys from the
Caspian Sea to the City of London*. New York: Verso Books, 2012.

Matsen, Egil, Gisle J. Natvik, and Ragnar Torvik. "Petro Populism." *Journal of Development Economics* 118 (January 2016): 1–12. https://doi.org
/10.1016/j.jdeveco.2015.08.010.

Mazur, V. L., and M. V. Timošenko. "Aktual'nye Èkonomičeskie Voprosy v
Metallurgičeskoj Otrasli Ukrainy." *Upravlenie Èkonomikoj: Teorija i Praktika* 6 (2012): 13–23.

Mazur, V. L., M. V. Timošenko, and C. V. Mazur. "Èkologičeskie, texnologičeskie i
èkonomičeskie aspekty razvitija metallurgii Ukrainy." *Èkologija i promyšlennost'* 4
(2014): 32–36.

Mazzuca, Sebastián L. "Lessons from Latin America: The Rise of Rentier
Populism." *Journal of Democracy* 24, no. 2 (2013): 108–22.

May, Paul, and Simon Cotton. *Molecules That Amaze Us*. Boca Raton, FL:
CRC Press, 2014. https://doi.org/10.1201/b17423.

Men, Rimma. "Steel Groups Extend Grip into Europe." *Kyiv Post*, March 1,
2006. https://www.kyivpost.com/article/content/business/steel-groups
-extend-grip-into-europe-23965.html.

Metinvest. "Annual Report and Accounts 2016." http://www.scm.com.ua/m
/documents/MET_27160_AR2016_AW_web.pdf.

Miesener, Thomas O., and William L. Leffler. *Oil and Gas Pipelines in Non-technical Language.* Tulsa: PennWell, 2006.

Miller, Tom. *The Panama Hat Trail: A Journey from South America.* New York: Morrow, 1986.

Milner, Helen V. *Interests, Institutions, and Information: Domestic Politics and International Relations.* Princeton, NJ: Princeton University Press, 1997.

Ministry of Economy of the Slovak Republic. "Report on the Results of Natural Gas Supplies Security Monitoring, 2015." http://www.economy
.gov.sk/sprava-o-vysledkoch-monitorovania-bezpecnosti-dodavok
-plynu—2015-/145946s.

Miseror. "Rohstoffe für die Energiewende." Aachen: Miseror, 2018. https://
www.misereor.de/fileadmin/publikationen/studie-rohstoffe-fuer-die
-energiewende.pdf.

Misík, Matús. "Crisis as Remedy? The 2009 Gas Crisis and Its Influence on the Increase of Energy Security within Visegrad Group Countries." *International Issues & Slovak Foreign Policy Affairs* 31, nos. 1–2 (2012): 56–73.

Mitchell, Timothy. *Carbon Democracy: Political Power in the Age of Oil.* London: Verso Books, 2011.

——. *Rule of Experts: Egypt, Techno-Politics, Modernity.* Berkeley: University of California Press, 2002.

Mitrova, Tatiana. "Changing Gas Price Mechanisms in Europe and Russia's Gas Pricing Policy." Presentation at International Association for Energy Economics 38th international conference, Antalya, May 2015.

——. *Shifting Political Economy of Russian Oil and Gas.* Lanham, MD: Rowman & Littlefield, 2016.

Moiseenko, Oleksandr. "Majže deržavnij. Šo bude z Privatbankom." *Ekonomichna Pravda*, December 16, 2016. https://www.epravda.com.ua
/publications/2016/12/16/614619/.

Moravcsik, Andrew. *Why the European Community Strengthens the State: International Cooperation and Domestic Politics.* Working Paper 52. Cambridge, MA: Center for European Studies at Harvard University, 1994. http://aei.pitt.edu/9151/.

Morris, Craig. "Germany Runs out of Dutch Gas." *Energy Transition*, March 1, 2017. https://energytransition.org/2017/03/germany-runs-out-of-dutch
-gas/.

Mulder, Kenneth, and Nathan John Hagens. "Energy Return on Investment: Toward a Consistent Framework." *AMBIO: A Journal of the Human Environment* 37, no. 2 (March 2008): 74–79. https://doi.org/10.1579
/0044-7447(2008)37[74:EROITA]2.0.CO;2.

Muratov, Aleksandr. *Kontrakt veka*. Film. Lenfilm Studio, 1985. http://www.imdb.com/title/tt0089438/.

Musaeva-Borovik, Sevgil', and Dmitrij Denkov. "Glavnyj oligarx èpoxi JAnukoviča: God spustja." *Ukrainskaya Pravda*, April 29, 2015. https://www.pravda.com.ua/cdn/cd1/2015year/akhmetov/index.html.

Mykhnenko, Vlad. *Rusting Away? The Ukrainian Iron and Steel Industry in Transition*. CEU International Policy Fellowship Programme Research Paper. Budapest: Central European University, 2004.

Naftohaz Ukraini. *Annual Report for 2015*. http://naftogaz.com/files/Zvity/Naftogaz_Annual_Report_2015_engl.pdf.

Najêm, Mustafa, and Sergìj Lešenko. "Sergìj Taruta: Lazarenko perekonav Kučmu, šo potrìbno postaviti Ânukoviča." *Ukraiskaya Pravda*, February 11, 2013. http://www.pravda.com.ua/articles/2013/02/11/6983216/.

Nalbandian, Herminé, and Nigel Dong. "Coal and Gas Competition in Global Markets." 2013. https://usea.org/sites/default/files/072013_Coal%20and%20gas%20competition%20in%20power%20generation%20in%20global%20markets_ccc220.pdf.

Narbel, Patrick A., Jan Petter Hansen, and Jan R. Lien. *Energy Technologies and Economics*. Berlin: Springer, 2014.

National Bank of Ukraine. "Dinamìka tovarnoï strukturi eksportu." Foreign trade statistics. https://bank.gov.ua/doccatalog/document?id=19257909.

National Resources Canada. "Frequently Asked Questions (FAQs) Concerning Federally Regulated Petroleum Pipelines in Canada." October 29, 2012. https://www.nrcan.gc.ca/our-natural-resources/energy-sources-distribution/clean-fossil-fuels/pipelines/faqs-federally-regulated-petroleum-pipelines-canada/5893#h-1-1.

National Transportation Safety Board. "Safety Recommendation Report: Natural Gas Distribution System Project Development and Review (Urgent)." December 6, 2018. https://www.ntsb.gov/investigations/AccidentReports/Reports/PSR1802.pdf.

Nazarov, Ivan. "Overview of the Russian Natural Gas Industry." In *Gazprom: An Energy Giant and Its Challenges in Europe*, edited by Andrey Vavilov. London: Palgrave Macmillan, 2015.

"Neftjaniki: Neft'i gaz." http://www.nftn.ru/oilfields/russian_oilfields/khanty_mansijskij_ao/vateganskoe/6-1-0-566.

Nefte Compass. "Russian Crude Oil Exports to NonCIS Markets, 2013." January 23, 2013. http://www.energyintel.com/pages/about_ncm.aspx.

Neilson, Jeffrey. "Value Chains, Neoliberalism and Development Practice: The Indonesian Experience." *Review of International Political Economy* 21, no. 1 (January 2014): 38–69. https://doi.org/10.1080/09692290.2013.809782.

Neilson, Jeffrey, Bill Pritchard, and Henry Wai-chung Yeung. "Global Value Chains and Global Production Networks in the Changing International

Political Economy: An Introduction." *Review of International Political Economy* 21, no. 1 (January 2014): 1–8. https://doi.org/10.1080/09692290 .2013.873369.

Nester, Leonid. "Krušenie xrustal'noj mečty, ili neskol'ko slov o mifax i realijax kaspijskoj nefti." *Zerkalo nedeli* 42/517, October 16, 2004.

Nesterov, Daniil, and Sergej Ljamec. "Pozvolit li Kabmin opustošit' trubopro-vody." *Ekonomichna Pravda*, June 25, 2014. https://www.epravda.com.ua /rus/publications/2014/06/25/470618/.

Neumann, Anne, Sophia Rüster, and Christian von Hirschhausen. "Long-Term Contracts in the Natural Gas Industry: Literature Survey and Data on 426 Contracts (1965–2014)." Deutsches Institut für Wirtschaftsforschung, Berlin, 2015. https://www.econstor.eu/handle/10419/108977.

Nikolajuk, Nikolaj N. "Ulučšenie Kačestva Èksportiruemoj Nefti Kak Faktor Povyšenija Konkurentosposobnosti Rossijskogo TÈK Na Ènergetičeskom Rynke ES." *Neft', Gaz i Biznes* 1 (2013): 20–22.

"Notiziario Marketpress." April 14, 2008. www.marketpress.info/notiziario _det.php?art=62386.

Nowak, Ondřej, and Jiří Hnilica. "Rafinérský průmysl v České republice a energetická bezpečnost v oblasti dodávek ropy." *Ekonomika a Management*, 2010.

Office of the Prime Minister of Ukraine. "Report for 2015 Following the Results of Monitoring Security of Natural Gas Supplies." September 2015. https:// www.energy-community.org/portal/page/portal/ENC_HOME/DOCS /3842350/2198FDD2CC031492E053C92FA8C0BE17.PDF.

Omelchenko, Volodymyr. *Ekonomicheskie novosti*, April 21, 2011. http://old .razumkov.org.ua/ukr/expert.php?news_id=2744.

Omonbude, Ekpen J. "The Transit Oil and Gas Pipeline and the Role of Bargaining: A Nontechnical Discussion." *Energy Policy* 35, no. 12 (December 2007): 6188–94. https://doi.org/10.1016/j.enpol.2007.06.001.

"OpenStreetMap." https://www.openstreetmap.org.

Orban, Anita. *Power, Energy, and the New Russian Imperialism*. Westport, CT: Praeger, 2008.

Organization for Economic Cooperation and Development. "Oil Import Prices, Historical Chart for Crude Oil Import Prices 2000–2016." https:// data.oecd.org/energy/crude-oil-import-prices.htm.

Orttung, Robert W., and Indra Overland. "A Limited Toolbox: Explaining the Constraints on Russia's Foreign Energy Policy." *Journal of Eurasian Studies* 2, no. 1 (2011): 74–85. https://doi.org/10.1016/j.euras.2010.10.006.

Osička, Jan, Filip Černoch, Tomáš Dráb, Tomáš Martanovič, and Jiří Vlček. *Natural Gas Reverse Flows in the Danube Strategy Region: Current State and Outlook*. Brno: International Institute of Political Science of Masaryk University, 2015.

Ostrom, Elinor. "How Types of Goods and Property Rights Jointly Affect Collective Action." *Journal of Theoretical Politics* 15, no. 3 (July 2003): 239–70. https://doi.org/10.1177/0951692803015003002.

O'Sullivan, Meghan. *Windfall: How the New Energy Abundance Upends Global Politics and Strengthens America's Power*. New York: Simon & Schuster, 2017.

Otkritie Capital. *Oil & Gas Yearbook 2013*. Available at www.securities.com and www.emis.com.

Oxford Institute for Energy Studies. "European Traded Gas Hubs: An Updated Analysis on Liquidity, Maturity and Barriers to Market Integration." 2017. https://www.oxfordenergy.org/wpcms/wp-content/uploads/2017/05/European-traded-gas-hubs-an-updated-analysis-on-liquidity-maturity-and-barriers-to-market-integration-OIES-Energy-Insight.pdf.

Pappe, Yakov. *Oligarkhi*. Moscow: Vyschaya Shkola Ekonomiki, 2000.

Park, Chris, and Michael Allaby. "Recoverable Resource." In *A Dictionary of Environment and Conservation*, 2nd Edition. Oxford: Oxford University Press, 2013.

Parker Follett, Mary. "Power." In *Dynamic Administration: The Collected Papers of Mary Parker Follett*, edited by Henry C. Metcalf and Lyndall Urwick. New York: Harper Brothers, 1942.

Penter, Tanja. *Kohle für Stalin und Hitler: Arbeiten und Leben im Donbass 1929 bis 1953*. Essen: Klartext, 2010.

Perečneva, Irina. "Samostojatel'naja rabota." *Èkspert Ural*, 28–31, no. 519 (2012). http://expert.ru/ural/2012/31/samostoyatelnaya-rabota/.

Perovic, Jeronim, Robert W. Orttung, and Andreas Wenger, eds. *Russian Energy Power and Foreign Relations: Implications for Conflict and Cooperation*. London: Routledge, 2009.

Peters, Stefan. "Beyond Curse and Blessing: Rentier Society in Venezuela." In *Contested Extractivism, Society and the State: Struggles over Mining and Land*, edited by Bettina Engels and Kristina Dietz. London: Palgrave Macmillan, 2017.

Pinto, B., V. Drebentsov, and A. Morozov. "Give Macroeconomic Stability and Growth in Russia a Chance: Harden Budgets by Eliminating Non-Payments." *Economics of Transition* 8, no. 2 (2000): 297–324.

Pirani, Simon. "Consumers as Players in the Russian Gas Sector." Oxford Energy Comment. University of Oxford, January 2013.

Pirani, Simon. *Russian and CIS Gas Markets and Their Impact on Europe*. Oxford: Oxford Institute of Energy Studies, 2009.

——. "Ukraine's Imports of Russian Gas: How a Deal Might Be Reached." University of Oxford, July 2014. https://www.oxfordenergy.org/publications/ukraines-imports-of-russian-gas-how-a-deal-might-be-reached/.

PKN Orlen. "Consolidated Management Board Report 2014." http://integratedreport.PKN Orlen.pl/en/financial-results/consolidated-menagerial-board-report.

———. "PNK PKN Orlen Facts, Figures, Comments 2014." http://integrated report.PKNOrlen.pl/sites/PKNOrlen14ar/files/pkn_PKNOrlen_facts _figures_comments_2014.pdf.

Pleines, Heiko. "Oligarchs and Politics in Ukraine." *Demokratizatsiya* 24, no. 1 (2016): 105–27.

Pochybova, Viera. "Yukos' Stake in Slovak Transpetrol." *Journal of East-West Busines* 11, nos. 3–4 (2006): 97–107.

Poussenkova, Nina. "From Rigs to Riches: Oilmen vs. Financiers in the Russian Oil Sector." In *The Energy Dimension in Russian Global Strategy* (Houston: James A. Baker III Institute for Public Policy of Rice University, 2004). https://scholarship.rice.edu/bitstream/handle/1911/91474/from -rigs-to-riches-oilmen-vs-financiers-in-the-russian-oil-sector.pdf.

"Publične akcionerne tovaristvo 'Avdiïvs'kij koksohimičnij zavod,' Rìčna infor-macìâ emìtenta cìnnih paperìv za 2012 rìk." http://akhz.metinvestholding .com/upload/akhz/shareholders/pao_akhz_-annual-report-_2012.pdf.

Pustišek, Andrej, and Michael Karasz. *Natural Gas: A Commercial Perspective.* Berlin: Springer, 2017. https://doi.org/10.1007/978-3-319 -53249-3.

Radetzki, Marian. "European Natural Gas: Market Forces Will Bring About Competition in Any Case." *Energy Policy* 27, no. 1 (1999): 17–24.

Radio Free Europe Ukrainian Service. *Rankova Svoboda* radio program, December 19, 2016. www.Radiosboboda.ua, https://ain.ua/2016/12/21/privatbank -chto-my-poteryali-i-alternativa.

Rees, Judith. *Natural Resources: Allocation, Economics and Policy.* London and New York: Routledge, 1990.

Reuters. "Special Report: Putin's Allies Channeled Billions to Ukraine Oligarch." https://www.reuters.com/article/russia-capitalism-gas-special-report -pix/special-report-putins-allies-channelled-billions-to-ukraine-oligarch -idUSL3N0TF4QD20141126.

———. "Update 2: Russia's Gazprom Expects Gas Exports to Drop by 16 percent in 2020." April 29, 2020. https://af.reuters.com/article/commoditiesNews /idAFL5N2CH2SR.

Ricardo, David. *On the Principles of Political Economy and Taxation.* London: John Murray, Albemarle-Street, 1817.

Rivoli, Pietra. *The Travels of a T-Shirt in the Global Economy: An Economist Examines the Markets, Power and Politics of World Trade.* Hoboken, NJ: John Wiley & Sons, 2005.

Rodgers, Allan. "Coking Coal Supply: Its Role in the Expansion of the Soviet Steel Industry." *Economic Geography* 40, no. 2 (April 1964): 113–50.

Rodrigue, Jean-Paul, Claude Comtois, and Brian Slack. *The Geography of Transport Systems.* New York: Routledge, 2017.

Rogers, Douglas. *The Depths of Russia: Oil, Power, and Culture after Socialism.* Ithaca, NY: Cornell University Press, 2015.

———. "The Materiality of the Corporation: Oil, Gas, and Corporate Social Technologies in the Remaking of a Russian Region." *American Ethnologist* 39, no. 2 (2012): 284–96. https://doi.org/10.1111/j.1548-1425.2012.01364.x.

———. "Petrobarter: Oil, Inequality, and the Political Imagination in and after the Cold War." *Current Anthropology* 55, no. 2 (2014): 131–53.

Ronneau, Claude. *Énergie, pollution de l'air et développement durable: Lectures universitaires.* Louvain-la-Neuve: Presses universitaires de Louvain, 2004.

"Rosneft, LUKoil Exchange Export Quotas." *Nefte Compass*, July 25, 2013. http://www.energyintel.com/pages/searchresult.aspx.

Ross, Michael L. *The Oil Curse: How Petroleum Wealth Shapes the Development of Nations.* Princeton, NJ: Princeton University Press, 2012.

———. "Oil, Drugs and Diamonds: The Varying Roles of Natural Resources in Civil War." In *The Political Economy of Armed Conflict: Beyond Greed and Grievance*, edited by Karen Ballentine and Jake Sherman. Boulder, CO: Lynne Rienner, 2003.

Rumer, Boris Z. *Soviet Steel: The Challenge of Industrial Modernization in the USSR.* Ithaca, NY: Cornell University Press, 1986.

Russian Federation. *Energetičeskaja strategia Rossii na period do 2020 goda: Utverždena rasporjaženiem Pravitel'stva Rossijskoj Federacii 28 avgusta 2003 g.* (Energy Strategy of Russia until 2020. Approved by the directive of the Government of Russian Federation on August 28, 2003, no. 1234).

———. *Energetičeskaja strategia Rossii na period do 2030 goda: Utverždena rasporjaženiem Pravitel'stva Rossijskoj Federacii 27 avrusta 2008* (Energy Strategy of Russia until 2030. Approved by the directive of the Government of Russian Federation on August 27, 2008).

———. "Resolution No. 218 of the Russian Government of March 29, 2011 ('Resolution No. 218'), Approving the Rules of Securing Non-Discriminatory Access to Services of State Natural Monopolies in Transportation of Crude Oil (Petroleum Products) via Trunk Pipelines."

Rutland, Peter. "Russian Railways: An Emerging Force." Oxford Analytica, 2012.

Safonova, Tamara JU. "Vlijanie de-èskalatorov po kačestvu na cenu rossijskoj nefti." *Neft', Gaz i Biznes* 4 (2013): 29–32.

Sagers, Matthew J. "Natural Gas Liquids and the Soviet Gas Processing Industry." Soviet Economic Studies Branch, Center for International Research, Bureau of the Census, U.S. Department of Commerce, 1986.

Sakova, Ekaterina. "V Ukraine snižaetsja dobyča nefti i ee pererabotka." http://www.capital.ua/ru/publication/33318-v-ukraine-snizhaetsya-dobycha-nefti-i-ee-pererabotka.

Salašenko, T. I., and G. M. Fedenko. "Energetična bezpeka Ukraïni u sferì nafto-pererobki." *Problemi ekonomìki* 4 (2014): 141–52. http://www.problecon .com/pdf/2014/4_0/141_152.pdf.

Samaêva, Ûliâ. "Subsidïï: Nova suspìl'na zmova." *Dzerkalo Tizhnia*, January 15, 2016. https://dt.ua/macrolevel/subsidiyi-nova-suspilna-zmova-_.html.

Sarna, Arkadiusz. "Ukrainian Metallurgy: The Economic Link in the Oligar-chic Power System." OSW Centre for Eastern Studies, May 2002. http:// pdc.ceu.hu/archive/00001679/.

Saržan, A. "Privatizacìâ vugìl'nih pìdpriêmstv Ukraïni: Dosvìd, problemi." *Novì storìnki ìstorìï Donbasu* 22 (2013): 76–86.

Sawyer, John E. "Natural Gas Prices Impact Nitrogen Fertilizer Costs." *Inte-grated Crop Management News*, April 14, 2003. https://lib.dr.iastate .edu/cropnews/1671.

Schlosser, Eric. *Fast Food Nation: The Dark Side of the All-American Meal.* New York: HarperCollins, 2002.

Schmidt, Friedrch. "Sind so teure Röhren." *Franlkfurt Allgemaine Zeitung*, February 14, 2019.

Schobert, Harold, and N. Schobert. "Comparative Carbon Footprints of Met-allurgical Coke and Anthracite for Blast Furnace and Electric Arc Furnace Use." 2015. http://www.blaschakcoal.com/wp-content/uploads/Carbon -Footprint-Archival-Report-v-4-September-2015.pdf.

Serletis, Apostolos, Govinda R. Timilsina, and Olexandr Vasetsky. "Interna-tional Evidence on Sectoral Interfuel Substitution." *Energy Journal* 4, no. 4 (2010): 1–29.

Shatokha, Volodymyr. "The Sustainability of the Iron and Steel Industries in Ukraine: Challenges and Opportunities." *Journal of Sustainable Metallurgy* 2, no. 2 (2016): 106–15.

Shiells, Clinton R. "Optimal Taxation of Energy Trade: the Case of Russia and Ukraine." 2005. http://www.etsg.org/ETSG2005/papers/shiells.pdf.

——. "VAT Design and Energy Trade: The Case of Russia and Ukraine." *IMF Staff Papers* 52, no. 1 (2005): 103–19.

Shokot, Tatiana. On radio program *Donbass realii*, November 8, 2016. http://www.radiosvoboda.org/a/28104142.html.

Sklyar, Mikhail G. "Ukrainian Coals: Resources, Output, Utilization." *Fuel* 73, no. 10 (1994): 1672–78.

Skorkin, Konstantin. "Ukraine's President Can't Avoid Showdown with His Oli-garch Backer." October 2, 2019. https://carnegie.ru/commentary/79972.

Sleptsova, Evghenia, and Elena Gnedina. "From Multi-Vector to Vectorless: Ukraine's Policy towards Russia and the European Union." In *Russia's Changing Economic and Political Regimes*, edited by Andrey Makarychev and Andre Mommen. New York: Routledge, 2013.

Smil, Vaclav. *Power Density: A Key to Understanding Energy Sources and Uses.* Cambridge: MIT Press, 2015.

Smith, Keith C. *Russian Energy Politics in the Baltics, Poland, and Ukraine: A New Stealth Imperialism?* Washington, DC: Center for Strategic and International Studies, 2004.

Spar, Debora L. *The Cooperative Edge: The Internal Politics of International Cartels.* Ithaca, NY: Cornell University Press, 1994.

Speight, James G. *An Introduction to Petroleum Technology, Economics, and Politics.* New York: John Wiley & Sons, 2011.

S&P Global Platts. "Steel for Windpower: A Burgeoning Market." *Metals Insight*, December 7, 2017, 1–7.

Starinskaja, Galina. "Štraf neft'ju: 'Transneft'' predlagaet sozdat' bank kačestva nefti, osnovannyj na ob"eme." *RBK*, 2013. https://www.rbc.ru/newspaper /2013/04/04/56c1afca9a7947406ea09dc8.

Steel Times International. "Basics of Iron and Steel Making." No date. www .steeltimesint.com/contentimages/features/Basics_of_Iron_and_Steel _Making.doc.

Stratfor. "Russia's New Export Routes Leave Czechs Short of Oil." April 14, 2012. https://www.stratfor.com/analysis/russias-new-export-routes-leave -czechs-short-oil.

Stern, Jonathan P. *The Future of Russian Gas and Gazprom.* Oxford: Oxford University Press, 2005.

——. "The Russian Gas Balance to 2015: Difficult Years Ahead." In *Russian and CIS Gas Markets and Their Impact on Europe*, edited by Simon Pirani. Oxford: Oxford University Press, 2008.

Stern, Jonathan, and Howard Rogers. *The Dynamics of a Liberalised European Gas Market: Key Determinants of Hub Prices, and Roles and Risks of Major Players.* Paper NG 94. Oxford: Oxford Institute of Energy Studies, 2014. https://ora.ox.ac.uk/objects/uuid:66b7bc5e-209f-433e-92fc-33efd1b6117c.

Stern, Jonathan, Simon Pirani, and Katja Yafimova. *The Russo-Ukrainian Gas Dispute of January 2009: A Comprehensive Assessment.* Paper NG 27. Oxford: Oxford Institute of Energy Studies, 2009. Available at https:// www.oxfordenergy.org.

Stern, Jonathan, and Katja Yafimova. *The EU Competition Investigation of Gazprom's Sales in Central and Eastern Europe: A Detailed Analysis of the Commitments and the Way Forward.* Paper NG 121. Oxford: Oxford Institute of Energy Studies, 2017. Available at https://www.oxfordenergy .org.

Stern, Marcus. "How to Prevent an Oil Train Disaster." *New York Times*, May 19, 2015. https://www.nytimes.com/2015/05/19/opinion/how-to-prevent -an-oil-train-disaster.html.

Strange, Susan. "Structures, Values and Risk in the Study of the International Political Economy." In *Perspectives on Political Economy*, edited by R. J. B. Jones. London: Francis Pinter, 1983.

"Study on Entry-Exit Regimes in Gas. Part A: Implementation of Entry-Exit Systems." DNV Kema, July 2013. https://ec.europa.eu/energy/sites/ener/files/documents/201307-entry-exit-regimes-in-gas-parta.pdf.

Sturgeon, Timothy J. "Global Value Chains and Economic Globalization: Towards a New Measurement Framework." Report to Eurostat, 2013. http://ec.europa.eu/eurostat/documents/54610/4463793/Sturgeon-report-Eurostat.

Swain, Adam. "Soft Capitalism and a Hard Industry: Virtualism, the 'Transition Industry' and the Restructuring of the Ukrainian Coal Industry." *Transactions of the Institute of British Geographers* 31, no. 2 (2006): 208–23.

Swain, Adam, and Vlad Mykhnenko. "The Ukrainian Donbas in 'Transition.'" In *Re-Constructing the Post-Soviet Industrial Region: The Donbas in Transition*, edited by Adam Swain. New York: Routledge, 2007.

"Sxemy magistral'nyx truboprovodov PAO. 'Transneft.'" http://transneft.ru/pipelines/.

Tabata, Shinichiro. "Russian Revenues from Oil and Gas Exports: Flow and Taxation." *Eurasian Geography and Economics* 43, no. 8 (2002): 610–27. doi:10.2747/1538-7216.43.8.610.

Talus, Tim. *EU Energy Law and Policy: A Critical Account*. Oxford: Oxford University Press, 2013.

"Tatneft' i Bašneft' prosjat V. Putina ne vvodit' položenie o 'banke kačestva nefti' v zakon o truboprovodnom transporte." March 13, 2002. *Higher School of Economics, Research and Educational Portal IQ*. https://iq.hse.ru/news/177807247.html.

Tchalakov, I., I. Hristov, and T. Mitev. *The Black Holes of Bulgarian Power Industry Transformation of Electric Power Sector after 1989*. Sofia: East-West Publishing House, 2013.

Tilley, Christopher. *The Materiality of Stone: Explorations in Landscape Phenomenology*. Oxford: Berg, 2004.

Transport & Environment. "Diesel: The True (Dirty) Story: Why Europe's Obsession with Diesel Cars Is Bad for Its Economy, Its Drivers & the Environment." September 2017. www.transportenvironment.org/sites/te/files/2017_09_Diesel_report_final.pdf.

Tynkkynen, Veli-Pekka. *The Energy of Russia: Hydrocarbon Culture and Climate Change*. Cheltenham, U.K.: Edward Elgar, 2019.

Ukrainian Institute for the Future. *The Future of Ukrainian Oligarchs*. Kyiv: Ukrainian Institute for the Future, 2018.

Ukrainian State Statistics Committee. *Statystychnyi shchorichnyk Ukrainy za 2002 rik.* Kyiv: Technical, 2003.

Ukrpromvnešèkspertiza, *Rynok koksujuščego uglja i koksa v Ukraine: Faktičeskie dannye za prošedšij mesjac i prognoz na 2 mesjaca №7 ot 15 ijulja 2011 goda.* Kyiv: GP Ukrpromvnešèkspertiza, 2011.

Ukrtranshaz. "Modernisation and Reconstruction of Urengoy-Pomary-Uzhgorod Gas Pipeline." https://www.energy-community.org/portal/page/portal /ENC_HOME/DOCS/3398175/0633975ADD357B9CE053C92F A8C06338.PDF.

"Ukrtransnafta načinaet vikačivat texnologičeskuju neft iz nefteprovodov." http://www.oilnews.com.ua/a/news/Ukrtransnafta_nachinaet_vikachivat _tehnologicheskuyu_neft_iz_nefteprovodov/212297.

Unipetrol. *Unipetrol Annual Report 2012.* https://www.unipetrol.cz/en /InvestorRelations/RegulatoryAnnouncements/Pages/Unipetrol-Annual -Report-2012.aspx.

——. *Unipetrol Annual Report 2013.* http://www.unipetrol.cz/cs/VztahyS Investory/vyrocni-zpravy/Documents/2013%20ANNUAL%20 REPORT/Unipetrol_Annual_Report_2013.pdf.

——. "Unipetrol loni prodělal 1,4 miliardy, tržby klesly o sedm procent." January 24, 2014. *iDNES.cz.* http://ekonomika.idnes.cz/hospodareni-unipetrolu -v-roce-2013-d4o-/ekoakcie.aspx?c=A140124_074254_ekoakcie_vez.

U.S. Congressional Research Service, "U.S. Sanctions on Russia." Updated periodically. https://fas.org/sgp/crs/row/R45415.pdf.

U.S. Energy Information Administration. "Energy Conversion Calculators." https://www.eia.gov/energyexplained/index.cfm?page=about_energy _conversion_calculator.

——. "Natural Gas Processing: The Crucial Link between Natural Gas Production and Its Transportation to Market." Office of Oil and Gas, January 2006. https://www.eia.gov/pub/oil_gas/natural_gas/feature_articles/2006 /ngprocess/ngprocess.pdf.

Vahabi, Mehrdad. "The Resource Curse Literature as Seen through the Appropriability Lens: A Critical Survey." *Public Choice* 175, nos. 3–4 (2018): 393–428. https://doi.org/10.1007/s11127-018-0533-5.

Vandewalle, Dirk. *Libya since Independence: Oil and State-Building.* Ithaca, NY: Cornell University Press, 1988.

Vavilov, Andrey, and David Nicholls. *Gazprom: An Energy Giant and Its Challenges in Europe.* New York: Palgrave Macmillan, 2014.

Vavilov, Andrey, and Georgy Trofimov. "A Phantom Energy Empire: The Failure of Gazprom's Downstream Integration." In *Gazprom: An Energy Giant and Its Challenges in Europe*, edited by Andrey Vavilov. London: Palgrave Macmillan, 2015.

Vernon, Raymond. *Sovereignty at Bay: The Multinational Spread of U.S. Enterprises.* New York: Basic Books, 1971.

Vixrov, Maksim, and Maksim Butčenko. "Fenomen 'narodnyx respublik' Donbassa." April 12, 2016. https://carnegie.ru/2016/04/12/ru-pub -63295.

Vlček, Tomáš. *Alternative Oil Supply Infrastructure for the Czech Republic and Slovak Republic.* Brno: IPS and Muni Press, 2015.

——. "The Petroleum Sector of the Czech Republic and the Involvement of the Russian Federation." Unpublished paper, 2016.

Wallerstein, Immanuel. *World Systems Analysis: An Introduction.* Durham, NC: Duke University Press, 2004.

Waltz, Kenneth, N. *Theory of International Politics.* New York: Addison-Wesley, 1979.

Wengle, Susanne Alice. *Post-Soviet Power: State-Led Development and Russia's Marketization.* Cambridge: Cambridge University Press, 2015.

——. "Power Politics: The Political Economy of Russia's Electricity Sector Liberalization." PhD diss., University of California, Berkeley, 2010. https://escholarship.org/uc/item/2pz5w0xh.

Westphal, Kirsten. "Institutional Change in European Natural Gas Markets and Implications for Energy Security: Lessons from the German Case." *Energy Policy* 74 (2015): 35–43.

Wikborg Rein. "Facilitating Reverse Flow Capacity from West to East." Memo to Naftohaz, June 2, 2015. http://www.naftogaz.com/files/Information /2015-06-02%20-%20Facilitating%20Reverse%20Flow%20Capacity%20 from%20West%20to%20East.pdf.

Williamson, Oliver E. *Contract, Governance and Transaction Cost Economics.* Singapore: World Scientific, 2017.

——. "The Vertical Integration of Production: Market Failure Considerations." *American Economic Review* 61, no. 2 (1971): 112–23.

Wirschaftsvereinigung Stahl. *Statististisches Jahrbuch der Stahlindustrie 2016/2017.* Düsseldorf: Verlag Stahleisen, 2016.

Woellwarth, Lydia. "Transneft Reduces Oil Transit through Ukraine Amid Crude Oil Quality Complaints." *World Pipeline*, May 15, 2018. https:// www.worldpipelines.com/business-news/15052018/transneft-reduces -oil-transit-through-ukraine-amid-crude-oil-quality-complaints/.

Woodruff, David M. *Money Unmade: Barter and the Fate of Russian Capitalism.* Ithaca, NY: Cornell University Press, 1999.

World Bank. *Mining Communities of Ukraine: Advancing Restructuring for the Benefit of All.* Washington, DC: World Bank, 2003.

——. *Ukraine: Coal Industry Restructuring Sector Report.* Washington, DC: World Bank, 1996. http://documents.worldbank.org/curated/en /1996/03/696696/ukraine-coal-industry-restructuring-sector-report.

World Coal Association. "Where Is Coal Found?" April 29, 2015. https://www.worldcoal.org/coal/where-coal-found.

World Nuclear Association. "Heating Values of Various Fuels." World Nuclear Association. September 2016.

World Steel Association. *Steel Solutions in the Green Economy: Wind Turbines.* Brussels: World Steel Association, 2012. https://www.worldsteel.org/en/dam/jcr:41f65ea2-7447-4489-8ba7-9c87e3975aab/Steel+solutions+in+the+green+economy%253A+Wind+turbines.pdf.

World Steel in Figures. "Donetsk Oblast." International Iron and Steel Institute, 2002.

Xusainov, F. I. *Reforma železnodorožnoj otrasli: Problemy nezaveršennoj liberalizacii.* Moscow: Higher School of Economics, 2014.

Yafimava, Katja. "Evolution of Gas Pipeline Regulation in Russia: Third-Party Access, Capacity Allocation and Transportation Tariffs." 2015. https://ora.ox.ac.uk/objects/uuid:88facaf3-3416-45ac-aad7-3d8f5543879a.

Yakovenko, Mikola. "Ukraine Oil Transit." Unpublished paper, September 2016.

Yegorov, Yuri, and Franz Wirl. "Ukrainian Gas Transit Game." *ZfE Zeitschrift für Energiewirschaft* 33, no. 2 (2009): 147–55. http://dx.doi.org/10.1007/s12398-009-0017-x.

Young, Robert A., and John B. Loomis. *Determining the Economic Value of Water: Concepts and Methods.* New York: Routledge, 2014.

Younger, A. H., and P. Eng. "Natural Gas Processing Principles and Technology, Part I: Adsorption / Physical Chemistry." Gas Processors Association, Tulsa, 2004.

Zachmann, Georg, and Dmytro Naumenko. "Ukraine Energy Update 2015/16." German Advisory Group Ukraine, Berlin/Kyiv, March 2016. http://www.beratergruppe-ukraine.de/wordpress/wp-content/uploads/2016/05/TN_01_2016_en.pdf.

Zajcev, Vadim. "Kak pojavilis' sorta Brent, WTI i Urals (Deržat' marku)." *Kommersant Vlast'* 13 (2013).

Zedalis, Rex J. *Singapore, the Energy Economy: From the First Refinery to the End of Cheap Oil, 1960–2010.* London: Routledge, 2012.

Zhadan, Serhiy. *Voroshylovhrad.* Kharkiv: Folio, 2010; also pub. in the United States—Dallas: Deep Vellum, 2016.

Zimmerman, Erich Walter. *World Resources and Industries: A Functional Appraisal of the Availability of Agricultural and Industrial Resources.* New York: Harper Brothers, 1933.

Zon, Hans van. "Is the Donetsk Model Sustainable?" *Geographia Polonica* 78, no. 2 (2005): 77–90.

——. "The Reform of Ukraine's Energy Complex and Its Consequences for Donetsk." In *Re-Constructing the Post-Soviet Industrial Region: The Donbas in Transition*, edited by Adam Swain. New York: Routledge, 2007.

——. "The Rise of Conglomerates in Ukraine: The Donetsk Case." In *Big Business and Economic Development: Conglomerates and Economic Groups in Developing Countries and Transition Economies under Globalization,* edited by A. E. F. Jilberto and B. Hogenboom. London: Routledge, 2007.

ZumBrunnen, Craig, and Jeffrey Osleeb. *The Soviet Iron and Steel Industry.* Totowa, NJ: Rowman & Allenheld, 1986.

Index

Figures, notes, and tables are indicated by *f*, *n*, and *t* following the page number.

221, 237; product differentiation for, 328n45; on refined oil products, 129–31, 237; 60-66-90-100 system, 328n44; in value chain analysis, 34
export quotas, oil, 133–35, 329n57

Favorov, Andrew, 247
fertilizers, 18, 62–63, 101–2, 120, 219, 315n109
Fico, Robert, 111
final energy and energy services, 47, 253
finished steel products, 169, 198, 200, 202, 266
Firtash, Dmytro: bribery investigations involving, 244; in chemical industry, 101–2, 120, 243, 363n20; defined, 271; in electricity generation, 208; profit sharing by, 102, 221–22, 316n112; and RosUkrEnergo, 100, 101, 208, 314n103
fixed delivery points, 105, 242, 257
fossil fuels: demand for, 5; future outlook for, 6; primary physical criteria, 24, 24t, 46–53; secondary features of, 53–64, 54t; supply interruptions, 42, 43t; use of term, 285n7. *See also* coal; natural gas; oil; unconventional fossil fuels
fracking, 6, 117, 248, 363n1
fractional distillation, 324–25n10
Franken I power plant, 114, 116–18, 208, 271, 323n175
Fukushima nuclear accident (2011), 38, 117
fungibility, 19, 48, 60, 253
furnaces: basic oxygen furnace (BOF), 191–92, 200, 264; electric arc furnace (EAF), 191,

192, 202–3, 265, 355n124, 360n171; open hearth furnace (OHF), 191–92, 265, 355n125, 355n127

gas. *See* natural gas; refined oil products
gas condensate, 83–85, 87, 257
Gas Directives (EU), 233, 234, 242, 321n163
gas-fired power plants, 111, 114, 116–18
gas-metering stations (GMSs), 92, 95–96, 108, 258, 313n85
gasoline: demand for, 127, 158; export duties on, 130, 131; gas condensate processed into, 85; oversupply of, 6, 124; refining of crude oil into, 31, 34, 159–60; shortages of, 130, 132
Gas-on-Gas (GOG) pricing mechanism, 368n55
gas release programs, 234
Gasunie, 114, 116, 271
Gaz de France, 113, 271
Gazprom: antitrust case against, 235, 240; and captive value chains, 361n2; as commercial node, 92, 114; contract model of, 82, 105; defined, 271; dispatch control, 91; disputes with, 96, 104, 110, 235–36; export strategies, 86–89, 310n60; joint ventures organized by, 113, 119, 120; lobbying power with European Commission, 234; market power of, 105, 233, 235, 246, 319–20n145; as monopoly, 6, 68, 86–89, 107, 121, 126, 212; native population engagement by, 306n22; pipeline construction by, 3, 208; Polish

oligarchs: in coal value chain, 167,
182–84, 192, 194, 203–4, 210;
emergence of, 21; in energy-
political system, 194, 218; in
nonenergy industries, 18, 101; in
oil value chain, 144–49; power
of, 62, 101, 204; privatization of
state subsidies by, 220; sanctions
directed at, 248; and value chain
disruptions, 243–45
OPAL (Ostsee-Pipeline-
Anbindungsleitung) pipeline:
capacity limitations, 74; defined,
274; Nord Stream access to, 112,
115–16, 222, 233–35, 240
open hearth furnaces (OHFs),
191–92, 265, 355n125,
355n127
open-pit mining, 171–72, 175, 178,
188, 266
operating costs, 124
opportunity costs, 66
Orange Revolution (2004), 7, 143,
145, 186, 218, 243
Organization for Economic
Cooperation and Development
(OECD), 81, 124, 135
Organization of Arab Petroleum
Exporting Countries (OAPEC),
9, 11, 287n19
Organization of the Petroleum
Exporting Countries (OPEC), 9,
11, 302n59
Ostchem, 101–2, 120, 274,
315n110

pandemic. *See* COVID-19 pandemic
Party of Regions, 102, 194, 248,
274
path dependencies, 5, 137, 192,
207–8, 222
Perry, Rick, 247

petroleum associated gas. *See*
associated gas
PGNiG, 236
physical nodes: in coal value chain,
176, 238; defined, 254; and
energy security issues, 158;
identification of, 18; importance
of, 34–35; interaction with
commercial and regulatory nodes,
35, 35f, 107, 214; in natural
gas value chain, 221; in oil value
chain, 134, 153; situational
coalitions formed around, 222
physical swaps, natural gas, 79, 225,
305n5, 363n23
pig iron: defined, 266; import
destinations for, 200; in
integrated steel plants, 345n9;
level of value added for, 202;
production of, 167, 169, 183,
191, 198; quality of, 180
Pinchuk, Viktor, 183, 187, 192,
203, 274, 360n171
pipelines: compressor stations for,
79, 91, 95–97, 109–11, 257,
313n90; as contractual space, 214;
EU regulation of, 74, 104–5,
115, 337n135; standard for, 58,
79–80, 84, 259; utilization rates
for, 55–56; working pressure
of, 98, 261. *See also* natural gas;
oil; third-party access; trunk
pipelines; *specific pipelines*
PKN Orlen, 124, 155–59, 275,
341nn179–80
point resources, 53, 254
political costs, 10
political power, 16–17, 21, 47, 136,
139, 218
Poroshenko, Petro, 145, 244
power: bargaining, 53, 62, 230,
232, 241; centralization of, 38,

GPSR Authorized Representative: Easy Access System Europe, Mustamäe tee
50, 10621 Tallinn, Estonia, gpsr.requests@easproject.com

www.ingramcontent.com/pod-product-compliance
Lightning Source LLC
Chambersburg PA
CBHW022130020426
42334CB00015B/834